The Cotingas

Bellbirds, umbrellabirds and other species

Frontispiece
A male Bearded Bellbird crouches in front of the female before making the mating leap
(*see page* 168)

The Cotingas

Bellbirds, umbrellabirds and other species

David Snow

COLOUR PLATES BY MARTIN WOODCOCK

British Museum (Natural History)
Comstock Publishing Associates, a division of
Cornell University Press
Ithaca, New York

Dedicated to the memory of
PAUL SCHWARTZ

For information address Cornell University Press
124 Roberts Place, Ithaca, New York 14850

First published 1982 by Cornell University Press

International Standard Book Number 0-8014-1490-3
Library of Congress Catalog Card Number 81-70704

Printed in Great Britain by W. S. Cowell Ltd, Ipswich, Suffolk

Contents

Preface

The cotingas are among the most diverse of passerine families. In size they range from the huge black Amazonian Umbrellabird, one of the largest of all passerines, down to the tiny Kinglet Calyptura, a bird about the size of a Goldcrest and not unlike a Goldcrest in plumage. They include two of the very few land-birds with wholly white plumage, others with uniquely deep purple and wine-coloured plumage, others that are brilliantly red or orange, and yet others that are of an unsurpassed shining blue. A few are completely drab. Their ornamentation includes bizarre wattles, extraordinary crests, and unusually modified wing-feathers. Though they do not quite approach the birds of paradise in the extravagance of their ornamentation they are, among the passerines, second only to the birds of paradise. They are diverse also in their way of life. Some live in pairs, some are polygamous, and one species at least lives in highly integrated social groups. Most pluck fruit from trees in flight or snatch insects from the foliage and branches, but within this framework their feeding habits are varied. In particular, some have entered into specialised coadapted relationships with the plants whose fruit they eat. The evolution of the family as a whole is intimately bound up with the evolution of the forest flora on which they depend.

In writing this book I have had two aims: first, to give a reasonably comprehensive account of what is known of the natural history of all the species of cotingas, with the emphasis on their behaviour and ecology; and second, to discuss the points of general biological interest raised by a study of the cotingas. As the family has not been previously monographed and the literature is widely scattered in ornithological journals and elsewhere, I hope that a bringing together of all available information will be useful. If it stimulates further field work and encourages wider interest in a family of birds that suddenly, in the last thirty years, after millions of years of evolution, are as threatened as the forests in which they have evolved, it will have achieved another of its purposes.

Acknowledgements

I am deeply indebted to the following, who have contributed either the whole or parts of the sections on cotingas of which they have unique first-hand knowledge: Theodore A. Parker III (*Ampelion*), Cesar E. Benalcazar & Fabiola Silva de Benalcazar (Andean Cock-of-the-rock), Barbara K. Snow (Calfbird, bellbirds), John W. Fitzpatrick (Black-faced Cotinga), Derek A. Scott & Michael de L. Brooke (Grey-winged Cotinga).

Very many other friends and correspondents, from nearly a dozen countries, have helped me in the preparation of this book. I am grateful to Thomas S. Schulenberg and Helmut Sick, who allowed me to incorporate unpublished observations on the breeding of the Chestnut-crowned Cotinga and Swallow-tailed Cotinga, respectively. Among the contributors I must make mention again of Ted Parker, who generously gave me the benefit of his unrivalled knowledge of Andean cotingas. Steven Hilty generously allowed me to use information from his still unpublished guide to the birds of Colombia (referred to in the text as Hilty, MS). For invaluable help in other ways I thank the following: W. Belton, R. Bleiweiss, J. I. Borrero, W. L. Brown, J. Bull, H. F. de A. Camargo, C. T. Collins, J. A. Dick, H. E. M. Dott, R. van den Elzen, J. M. Forshaw, F. B. Gill, J. L. Gulledge, F. Haverschmidt, D. T. Holyoak, J. Ingels, L. B. Kiff, T. E. Lovejoy, A. L. Mack, G. F. Mees, R. M. de Schauensee, J. R. Northern, F. Novaes, J. P. O'Neill, K. C. Parkes, R. A. Paynter, W. H. Phelps Jr., J. V. Remsen, D. M. Richardson, M. B. Robbins, H. Romero Z., P. Schwartz, L. L. Short, C. G. Sibley, H. Sick, A. F. Skutch, E. H. Stickney, F. G. Stiles, E. Sutter, O. Tostain, E. O. Willis, H. Wolters.

I am indebted to the following societies for permission to quote passages and reproduce figures from periodicals published by them: American Ornithologists' Union (passage on pp. 114–117, and Fig. 9); British Ornithologists' Club (pp. 61–64); British Ornithologists' Union (Figs 7 and 8); Cooper Ornithological Society (passage on p. 117); New York Zoological Society (passages on pp. 95–97 and 150–151).

Origin, classification and distributional history of the cotingas

Some time in the Cretaceous period, when the great southern continent, Gondwanaland, broke up, the land-mass that is now South America split off from what is now Africa; it drifted northwestwards with extreme slowness until it came up against Central America and a permanent land-bridge — now Panama and Costa Rica — was formed in the late Pliocene. This, in simple terms, is the broad picture that emerges from recent research on continental drift and ocean-floor spreading. The evidence at present indicates that the splitting of South America from Africa was completed about 110 million years ago, and the junction with Central America took place about 4 million years ago (Cracraft 1973, Haffer 1974, Buffetaut & Taquet 1979). There was thus a period of about 100 million years when South America was an isolated island-continent.

It was, it seems, a continent of low relief, enjoying a moist and equable tropical climate and covered with forest. It was not until the very end of the Pliocene and the early Pleistocene that the main uplift of the Andes took place, creating extensive subtropical and temperate zones and, locally, ice-caps and deserts.

As it separated from Africa, the land-mass must have carried with it descendants of the Gondwana avifauna, including some primitive passerines. The cotingas are modern representatives of this early passerine stock. Other descendants are the manakins (Pipridae) and tyrant-flycatchers (Tyrannidae), two families fairly closely related to the cotingas, and, more distantly related, the woodcreepers, ovenbirds, antbirds and their allies (Dendrocolaptidae, Furnariidae, Formicariidae and Rhinocryptidae). Two other small families — the single species of sharpbill (Oxyruncidae) and the three species of plant-cutters (Phytotomidae) — complete the list of modern bird families descended from the original stock of South American passerines that evolved and differentiated during the continent's long period of isolation. The 18 other passerine families that now occur in South America are almost certainly of northern origin, and spread south into South America when the Central American land-bridge was formed. These families of northern origin all belong to the oscine division of the passerine order (the true 'song-birds'), characterized by a more complex syringeal musculature which seems to be the anatomical basis of their more complex songs. They are usually thought of as the more advanced of the two divisions, while the southern group of Gondwanaland origin, the suboscines, are held to be more primitive.

The classification of the South American suboscines, the details of whose evolutionary history will never be known, is still controversial and is likely to remain so for a long time. The cotingas, with the manakins, tyrant-flycatchers, sharpbill and plant-cutters, are currently placed in a superfamily, Tyrannoidea, within the suborder Tyranni, of the order Passeriformes. The woodcreepers, ovenbirds, antbirds and their allies are placed in another superfamily, Furnarioidea, within the same suborder. This classification reflects an important early divergence between two main lines of specialization in the adaptive radiation of the isolated South American forest avifauna. One line of specialization led to the evolution of fruit- and insect-eaters that plucked fruit on the wing and caught insects in the air or snatched them from the trees in flight-sallies — the tyrannoid assemblage; the other led to insect-eaters that foraged on the forest floor and in the undergrowth, searched the tree-trunks, and gleaned insects from the branches and twigs — the furnarioid assemblage. The tyrannoid assemblage exploited the feeding opportunities offered by the forest canopy and the middle layers of the forest, the furnarioids dominated the trunks and large branches, the lower layers of vegetation and the ground beneath. In the tyrannoid assemblage, those stocks that most effectively exploited the many and varied opportunities for insect-eating gave rise to the tyrant-flycatchers, those that specialized on the smaller fruits of under-storey trees and shrubs gave rise to the manakins, and those that specialized on the larger fruits of the forest trees gave rise to the cotingas. When the Andes had been uplifted high enough for the development of subtropical and temperate woodlands it was the cotingas, not the manakins, that evolved new forms to exploit the fruits of the new montane habitats.

I have sketched the probable course of events in this rather general way in order to emphasise that the cotinga family, as it is recognized today, may not be monophyletic – that is to say, all cotingas may not be descended from a common stock the members of which are more closely related to one another than they are to any of the tyrant-flycatchers or manakins. It may be that two or more evolutionary lines leading to the development of specialized frugivores separated off independently from the common tyrannoid stock. If this was so, it would help to explain why it has proved so difficult to divide the cotingas from the manakins and tyrant-flycatchers on the basis of structural characters, as discussed in the following section.

The limits of the family

The delimitation of the Cotingidae from the other families that make up the Tyrannoidea has been debated for over 100 years. A typical cotinga is very different from a typical manakin, and even more different from a typical tyrant-flycatcher; but there are a relatively large number of genera whose allocation is problematical. Systematists have been concerned to find structural characters that would reliably separate the families, but in fact it seems that no one character, or group of characters, identifies a bird as a cotinga. The reader is referred to Sibley (1970) and Ames (1971) for excellent reviews of the vicissitudes of previous attempts at the classification of the tyrannoid assemblage. Here only a summary account is given.

Sclater's *Catalogue of Birds in the British Museum*, vol. 14 (1888), may be taken as the starting point. He recognized 31 genera in the Cotingidae, dividing them from the Tyrannidae and Pipridae on the basis of tarsal scutellation. The relevant part of his key is as follows:

a. Tarsus exaspidean.*
   á. Toes nearly free (as in the *Oscines*).
      Bill incurved, hooked . . 1. **Tyrannidae**
      Bill straight, pointed. . . 2. **Oxyrhamphidae**
                      [= **Oxyruncidae**]
   b́. Toes more or less united . 3. **Pipridae**
b. Tarsus pycnaspidean.
      Bill elongated, compressed,
        not serrated . . . . . 4. **Cotingidae**
      Bill short, conical,
        serrated . . . . . 5. **Phytotomidae**

Ridgway (1907), in prefacing his very detailed key to the family Cotingidae, pointed out that the nature of the tarsal scutellation is not so invariable within the families as Sclater had supposed. Nevertheless he followed Sclater's arrangement closely. He gave what is still the only attempt at a verbal definition of the cotingas in the following words: 'Haploophone, catacromyodous, heteromerous Mesomyodian Passeres with the tarsal envelope pycnaspidean, holaspidean or modified taxaspidean (never exaspidean), first (basal) phalanx of middle toe never wholly united to inner toe, nor second phalanx of middle toe coherent with outer toe (or else, in genus *Phoenicircus* only, with inner side of tarsus feathered)'. Readers who are baffled by the string of technical terms* may take comfort in the fact that most professional ornithologists would be hard put to it to define them all without recourse to a library. Here we may only note that, in addition to the nature of the toes and tarsal scutellation used by Sclater, they refer to the structure of the syrinx and its musculature, and to the arteries of the thigh.

When Hellmayr dealt with the Cotingidae in Part VI of the *Catalogue of Birds of the Americas* (1929), a work which, 50 years later, is still a necessary starting point in any systematic study of the family, he followed Sclater and Ridgway closely, admitting 31 genera – 6 more than we admit here. His classification was for long accepted as standard, and it was not until 1970 that a major change was made, when Meyer de Schauensee, in his *Guide to the Birds of South America*, removed several genera

---

*The following definitions are modified slightly from Ridgway (1907):

Catacromyodous: the vocal muscles inserted on the dorsal end of the bronchial semi-rings.

Exaspidean: the anterior envelope extending entirely across the outer side of the tarsus and around the posterior side.

Haploophone: having the syrinx simply broncho-tracheal (typically passerine).

Heteromerous: the main artery of the thigh is the femoral instead of the sciatic.

Holaspidean: the broad plantar surface of the tarsus occupied by a single series of broad, more or less quadrate or rectangular scutella.

Mesomyodian: the syringeal muscles (if present) attached to the middle or either end (but not both ends) of the bronchial semi-rings.

Pycnaspidean: the broad plantar surface of the tarsus broken up into numerous small irregular or roundish scutella or granules.

Taxaspidean: the broad plantar surface of the tarsus occupied by two, or rarely three, series of small quadrate or hexagonal scutella.

and placed them in the Tyrannidae. These were the mourners (*Rhytipterna* and *Laniocera*), the attilas (*Attila* and *Pseudattila*), and *Casiornis*, genera about which doubts had previously been expressed and which recent anatomical research had shown to be typically tyrannine in the structure of the skull (Warter 1965) and syrinx (Ames 1971). A further reduction in the number of genera included in the family has recently been made with the publication of volume 8 of Peters' *Check-list of Birds of the World* (1979), in which the tityras (*Tityra*) and becards (*Pachyramphus*, including *Platypsaris*) are also removed from the Cotingidae and placed in the Tyrannidae. The tityras and becards had never been easily accommodated in the Cotingidae. In general behaviour and nesting habits they are untypical of the family, and on the basis of skull structure both groups, and the becards also on syringeal structure, are closer to the tyrant-flycatchers.

One final change from Hellmayr's treatment has been to place the cocks-of-the-rock (*Rupicola*) back in the family. *Rupicola* has been placed in and removed from the Cotingidae a number of times. Long ago Garrod (1876) found that in *Rupicola* the main artery of the thigh is the sciatic (as in the Tyrannidae) and not the femoral (as in the other cotingas studied). In spite of this, Sclater kept *Rupicola* in the Cotingidae; but Ridgway placed it in a separate family, on the basis of the thigh arteries, and Hellmayr followed him presumably for the same reason. Subsequent authors have not been consistent: for instance, Meyer de Schauensee (1966, 1970) maintains the family Rupicolidae, while Sibley (1970) places *Rupicola* in the Cotingidae. For our present purpose there is a great advantage in including the cocks-of-the-rock, as they show in extreme form the tendency to marked sexual dimorphism, associated with elaborate courtship displays, that is such a feature of the cotingas; they are, in fact, one of the culminating points in the evolution of tropical American frugivorous birds.

The removal of the mourners, attilas, becards and tityras results in a more homogeneous – though still very diverse – family. Its diversity has been increased by two new discoveries since Hellmayr's time, both from Peru: the very distinct Black-faced Cotinga *Conioptilon mcilhennyi*, for which a new genus has had to be created, and the high Andean White-cheeked Cotinga *Ampelion stresemanni*, originally described as a new genus *Zaratornis* but here placed in the Andean genus *Ampelion*.

Divisions and relationships within the family

More than half of the genera of cotingas (13 out of 25) are monotypic – that is, they contain a single species. In addition there are four genera consisting of two or three allopatric species that are so closely related that 'lumpers' might well treat them as conspecific. About two-thirds of the genera (17 out of 25) are thus effectively monotypic. Moreover, nearly all of the 25 genera are very distinct, so that there has never been any doubt of their generic status and it is not easy to suggest what their nearest relatives might be. These figures serve to emphasize the extreme heterogeneity of the family. It is not surprising that attempts to recognize subfamilies within the Cotingidae have had only limited success. Here we do not formally recognize subfamilies, but the latest subfamilial classification, proposed by Warter (1965) and based primarily on skull structure, is a convenient basis for discussion of relationships within the family. The thorough examination by Ames (1971) of the syrinx of 16 of the 25 genera has provided another important source of comparative anatomical data.

The largest group recognized by Warter are the 'typical' cotingas (Cotinginae), consisting of *Pipreola*, *Cotinga*, *Xipholena*, *Carpodectes*, *Ampelion*, *Tijuca*, *Carpornis*, *Porphyrolaema* and *Ampelioides*. On skull structure the first five of these form a fairly natural group; the skulls of the last four were not examined but they were included on the basis of other characters. Recent evidence, discussed on p. 109, suggests, however, that *Tijuca* should not be a member of this group. (*Conioptilon* had not been discovered when Warter wrote. On its skull structure it is closest to this group (Lowery *et al.* 1966).) The validity of Warter's grouping is reasonably well supported by evidence from the syrinx and its musculature: *Pipreola*, *Cotinga*, *Xipholena* and *Ampelion* are all similar in their syringeal structure. Ames placed *Carpodectes*, however, with *Querula*, a grouping that is not supported by any other characters; the other three genera were not examined. On general grounds Warter's group of 'typical' cotingas seems well founded; they include the very brightly coloured, sexually dimorphic, medium-sized fruit-eaters of lowland tropical forest, and the less brightly coloured (mainly green, yellow and black) fruit-eaters of the Andes and eastern Brazilian highlands. In view of the comparatively recent elevation of these mountains, the montane genera should be the most recently evolved.

Warter placed *Gymnoderus* in a subfamily of its own (Gymnoderinae). Its skull is a large form of 'cotingine' type, but the genus has many peculiar features, including well-developed powder-down tracts. On its syringeal characters Ames placed *Gymnoderus* with the fruit-crows.

The fruit-crows (Querulinae) constitute the only

other substantial subfamily in Warter's classification. He includes in this group *Querula*, *Pyroderus*, *Haematoderus*, *Perissocephalus*, *Cephalopterus* and *Lipaugus*. Ames recognizes a similar group on syringeal structure, but includes in it *Gymnoderus*, as mentioned above, and the recently discovered *Conioptilon*, and excludes *Lipaugus*. The first five genera included by Warter are all large or very large cotingas with heavy crow-like beaks and (except for *Perissocephalus*) mainly black or black and crimson plumage. Three of them utter far-carrying booming or bellowing calls and have some form of lek display. *Querula*, the smallest of the group, is very different in voice and social organization, while *Haematoderus* is almost unknown in life.

Warter proposed a new subfamily, Procniatinae, for the bellbirds *Procnias*. Of all the cotinga skulls that he examined, that of *Procnias* is the most highly modified. In syringeal structure it is also unique.

Finally, Warter provisionally placed *Rupicola* in a family of its own, noting that if further evidence showed that it should be included in the Cotingidae it should be placed in a subfamily of its own, Rupicolinae.

Warter's classification omitted the genera *Iodopleura*, *Calyptura*, *Phoenicircus*, *Phibalura* and *Laniisoma*, whose skulls (in addition to those of four genera placed in the Cotinginae) were not available for examination. Of these, *Iodopleura* is more like a tyrant-flycatcher than a typical cotinga in its syrinx; the syringeal structure of the others is either unknown or not well enough known to help in determining their affinities. We place these five diverse genera at the beginning of the sequence, in recognition of the fact that on present knowledge they cannot be linked with any of the main groups of genera.

Further than this one cannot go with any assurance, on the evidence at present available. The most that can be claimed is that the sequence of genera adopted here is in accordance with the available anatomical and other evidence, so far as it is not conflicting. The sequence differs slightly from that adopted in volume 8 of Peters' *Check-list*, the main change being to bring together all the genera of 'typical' cotingas, according to Warter's classification, with the exception of *Tijuca* which is placed next to *Lipaugus*.

Species limits

There are a number of cases in the cotingas, as there are in practically all bird families, where closely related but distinct forms occupy separate geographical areas. All such cases pose a problem for the taxonomist, who has to decide whether to treat the different forms as separate species or as subspecies of a single species. The decision often has to be more or less arbitrary, as it is not known whether the forms in question would prove to be reproductively isolated from one another if they came into contact. In the special case of 'parapatric' forms, however, the decision is easier. These are forms whose ranges approach very closely or actually abut, so that it seems that the range of each is limited by the presence of the other; the inference is that the two forms are reproductively isolated from one another, but too similar ecologically to be able to coexist. They qualify for specific status, but have probably achieved it relatively recently. There are only two clear cases of parapatry in the cotingas (*Phoenicircus* and *Xipholena*; Maps 1 and 17, pp. 32 and 94), and perhaps a third (*Cotinga maynana* and *C. cotinga*; Map 14, p. 84). There are many more cases where closely related forms, differing to about the same degree as these parapatric species, are separated either by a tract of unsuitable country or, in a few cases, by an area that appears suitable but is unoccupied. In these cases also it seems best to give specific status to each. Such a treatment has the merit of uniformity; in the absence of critical evidence it indicates differences that appear to be of specific significance, and distinguishes them from the minor differences of size and colour that are characteristic of subspecies.

Distributional history

There is no reason to think that the distributional history of the cotingas has followed a radically different course from that of other groups of South American forest birds. It would be foolish to draw far-reaching zoogeographical conclusions from the analysis of the distribution of a comparatively small number of species, when much sounder conclusions could be reached from a consideration of the whole of the forest avifauna. For this reason I discuss here only the salient points in the distribution of the cotingas and draw a few tentative conclusions from them.

There seems no doubt that practically the whole evolution of the family took place in South America, Central America having probably been colonized only after the Panama land-bridge was established. Thus in Central America there is no endemic cotinga genus, and no very strongly differentiated species within any genus. *Carpodectes*, the only genus confined to Central America and adjacent parts of South America, might have evolved either in the trans-Andean forests of western Colombia or in

Central America; its limited northward extension in Central America suggests the former. The only montane forest species in Central America, the Bare-necked Umbrellabird *Cephalopterus glabricollis* and Three-wattled Bellbird *Procnias tricarunculata*, are both outlying representatives of widespread South American genera and seem likely to have colonized Central America by long-distance dispersal from the western Andean slopes (umbrellabird) and northern Venezuela (bellbird).

The family may be conveniently divided into two main distributional groups: (1) lowland forest species; and (2) montane species, including species whose distribution is montane in a broad geographical sense but which occur on the lower slopes or in the foothills, in many cases at tropical levels. Some species in this last category undertake vertical migrations, breeding at higher levels and moving down to the foothills or neighbouring lowlands in the off-season. For the most part the members of the two groups belong to different genera; only two genera, *Lipaugus* and *Cephalopterus*, have species in both groups. Judging from the varying extent to which the different genera have become specialized along the lines that are most characteristic of the family — specialized frugivory, associated with marked sexual dimorphism and the evolution of elaborate courtship displays — it might be supposed that the most primitive cotingas are to be found in the montane group. The montane genera include several which seem to be the least specialized, such as *Carpornis*, *Pipreola*, *Ampelioides* and *Laniisoma*. They arc mostly medium-sized birds, with mainly green, yellow and black plumage and without extreme sexual dimorphism, and some of them are known to live in pairs (the social organization of the rest being unknown). Any such conclusion must, however, be treated with caution, for if environmental conditions in mountains favour the plumage colours, slight sexual dimorphism, pair-formation and other characters that we now see in the montane species, the evolutionary history could just as well be interpreted the other way; in other words, the montane forms might have been derived from lowland forest ancestors. Any sound conclusion on this question should be based on evidence that is, so far as possible, independent of present-day ecologies and distributions. The geological evidence, indicating that the Andes reached heights suitable for the development of temperate forest only in the last 2 million years (Haffer 1974), suggests that *Ampelion*, the cotinga genus that lives at the highest altitudes, may be relatively recently evolved, and *Pipreola* and *Ampelioides* are unlikely to be very ancient.

Lowland forest species

Most of these occur in the great Amazonian forest block, with its extensions north to the upper drainage of the Orinoco and the Guianas. Only two Amazonian species, *Lipaugus vociferans* and *Querula purpurata*, have ranges extending beyond Amazonia: *L. vociferans* occurs also in the eastern Brazilian coastal forests, and *Q. purpurata* occurs west of the Andes and in Central America, in both cases without noticeable subspecific differentiation. The eastern Brazilian lowland forests contain only three other near relatives of Amazonian species, specifically distinct but in two cases closely enough related to be linked in a superspecies with an Amazonian counterpart: *Cotinga maculata* (Amazonian allospecies *C. cotinga*), *Xipholena atropurpurea* (Amazonian allospecies *X. lamellipennis* and *X. punicea*), and *Iodopleura pipra* (Amazonian relatives *I. isabellae* and *I. fusca*). The trans-Andean and Central American lowland forests also contain species in three genera (two lowland forest, one montane) that are closely related to Amazonian species: *Lipaugus unirufus* (Amazonian allospecies *L. vociferans*), *Cotinga nattererii* and its Central American close relatives (Amazonian relatives *C. maynana* and *C. cotinga*); and *Cephalopterus penduliger* and *C. glabricollis* (Amazonian allospecies *C. ornatus*). In addition the trans-Andean genus *Carpodectes* may share a common origin with *Xipholena*, but the two genera are certainly not recently differentiated (see p. 99). This analysis, summarized in Table 1, suggests that both the trans-Andean and the eastern Brazilian lowland forests received most of their cotingas from Amazonia, and that the connection between the Amazonian and eastern Brazilian forests was the more recently broken. The trans-Andean forests may themselves have been a minor evolutionary centre, being perhaps the area of origin of *Querula* as well as *Carpodectes*. The absence of *Querula* from the eastern Brazilian forests, its absence from part of Amazonia and the Orinoco drainage where all other widespread Amazonian genera occur, and its abundance in the trans-Andean forests, together with the lack of any subspecific distinction east and west of the Andes, all suggest that it may have originated west of the Andes and colonized Amazonia relatively recently.

It is noteworthy that the lowland forests of Venezuela north of the Orinoco, including the forests round the south end of Lake Maracaibo, lack all of the Amazonian cotingas. The cotingas that occur in this part of Venezuela are all montane species. This must surely indicate that the llanos region of central Venezuela and eastern Colombia has been a barrier to forest birds of very long standing, and that the narrow forest belt along the eastern base of the Andes, which stretches through Colombia into Venezuela and provides a tenuous link with the Amazonian forest, has not been adequate, or of long enough standing, to serve as a corridor for the spread of any of the lowland forest cotingas into northern Venezuela. One submontane cotinga, *Laniisoma elegans*, has reached Venezuela along this corridor, as have a number of Amazonian species of other families, for example the Wire-tailed Manakin *Pipra filicauda*.

Dr Jurgen Haffer's interpretation of speciation patterns in American tropical forest birds may be applied to the cotingas; indeed, two cotinga genera were among the examples that he used to illustrate his thesis in his first major paper on the subject (Haffer 1970). According to this hypothesis, at various times in the Pleistocene (approximately the last 2 million years, excluding the last few thousand) there were periods of aridity when the lowland forests of tropical America were reduced to a number of small isolated patches, generally corresponding to areas where rainfall is very high today. The arid periods were probably synchronous with glacial periods in the northern hemisphere, but this is not certain. The remaining forest patches served as refuges for the fragmented lowland forest avifauna. Populations of birds, isolated in these refuges, underwent differentiation to greater or lesser extents. When humid conditions were re-established and the forests spread and coalesced, the birds spread with them and thus related populations which had been isolated in different refuges came together again. The results of these secondary contacts, following the latest spread of forests some 10 000 years ago, have produced the geographical species patterns that we see today. Populations that had not differentiated much in isolation may have simply merged, leaving little or no trace of their former separation, while those that had differentiated sufficiently to be reproductively isolated from one another maintained their separate identities on meeting again. A characteristic distribution pattern resulted from secondary contact between populations that were reproductively isolated from one another but too similar ecologically to be able to coexist. In such cases they persisted as separate species with closely abutting ranges, each apparently keeping the other out of its own range. Haffer (1970) cited the cotinga genera *Phoenicircus* and *Xipholena* as examples of distribution patterns explicable in this way, and later (Haffer 1974) the genus *Cotinga*.

Haffer (1974) recognized 16 main lowland forest refuges. They provide a satisfactory explanation of the geographical patterns of differentiation in six groups of closely related cotinga species, as set out in Table 2. In particular, the present distributions of *Cotinga* and *Carpodectes* west of the Andes and in Central America agree closely with the postulated positions of forest refuges. A few species which are very widespread today cannot be assigned to a single refuge. Groups of species that are not listed in Table 2 seem too distantly related to be the result of isolation caused by the contraction of forests in the last few tens of thousands of years. Thus the distribution of the four bellbird species (*Procnias*), or of the two cocks-of-the-rock (*Rupicola*), must surely be the result of speciation processes that antedated the last change from arid to humid conditions.

Montane species

This is a very heterogeneous group of genera and species, sharing little except that their distribution is montane, at various levels, either at all times or at least for part of the year. As mentioned above, they belong to genera which, except for *Lipaugus* and *Cephalopterus*, are unrepresented in lowland forest — a fact which suggests that it is difficult for birds adapted to lowland forest to colonize montane habitats, and vice versa. The genera and species recognized as montane are listed in Table 3.

The question whether some of these montane genera are 'primitive', *i.e.* closer to the ancestral

Table 1
Trans-Andean and eastern Brazilian representatives of Amazonian forest cotingas

Trans-Andean species	Amazonian species	Eastern Brazilian species
	Iodopleura isabellae	*I. pipra*
L. unirufus (su)	*Lipaugus vociferans*	*L. vociferans*
C. amabilis, ridgwayi, nattererii	*Cotinga cotinga*	*C. maculata* (su)
Carpodectes spp. ?	*Xipholena lamellipennis, punicea*	*X. atropurpurea* (su)
Q. purpurata	*Querula purpurata*	
C. penduliger (su)	*Cephalopterus ornatus*	

Note. (su) = placed in superspecies with Amazonian species forms of cotingas than the lowland forest genera, has been discussed above. Another point deserving investigation is whether, or to what extent, there is any relationship between the endemic eastern Brazilian and Andean genera. For instance, there is a superficial resemblance between the larger *Pipreola* species, especially *P. arcuata* and *P. riefferii*, and *Carpornis melanocephalus* of eastern Brazil; and *Phibalura* has a partly concealed reddish nuchal crest not unlike that of *Ampelion* species.

Several considerations lead to the conclusion that some at least of the montane genera are able to colonize distant areas across extensive lowland gaps. *Phibalura* is almost certainly of eastern Brazilian origin but has a foothold, apparently of very small extent, on the Bolivian slopes of the Andes (Map 5, p. 47). *Laniisoma* is probably an example of a less recent colonization of the eastern slopes of the Andes from eastern Brazil (Map 2, p. 36). The ancestors of *Pipreola whitelyi*, endemic to the tepuis of the Guiana highlands, must have reached there by chance dispersal from the Andes to the west or

northwest (Mayr & Phelps 1967). *Procnias tricarunculata* probably colonized Central America by long-distance dispersal from northern Venezuela, a feat that seems less surprising in the light of the fact that *P. alba* (p. 195) is known to have wandered to Trinidad, from the Guiana highlands some 400 km to the south, at least three times in about 100 years.

Table 2

Probable areas of origin (Pleistocene forest refuges) of lowland forest cotingas

Phoenicircus carnifex	Guiana
Phoenicircus nigricollis	Napo (E. Ecuador)
Iodopleura fusca	Guiana
Iodopleura isabellae	? (species now widespread)
Lipaugus vociferans	? (species now widespread)
Lipaugus lanioides	Serra do Mar (S. E. Brazil)
Lipaugus unirufus	Pacific Colombian or a Central American refuge
Cotinga amabilis	Guatemala–Honduras or Caribbean Costa Rica
Cotinga ridgwayi	Pacific Central American
Cotinga nattererii	Pacific Colombian
Cotinga maynana	Napo (E. Ecuador)
Cotinga cotinga	Guiana or Belém
Cotinga maculata	Serra do Mar (S. E. Brazil)
Xipholena punicea	Guiana
Xipholena lamellipennis	Belém
Xipholena atropurpurea	Serra do Mar (S. E. Brazil)
Carpodectes nitidus	Caribbean Costa Rica
Carpodectes antoniae	Pacific Central American
Carpodectes hopkei	Pacific Colombian

Table 3

Montane cotingas and their distribution

Laniisoma elegans	S.E. Brazil[1] and Andes; mainly low altitudes, tropical zone; possibly with vertical migrations. Perhaps a recent colonist of Andean part of range.
Phibalura flavirostris	S.E. Brazil and Andes (Bolivia only, one known locality). Migratory in eastern part of range. Almost certainly colonised Andes from the east.
Tijuca spp.	S.E. Brazil, restricted to high altitudes.
Ampelion spp.	Andes, subtropical and temperate levels.
Carpornis spp.	S.E. Brazil, not restricted to high altitudes.
Pipreola spp.	Andes (10 spp., tropical to temperate levels) and Guiana highlands (1 sp., subtropical).
Ampelioides tschudii	Andes, upper tropical and subtropical levels.
Calyptura cristata	S.E. Brazil (very restricted range, little known).
Lipaugus spp.	S.E. Brazil (*L. lanioides*), Andes (*L. fuscocinereus*, *L. subalaris*, and *L. cryptolophus*, tropical to temperate levels), and Guiana highlands (*L. streptophorus*). Also two species in lowland forest.
Chirocylla uropygialis	Andes (very local in Bolivia, subtropical).
Pyroderus scutatus	S.E. Brazil, Andes, and locally in Guiana region; various altitudes, tropical to temperate. Only species occurring in all three montane regions.
Cephalopterus spp.	W. Andes (*C. penduliger*, tropical and subtropical) and C. American highlands (*C. glabricollis*, tropical and subtropical; vertical migrations). Third member of genus (*C. ornatus*) in Amazonian forest.
Procnias spp.	S.E. Brazil (*P. nudicollis*), N.E. Brazil, Guiana highlands and Venezuelan Andes (*P. averano*), Guiana highlands (*P. alba*), and C. American highlands (*P. tricarunculata*). Tropical and subtropical; vertical migrations.
Rupicola spp.	Andes (*R. peruviana*) and Guiana highlands (*R. rupicola*); tropical and subtropical.

[1]S.E. Brazil includes, in some cases, adjacent parts of E. Paraguay and N.E. Argentina.

Evolutionary radiation and sociobiology

All of the cotingas, so far as their diets are known, feed on fruit to a greater or lesser extent. Most also take a proportion of insects; some feed entirely on fruit, except perhaps for an occasional special supplement – thus one of the wholly frugivorous bellbirds has been recorded eating snail shells, probably for their calcium content. Within the limits imposed by a diet of fruit and insects the family has undergone a considerable adaptive radiation in feeding ecology; they do not all take the same kinds of fruits, and their methods of catching insects differ.

Knowledge of feeding ecology is basic to an understanding of the adaptive radiation of the family, but for a full understanding of any species one must know about much in addition to its feeding ecology: the site and structure of the nest, breeding behaviour, social organization, defence against predators, survival rates, and other aspects of the natural history of a species are all linked with feeding ecology in an adaptive web. So little is known about many cotinga species that little or nothing can be said under any of these headings; for even the best known only a tentative account can be given. The details for each species, as far as they are known, are summarized in the systematic chapters; here an attempt is made at a general synthesis.

Size, structure and proportions

The cotingas have the widest size range of all passerine families, the largest species being about 80 times as heavy as the smallest, and about 6 times as large in wing-length. The great majority of them share, however, an important behavioural character: they take most of their food, both fruit and insect, by plucking or snatching it in short flight-sallies. They tend not to be agile on their legs, which are relatively short. Thus when foraging they do not usually climb or hop about among the branches but perch motionless, looking about, until they see a food item and fly to take it. To this rule the Bare-necked Fruit-crow *Gymnoderus foetidus* is a striking exception.

The relationship between weight and wing-length is shown in Figure 1. Not all species are included, as there are some for which weights are not available. The general trend of the relationship is much as in other birds: weight is proportional to the cube of the wing-length (Greenewalt 1962). Some genera, however, stand out as having distinctly long or short wings for their weight, by comparison with most members of the family. Thus the Dusky Purpletuft *Iodopleura fusca* is very long-winged for its weight. The purpletufts are peculiar among cotingas in feeding largely by hawking for flying insects from tree-tops, and they are correspondingly swallow-like in proportions. The Purple-throated Fruit-crow *Querula purpurata* is also very long-winged for its weight (and also has very broad wings); its agility in flight, which doubtless depends on these wing proportions, appears to be an important adaptive character in its unique social organisation (p. 134). Of the cotingas that are relatively short-winged for their weight the red cotingas (*Phoenicircus*) and *Ampelioides* stand out as the most extreme, but so little is known of them in life that no interpretation can be suggested.

There is a moderate amount of interspecific variation in other body proportions. Details are set out in the systematic section, at the end of the account of each genus. In most species tail-length is 45–75% of wing-length; in only one genus (*Phibalura*) is the tail markedly longer than the wing, and in another (*Chirocylla*) it is slightly longer. The long swallow-like tail of *Phibalura* probably gives it added manoeuvrability in flight; it is the only genus, besides *Iodopleura*, that regularly hawks flying insects. The unusually high tail:wing ratio of *Chirocylla* is due, at least in part, to the short rounded wing, with modified outer primaries, in this little known genus.

Beak-length (measured from the tip to the posterior margin of the nares) varies from about 9% of the wing-length, in some of the small and medium-sized species, to about 16–17% in some of the large fruit-crows (*Cephalopterus* and *Perissocephalus*). In nearly all genera the beak is relatively wide at the base for the size of the bird — an obvious adaptation for swallowing fruits whole — but there is a considerable range of variation in other respects. Three main types may be distinguished:

(1) Beak short, moderately hooked at tip, not greatly compressed. This apparently un-specialized beak shape is found in such genera as *Carpornis* and *Pipreola*; it seems to be adapted to a diet of smallish fruits.

(2) Beak very wide and short, much com-pressed. This beak shape is seen in its most extreme form in the bellbirds (*Procnias*), and in less extreme form in *Xipholena* and other medium-sized frugivores that feed on relatively large fruits.

(3) Beak relatively long, strong and crow-like. This beak shape, typical of the fruit-crows, seems to be adapted to a mixed diet of large fruits and large insects.

Relative tarsus-length varies less than the pro-portions discussed above; in the great majority of species it ranges from 17% to 25% of the wing-length. It is especially long in *Calyptura* (31%), the smallest cotinga, and in the red cotingas (*Phoeni-circus*) (28%). The combination of short wings and long tarsus in the red cotingas suggests that they may have a courtship display involving jumps from perch to perch, perhaps reminiscent of the display actions of manakins of the genus *Manacus*, which also have relatively short wings and long legs. The shortest relative tarsus-length is found in the fruit-crows *Querula* and *Haematoderus* (both 13%). In the

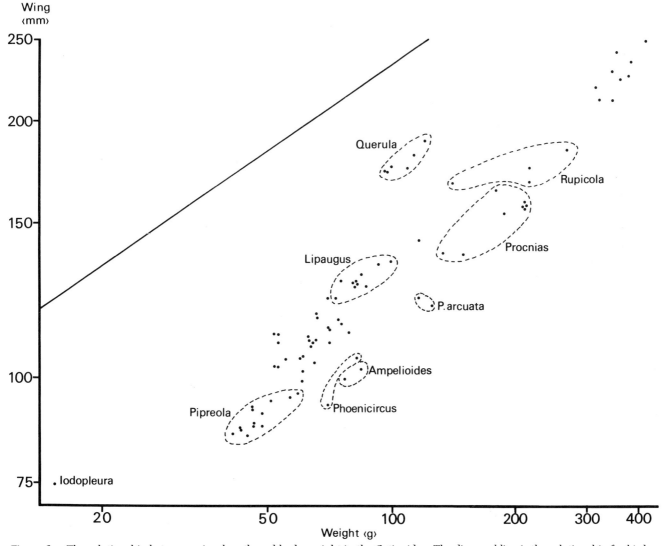

Figure 1   The relationship between wing-length and body-weight in the Cotingidae. The diagonal line is the relationship for birds in general, from Greenewalt (1962); the displacement of the cotinga data below the line is due to the fact that Greenewalt's data are based on wing-span/2 and the cotinga data on the conventional measurement of the wing from the carpal joint.

former, an aerially highly manoeuvrable bird, it is combined with relatively long and broad wings, as discussed above. In the Crimson Fruit-crow *Haematoderus militaris* wing-length relative to overall size seems to be about the same as in the other very large fruit-crows (no weights are available for *Haematoderus*), but the other large fruit-crows have relatively much longer tarsi (18–20%). The reason for this difference is unknown, as nothing is known of the feeding or any other aspect of the behaviour of the Crimson Fruit-crow. It is noteworthy that the Bare-necked Fruit-crow, which is quite atypical of the family in the agility with which it hops and runs along tree branches, also has a relatively short tarsus.

Table 4
Sexual size dimorphism: female measurement as a percentage of male measurement

	Wing-length	Weight[1]
Phoenicircus	114–117	–
Laniisoma	98	–
Phibalura	99	–
Iodopleura	98–103	–
Tijuca	98	–
Carpornis	98	–
Ampelion	97–100	97–100
Pipreola	95–101	96–108
Ampelioides	97	91
Porphyrolaema	104	–
Cotinga amabilis	98	–
C. ridgwayi	101	122
C. nattererii	100	–
C. cotinga	95	–
C. maculata	97	–
C. maynana	105	–
C. cayana	98	103
Xipholena	95–97	94
Carpodectes	89–93	–
Lipaugus vociferans etc.[2]	95–99	99–101
L. fuscocinereus	100	–
L. streptophorus	99	–
L. subalaris	101	–
Chirocylla	109	–
Conioptilon	95	–
Gymnoderus	91	–
Haematoderus	97	–
Querula	94	85–96
Pyroderus	92–95	–
Cephalopterus	84–89	–
Perissocephalus	93	89
Procnias	85–89	–
Rupicola	95–96	83[3]

[1] Minimum sample: 3 weights of each sex, except for *Rupicola*.
[2] Includes *L. vociferans*, *unirufus* and *lanioides*.
[3] Based on only one male, three females (*R. peruviana sanguinolenta*).

Sexual dimorphism in size and proportions

In the majority of cotinga species the wing-length of females averages 93–99% of that of males. Available weights indicate that females tend to be somewhat heavier than males, relative to their wing-length. Too few weights are available, however, for a thorough examination of sexual differences in absolute size. The data are summarized in Table 4, and only a few of the salient points are discussed here.

The greatest degree of sexual size dimorphism, as measured by wing-length, is found in two of the umbrellabirds (*Cephalopterus*, 84 and 89%) and the four bellbirds (*Procnias*, 85–89%). These are all birds with highly developed male ornamentation associated with striking courtship displays. Probably in all of them, males defend traditional display perches against other males, so that there may be a selective advantage in large size. It is noteworthy that in *Pyroderus* and *Perissocephalus*, the two genera that are mostly closely related to *Cephalopterus*, sexual size dimorphism is considerably less; in both of these genera the male and female plumages are very similar. The differences in sexual dimorphism between these three genera of very large fruit-crows are presumably related in some way to their social organization and displays, but too little is known about them for any plausible suggestion to be proposed.

At the other extreme of the range, females are larger than males in at least one species of *Cotinga*, in the related genus *Porphyrolaema*, probably in *Phoenicircus*, and possibly in *Chirocylla*. In *Cotinga* there are differences between the species. In *C. maynana* females are on average larger than males in all measurements; in *C. ridgwayi* females exceed males in most measurements and are considerably heavier; and in *C. cotinga* and *C. maculata* males are distinctly larger than females. With the almost complete lack of knowledge of the social organization and displays of these species, no reasons can be suggested for the interspecific differences. In *Phoenicircus* females are very considerably longer-winged than males. They are also longer-legged, and so probably larger overall, but weights are not available for both sexes. In this genus it may well be that the reduced size of the adult male is associated with a highly active display, as it is in manakins of the genus *Pipra*. In *Chirocylla*, for which few measurements are available, the sexual difference in wing-length may be due to the fact that the primaries are abbreviated and modified to a greater degree in the male than in the female.

Throughout the family there is a clear tendency for the tail to be shorter, relative to the wing, in males than in females. Details can be obtained from the measurements tabulated at the end of the species accounts. The difference is most marked in genera with a high degree of sexual plumage dimorphism (e.g. *Procnias*, *Rupicola*, some *Cotinga* spp.), but it is not confined to such genera. *Phibalura*, the only genus with an elongated swallow-shaped tail, is the only one in which the male's relative tail-length is considerably greater than the female's.

Whether the marked size difference between the sexes in extreme cases such as the umbrellabirds and bellbirds is associated with any sexual difference in feeding ecology is a question for future investigation. It seems unlikely that there would be any easily detectable differences in other cotingas. If there are any such differences they would be expected to involve the upper size limits of fruits that can be swallowed whole. Certainly there is sufficient difference in the width of the gape in male and female umbrellabirds to suggest that the two sexes may select a different range of fruits.

Food

For the fruit part of their diet the cotingas depend very largely on a small number of plant families. The fruit-crows and other large species feed especially on the fruits of palms (Palmae) and trees of the incense family (Burseraceae) and laurel family (Lauraceae). Of the incense family three genera (*Dacryodes*, *Protium* and *Trattinickia*) seem to be especially important. Fruits of the widespread and often abundant matchwood tree (*Didymopanax morototoni*), belonging to the Araliaceae, figure prominently in their diets, when available, and in montane forest other araliaceous trees are probably important.

With the exception of the palms, which they have not been recorded taking and may be unable to pluck with their very short and rather weak beaks, the same plant families and genera are important in the diet of the wholly frugivorous bellbirds. Probably the Lauraceae is the most important family for them. In her detailed study of the food of the Bearded Bellbird *Procnias averano* in Trinidad, B. K. Snow (1970) found that 30% of all recorded fruits were from this family, and represented eight species (a greater number of species than was recorded for any other plant family) which between them provided fruits in 10 of the 12 months of the year. The laurels are especially numerous in individuals and species in lower montane forest, at about the levels where bellbirds occur. The upper size limits of their fruits closely match the bellbirds'

gape width (Snow 1973a), a correspondence which is likely to have resulted from long coevolution between the trees and their avian dispersal agents.

The high nutritive quality of the pericarps of the fruits of palms, laurels and other tree families on which the larger cotingas feed is also, it seems, the result of coevolution between tree and dispersal agent. The tree invests a relatively large amount of its resources in each fruit, and in exchange it obtains from the bird relatively efficient dispersal of the seed within the fruit. The cotingas are not the only birds involved in this interaction, but they are certainly among the most important in the American tropics. Coevolutionary relationships between frugivores and their food plants have been the subject of much research, both practical and theoretical, in recent years, and a full review is beyond the scope of this chapter. The reader is referred to discussions by Morton (1973), McKey (1975) and Snow (1971d, 1981).

Little is known about the fruits taken by most of the medium-sized and smaller cotingas. There is some evidence, summarized on p. 83, that the blue cotingas (*Cotinga* spp.) show a distinct preference for figs (*Ficus* spp.), which do not figure prominently, if at all, in the diets of the larger species. The purple-tufts (*Iodopleura* spp.) are said to feed largely on mistletoe fruits. Mistletoe fruits are also a preferred food of the Swallow-tailed Cotinga *Phibalura flavirostris* of southeastern Brazil, and have recently been found to be the only kind of fruit eaten by the White-cheeked Cotinga *Ampelion stresemanni* of the Peruvian Andes. The relationship between this bird and its food supply, described on p. 62, is one of the most remarkable cases known of coevolution between a frugivore and its food plant. It is not known whether any of the mistletoe-eating cotingas have their alimentary tracts modified for such a diet, as have the tanagers of the genus *Euphonia* and some of the oriental and Australian flowerpeckers (*Dicaeum* spp.).

Sociobiology

Some important conditions of life are probably common to many of the cotingas of tropical and subtropical forest. Except for occasional periods of scarcity, nutritious fruit is likely to be easily available, so that a sufficient quantity for a bird's daily needs can usually be obtained in a small fraction of the daylight hours. Field observations in support of this statement are summarized on pp. 115 and 167, and comparable data for the mainly frugivorous manakins are given in Snow (1962a, 1962b). It is probable that adults have a high annual survival rate, and that the annual rate of production of young is very low. This has been found to be so for other tropical forest birds (e.g. Fogden 1972, Snow & Lill 1974, for adult survival rates; Skutch 1976, Snow & Snow 1979, for reproductive rates) but not for any cotingas, since difficulties of field work have so far stood in the way of quantitative studies. The low reproductive rates are almost certainly attributable to nest predators; hence there should be strong selection for adaptations of nest structure, nest site and parental behaviour which minimize predation rates.

These various factors acting together have, it seems, tended to produce the kind of adaptive 'syndrome' shown by bellbirds, and probably closely paralleled by the umbrellabirds (*Cephalopterus*), blue cotingas (*Cotinga*), white-winged and white cotingas (*Xipholena* and *Carpodectes*) and some other medium-sized or large cotingas that are sexually highly dimorphic. The nest is reduced in size to an absolute minimum, for inconspicuousness; family size is reduced to only one or two young (the most that the nest can hold), which the inconspicuous female alone can tend and feed. The male, being no longer needed at the nest and being able to feed himself in a short period each day, is freed to devote most of his time to attracting mates. Competition between males is consequently intense and leads to the evolution of striking ornamentation and extravagant courtship behaviour. To what extent the selective force involved in the evolution of these male characters is the active 'choice' of the most highly endowed males by the females (sexual selection in the orthodox sense), and to what extent it is the ability of the best endowed males to out-compete their fellows and thus obtain the dominant position within the local group, and with it the right to mate with the available females, is a debated question for whose solution the cotingas, in the present state of knowledge, can offer no critical evidence.

Not all the tropical and subtropical forest cotingas have followed this evolutionary pathway. For reasons that are not apparent, some show all the features of the bellbird syndrome except that sexual dimorphism is reduced or virtually absent. The two lowland forest pihas (*Lipaugus*), the Calfbird *Perissocephalus tricolor* and the Red-ruffed Fruit-crow *Pyroderus scutatus* are the outstanding examples. In all of them a striking or very loud call is an important element in the male's courtship behaviour, and it may be that this reduces his need for visual distinctiveness; but very loud calls are also a feature of the bellbirds, and in them they are combined with striking sexual dimorphism. A much more complete understanding of the behaviour and ecology of these genera will be needed before the different degrees of sexual dimorphism can be explained.

Two other variables in the organization of male displays may be briefly mentioned. Males may display singly, or in leks; and the display areas may be traditional, persisting from year to year, or they may shift. Among the cotingas, the Guianan Cock-of-the-rock *Rupicola rupicola* provides the prime example of lek displays of the classical type, in which each male owns and displays on its own 'court' within the general area of the lek. The parallel with such well-known lek birds as the Black Grouse *Lyrurus tetrix* and Ruff *Philomachus pugnax* is close, though the ecological conditions that have led to their evolution are of course quite different. The red cotingas (*Phoenicircus*) may turn out to have lek displays of much the same kind, as discussed above. Other species, such as the Calfbird, Screaming Piha *Lipaugus vociferans* and Red-ruffed Fruit-crow, may be broadly classed as lek birds, but all need further study before their display systems are properly understood. In the bellbirds (*Procnias*) and probably the umbrellabirds (*Cephalopterus*) the system may be described as a dispersed lek: males have individual display perches well separated from one another, but they are grouped together in a loose assemblage, within earshot if not within sight of one another.

The Andean Cock-of-the-rock *Rupicola peruviana* has a display organization of an unique type. If one may generalize from the single case that has been studied in detail, males display in leks, but within the lek they are paired and members of a pair direct most of their displays at one another. In the only lek studied, one male was dominant not only over his display partner but over all the other males, and he was the only one to mate with visiting females. In such a case, it seems that subordinate males effectively enhance the display of the dominant male without themselves getting any immediate advantage. It may be that the best 'strategy' for a subordinate male is to be ready to take over the dominant role if the leading male dies or for any reason is unable to maintain his position. The Calfbird's lek system may well be similar, and the coordinated vocal display of the Black-and-gold Cotinga *Tijuca atra* may be another manifestation of a system in which a dominant male has his performance enhanced by subordinate birds. Close parallels are found in some manakins, for example the blue-backed manakins (*Chiroxiphia*) and the Wire-tailed Manakin *Pipra filicauda* (Snow 1976b, Schwartz & Snow 1979).

It appears to be the rule for display areas, whether leks, dispersed leks, or single perches, to be traditional, persisting from year to year as long as they and the surrounding forest remain suitable. And it may also be the rule — though far more observations are needed to confirm it — for certain strategically placed, or otherwise especially suitable, display perches or courts within the lek areas to be most sought after. It is probable, however, that there are some species in which the displaying males are not confined to a traditional area, and the fundamental reason for this may be that the population needs to follow a seasonally shifting food supply. Such may be the case in the genera *Xipholena*, *Carpodectes* and *Cotinga*. What little is known of these cotingas indicates that males make themselves conspicuous by flight displays above the forest canopy, a method suited for long-distance advertisement and thus appropriate for birds that need to range widely for their food, and in strong contrast to the cock-of-the-rock's system of traditional display areas beneath the forest canopy.

The conditions of life in montane forest, especially at the higher levels, have tended to produce a very different kind of social organization. Possibly nest predation is less intense; possibly the lower temperatures make a larger and better insulated nest necessary; possibly nutritious food both for adults and for nestlings is less easily obtained. All this is speculative in the absence of knowledge, but whatever the complex of conditions that has shaped their evolution, the cotingas living at these levels tend to show slight to moderate sexual dimorphism and those that have been studied have been found to live in pairs, both sexes attending the nest.

There are also a few examples of less usual kinds of social organization in the family, but they are too poorly known for useful discussion here. Purple-throated Fruit-crows *Querula purpurata* are highly social birds, living in groups, all members of which may attend a single nest. They also defend the nest vigorously against potential predators, a trait that is unusual and perhaps unique in the family (but see p. 143), and this seems to be linked with their high aerial manoeuvrability and perhaps with their black plumage. The purpletufts (*Iodopleura*) are also highly social birds, perhaps breeding in groups, but their organization has not been properly studied. It is reasonable to suppose that it is linked in some way with their feeding ecology, which sets them apart from all other cotingas. Finally, there is some evidence that the Swallow-tailed Cotinga *Phibalura flavirostris* may have an unusual breeding system in which male and female of a pair each attends a separate nest. It is a certain prediction that future studies of cotingas in the field will bring to light a richer and more diverse array of social systems than we can envisage with the very inadequate knowledge at our disposal.

Colour, ornamentation
and other display structures

Deep reds and unusual shades of mauve and purple are a notable feature of the plumage of many cotingas. Shining blues of different shades are the special glory of the blue cotingas (*Cotinga* spp.), and are found in no other members of the family. Greens and yellows are prominent in the plumage of many of the montane genera which might be considered 'primitive', a controversial point that is discussed in a previous chapter (p. 13). Blacks, browns and greys are widely distributed through the family. The males of two species of bellbirds (*Procnias*) are among the very few kinds of land-birds with wholly white plumage, while the males of the white cotingas (*Carpodectes* spp.) are nearly white all over. Some of these colours are produced by pigments, some by modifications of the fine structure of feathers, and some by a combination of both. Other structural modifications of feathers enhance the effect of the pigments, and in some species areas of bare coloured skin and wattles produce striking visual effects. Finally, in several genera some of the wing-feathers are curiously modified. All of these features are developed to the highest degree in adult males, and as far as known all are associated with male advertisement and courtship display. Together they represent a wealth of colour and ornamentation which in its variety surpasses all other passerine families except the birds of paradise. Not surprisingly, the chemistry of the pigments and structure of the feathers of cotingas have been the subject of a number of investigations. What follows is a summary of these and related studies.

Colours

Görnitz & Rensch (1924) were the first to investigate the red and violet colours of cotinga feathers. They described a carotenoid (lipochrome) pigment, found in granular form in the feathers of *Xipholena* and *Cotinga*, which they named 'cotingin'. In *X. atropurpurea* the very dark blackish purple colour of the feathers is produced by a darker form of this pigment concentrated under the shiny surface of the barbs; there is no melanin (black or brown pigment). Görnitz & Rensch noted that on being broken down by treatment with heat and chemicals 'cotingin' changes colour, from violet through red to orange.

Völker (1952) carried the examination of cotinga feather pigments much further. He identified a number of different carotenoids in the feathers of various genera, and pointed out that the purple-red and violet pigments are structurally not very different from other red feather pigments, and that there is no need to give them a special name. Völker noted that the colour change of deep red and violet pigments through red to orange can be produced either by heat or by treatment with weak acid or alkali. The effect of heat was, in fact, known to some of the old collectors; there are old skins in museum collections which are discoloured in this way, probably because they were placed too close to a fire when they were being dried. In what is apparently the earliest published reference to this point, Quelch (1896) reported that mechanical pressure as well as heat can cause the colour change.

Brush (1969) made a much more detailed examination of the deep wine-red colour of males of *Xipholena punicea*. He found that it is produced by a mixture of carotenoids in combination with structural blue, and he agreed with Völker that 'cotingin' is not a useful term. Olson (1970) examined the modifications of feather structure found in several cotinga genera with deep red, purple and violet plumage colours. In all of them, heavy deposition of carotenoids is associated with modification of the barbs of the feathers in which they occur; characteristically the barbs are flattened and lack barbules. This condition reaches an extreme in the plumage of *Xipholena*.

There is little doubt that, in common with all other birds, cotingas are unable to synthesize carotenoids *de novo*, but are dependent for them on their diet. Presumably they obtain most of the carotenoids that they need from fruits. There is a general relationship in birds as a whole between diet and plumage colour, red and yellow and mixtures thereof being associated with fruit- and seed-eating; but within the cotinga family the relationship is not obvious. Certainly the cotinga species with the greatest extent or intensity of carotenoids in the plumage are specialized fruit-eaters, but all species are fruit-eaters to some extent and some of the most specialized (e.g. the bellbirds) lack carotenoids.

Although birds are dependent on their diet for these brilliant pigments, they can modify the chemical structure of the pigments once they have been assimilated, and thus the colours that they produce. Hence the various forms of carotenoids that have been identified in cotinga feathers need not have been present in their food in the same form.

Melanins are present in the feathers of many cotingas, as they are in the feathers of most birds. They are responsible for all black and brown feather colours, and in combination with carotenoids produce greens, olives and red-browns. Völker (1938) reported the presence of porphyrins (purplish pigments) in feathers of *Cotinga, Xipholena, Ampelion* and *Pipreola*. At that time porphyrins had not been found in the feathers of any other passerines, and apparently they still have not been; but they have been found in the feathers of a variety of non-passerine birds (Brush 1978). They are present only in very small amounts and, whatever their function, their colour does not contribute significantly to the appearance of these cotingas.

The blue of the plumage of *Cotinga* species is a structural colour, caused by Tyndall scattering, *i.e.* the scattering of the shorter light waves by sub-microscopic 'particles' (in fact minute air spaces) just below the surface of the barbs, the blue colour thus produced being intensified by a backing of melanin (Fox & Vevers 1960). The bright greens of *Pipreola* species are probably produced by a combination of yellow carotenoid with structural blue. Whiteness is also structural, and is produced by the reflection of light from the surface and from interior air spaces of barbs that lack pigment.

The blue of the bare head and neck of the Bare-necked Fruit-crow *Gymnoderus foetidus* and the blue-green of the bare throat of the Bare-throated Bellbird *Procnias nudicollis* must be caused by Tyndall scattering, but they have not been investi-gated. The redness of the throat of the Bare-necked Umbrellabird *Cephalopterus glabricollis* is presumably caused by small blood vessels near the surface of the skin; the colour disappears in preserved specimens. On the other hand, the orange or red which pervades the skin (as well as the beak and legs) of male cocks-of-the-rock (*Rupicola*) is clearly the same as the carotenoid in the feathers.

Modified feathers

Modifications of feather structure that enhance the visual effect of red and purple carotenoids are found in several genera, reaching an extreme in *Xipholena* as mentioned above. They are described and some of them are figured by Olson (1970); the complexity of their microscopic structure is too great for a brief summary. In several genera such feathers are also obviously modified in their gross structure; thus the most highly glossed and deepest crimson feathers of the Crimson Fruit-crow *Haematoderus militaris* are very elongated and lanceolate, and the red feathers on the throat of the Red-ruffed Fruit-crow *Pyroderus scutatus* are curiously crimped along the outer edge. The Guianan Cock-of-the-rock *Rupicola rupicola* has the most elaborately modified feathers of all the cotingas, especially the inner secondaries. The visual effect is complex and depends in part on the long silky fringe on the outer edge of the feather, which stirs in the slightest breeze (see p. 184). The back and rump feathers are modified in a similar way but to a much smaller degree than the inner secondaries. It seems probable that the modification originated in the secondaries and spread to the body plumage, as the secondaries (but not the back feathers) are modified in the Andean Cock-of-the-rock *R. peruviana* but much less strikingly.

In several genera one or more of the primary feathers are peculiarly modified (*Phoenicircus, Lanii-soma, Chirocylla, Cotinga, Procnias, Rupicola*). For descriptions and illustrations the reader is referred to the chapters on these genera. A minor modifica-tion is found in the Cinnamon-vented Piha *Lipaugus lanioides* but not in other members of the genus (p. 112). Most of these modifications involve the emargination of the feather tip and its reduction in length; in some cases the modified feathers are markedly curved, and in one (*Phoenicircus*) they are twisted. In *Cotinga* it seems that the emargination of one or more of the primaries is responsible for the rattling or twittering sound made by adult males in flight (a sound which some observers have thought to be vocal), and this presumably has some function in the male's advertisement or display. In the other species it is a reasonable assumption that the feather modifications have a similar function, but there is no evidence to support such an idea.

The extraordinary modification of the 7th primary in *Phoenicircus* may well be used for sound production in some kind of jumping display rather than in flight. The 7th primary is also modified in *Laniisoma*, but in a different way. Whether this indicates any affinity between these two genera is an open question, further discussed on p. 35.

Wattles and other appendages

These occur in the Bare-necked Fruit-crow, the umbrellabirds, and bellbirds. There seems little doubt that they were independently evolved in each of them. In the Bare-necked Fruit-crow the folds of bare skin on the male's head and neck are not known to be extensible or erectile, but in the umbrellabirds and bellbirds the displaying male has the ability to alter the size of the appendages surprisingly rapidly. The histology of the umbrellabird's wattle and its relationship to other structures have not been investigated, but it is clear from Cordier's account of the Bare-necked Umbrellabird (p. 150) that in this species at least it is inflated with air during display, and it is unlikely that its anatomy and functioning are fundamentally different in the other two species. The single wattle of the White Bellbird *Procnias alba* was formerly thought to be inflatable, but Burton (1976) has shown that it is isolated from the buccal cavity, respiratory tract and the pneumatic spaces in the skull. It is richly vascularised and contains longitudinal muscle bundles. Its extension, which takes 3–5 seconds, is probably brought about by engorgement of the blood vessels; its contraction, which is slightly more rapid, is probably caused by emptying of the blood vessels accompanied by elastic recoil and contraction of the longitudinal muscles.

Breeding and the annual cycle

Published information on the breeding of the cotingas is very scanty. There are in fact only three species for which one can give a reasonably accurate idea of the breeding season, and that only for one area each: the Bearded Bellbird *Procnias averano* in Trinidad, the Rufous Piha *Lipaugus unirufus* in Central America (Costa Rica and Panama), and the Guianan Cock-of-the-rock *Rupicola rupicola* in Guyana. Details for these, and the scattered information that exists for other species, are given in the accounts of genera and species: here a summary is given, with a brief discussion, of the breeding of the cotingas and the related events of the annual cycle.

The nest

With the exception of the two species of *Rupicola*, all of the cotingas whose nests are known – and this now includes 15 of the 25 genera – build open nests which they place in trees or shrubs. Some of the large and medium-sized species of tropical forest build extraordinarily small and flimsy saucer-shaped structures, supported by twigs or small branches, which have sometimes astonished the finder. *Procnias*, *Lipaugus* and *Xipholena* are outstanding examples; the nests of *Perissocephalus* and *Cephalopterus* are in the same category, but less extreme. Others build equally flimsy pads which rest on a more substantial base, such as a thick branch or a mass of epiphytes; *Gymnoderus* and *Cotinga* are examples. When the materials used in such nests have been carefully studied it has been found that they consist of twigs or tendrils from a few kinds of plants, whose structure is such that they interlock and hold together much more strongly than would at first sight seem possible. Whether the distribution of plants that provide suitable nest-materials is ever a factor governing the local distribution of these and other cotingas is a subject well worth investigating.

It seems certain that these very small nests have evolved under the selective pressure of nest predation; inconspicuousness is one of the obvious ways of avoiding predators. In the few species that have been watched at the nest, the behaviour of the parent bird and of the nestlings is beautifully adapted to draw as little attention as possible to the nest and its contents. Undoubtedly this is why so few nests of these cotingas have ever been found.

The Purple-throated Fruit-crow *Querula purpurata* is a striking exception to all of the above generalizations. Its nest is not very small nor very inconspicuous; several adults attend a nest, and their behaviour when doing so is highly conspicuous. Their strategy, an uncommon one in birds of tropical forest, is to protect the nest by mobbing any potential predator that may approach it. Possibly the Red-ruffed Fruit-crow *Pyroderus scutatus* uses the same method of nest defence (p. 143). Both of these species are made conspicuous by their mainly black plumage.

On the basis of existing knowledge few generalizations can be made about the structure of the nest in the other genera of cotingas and the ways in which they are adapted to their environment. Besides those mentioned above, the nest of only one other cotinga of lowland forest is known. The single recorded nest of the White-browed Purpletuft *Iodopleura isabellae*, one of the smallest of the cotingas, was a tiny cup bound by cobwebs to a thin horizontal branch in the crown of a tree and reminiscent of a hummingbird's nest (Sick 1979). Such a nest must depend for its safety on both inconspicuousness and inaccessibility.

The nests of only three montane genera are known. The Swallow-tailed Cotinga *Phibalura flavirostris* of the southeast Brazilian highlands builds a flimsy cup nest of lichens, mosses and similar materials in an upright tree-fork or on a horizontal branch. The Andean genera *Pipreola* and *Ampelion* build more substantial cup nests in shrubs and small trees. These latter more 'conventional', unspecialized nests, similar to those of many passerine birds of other families, might be thought to be the ancestral kind, from which the specialized nests of the lowland forest species were evolved.

25

Such an argument may well be fallacious, however. In the cooler montane conditions, where nest predators are probably less numerous than in tropical forest, selection for inconspicuousness may be relaxed, while the insulating properties of a nest may be more important. The bulky cup nest is probably equally well adapted to environmental conditions as are those of tropical forest, and the evolutionary sequence may be read either way.

Finally, the cocks-of-the-rock plaster their bracket-shaped nests of vegetable matter and mud onto more or less vertical rock faces, the Andean species often above mountain torrents and the Guianan species usually in shallow caves or among giant boulders. These are clearly examples of nests which depend for their safety on their inaccessibility to most predators.

The eggs

Cotinga eggs are typically buff, khaki or olive in ground colour with spots and blotches of darker browns, sepia, ashy violet and similar colours, often concentrated more thickly round the broad end. Almost certainly the colour scheme is cryptic, though no definite evidence can be given in support of this statement. *Rupicola*, whose rock nests are often in semi-darkness and must be safe from many of the predators that threaten tree nests, has eggs similar to other members of the family but with paler ground colour.

The clutch consists of a single egg in all the medium-sized and large tropical-forest cotingas which build small saucer-shaped nests in trees, in the genera *Lipaugus*, *Cotinga*, *Xipholena*, *Cephalopterus*, *Perissocephalus* and *Procnias*. It consists of 2 eggs in *Rupicola* and *Pipreola*; and of 2–3 eggs in *Phibalura* and the Andean genus *Ampelion*. In the present state of knowledge interpretation must be tentative. In *Pipreola*, *Phibalura* and *Ampelion* both parents attend the nest and feed the young; and in all the other genera listed above only the female attends the nest. It might seem therefore that clutch-size depends mainly on whether one or both of the parents feeds the young; but this explanation is not necessarily correct, as clutch-size is also related to the structure and size of the nest. The substantial cup nests of *Pipreola* and *Ampelion* can accommodate two or three young, while the very small structures of *Lipaugus* and the other tropical-forest cotingas are unsuited for holding more than one well-grown young. For further discussion of this point the reader is referred to pp. 19–20, where the single-egg clutch is related to the whole adaptive strategy of the specialised frugivorous cotingas.

In his book *Ecological adaptations for breeding in birds* Lack (1968) examined the relationship between egg size and body size in the different families of birds. The general relationship which he found for passerine birds is shown in Figure 2, together with the relationship in those cotingas for which both egg weights and body weights are available. On this showing the cotingas have unusually large eggs for passerine birds; the relationship between egg size and body weight is in fact similar to that for some non-passerine families, for example the kingfishers and rollers. No obvious reason can be suggested, but it may be that a large egg size is related to a long incubation period (see next section), both of these being adaptations enabling the young bird to complete as much as possible of its growth in the egg. As may be seen from Figure 2, in which species laying a single-egg clutch are distinguished from species laying 2 or more eggs, there is no evidence that a small clutch-size has favoured a compensatory increase in egg size.

Incubation and fledging periods

These are very incompletely known. The following tabulation summarizes the available information, the periods being given to the nearest whole day:

	Incubation	Fledging
Pipreola riefferii	19–20	21 (captive breeding)
Pipreola jucunda	17	25 (captive breeding)
Lipaugus unirufus	25–26	28–29
Querula purpurata	25	33
Perissocephalus tricolor	26–27	–
Procnias averano	23	33
Rupicola rupicola	27–28	–
Rupicola peruviana	28	42–44

Compared with those of oscine passerine birds of similar size, the incubation periods are very long; the fledging periods are also long but not so markedly different. As Lack (1968) suggested for the related manakins, which also have unusually long incubation periods for their size, it may be that the young hatch at a relatively advanced stage of development, which would tend to lengthen the incubation period at the expense of the fledging period; and the reason might be that it is safer for the young bird to complete as much as possible of its development in the egg; but there is no information with which this suggestion can be tested.

The nestling

Except for *Rupicola*, in which the nestling down is long but sparse, cotinga nestlings are thickly covered with down. The details, where known, are described in the accounts of genera and species. While no comprehensive account of cotinga nestlings can yet be given, it is clear that there is an extraordinary diversity in their appearance, and it seems that some at least of this diversity involves adaptations for the camouflage of the nestling. The nestling of the Shrike-like Cotinga *Laniisoma elegans*, perhaps the most striking of all (Plate 2, p. 34), is apparently camouflaged to resemble moss covered with fruiting bodies; its nest and nest-site are unrecorded. The nestling of the Bare-necked Fruit-crow *Gymnoderus foetidus* has an extraordinary resemblance to lichen (p. 130), an appropriate camouflage as the nest is a small pad on a thick tree branch. Why the nestlings of the Bearded Bell-bird and the blue cotingas (*Cotinga* spp.) should be covered with thick whitish down, the nestling of the Calfbird *Perissocephalus tricolor* with bright orange down, and the nestling of the Rufous Piha with grey down, is less easy to explain, as these colours do not match their nests or nest-sites. In the case of the bellbird, the thickness of the down may be connected with the fact that the female broods the nestling very little after the first few days, so that efficient heat conservation may be more important for it than for nestlings which receive more brood-ing. The study of cotinga nestlings will certainly be important for a better understanding of the natural history of the family, but progress is bound to be very slow.

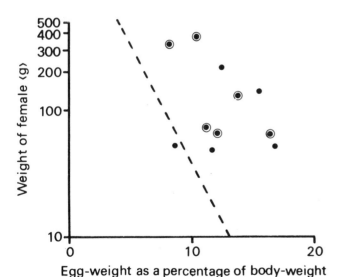

Figure 2   Proportionate egg-weight in relation to body-weight in 11 species of cotingas. Species laying one-egg clutches are shown by encircled symbols, those laying two or more eggs by plain symbols. The broken line is the general relationship for passerine birds from Lack (1968, Fig. 1, p. 184).

Breeding seasons

In general, the breeding seasons of cotingas appear to be similar to those of other passerine birds in the areas where they occur. Thus in Panama and Costa Rica there are 8 records of egg-laying (*Cotinga* and *Lipaugus* spp.) in the months February–May, the main breeding season for most land-birds, and a single late record in August. In Trinidad, the Bearded Bellbird has a long breeding season, apparently with a major peak in May and a minor peak in October–November, much the same as the long, double-peaked breeding season of forest thrushes and other species. South of the Equator, in southeastern Brazil, the sparse data indicate a breeding season at a time of year equivalent to that in Central America, i.e. different by about 6 calendar months. At low latitudes, near the Equator, there are too few records for any generalization to be possible.

In relation to climate, breeding seasons begin in the latter part of the dry season and extend to varying extents into the wet season. Studies in Central America, Trinidad, and southeastern Brazil are all in broad agreement in showing that the peak of abundance of fruits is in the dry season or early in the wet season, and the peak of abundance of insects is in the wet season (Snow 1976a). The period round the end of the dry and beginning of the wet season seems to be the time of year when feeding conditions are most favourable for frugivores which also take some insects.

There is little information on how many nesting attempts an individual female makes in the course of the breeding season, but it is probably the rule that repeated attempts are made. The only positive evidence is for the Bearded Bellbird, Rufous Piha and Natterer's Cotinga *Cotinga nattererii*. The point is an important one in relation to population and survival statistics, since the evidence suggests that a high proportion of nesting attempts end in failure.

Moulting seasons

Like most birds, the cotingas undergo a complete moult immediately after the end of the breeding season. This, at least, is true of the females of all the species, so far as known, and of both sexes of those species in which both male and female attend the nest; but in those species in which the males are emancipated from nesting duties, the males moult well in advance of the females, in some cases so far in advance that it is clear that they must begin to moult while they are still courting and mating. The evidence for this is far from complete for all species; the following are the best substantiated cases.

In the Guianan Cock-of-the-rock, in Guyana, egg-laying takes place mainly in March and April. For 8 females from Guyana and adjacent areas of Bolivar, southeastern Venezuela, the calculated dates of the onset of moult are from the extreme end of March to July; for 8 males the calculated dates are all in February and March.

The recorded egg-laying dates of the Rufous Piha in Costa Rica extend from early March to early August. The calculated dates of onset of the moult for females from Costa Rica and adjacent Nicaragua are in the months April–August, and for males in the months February–May.

In Trinidad the Bearded Bellbird lays from April to August, and after a break (probably coinciding with the period when most females are moulting) there is a second, minor laying period in October and November. There are hardly any records of the moult of females, but for all of the 11 records for males the calculated dates of onset of moult are in the months March–June.

It will be noted that in these cases the males must moult during, or even before, the females' period of egg-laying, and that the moulting dates for the females too are earlier than might be expected from knowledge of the breeding season. It seems that some females, perhaps young birds breeding for the first time, must begin to moult at once, following an early nest failure. The data do not justify the conclusion that females moult while they are attending a nest, though successful breeders may well begin immediately after their young have fledged.

If the breeding season is timed to coincide with the period when the food supply is most favourable, as discussed in the previous section, it is reasonable to suppose that males that have no nesting duties should begin to moult at the same time as the females are breeding, for both breeding and moulting are energy-demanding activities. For the females, the best strategy should be to moult as soon as possible after the extra energy demands of breeding have finished. Young females, whose chances of successful breeding may be low, may do better to moult at once after an early nest failure rather than to make another attempt and delay their moult until feeding conditions are less favourable.

The following tabulation, modified from Snow (1976a), summarizes the sex differences in the timing of moult in all the genera for which there are adequate records:

Phibalura	The only genus in which there is evidence that females moult earlier than males (females, Oct.–Dec., 6 records; males, Nov.–Feb., 8 records). This difference, if substantiated, may be related to what seems to be a unique breeding strategy in this genus (see p. 48).
Carpornis	Females on average about a month later than males in *C. cucullatus*; probably later in *C. melanocephalus* but records inadequate.
Ampelion	Females on average later than males; but moult is very un-seasonal in this genus throughout most of its range, and the difference is apparent only in one of the northern-most populations.
Pipreola	Females on average about a month later than males, but moult not well synchronized in this Andean genus and the difference is apparent only in northern populations.
Lipaugus	In *L. unirufus* and *L. vociferans* females are consistently later than males by two or three months on average, but there is considerable overlap. Records for the other species are inadequate.
Tijuca	Few records, but females later than males by nearly two months on average; no over-lap.
Cotinga	No difference apparent, but samples are rather small from all areas.
Xipholena	Males apparently well in advance of females, but most of the range of the genus is at low latitudes where moult is not well synchronized.
Carpodectes	Males on average considerably in advance of females, but much overlap.
Gymnoderus	Most of the range is at low latitudes where moult is not well synchronized, but in the extreme south, in Bolivia, records for females are about a month later than males.
Querula	Females on average later than males, but much overlap.
Pyroderus	No difference between the sexes apparent.

Perissocephalus Females apparently later than males, but samples inadequate.

Procnias Females on average later than males, but too few records for estimate of extent of difference (onset of moult dependent on age, at least in males – see p. 170).

Rupicola Females on average 2–3 months later than males, with some overlap.

Breeding success

The records are so far quite inadequate for any reliable assessment of the breeding success of any of the cotingas. Only a handful of nests have been found while they were being built or when they had eggs, and then observed until their outcome was known. Of ten such nests, for which there are satisfactory records (*Procnias averano*, *Lipaugus unirufus*, *Cotinga nattererii*), two were successful in producing fledged young. Obviously no conclusion can be drawn from these figures, except that they suggest that cotingas which build very flimsy tree nests may have a low rate of success, as do many species of birds in tropical forest.

Note on the systematic section (pages 31–185)

The following accounts of the genera and species of cotingas are arranged under headings that are very largely standardized, but in some cases modified to suit particular needs. It has not been considered necessary to give detailed plumage descriptions of each species; their appearance is adequately shown by the colour plates, and full descriptions, if needed, are available in standard handbooks. The inclusion of such descriptions would have considerably lengthened the text and would have meant omitting information of more value. Plumage changes and moult sequences are, however, described in some detail, as these are mostly not available from other sources. Measurements are given for all species, and weights where available. Wing (flattened against the rule, and straightened), tail and tarsus measurements were taken in the standard way; culmen measurements are from the bill-tip to the posterior margin of the

nares. Measurements, preceded by the sample size in parentheses, are given as the range and mean, or (in the case of very small samples) as single measurements.

In the interest of readability the English names of the cotingas are used in the longest sections dealing with ecology, behaviour and breeding. No innovations have been made in these English names, which follow those used in recent standard works; but as complete uniformity of usage has not yet been achieved, a few alternatives are given. The English name proposed for the newly discovered *Tijuca condita*, Grey-winged Cotinga, is based on the field character that was found to be most distinctive by the only two ornithologists to have seen it in life. In the sections on distribution, plumages and moults, and structural characters, scientific names are used.

MWWoodcock

Genus *Phoenicircus* – the red cotingas

Phoenicircus carnifex – Guianan Red Cotinga
Phoenicircus nigricollis – Black-necked Red Cotinga

Phoenicircus is a genus of uncertain position. Although very different in other ways, it shares two characters with *Laniisoma*: the outer toe is united to the middle toe for most of its length, and the 7th primary is modified (but not in the same way in the two genera). A unique character is that the tarsus is feathered along its inner side. The foot structure is typical of manakins rather than cotingas, and it may be that the red cotingas are in fact overgrown manakins. Recent classifications have kept *Phoenicircus* in the Cotingidae, as we do here with some reservations.

The brilliantly coloured males apparently display in leks, but the single report of their behaviour is tantalizingly brief and lacking in detail. One may suspect, from the fact that adult males are distinctly smaller than females and immature males, that their display involves agility and quick flight movements, just as male manakins of the genus *Pipra*, whose displays involve jumps and rapid aerial manoeuvres, are smaller than the females. Little is known about any aspect of the natural history of the red cotingas.

The genus consists of two allopatric species which together constitute a superspecies. They are very similar to one another, differing mainly in the development of black in the male plumage, and in size (*nigricollis* being the larger of the two). They

might almost be treated as conspecific except for evidence, admittedly slight, that where their ranges meet they behave as good species.

Distribution (Map 1)

The two species between them occupy most of the lowland forest of Amazonia and the Guianas. The absence of either from most of southern Venezuela seems well founded, as a good deal of collecting has been carried out there; the apparent absence of *nigricollis* from southeastern Peru and Bolivia is perhaps more likely to be due to insufficient collecting in lowland forest areas.

P. nigricollis occupies upper Amazonia; north of the Amazon it extends east to the Rio Negro (records from the south bank only of the lower Negro, but from both sides upstream from about 65°W), but south of the Amazon it has been recorded as far east as the Rio Curuá, between the Tapajós and the Xingú. *P. carnifex* replaces it over most of lower Amazonia and in the Guianas; on the south side of the Amazon it occurs along the lower courses of the Tapajós, Xingú and Tocantins rivers, and in this area it comes into close proximity or contact with *nigricollis*. Specimens of both species are recorded from both sides of the lower Tapajós, but they were taken mainly by commercial collectors, possibly over a wider area than indicated by the localities on the labels, and so do not afford critical evidence that the two species are truly sympatric (see Appendix 3). The most likely interpretation of their distributional relationship is that they are too similar ecologically to be able to coexist, but ethologically distinct enough not to hybridise when they come into contact along the borders of their ranges. A field study of the red cotingas along the lower Rio Tapajós would be of the greatest interest.

Haffer (1970) has suggested that the two species differentiated in isolation during a past arid climatic period, *nigricollis* in a forest refuge centred on eastern Ecuador (the Napo refuge) and *carnifex* in a Guiana forest refuge; and that both of them spread with the subsequent spread of the forests until they

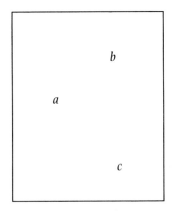

Plate 1
The red cotingas
(*Phoenicircus*)

a and b: Guianan Red Cotinga *P. carnifex*, male and female
c: Black-necked Red Cotinga *P. nigricollis*, male

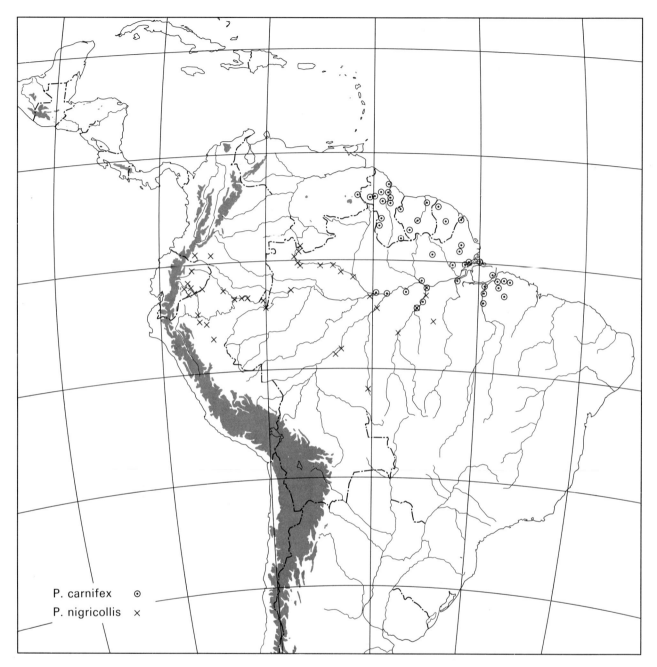

Map 1   Distribution of the Guianan Red Cotinga (*Phoenicircus carnifex*) and the Black-necked Red Cotinga (*P. nigricollis*).

met at their present border and halted each other's advance. This hypothesis is further discussed on p. 14.

Habitat and food

Both species are confined to lowland evergreen forest. They appear to be exclusively fruit-eaters, but few details have been recorded. Schomburgk (1848) reported that the Guianan species was fond of the fruits of figs (*Ficus* spp.), and Snethlage (1908) mentioned the fruits of a species of Passifloraceae. The stomachs of three specimens of Guianan Red Cotingas in the collection of the Museu Nacional, Rio de Janeiro, are recorded as containing the fruits of *Euterpe* palms (locally known as 'assahy'). Schubart *et al.* (1965) record that one specimen of the Black-necked Red Cotinga contained relatively large seeds, unfortunately unidentified.

Behaviour

Olalla (1943) reported that the Black-necked Red Cotinga performs communal displays like those of manakins. Up to 12 males may assemble, apparently called up by one male; they make short flights between the trees and utter monosyllabic calls; then disperse, to reassemble elsewhere. They are said to be very tame when 'dancing'. This brief account can only serve as an incentive to some ornithologist to find the red cotingas' display grounds and make a proper study of what must surely be a spectacular performance.

Breeding and annual cycle

Nothing is known of the nesting of either species and no very young birds seem to have been collected. The small number of moulting specimens examined, from widely scattered localities, are insufficient to indicate the pattern of timing of moult.

Plumages and moults

Nestling and juvenile plumages unknown. Immature male plumage like female, but with deeper red colouration and shorter wings (but not as short as adult males), the primaries nearly concealed by the secondaries in the closed wing. Apparently no subadult male plumage.

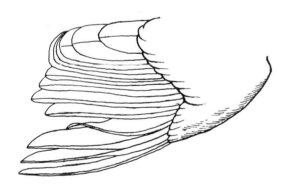

Figure 3 Wing of adult male *Phoenicircus nigricollis*.

Physical characters

Structure

Bill short, wide at base, slightly hooked; nostrils large, oval, half concealed by forwardly directed feathers of forehead; rictal bristles slightly developed and prominent bristly feathers round base of both mandibles. Tarsi feathered on inner side; outer toe united to middle toe except for terminal phalanx. Crown-feathers glossy and plush-like in adult male. Primaries in adult male as follows: 1–5 normal; 6th normal in shape but short (6–7 mm shorter than 5th); 7th very short (4–5 mm shorter than 6th), with attenuated, stiffened and strongly recurved tip (Fig. 3); 8–10 longest, about equal in length, somewhat stiffened, very narrow at base, broadest in middle, and narrowing towards tip (especially 10th).

Unfeathered parts

Similar in both species.

Iris: adult male, dark red; female, red-brown.

Bill: brown, lower mandible paler. Gape and mouth lining yellow.

Feet and legs: pale yellowish brown.

Measurements

P. carnifex

ad ♂♂ (14)   Wing 90–98, 94.2.   Tail 70–77, 74.0.
   Tarsus 25–27.5, 26.3.   Culmen 9.5–11.5, 10.5.

im ♂♂ (7)   Wing 97–110, 103.6.   Tail 78–81, 79.3.

♀♀ (11)   Wing 103–114, 109.9.   Tail 84–94, 88.8.
   Tarsus 27–28.5, 27.7.   Culmen 11–12.5, 12.0.

Weights: 1 ad ♂ 70 g (wing-length 93 mm).
   4 im ♂♂ 75–85, 82.0 g (mean wing 105.8 mm).

P. nigricollis

ad ♂♂ (10)   Wing 95–105, 98.9.   Tail 74–82, 76.8.
   Tarsus 26–27, 26.7.   Culmen 12–13, 12.4.

im ♂♂ (3)   Wing 103–106, 104.3.   Tail 81–83, 82.0.

♀♀ (6)   110–119, 113.2.   Tail 82–92, 86.7.   Tarsus 27.5–29, 28.3.   Culmen 12–12.5, 12.3.

MWWoodcock

Genus *Laniisoma*

Laniisoma elegans – Shrike-like Cotinga

This is in every way an unsatisfactorily known genus, principally, it seems, because the single species, although widespread, occurs in low densities in a habitat difficult for field work, dense hill forest at tropical levels. It is one of several cotinga genera that probably originated in the southeastern Brazilian highland area, two of which (*Laniisoma* and *Phibalura*) subsequently spread to the eastern flanks of the Andes; but it is not closely related to the other three, and indeed it has in the past been placed in the related family Pipridae (manakins) on the basis of its foot structure.

The Shrike-like Cotinga owes its English name to a translation of its not very appropriate generic name (*Lanius* = shrike, *soma* = body, form). There is nothing to suggest that it is in fact shrike-like in any way. It is a medium-small cotinga with moderate sexual dimorphism in plumage colour. It has two structural peculiarities: the outer toe is extensively joined to the middle toe, only the two distal phalanges being free (a condition typical of the manakins); and in the male the 7th primary is modified, being emarginated, narrow at the tip, and slightly recurved (Fig. 4). Both of these characters suggest affinity with *Phoenicircus*, which also has a manakin-like foot and, in the male, has the 6th and 7th primaries modified, but not in the same way as *Laniisoma*.

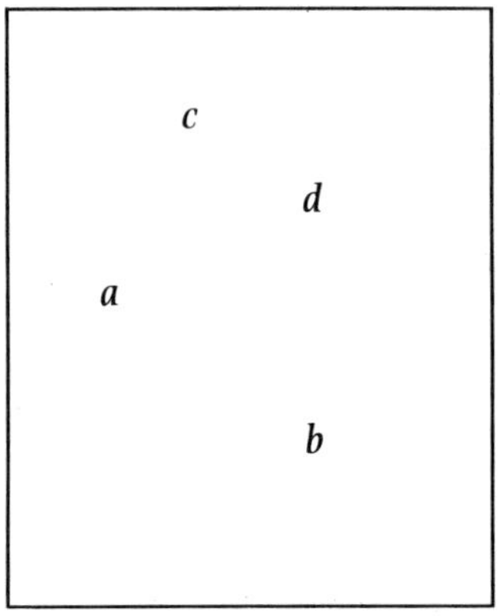

Distribution (Map 2)

Laniisoma elegans has been known since 1823 from the eastern Brazilian coastal mountains, where it has a limited range in the states of Espirito Santo, Rio de Janeiro and São Paulo. Its occurrence on the eastern slopes of the Andes was first made known in 1854, from specimens collected in Ecuador. It was subsequently found in Bolivia in 1934, in Venezuela in 1941, in Colombia in 1959, and in Peru in 1961. All records are from tropical levels along the eastern (or in Venezuela the southern) base of the Andes. With the increase in field work in Peru in recent years it is becoming apparent that the species may, locally at least, be more common than has been supposed. The possibility of vertical migration up and down the Andean foothills is discussed in the next section.

Ecology

Nothing is known of the ecology of the eastern Brazilian population, specimens of which have been taken mainly at about 3000 ft (900 m) and some at lower levels. Bolivian records are from 2200 ft (700 m), 'in heavy forest, amongst the undergrowth' (Carriker 1935), and from 4500 ft (1370 m). The first Peruvian specimen was collected in tropical rain forest at 350 m above sea level, and later specimens have been collected

Plate 2
Shrike-like Cotinga
Laniisoma elegans

a and b: southeastern Brazilian race (*elegans*), male and female
c and d: Andean race (*buckleyi*), female and nestling

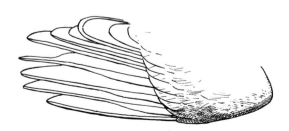

Figure 4 Wing of adult male *Laniisoma elegans*.

35

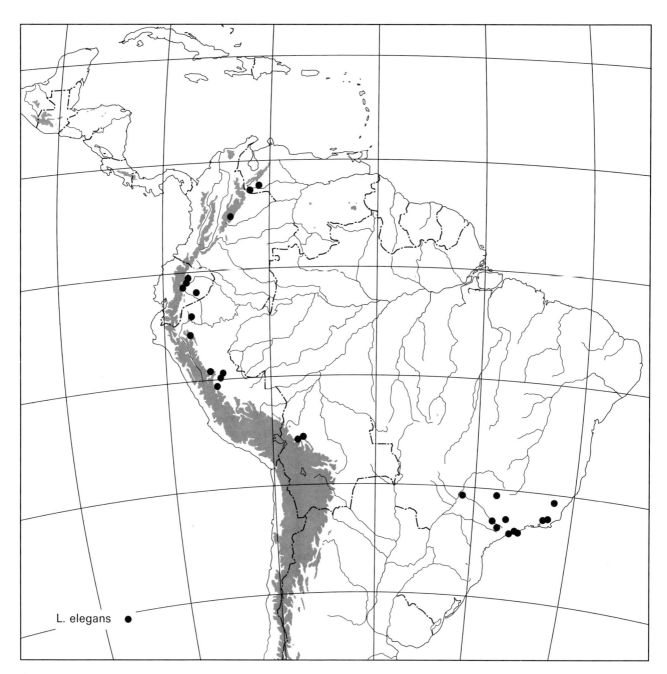

Map 2   Distribution of the Shrike-like Cotinga (*Laniisoma elegans*).

at about 1800 m (Snow 1975, Thoresen 1974). T. A. Parker, whose recent observations on the bird's behaviour are quoted in the following section, found it at 3500 ft (1100 m) in upper tropical zone cloud forest. Ecuadorian and Venezuelan specimens have been collected in the upper tropical zone.

All the Andean records indicate that the Shrike-like Cotinga is restricted to a narrow belt along the eastern (or in Venezuela the southern) base of the Andes. There is no obvious reason why a bird that is resident as low as only a few hundred metres above sea level in tropical forest at the base of the Andes should not extend much more widely into the lowlands; but if the Shrike-like Cotinga undertakes a seasonal migration to high altitudes, perhaps to breed, its limited range is explicable. Parker's observations of male territorial behaviour in upper tropical zone cloud forest in late August and early September, presumably the beginning of the breeding season, give some support to this suggestion. Unfortunately the altitude of Pindo in Ecuador, where Clarence Buckley collected the remarkable nestlings described and figured by Sclater & Salvin (1880), is not known.

The stomach of the only specimen whose stomach contents were recorded (rain forest at 3500 ft, Peru) contained insect remains. In the area where he made the observations quoted in the next section Parker saw birds regularly visiting fruiting melastomes in secondary growth around the forest edge. Probably, therefore, the Shrike-like Cotinga's diet, like that of most other unspecialised members of the family, consists of a mixture of fruits and insects.

Behaviour

In late August to mid-September 1977, T. A. Parker located two territorial males in upper tropical zone cloud forest 80 km northwest of Rioja (Dept. San Martin) on the road to Pomacochas, at a height of 3500 ft. They were noticed because of their peculiar calls, very thin, high-pitched notes repeated over and over: *psiiiiiiiiieeeee*, which they delivered from the subcanopy of tall cloud forest with sparse undergrowth. In response to song playbacks one male flew down to within 30 ft of him and sat upright, peering from side to side with the throat-feathers slightly puffed out. No calls were given by this or the other bird away from the subcanopy or canopy. The 'song' was heard almost constantly throughout the morning and early afternoon. The two males were found about 2 km apart and both ranged about 100 m from several preferred calling perches. These individuals, and also females, were apparently regularly visiting fruiting melastomes in neighbouring secondary growth.

Breeding and annual cycle

Buckley collected two nestlings in eastern Ecuador together with a female (presumably their parent). Their remarkable plumage is described in the next section and illustrated in Plate 2; but most unfortunately the specimens were accompanied with no information, neither of date nor of nest or nest-site.

A little information on the annual cycle can be gained from examination of moulting specimens. Two eastern Brazilian specimens (both males) in advanced stages of moult in November indicate a start of moult in August and September. Two Venezuelan specimens (also males), one in the middle of its moult in September and the other very near the end of its moult in November, both indicate a start of moult about July. These latter two are in accord with the general moult season for cotingas in their area, but the Brazilian specimens are unusually early, as the moult of male cotingas in their area (São Paulo) mostly begins considerably later, in October–December.

Plumages and moults

The two nestlings collected by Buckley were described by Sclater & Salvin as follows: 'The plumage is most remarkable: the upper surface, including the whole of the head, is of a cinnamon colour spotted with black, each black spot on the head being tipped with white; the under surface is black, banded with narrow white bars. From the top of the head proceed fine black filaments more than an inch long, each tipped with white.'

The nestlings, which are in the British Museum collection, are indeed remarkable, but Sclater & Salvin's description is misleading. They are, in fact, acquiring their juvenile plumage, and the nestling down is still adhering to the tips of the feathers of the upper parts (apparently it has worn off the underparts except for traces on the flanks); their wing-feathers are about half-grown, and the tail-feathers just sprouting from the sheaths. The filamentous down feathers, branched from the base, are black with white tips on the head, shading to cinnamon with white tips on the back; the down of the head is up to about 26 mm long, and that of the back up to about 20 mm long. The white base of the down feathers gives the appearance of a white spot on the tips of the juvenile feathers, but they are not in fact white-tipped, as Sclater & Salvin say. The juvenile plumage of the upper parts and throat is fluffy, the feathers being bright cinnamon with black tips; below, the juvenile feathers are barred blackish and white, becoming cinnamon towards the flanks and vent. The wing-coverts are olive-green basally, and cinnamon with a black tip distally. Primaries and secondaries are olive-green.

The juvenile plumage is apparently soon replaced by a plumage that resembles the adult plumage closely, except that the juvenile flight-feathers and some cinnamon-tipped wing-coverts are retained.

Physical characters

Structure
Bill rather long, with straight culmen ridge,

abruptly hooked at tip; nostrils covered by forwardly directed frontal bristles; rictal bristles well developed. Tarsus slender; outer toe partly united to middle toe, only the two distal phalanges free. 7th primary (male only) attenuated distally, slightly recurved, and projecting a little beyond the 6th and 8th (Fig. 4).

Unfeathered parts
Sexes apparently similar.
Iris: brown. Orbital flesh green.
Bill: upper mandible black, lower mandible pale bluish horn or grey.
Legs and feet: olive, bluish olive or grey.

Geographical variation
Geographical variation is surprisingly slight, considering the wide distributional gap that separates the Andean from the eastern Brazilian populations. The Andean populations differ from the eastern Brazilian populations most noticeably in the female plumage; the crown is sooty in eastern Brazil, but in the Andean populations only a little darker than the olive-green of the back. Andean birds are also on average smaller, and the underparts are less heavily barred.

There is some geographical variation among the Andean populations, but too few specimens are available to enable it to be properly worked out. Venezuelan birds are apparently slightly different in colour from those further south in the Andes, and there is probably some size variation throughout the Andean range. Three subspecies names are in use for these populations, *venezuelensis* for Venezuelan birds, *buckleyi* for those from Ecuador and Peru, and *cadwaladeri* for the single known Bolivian specimen (see Appendix 1). It is likely that further knowledge will lead to a revision of this arrangement.

Measurements
L. e. elegans
♂♂ (16)   Wing 100–107, 103.9.   Tail 62–68, 63.9.
      Tarsus 21–22.5, 21.7.   Culmen 11.5–13.5, 12.4.
♀♀ (6)   Wing 99–103, 101.5.   Tail 60–63, 62.0.
      Tarsus 21–23, 22.3.   Culmen 13–14, 13.5.

L. e. venezuelensis
♂♂ (5)   Wing 91–97, 93.4.   Tail 53–55, 54.5.

L. e. buckleyi
♂♂ (3)   Wing 95–101.5, 97.8.   Tail 53–67.5, 59.7.
♀♀ (4)   Wing 98–101, 99.0.   Tail 60–67, 62.3.
Weights: 1 ♂   46 g (wing 101.5 mm).
      2 ♀♀   45.8, 51 g (wings 98, 99 mm).

L. e. cadwaladeri
♂ (type)   Wing 102.   Tail 65.

Genus *Calyptura*

Plate 3, page 42

Calyptura cristata – Kinglet Calyptura

From its size and plumage one might suppose that *Calyptura cristata* should be placed in the manakin family (Pipridae) or the tyrant-flycatchers (Tyrannidae). Its allocation to the Cotingidae is based on its tarsal scutellation and foot structure, which are typical of the cotingas: its tarsus is pycnaspidean (not exaspidean, as in the manakins and flycatchers – see p. 10) and its toes are free (not more or less united, as in the manakins). Its allocation to the cotingas has always been accepted, but its remoteness from the rest of the family in nearly all external characters supports the view that the cotingas may be an association of diverse phylogenetic lines that arose from the primitive tyranniform stock before the main lines leading to the flycatchers and manakins were recognizable.

The Kinglet Calyptura is much the smallest of the cotingas, and is further remarkable for having one of the smallest ranges of any cotinga and for being one of the least known species. Indeed, not only has no living ornithologist seen it but it seems that it has not been found in this century. There exist only a handful of specimens in a few museums. It is a tiny bird, something like a brightly coloured, thick-billed and very short-tailed Goldcrest *Regulus regulus*. Except that the black and vermilion crown-patch is reduced in the female, the sexes are similar. The only account of its habits, by Descourlitz (1852), may not be altogether reliable but at least suggests the kind of habitat where it would be worth searching for it.

Distribution (Map 3)

The original specimen was collected in the vicinity of Rio de Janeiro. Cantagalo and Nova Friburgo, two places about 40 km apart in the eastern part of the Serra dos Orgãos, in the State of Rio de Janeiro, are the only other known localities. They lie in valleys, at altitudes of about 150 and 900 m respectively, among mountains that rise to 750–1500 m, and it was presumably in the surrounding mountains that the specimens were collected, if Descourlitz is correct in stating that the Calyptura 'recherche les lieux les plus élevés et les plus sauvages'.

Habitat and food

Under this heading one can again only quote Descourlitz, who says that the bird is found in virgin forest but also, and apparently more usually, in the thick secondary growth of abandoned clearings (the kind of vegetation known in Brazil as *capoeira*); and that it keeps to middle heights in the vegetation, never going up into the crowns of the trees. He describes it as climbing about in all directions on the lianas, taking insects or small berries according to the season, or exploring the rosettes of leaves of bromeliads in which the dew collects. He further stated that it had a special liking for the fruits of an 'arborescent Belladonna (*Marianeira*)' and seemed most abundant when they were ripe. *Marianeira* is a Brazilian name applied to two solanaceous shrubs, *Acnistus cauliflora* and *Bassovia* (= *Aureliana*) *lucida*, both of which grow to a height of about 3 m.

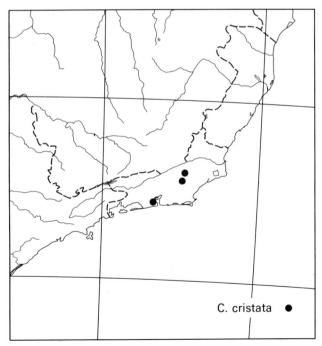

Map 3 Distribution of the Kinglet Calyptura (*Calyptura cristata*).

39

Behaviour

According to Descourlitz, the Kinglet Calyptura is usually found in pairs, and has a surprisingly loud call for its size which he described as 'bref, rauque et désagréable'.

Physical characters

Structure
Bill conical, culmen strongly arched; nostrils oval, exposed; rictal bristles moderately developed. Tail very short (less than 50% of wing). Crown-feathers somewhat elongated. Legs and toes slender.

Unfeathered parts
Colours not recorded, but bill and legs apparently dark.

Measurements
♂♂ (4) Wing 47–48, 47.8. Tail 22–24, 23.3. Tarsus 15–15.5, 15.1. Culmen 5–5.5, 5.1.
♀♀ (2) Wing 48, 49. Tail –, 23.

Genus *Iodopleura* – the purpletufts

Plate 3, page 42

Iodopleura isabellae – White-browed Purpletuft
Iodopleura fusca – Dusky Purpletuft
Iodopleura pipra – Buff-throated Purpletuft

Iodopleura is an isolated genus of uncertain affinities. Its most striking character is the tuft of long, silky violet feathers on either side of the breast in the male. On the basis of its syringeal structure, which is very different from that of any other cotinga, it appears to be allied to the Tyrannidae (Ames 1971); but it differs from the tyrant-flycatchers in beak shape, and the violet colour of the male's flank-feathers is produced by a pigment similar to the plumage pigments of *Xipholena* and *Cotinga* (Völker 1952). In physical proportions and general behaviour the purpletufts are most unlike other cotingas; they are among the smallest members of the family, relatively long-winged and short-tailed, and habitually perch on exposed tree tops from which they make aerial sallies to capture flying insects. They are also (and probably predominantly) frugivorous, one species at least taking mistletoe berries especially. Sexual dimorphism is slight, females being on average slightly smaller than males (a difference not always apparent in small samples) and having shorter, white flank-feathers in place of the violet tuft.

We recognize three species. *I. isabellae* and *I. fusca* are a closely related pair, differing mainly in the greater depth and extent of the dark pigment in the plumage of *fusca*. They may prove to be conspecific; but there is an extensive area in northern Brazil, southern Venezuela and the Guianas where neither has been found, and until something is known of the situation in this area it seems best to keep them separate. *I. pipra* is a smaller species, with a relatively longer tail and tarsus and a relatively shorter beak. It is less deeply pigmented, and has a buff-coloured throat and under tail-coverts. It replaces the *isabellae-fusca* group in southeastern coastal Brazil, an area rich in endemic species, and on the basis of two old specimens (more fully discussed below) is also generally supposed to occur in Guyana. There is some doubt, however, whether these two specimens really came from Guyana, and in any case their exact place of origin is unknown. Hence uncertainty remains as to whether more than one species of *Iodopleura* occurs in any area.

Distribution (Map 4)

The genus is South American, not extending west of the Andes. *I. isabellae* is widespread in the Amazon basin, north to south-central Colombia and southern Venezuela, and south to southern Peru, northern Bolivia, and the upper drainages of the Tapajós, Xingú and Tocantins rivers. It is replaced in the Guianas by the closely related *I. fusca* which, as mentioned above, may be only subspecifically distinct.

The distribution of *I. pipra* is still incompletely known. The main part of its range is in coastal Brazil from Espirito Santo to São Paulo. All except one of the known localities are close to the coast, suggesting that the species is confined to the very humid coastal strip. The single inland record, from secondary forest ('capoeira') at Lagoa Santa in Minas Gerais, was doubted by Hellmayr (1929) but accepted by Camargo & Camargo (1964), who reviewed the Brazilian distribution of the species. The occurrence in Guyana of a distinct subspecies of *I. pipra, leucopygia*, is based on two specimens obtained by Salvin in 1877 from H. Whitely senior, a London dealer in natural history specimens. They were believed by Salvin to come from British Guiana (they no longer have Whitely's original label), and Hellmayr (1929) described them as 'trade skins of the characteristic "Demarara" preparation'. It is puzzling that although there are many specimens in the British Museum collection supplied by Whitely the only other ones that come from British Guiana were collected by his son, between 1879 and 1892. On the other hand Whitely senior supplied many skins from eastern Brazil, apparently from the Bahia area. There thus seems to be at least a possibility that the two specimens of *I. pipra leucopygia*, in spite of their manner of preparation, may have originated from the eastern Brazilian coastal area somewhere to the north of the range of *I. p. pipra*.

MWWoodcock

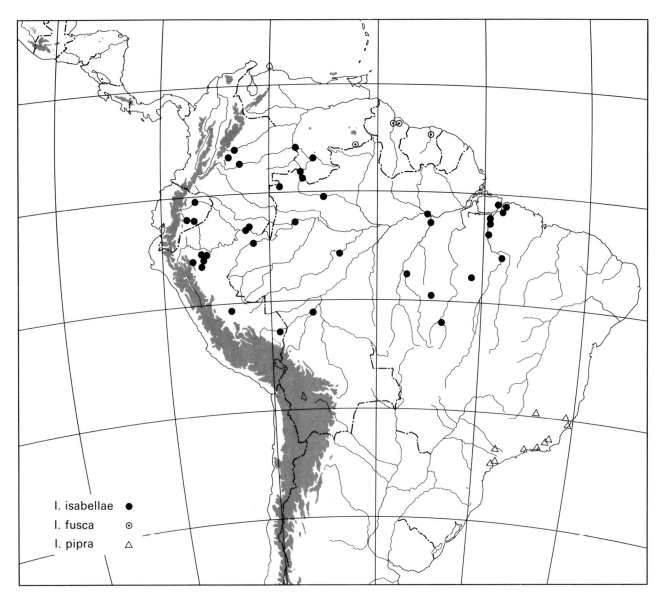

Map 4 Distribution of the purpletufts (*Iodopleura* spp.).

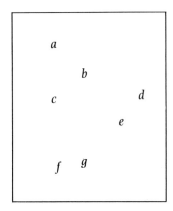

Plate 3
The purpletufts and
Kinglet Calyptura

a and b:White-browed Purpletuft *Iodopleura isabellae*, male
  and female
c: Dusky Purpletuft *I. fusca*, male
d and e: Buff-throated Purpletuft *I. pipra*, male and female
f and g: Kinglet Calyptura *Calyptura cristata*, male and female

Ecology

Very little information is available. The general impression gained from the fragmentary published reports is that purpletufts are birds of secondary forest and the forest edge, that they live in small parties made up of a number of pairs, feed mainly on fruits, are usually rather scarce, and do not associate with other species. According to Camargo & Camargo, the Buff-throated Purpletuft prefers the fruits of mistletoes (Loranthaceae), *Struthanthus* (= *Steirotis*) *concinnus* having been identified in stomach contents. For the two other species there seem to be no identifications of the fruits eaten; Layard (1873) mentioned that a specimen of the White-browed Purpletuft collected near Belém contained a single large berry, completely filling its stomach. A few of the recorded stomach contents also include insects; Schubart *et al.* (1965) mention ants, doubtless captured in flight.

In November 1972 (in secondary forest near Belém) D. Goodwin and I observed a party of White-browed Purpletufts consisting of four adults, apparently in two pairs, and a recently fledged juvenile. The adults were making regular aerial sallies to catch flying insects from tree-top perches 50–65 feet up. Several times an adult was seen to feed the juvenile, apparently by regurgitation as no food could be seen in the beak. Probably, as in other cotingas, adults feed the young on proportionately more insects than they eat themselves.

Behaviour

Little has been reported of the calls or displays of any of the purpletufts. Sick (1979) refers to the White-browed Purpletuft betraying its presence in the tree tops by its very high-pitched call which he transcribes as 'Üiht'. Hilty (MS) describes what may be the same call as 'a high weak *jee-jee-jee*'. Descourlitz (1844, quoted by Camargo & Camargo 1964) mentioned that a male Buff-throated Purpletuft, obtained alive, raised and spread its violet flank feathers when it was aroused; when it was calm they were half covered by the dark breast feathers. Doubtless these modified feathers are exhibited by the male in courtship.

Brief reports by several observers indicate that purpletufts live in pairs which associate together in small parties. Our observations of four adults accompanying a single fledged young bird suggested cooperative breeding, but it was not certain that more than two of the adults were feeding the young; certainly at least two of them were doing so. When the young bird flew from one tree to another it was escorted closely by an adult on either side. For most of the period of observation the four adults behaved as if they consisted of two pairs.

Perched in the usual upright position the White-browed Purpletuft's general appearance, with a rather large head, distinct neck, long wings and short tail, is martin-like. Layard (1873) mentioned that on the only occasion when he saw a pair, near Belém, he at first thought that they were swallows. In direct flight from tree to tree the birds that we watched flew with deep wing beats, but when making aerial sallies after insects their flight was more fluttering, the wing beats shallow and slower than would be expected for a bird of their small size.

Breeding and annual cycle

Breeding

No nest of any purpletuft had been recorded until Sick (1979) described a nest of the White-browed Purpletuft found at an early stage of building near Belém. On 26 November 1977 Dr Sick discovered two birds at work on the foundation of a nest 18 or 19 m up in the bare crown of a dead leguminous tree. On this date a thin pad of spider's web was being laid down on a slender horizontal branch. The two birds, presumably a pair, visited the site together; a third bird, possibly a young one from a previous nesting, kept company with them but showed no concern in the nest. The building birds brought cobweb in the bill and applied it to the branch by tapping with the underside of the bill. Observations were continued over two weeks, at the end of which the nest appeared finished but no egg had been laid. As no further observations were possible, the nest was then collected. It was a minute cup-shaped structure, fastened saddle-like on the branch and very like a hummingbird's nest. The external dimensions at the rim were 3 × 3.4 cm, and the depth was barely 1 cm; the branch to which it was attached was 2 cm in diameter. On the outside it was coated with cobweb so thickly that the underlying materials could not be seen; the smooth surface resembled papier maché, its texture suggesting that saliva might have been used to mat the cobweb together. Inside it was unlined, and probably not finished; the interior material consisted of black fibres, probably the threads of the fungus *Marasmius*.

The minute size of this nest strongly suggests that the three eggs described by Schönwetter (1969) and attributed to the Dusky Purpletuft, a species of about the same size as the White-browed, were wrongly identified. Schönwetter gives the measurements of a clutch of 3 eggs as 19.0–19.1 × 13.9–14.0 mm. It would be completely impossible for more than a single egg of this size to fit into the nest described by Sick; a clutch of 2 eggs is probably the maximum that such a nest could hold, and they would have to be much smaller than those described by Schönwetter.

Annual cycle

The young bird that we saw near Belém on 20 November was still stub-tailed and thus probably not long out of the nest, suggesting a laying date in October. A juvenile in the collection of the Department of Zoology at São Paulo, also from near Belém, is dated 21 October, suggesting a September laying date. No other dated juvenile specimen has been examined. Sick's observations, quoted above, suggest that egg-laying would have taken place in December.

Using an estimated duration of moult in the

individual of 100 days (Snow 1976*a*) the calculated months of onset of moult for four adult *I. isabellae* collected in the Belém area are June (1), November (2) and December (1). For three birds collected in Peru south of 6°S the calculated months are October (2) and November (1). Moult records of birds collected near the Equator in the middle and upper Amazon basin show no clear seasonal pattern. For the two available moult records of *I. pipra* from São Paulo, southeastern Brazil, the calculated months of onset of moult were August and September. Except that the São Paulo moult records are a little early, these records indicate an annual cycle with basically the same timing as in other cotingas.

Plumages and moults

Nestling plumage unknown. Juvenile plumage distinguishable from adult's as follows: feathers of upper parts white-tipped (tips soon wearing off and becoming less apparent), especially on lower back; wing coverts very pale, basally pale brown grading to broad whitish tips; primaries and secondaries with well-defined white tips (tail-feathers not white-tipped); dark feathers of underparts broadly fringed with whitish. This plumage replaced by a plumage nearly or quite indistinguishable from fully adult plumage.

Physical characters

Structure
Bill widely expanded at base, slightly hooked at tip, nostrils more or less rounded with raised rim, concealed by feathering. Wings relatively long, flight feathers unmodified; tail short, extending only 5–10 mm beyond tail-coverts.

Unfeathered parts
Apparently the same in all three species.
Iris: dark brown.
Bill: black, leaden below.
Legs and feet: dark leaden.

Geographical variation
Iodopleura isabellae
Todd (1950) described a race, *paraensis*, from Benevides (near Belém), Pará, distinguishing it from *isabellae* (type locality San Carlos, Amazonas, Venezuela) by its having 'underparts with less mesial white, and sides and flanks with more brownish white barring and mottling, giving a decidedly duller effect'. The populations of the eastern part of the Amazon basin, west at least to the Tocantins, show the differences described by Todd which, though rather slight, seem to merit subspecific recognition.

Iodopleura fusca
None recorded.

Iodopleura pipra
The two specimens of the race *leucopygia* (both males) supposedly from Guyana (see above) are undoubtedly distinct from the populations from Espirito Santo south to São Paulo. They are smaller (wings 54 and 56 mm, cf. 56–62 in S.E. Brazilian birds), have a broad white rump band which is totally lacking or at most faintly adumbrated in S.E. Brazilian birds, and the buff area of the throat is purer in colour (less suffused with grey) and more extensive.

Measurements
Iodopleura isabellae
♂♂ (13) Wing 75–81, 77.5. Tail 35–40, 38.5.
    Tarsus 13–15, 13.8. Culmen 7–9, 7.8.
♀♀ (7) Wing 73–78, 75.9. Tail 37–40, 38.2.
    Tarsus 14. Culmen 7–8.5, 8.0.

I. fusca
♂♂ (4) Wing 73–77, 75.0. Tail 36–39, 37.7.
    Tarsus 13.5–14, 13.8. Culmen 7–8, 7.7.
♀♀ (4) Wing 76–78, 77.0. Tail 37–39, 37.9.
    Tarsus 14–15, 14.5. Culmen 7–8, 7.5.
Weight: 1 ♂ 15.3 g (wing 75 mm).

I. pipra pipra
♂♂ (12) Wing 56–60, 58.3. Tail 29–34, 31.1.
    Tarsus 13–15.5, 14.4. Culmen 5–6, 5.5.
♀♀ (5) Wing 55–59, 57.2. Tail 31–32, 31.5.
    Tarsus 14–14.5, 14.1. Culmen 5–6, 5.5.

I. pipra leucopygia
Type and co-type (both ♂) Wing 54, 56. Tail 29, 29. Tarsus 14, 14.5. Culmen 6, 6.

Genus *Phibalura*

Plate 4, page 50

Phibalura flavirostris – Swallow-tailed Cotinga

Phibalura is superficially a very distinct genus, mainly because of its elegantly elongated, swallow-like tail; but in some of its characters it resembles *Ampelion*, which may be its nearest relative. Thus *Phibalura*, *Ampelion rubrocristatus* and *A. rufaxilla* all have mainly black or blackish crowns with erectile nuchal crests of much the same red colour, a character not found in any other cotingas. *Phibalura* is a specialist on mistletoe fruits and also hawks for flying insects, both of which are unusual feeding habits for a cotinga but are paralleled in *Ampelion* species.

For a long time *Phibalura* was known only as one of the endemic species of the eastern Brazilian region, but in 1926 it was reported from a locality in Bolivia, on the eastern slopes of the Andes (Chapman 1926). The two Bolivian specimens subsequently proved to be subspecifically separable from the eastern population (Chapman 1930). The occurrence of the species in the Andes is still based on these two specimens.

The Swallow-tailed Cotinga is an aerially active bird, apparently living in pairs and showing only slight dimorphism in plumage. Its unusual nest was described in the last century (Goeldi 1894), but it has remained little known, and only very recently have observations been made that suggest that it has a breeding system unique in the Cotingidae.

Distribution (Map 5)

The Swallow-tailed Cotinga has an extensive range in eastern Brazil, mainly in coastal areas from Minas Gerais in the north to Rio Grande do Sul in the south. Inland it has been recorded west to south-central Goias in the north, and to eastern Paraguay in the south. Since it is migratory, breeding in the mountains and descending to lower levels in winter, it may well be that outlying records, especially those from Goias, refer to migrants in the off-season. In Rio Grande do Sul, at the extreme southern end of its range, all records are between 23 September and 24 March (W. Belton, *in litt.*).

By contrast, the Bolivian population is known only from a single locality, Atén (south of Apolo) in the Department of La Paz. The altitude was not recorded with the specimens, but Atén is at about 2000 m on the eastern slopes of the Andes. Presumably the Bolivian population was founded by stragglers dispersing farther than usual from the species' main area of distribution to the east.

Habitat and food

Goeldi (1894), who wrote what is still the best published account of the species, was at pains to make it clear that the Swallow-tailed Cotinga is not a forest bird, but is found in open areas with trees, such as meadows, road-sides and even gardens. In such places 'it resorts to the dense and shady foliage of trees of moderate height, and, in one word, is a bird easily overlooked by persons not trained in ornithological investigations'. Goeldi discovered that it was a summer visitor and nesting bird in the mountains of the coastal region of the states of Rio de Janeiro and São Paulo; in the winter months it was absent and found in the adjacent lowlands.

The Swallow-tailed Cotinga feeds predominantly on fruits, and to a lesser extent on insects, both kinds of food being apparently taken in flight. According to Goeldi, the main food consists of berries of various species of mistletoe (Loranthaceae); *Struthanthus* (= *Steirotis*) *marginatus* and *S. coccineus* are mentioned. No other identified fruits have been recorded. There is a record of stomach contents including in addition to fruit the remains of a beetle of the genus *Macrodactylus* (Hempel 1949), and Mitchell (1957) saw birds feeding at a flying termite swarm.

Behaviour

Little has been recorded of the Swallow-tailed Cotinga's general behaviour. In appearance they are somewhat like large barred and spotted swallows. They live in pairs, are excellent fliers, and their calls are seldom uttered and not loud enough

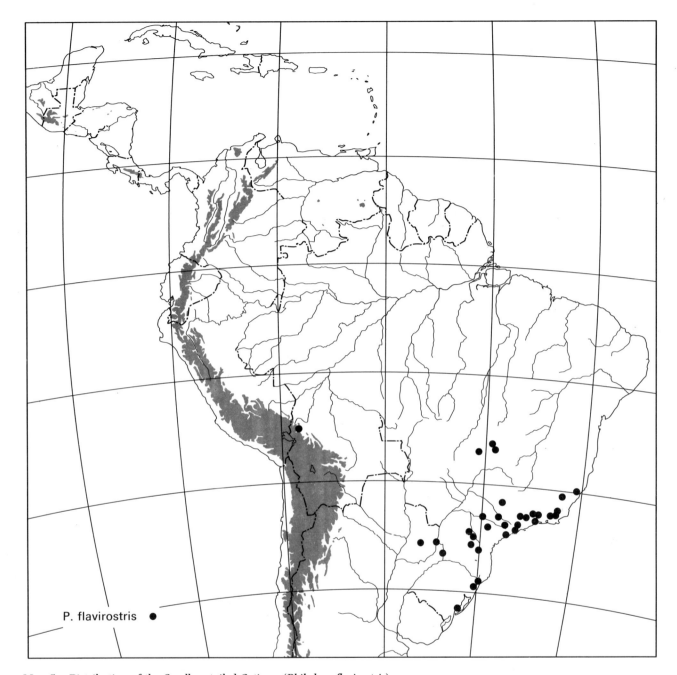

Map 5   Distribution of the Swallow-tailed Cotinga (*Phibalura flavirostris*).

to be audible at any great distance. The pair whose nesting Goeldi observed (see next section) were tame and undisturbed by the noisy activities of a saw-mill only a few yards from their nest.

Breeding and annual cycle

Nesting
Goeldi (1894) was the first ornithologist to describe the nest and eggs of the Swallow-tailed Cotinga. He watched a pair nesting near where he lived, at a height of 800 m in the Serra dos Orgãos not far from Rio de Janeiro. The nest was about 14 m above the ground, in a fork of the branches of a densely foliaged tree. Both male and female took an equal part in building. The nest was a very simple construction made entirely of pieces of the lichen *Usnea longissima*, arranged in a flattened cup of irregular shape; it was placed in an upright fork formed by four diverging branches, and was difficult to see from below. The birds collected the material from tree limbs, clinging while they pulled

it off. The clutch consisted of 2 eggs, measuring 23 × 19 and 22 × 19 mm. The eggs were very clear greenish blue in ground colour, and had around the broad end 'an irregular crown of spots of a neutral tint, larger at the end and becoming smaller and more indistinct towards the middle'. Later in the same season Goeldi collected two nestlings, which he kept alive for some time on a diet of mistletoe berries, but most unfortunately, as will become apparent below, he did not mention the circumstances under which he found them.

I am indebted to Dr Helmut Sick for further details of the nesting of the Swallow-tailed Cotinga from his unpublished notes extending over many years. The several nests that he has seen were from 3 to 18 m high (mostly at the higher end of this range) and were placed on thick horizontal branches. They were small flat structures made mainly of lichens, and quite invisible among the surrounding epiphytes. The incubating female is fed by the male. The nestlings, 2 or 3 in number, are fed by both parents, who bring solid food-balls, so big that they cannot close the bill, which they push deep into the nestlings' gapes. Once a male, curving its neck down and to the side, offered its widely open mouth patiently to a nestling which pecked into it several times, apparently obtaining material from the crop.

Dr Sick's observations show that the Swallow-tailed Cotinga's breeding behaviour may be conventional, with both parents cooperating in rearing the young. That the species may also employ a breeding system of a very unusual kind is suggested by the following observations (T. A. Parker, *in litt.*). On 1 November 1977 an employee of the museum in Itatiaia National Park (Rio de Janeiro/Minas Gerais border) showed T. A. Parker, Susan Allen Parker, and Peter Alden two nests of this species. One was in a solitary tree on the lawn at the edge of a parking lot; it was about 2 m above ground in the fork made by the branching of several limbs. The nest was a flat, flimsy structure of lichens, mosses and a few slender twigs approx. 5–8 cm long. One downy young was in this nest; it held its eyes tightly closed even while being touched; it was covered with tufts of white down, and the mouth was orange with two purple spots on the roof. The other nest and young were nearly identical; they were located about 15 m away, at the same height, in the same kind of tree. A male-plumaged adult attended the first nest, while a female-plumaged bird was seen about the second.

In the light of these observations, two specimens of Swallow-tailed Cotingas in the Stockholm Museum are of considerable interest. They were collected in November 1930 in the state of Santa Catarina (exact locality not recorded), one on the 16th and the other on the 23rd. The first, a male, was taken at a nest with 2 eggs, and the second, a female, at another nest with 2 eggs. Most unfortunately it was not recorded how far apart these two nests were, but it seems at least highly likely, since nests of this species are not readily found, that they were close together and perhaps built in similar sites.

To complete the record, it is worth noting that the pair of birds whose nest was collected by Goeldi were first seen building at another site, after which they switched their attention to the site from which he later collected the nest and eggs. He says nothing further about the first site. About two months later in the same season he collected two nestlings of about the same age, but on different days, suggesting that they were from different nests; but again he says nothing about the circumstances.

Although they are tantalisingly incomplete, taken together these observations strongly suggest that a breeding pair of Swallow-tailed Cotingas may build two nests in each of which the female lays a clutch, and that male and female then tend the two nests separately. Under certain conditions, and especially if one parent is able to feed the young adequately, this should be an evolutionarily sound breeding strategy, but it appears not to be known in any passerine bird.

Annual cycle

Known or calculated laying dates for southeastern Brazil, from Goeldi and other sources, are in the months October–January. A female specimen collected in eastern Paraguay on 14 October, containing a 'ripe' egg, indicates an October laying; while a young bird with wings and tail not fully grown, collected in Minas Gerais in November (no exact date), indicates a September or October laying.

The moult evidently begins soon after breeding. Neither of the two birds collected at nests with eggs, mentioned in the previous section, had begun their wing-moult. Birds in early stages of wing-moult have been collected from early November to February (with one late record in May), and birds with their wing-moult almost complete in April and May. It seems that moult takes about 120 days in the individual, and if this is correct, calculation of the date of onset of moult indicates that most birds begin in the months November-January, with a few late ones in February–April. The records suggest that females begin to moult somewhat earlier than males (females, Oct.–Dec., 6 records; males, Nov.–Feb., 8 records; the single April record unsexed). This difference, if substantiated, is most unusual in the family, as in most cotingas the males moult earlier than the females. Possibly it is related to the Swallow-tailed Cotinga's breeding system, discussed in the previous section.

Plumages and moults

Nestling down white. First generation of juvenile head- and body-feathers: upper parts drab brown with pale feather tips, darker on crown than on back and feathers of lower back pale with two dark bars, one subterminal, tips white; underparts whitish with dark crescentic feather bars, throat whitish. This plumage soon replaced by second generation of feathers as follows: body feathers barred blackish and white, tips whitish, throat mainly white; crown black with whitish feather fringes; wing-coverts, three innermost secondaries (tertials) and tail-feathers conspicuously tipped white or very pale yellow; wing and tail feathers with yellow-green outer edges. Head and body plumage, most or all wing-coverts and most or all tertials soon replaced by immature plumage.

Immature plumage: like adult plumage but black areas duller and browner, more heavily barred and scaled below, feathers of throat black-spotted, and wing and tail feathers green-edged.

Physical characters

Structure

Bill very short, broad at base; nostrils oval, partly concealed by feathers of forehead; rictal bristles absent, but bristly feathers round base of upper mandible and a few at base of lower mandible. Legs and feet slender; tarsus taxaspidean. Tail long and forked, outer feathers progressively more elongated and pointed. Wing feathers unmodified; wing rather long and pointed. Yellow feathers of throat brush-like, with short shafts and long barbs.

Unfeathered parts

Similar in both sexes.
Iris: dark chestnut-brown.
Bill: pale straw-coloured.
Legs and feet: pale ochre-yellow.

Geographical variation

The Bolivian population, known from a single male and female, is longer-tailed than the southeastern Brazilian population and differs in some details of plumage. It has been described as a distinct subspecies, *P. f. boliviana* (Chapman 1930). The main colour differences are as follows. The male has less yellow on the throat; the white post-auricular area is wider and unmarked; and there are fewer bars below, the abdomen being unmarked. The bird sexed as female resembles the male below (the abdomen with only a few black streaks, not barred as in the female of *flavirostris*); on the upper parts it resembles *flavirostris* females. There must be some doubt whether this bird was correctly sexed or was perhaps a young male.

Measurements

P. f. flavirostris

♂♂ (14) Wing 96–108, 101.4. Tail 106–125, 114.4. Tarsus 18–20, 18.9 Culmen 8.5–9.5, 9.0.
♀♀ (10) Wing 94–105, 100.5. Tail 96–104, 100.9. Tarsus 18–19, 18.6. Culmen 8.5–9.5, 9.1.
Weight: 1 ♀ 52 g (wing 103 mm).

P. f. boliviana (from Chapman 1930)

♂ Wing 101. Tail 131.
♀ Wing 100. Tail 110.

MWWoodcock

Genus *Carpornis* – the berry-eaters

Carpornis cucullatus – Hooded Berry-eater
Carpornis melanocephalus – Black-headed Berry-eater

Carpornis consists of two closely related species, both of them confined to the forested southeastern Brazilian coastal belt. They are medium-sized cotingas, apparently exclusively frugivorous; they may be ecological counterparts of the larger forms of *Pipreola* of the Andes, and some similarities of plumage, as well as of morphology, suggest a relationship between these two genera. Little is known of the life histories of the berry-eaters; they are not rare birds, but their inconspicuous behaviour and the difficulties of field work in the forests where they live have so far resulted in little except a few casual observations.

Like the other eastern Brazilian endemic cotingas, the berry-eaters are mainly olive-green, yellow and black, except for the deep chestnut patch on the back of *C. cucullatus*. They show rather slight sexual dimorphism.

Distribution (Map 6)

The genus is confined to the wooded mountains of southeastern Brazil and the coastal strip between the mountains and sea. The range of *melanocephalus* is mainly to the north of that of *cucullatus*, but they overlap widely, from Espirito Santo south to Santa

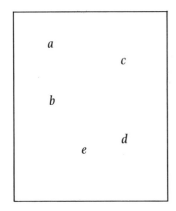

Plate 4

a and b: Hooded Berry-eater *Carpornis cucullatus*, male and female
c: Black-headed Berry-eater *C. melanocephalus*, male
d and e: Swallow-tailed Cotinga *Phibalura flavirostris*, male and female

Catarina. *C. melanocephalus* is the only one recorded from Bahia in the north, and *C. cucullatus* the only one recorded from Rio Grande do Sul in the south. Whereas *melanocephalus* seems to be rather closely confined to the coastal belt, *cucullatus* ranges further inland. An old record of *cucullatus* from 'Rio Claro, Goyaz' (specimen in British Museum) needs confirmation.

Ecology

Little is known. Both species have been recorded from sea level to well up in the mountains. Probably the Hooded Berry-eater ranges higher than the Black-headed; thus in the Serra dos Orgãos we have seen it up to 1600 m, in the Serro do Mar further south they have been collected up to 1150 m, and in the extreme south of the range, in Rio Grande do Sul, up to 900 m. Recorded altitudes for the Black-headed Berry-eater are few, and I have found none over about 700 m.

The few published remarks on their food agree that they are exclusively fruit-eaters. Descourlitz (1852), in his only partially reliable account of the habits of Brazilian birds, wrote that the Hooded Berry-eater feeds only on soft fruits, and this seems to be true. Thus in the Serra dos Orgãos, during many hours of watching at fruiting lauraceous trees, at which Black-and-gold Cotingas, thrushes and toucans were feeding, we never saw Hooded Berry-eaters come to the trees although they were quite common in the area. On the other hand, we watched a Hooded Berry-eater regurgitating seeds that were coated with a sticky substance. The seeds, regurgitated one by one, hung from the beak on long sticky threads and had to be wiped off against the branch on which the bird was perched. Almost certainly they were from the soft fruit of some epiphyte. Males calling in their territories (see next section) were twice seen to pluck fruit in flight, in both cases from unidentified vines. It may well be that fruits of epiphytes and vines, rather than of trees and shrubs, are the staple diet of this species. This might explain the fact that it is most abundant in the very humid

Map 6   Distribution of the Hooded Berry-eater (*Carpornis cucullatus*) and Black-headed Berry-eater (*C. melanocephalus*). The range of the Hooded Berry-eater extends south to just off the map (see Appendix 3, p. 195).

coastal mountains, where the forest trees are laden with epiphytic plants.

Black-headed Berry-eaters, occurring predominantly in forests at lower altitudes where epiphytic growth is less, may have rather different feeding habits. That they take mainly different kinds of fruit from the Hooded is suggested also by the shape of the bill, which is distinctly wider and more compressed dorso-ventrally. To judge from the few weights that are available (p. 54), they are lighter than Hooded Berry-eaters, though almost the same in wing-length, and have relatively shorter tails. The lower wing-loading suggests that they may take more of their fruit in flight.

Behaviour

Almost as little is known about the berry-eaters' behaviour as about their ecology. In October and November 1972 I spent many hours watching Hooded Berry-eaters in the Serra dos Orgãos (Rio de Janeiro) and Serra do Mar (São Paulo) in an attempt to find out something about their behaviour and social organization. Hamilton's (1871) old account proved accurate as far as it went: 'The hollow and rather mournful note of this bird is frequently the only sound one hears in passing through the depth of the forest, especially at midday, when almost every creature is silent. The bird itself, however, is not very easily noticed, as it remains almost motionless on its perch.'

The males occupied calling territories in the forest, where they could be found day after day during the period of our stay. Territories were well spaced; sometimes two birds were within earshot at the same time, but more often only one was audible. They appeared to be fairly evenly distributed through suitable tracts of forest. Calling perches were all below the forest canopy, at heights of 25 to 50 feet. The call is a stereotyped 4-syllabled phrase which I transcribed as *wo-op*, *wot-chú*, soft, mellow and, as Hamilton noted, of a somewhat hollow quality. When it calls the bird perches upright with the wings a little drooped, draws its head back for the *wo-op*, and then backwards again with a more marked jerk for the *wot-chú*. Calls are given in irregularly spaced series interspersed with silent periods, the bird moving round his territory between bouts of calling. The longest series of calls recorded numbered 24. Typically, the intervals between the calls in a series are of 10–26 seconds (55 records out of 70); shorter intervals, of 8 and 9 seconds, were recorded once each.

Males were twice seen taking fruit in their calling territories, and there was no evidence that they flew off to feed elsewhere. Once a female was seen with a male. For most of the time she perched quietly near him, occasionally uttering a low, inward grating note. The male also perched quietly for a time, uttering a similar note, then moved round the female, flying a few yards and perching, and then flying on to another perch, in a roughly circular course round her. The female eventually flew off out of sight and after a short time the male flew off in the same direction. On a later visit to the Serra do Mar, in October 1979, I briefly watched a male, with a bright red fruit held in its bill, pivoting jerkily from side to side while perched a few inches from a female on the same branch, about 18 ft up in a small forest tree. The male then abruptly flew off, leaving the female on the perch where she remained for 2 minutes before flying off in the same direction as the male. Later, the male called persistently in the same general area.

It is impossible from these brief observations to tell in either case whether the birds were a pair, or whether the female was visiting a solitary calling male. Evidence from the moult cycles, given in the next section, suggests that the males do not participate in nesting duties, which in turn suggests that females may visit the males in their calling territories for mating without forming lasting pairs.

Breeding and annual cycle

Von Ihering (1900) described the egg of the Hooded Berry-eater as ashy yellow ('cinzento-amarillo' – clay-coloured?) in ground colour, covered with numerous ash-brown splashes and spots, and measuring 34×23 mm. He gave no information on the nest, and this apparently remains the only information on the breeding of either of the berry-eaters.

The annual cycle can be assessed from a study of moult. For the Hooded Berry-eater, the calculated months of onset of moult in 8 males are October (2), November (5) and December (1); for 6 females the months are November (2), December (3) and January (1). This suggests that males begin to moult on average a month or two earlier than females, a difference similar to that found in other cotingas in which the males take no part in nesting duties. This question is discussed more fully elsewhere (p. 27). For the Black-headed Berry-eater almost all available moult records are from males, and they show that the moult begins mainly in September (8) and October (3 records). The remaining records are one each for May, August, November and December. This indicates a considerably earlier onset of moult than in the Hooded Berry-eater, and less synchronization.

Plumages and moults

Nestling plumage unknown. Juvenile plumage (known in *C. cucullatus* only) pale drab, fluffy, over both head and body. Immature plumage like that of female, but with black on head even less developed, wing-coverts green (not blackish with green edges), throat and breast more barred and yellow duller.

Physical characters

Unfeathered parts
C. cucullatus.
Iris: generally recorded as dark brown, but as 'bleu' in three males collected by A. Robert, and as 'feuerrot' (fiery red) in one female collected by H. Sick.
Bill: blue, grey-blue, or violet-blue.
Legs and feet: blue, grey-blue or violet-blue, claws grey.

C. melanocephalus.
Sexes apparently similar.
Iris: brick-red or fiery red.
Bill: blackish, base of lower mandible plumbeous.
Legs and feet: grey.

Measurements
C. cucullatus
♂♂ (17)   Wing 109–123, 116.2.   Tail 91–104, 96.2.
Tarsus 23.5–25, 24.2.   Culmen 10–11.5, 10.6.
♀♀ (15)   Wing 109–120, 113.3.   Tail 86–97, 92.2.
Tarsus 23–25, 23.8.   Culmen 10–11, 10.4.
Weights: 6 ♂♂ 74–80, 77.9 g (mean weight and wing-length of 4: 78.6 g, 113.0 mm).
2 ♀♀ 67, 74 g (wings 110, 110 mm); 84.4 g (probably breeding).

C. melanocephalus
♂♂ (12)   Wing 111–121, 115.1.   Tail 79–94, 86.8.
Tarsus 19.5–23, 21.8.   Culmen 10–11.5, 10.6.
♀♀ (12)   Wing 109–116, 112.3.   Tail 83–91, 87.5.
Tarsus 21.5–23, 22.3.   Culmen 10–11, 10.5.
Weights: 1 ♂   62.7 g (wing 112 mm).
1 ♀   64 g (wing 110 mm).

Genus Ampelion – Andean cotingas

Plate 5, page 58

Ampelion rubrocristatus – Red-crested Cotinga
Ampelion rufaxilla – Chestnut-crowned Cotinga
Ampelion (Doliornis) sclateri – Bay-vented Cotinga
Ampelion (Zaratornis) stresemanni – White-cheeked Cotinga

These four cotingas seem to form a natural group, but their generic treatment is debatable. We think it best to unite them in a single genus, but give above, in parentheses, the two generic names that are generally used for *sclateri* and *stresemanni*. They are structurally similar, share some plumage characters, are rather alike in general behaviour and voice, and are all confined to temperate or upper subtropical levels in the Andes.

They are rather inactive birds and lack brilliant colours; but the nuchal crest, when spread, can be striking. In *A. rubrocristatus*, but not in the other species, the tail is also conspicuously marked: the inner webs of all the tail-feathers except the middle pair have large subterminal white spots which are conspicuous in flight but concealed when the tail is folded. All are predominantly frugivorous, and apparently live in pairs. The sexes are alike in plumage.

Taczanowski (1874), in his original description, admitted the nearness of *Doliornis* to *Ampelion*, but it was maintained as a separate genus until Bond (1956) suggested that both it and *Zaratornis* should be merged with *Ampelion*. *Doliornis* has the same general plumage colours as *A. rubrocristatus* (grey, black and red-brown), and they agree closely in their partly concealed red-brown nuchal crest. The main external structural difference is that *Doliornis* has a narrower and less hooked bill; its internal anatomy has not been studied. It seems most likely that *sclateri* has been derived from an isolated fragment of *Ampelion* stock, and its generic separation seems unnecessary.

The best treatment of *Zaratornis* is more difficult to decide. We follow Bond, who recommended merging it with *Ampelion* because of the general similarity of its plumage; its upperparts strikingly resemble those of juveniles of *A. rubrocristatus*, and its underparts are like those of *A. rufaxilla*. The red-brown nuchal patch is present, though vestigial. Lowery & O'Neill (1966), however, state that its skull is 'so distinct as to preclude making *Zaratornis*

congeneric with *Ampelion*'. Nevertheless they place its skull next to that of *Ampelion* in what they describe as a 'nicely graded series' of six genera. Without knowing to what extent skull structure can be modified in response to differences in feeding behaviour in closely related forms, it is not possible to weigh the skull differences against other evidence that suggests close relationship with *Ampelion*.

As is apparent from Maps 7 and 8, *A. rubrocristatus* is the most widely distributed of the four species. *A. rufaxilla* is also widespread, but appears to be absent from the Eastern Andes of Colombia and their extension into Venezuela, and has not yet been recorded from Ecuador but must almost certainly occur there. *A. stresemanni* and *A. sclateri* have restricted ranges in central Peru, the former along the arid western cordillera and the latter in the humid eastern mountains. The known ranges of these two species have been considerably extended in recent years.

The biology of this interesting group of species has been little studied. Probably the only ornithologist to have seen all four species in life is Theodore A. Parker, who has contributed part of the following accounts of the Red-crested and Chestnut-crowned Cotingas and the whole of the accounts of the Bay-vented and White-cheeked Cotingas.

Ampelion rubrocristatus – Red-crested Cotinga

Ecology and behaviour (by Theodore A. Parker)

This is probably the most frequently observed cotinga of the Andes, where it is a characteristic bird of the humid Temperate Zone, in an elevational range of about 2700 to 3700 m. The habitat varies from the edge of undisturbed cloud forest to groves of trees (especially alders, *Alnus* spp.) bordering agricultural land. In western Peru the Red-crested Cotinga occurs in relictual woodlands of trees such as *Polylepis*, *Escallonia* and *Oreopanax*. In all habitats

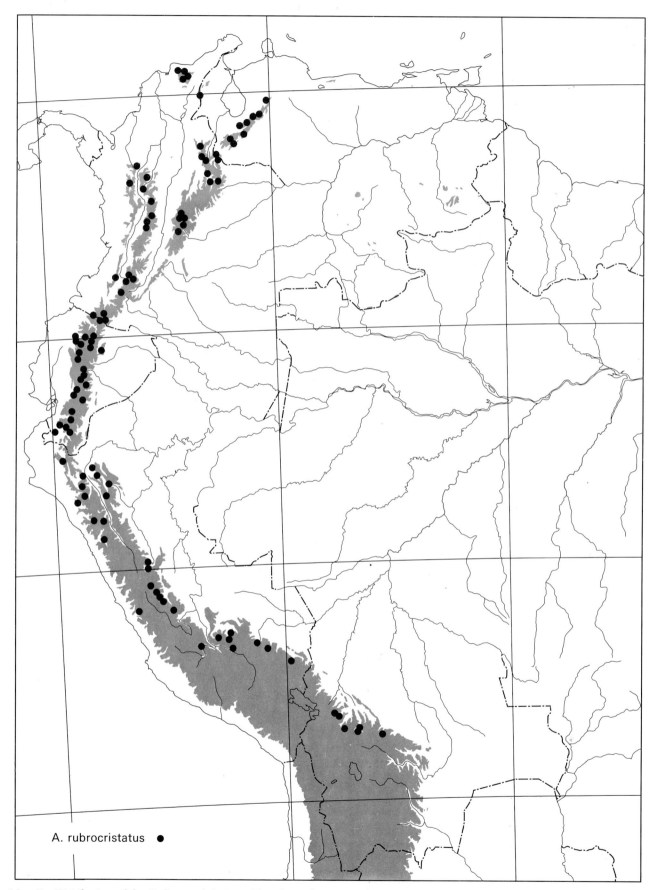

Map 7   Distribution of the Red-crested Cotinga (*Ampelion rubrocristatus*).

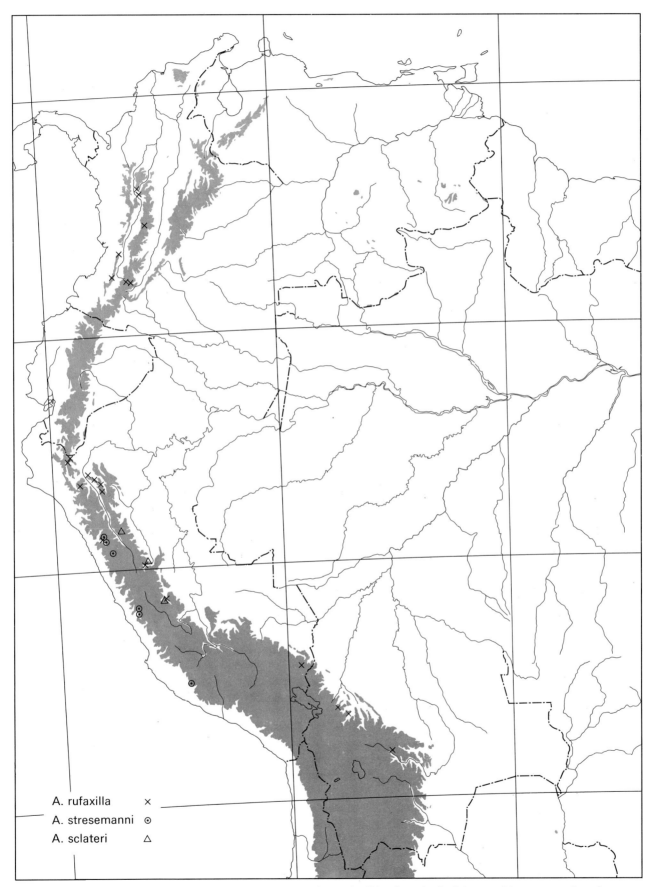

Map 8   Distribution of the Chestnut-crowned Cotinga (*Ampelion rufaxilla*),White-cheeked Cotinga (*A. stresemanni*) and
Bay-vented Cotinga (*A. sclateri*).

MWWoodcock

these cotingas are usually first seen perched conspicuously atop a tree. They are sluggish and not very vocal, but their calls are very distinctive. Most frequently heard of these are short, guttural, frog-like notes (*rrreh*), which are sometimes prolonged and given at a higher pitch. I have not heard this species give a long, patterned vocalization like that of the White-cheeked Cotinga (see below), but the calls of both are similar in quality. Also given by the Red-crested Cotinga, especially when agitated by conspecifics in feeding trees, are series of nasal, soft notes (*eh-eh-eh-eh-eh*).

This cotinga perches very upright, and spends long periods motionless. In flight it drops from a tree and flies with rapid, constant wingbeats to the next perch; a soft rattling sound is produced by the wings of (all?) flying birds. The white tail markings are quite conspicuous as the species passes overhead.

Though I have most often found Red-crested Cotingas singly, in pairs (male and female) or family groups of 3 to 4 individuals, I have also observed up to 6 adults together in the crowns of fruiting trees. At such times intra-specific conflicts are frequent; males will face each other, perching a few inches apart, and with conspicuously raised crests and bobbing heads they call loudly and flick their wings and tail, thus exposing the white markings in the latter. Chases are also frequent.

In Peru Red-crested Cotingas feed on fruits of several species of the mistletoe genus *Phrygilanthus*, but they are also common in areas where mistletoes are either scarce or absent, and I have seen the birds take other unidentified fruits. Peters & Griswold (1943) report that they feed on wild blackberries (*Rubus* sp.). The species also hawks insects from the air within a few feet of exposed perches.

Little has been published on the nesting behaviour of this cotinga. A nest mentioned by Peters & Griswold (1943) was found in central Peru in March, about 1.3 m above ground in a bush. The only other nest account in the literature is of a cup constructed of twigs and lichens placed 1.7 m above the ground in a small tree. Found in the Bolivian Andes on 24 December, this nest contained a single, fully-feathered young that weighed 53.4 g (Vuilleumier 1969). In mid-February 1975 I found a nest in the Department of Huanuco, central Peru; it was a large cup of mosses, lichens and twigs built on a *Polylepis* branch about 3 m above ground. I flushed a female from this empty structure, but later observed what I believed to be the same bird feeding two recently-fledged young nearby. An adult male was also in the vicinity, but it was not seen to feed the young. Vuilleumier (*op. cit.*) reported that two adult birds (presumably male and female) approached him closely as he examined the Bolivian nest, and this agrees with my observations of White-cheeked Cotinga adults near nests (see below).

Annual cycle

The two breeding records from Peru and Bolivia, mentioned above, indicate egg-laying in November and January. Morrison (1948) recorded a bird with a beakful of moss, apparently building, in Peru in October, and a 'breeding' female was collected in Ecuador in May. No generalization about breeding seasons can be based on these few records. Moult records, which are numerous, suggest that there is no well-defined season of moult in any part of the range; from the extreme north to the extreme south of the range they indicate that the moult may begin at any time of year. Probably the lack of a clear seasonal pattern is a reflection of the equable climatic conditions prevailing in the humid upper temperate zone of the Andes from 10°N to 18°S.

Plumage sequences

Nestling down whitish. Juvenile plumage paler than adult, with extensive pale fringes to the feathers: crown sooty, sides of feathers washed with rufous; back feathers with sooty centres and olive or red-brown lateral fringes; underparts streaked, feathers with dark centres and yellowish-green fringes. Secondaries and wing-coverts with whitish edges. Older juveniles show rufous colour concentrated on the back of the crown, scapulars, and lesser wing-coverts, and the lower back is paler than the rest of the upperparts (wider pale fringes to the feathers). The rufous nape and streaked abdomen are apparently the last juvenile characters to be retained, but details of plumage changes have not been worked out.

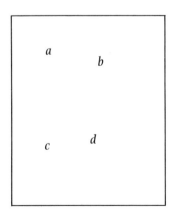

Plate 5
Andean cotingas
(*Ampelion*)

a: Chestnut-crowned Cotinga *A. rufaxilla*
b: Red-crested Cotinga *A. rubrocristatus*
c: White-cheeked Cotinga *A. stresemanni*
d: Bay-vented Cotinga *A. sclateri*

Ampelion rufaxilla – **Chestnut-crowned Cotinga**

This species is probably more closely related to *A. rubrocristatus* than the superficial appearance of the adult suggests. The red-brown colour of the wing-coverts, which is present in the juvenile of *rubrocristatus*, is retained and brightened in the adult of *rufaxilla*, and the same colour is also developed on the throat as well as round the nape (where also it occurs in the juvenile of *rubrocristatus*). The red crest is developed exactly as in *rubrocristatus*. The pale, dark-streaked underparts are reminiscent of the underparts of *rubrocristatus* juveniles. The adult plumage of *rufaxilla* thus appears to have evolved by retaining elements of the juvenile plumage of the genus and intensifying the colours.

Ecology and behaviour (by Theodore A. Parker)

Behaviourally and vocally this species is very like *A. rubrocristatus*, but it is more a forest bird, occurring generally at lower elevations but with some overlap. The Chestnut-crowned Cotinga seems to be uncommon and local. Like its relative, this cotinga is usually seen perching in the tops of trees at forest edge. The vocal repertoire includes short *reh* notes and a longer *eh-eh-eh-rrrrrreh*. I have seen males displaying in the manner described in the accounts of the Red-crested and White-cheeked Cotingas.

Little information is available on feeding behaviour. The stomach of three LSUMZ specimens collected in Bolivia and Peru contained fruits of unidentified plants (one stomach with a single large seed, measuring 16×14 mm). Niethammer (1956) recorded that a bird which he collected in Bolivia was catching insects in the air like a flycatcher; its stomach contained only insects.

The recorded elevational range of the species is 1980–2740 m in Colombia, 1860–2740 m in Peru, and 2300–2400 m in Bolivia.

Breeding and the annual cycle

Nothing was known of the breeding of this cotinga until December 1980, when Thomas S. Schulenberg found a nest in extreme southeastern Peru. The nest was situated in the crown of a broad-leaf evergreen tree, about 12 m high, at the edge of cloud forest and the second-growth of a large clearing, 2000 m above sea level. A pair of birds attended the nest, which was still being built when first found on 2 December and on the following day. The role of the sexes in building could not be determined, but only one bird was seen to build on each occasion. As observations had to finish on the

6th, the adult birds (a male and female) and the nest were collected. The nest contained one egg, measuring approximately 31×23 mm (too badly broken for precise measurement), closest to Ridgway's Greenish Glaucous in ground colour and heavily marked with dark spots varying in size from mere dots to markings about 2×3 mm. The nest, which was placed in a rather open situation within the tree, on the exposed upper surface of a large branch (c. 12 cm in diameter), was almost exclusively made of fruticose lichens, with some slender twigs woven into the lower part of it. It was remarkably simple in form, only 4 cm deep and about 15 cm across at its widest point, and there was no lining to the cup, which was merely a small depression 6 cm long, 4 cm wide and 2 cm deep.

A female with an enlarged ovary, collected in southern Colombia in early April, provides what seems to be the only evidence of the breeding season in the northern part of the species' range. The season of moult is probably not well defined. Judging from the stages that they had reached, five moulting specimens from Colombia began their moult in the period January–July, and three Peruvian specimens in the period August–December. It is noteworthy that the male of the pair at the nest in Peru, described above, had fresh flight feathers and was in heavy body moult, whereas the female had worn flight feathers and was in light body moult.

No juvenile or immature plumage stages have been seen.

Ampelion (Doliornis) sclateri – **Bay-vented Cotinga** (by Theodore A. Parker)

From the time of its description in 1874 until 1972, the Bay-vented Cotinga was known from only two specimens, a male and female collected by Jelski at Maraynioc (3000 m), in the Department of Junin, central Peru, and three specimens collected at the same locality, at 3300 m, by Harry Watkins in 1921. Following the Harvard Peruvian Expedition of 1923 to that locality Griswold wrote: 'It was mainly in the hope of getting this rare bird that I spent three months at Maraynioc, in which attempt, I might as well admit at once, I failed' (Peters & Griswold 1943). Then in 1972 Manuel Villar, a native collector, discovered this species in the Carpish Mountains of the Department of Huanuco (specimens in the Field Museum), and the following year Dan and Erika Tallman of the Louisiana State University Museum of Zoology and local guides found it in the same area. More recently, LSUMZ workers have found the Bay-vented Cotinga even farther north, in the Eastern Cordillera of Dept. La Libertad, east of Tayabamba.

In the three known localities the species inhabits the upper limit of temperate zone cloud forest, at or not far below treeline, from 2500 to 3300 m. In this moss-bound, almost impenetrable habitat, this cotinga is a very inconspicuous bird, and one cannot expect to find it easily even in the preferred habitat, which is at this time accessible mainly by steep, usually muddy trails.

In the Carpish Mountains (Zapatagocha, Huaylaspampa, Quilluacocha and Unchog are the known collecting sites within this mountain range) and east of Tayabamba, I encountered these cotingas in pairs perched quietly atop trees at or near the forest edge. They seem to be less active and vocal than the three other *Ampelion* species. Occasionally they remain in a clump of trees or bushes for several hours, and they appear to be quite sedentary in a particular woodlot even over a period of weeks. The only vocalization I ever heard this species utter is a raspy *shhh* note, which varies in length and intensity. Often, as in the White-cheeked Cotinga, when one individual gives this call, one or more distant birds answer with the same. Though normally quite phlegmatic, one male observed in La Libertad sat very upright and bobbed its head in response to playbacks of the above described call. When disturbed, these cotingas drop from a perch and fly up to fifty yards to another prominent perch, much in the manner of their relatives.

In the Carpish region I saw a pair of Bay-vented Cotingas feeding on small purplish or dark blue fruits of a melastome shrub at the forest edge. No other observations of foraging have been obtained to my knowledge. Stomachs of five of eight specimens with data (in LSUMZ) contained fruit pulp; another of this series had the stomach full of blue berries, and one contained 'seeds and many insects'.

The only available information on nesting behaviour was obtained from one of my Peruvian field assistants, Reyes Rivera, who reported (pers. comm.) that in 'April or May 1977' he flushed an adult from a nest (presumably a cup) placed on the fork of a slender branch about 4 m above ground, in a tree at the wood edge of Zapatogocha. Rivera, whose accounts of bird behaviour are quite reliable, recalled that the attendant bird perched atop a nearby tree and called loudly (a prolonged version of the *shhh* note). Unfortunately he did not climb the tree and examine the nest.

Of ten LSUMZ specimens of *A. sclateri* four show signs of moult. A male and female collected on 27 January were undergoing body moult. A male collected on 23 June was finishing its wing and tail moult, and a male taken on 18 July had very fresh wing and tail feathers. The nestling, juvenile and immature plumages are unknown.

Obviously much remains to be learned of this cotinga. My general impression of this species is that it resembles its relatives fairly closely in terms of behaviour and (probably) ecology, but it is rather divergent vocally. It should be mentioned here that *Ampelion rubrocristatus* occurs syntopically with *A. sclateri*, and also with *A. stresemanni* in at least one locality.

Ampelion (Zaratornis) stresemanni — White-cheeked Cotinga (by Theodore A. Parker*)

One of the most exciting discoveries made by Maria and Hans-Wilhelm Koepcke during their explorations of the relict Temperate Zone woodlands that occur on the western slopes of the Cordillera Occidental of the Peruvian Andes was the previously undescribed White-cheeked Cotinga. This thrush-sized bird was found, surprisingly, less than 70 air kilometers east of Lima in the *Oreopanax* association forest of Zarate, above the Rimac River valley at 2700 m. The species was described from two female specimens collected in October 1953 (Koepcke 1954). When news of the discovery reached American ornithologists in 1954, another specimen, a female collected by M. A. Carriker above Yánac in northern Ancash in March 1932, was discovered in the collection of the Philadelphia Academy of Sciences, where it had been overlooked for more than 20 years (Bond 1956).

Males of this cotinga were not known until 1966, when they were found in an isolated *Polylepis* woodland in the upper Santa Eulalia Valley, the next valley north of the Rimac, at more than 4000 m (Luthi 1970). Until I visited Yánac in 1976, the sexes had never been found together, and there was speculation that long distance migrations (e.g. across the Rimac Valley) must join them for the reproductive period (Luthi, *op. cit.*).

Furthermore, the apparent separation of males and females into two distinct habitats, with the former occurring in higher *Polylepis* and the latter in *Oreopanax*, led the Koepckes to conclude that if either habitat were destroyed by man the species might become extinct. This seemed corroborated by the fact that *Zaratornis* (I use the old generic name for convenience) could not be found by them above Yánac where the *Oreopanax* groves just above the village had been greatly reduced by local people. I now believe that this interesting bird is more or less resident in one habitat, *Polylepis* woodland, and that post-breeding dispersal accounts for individuals or

*Abridged, with permission, from Parker (1981).

groups of individuals that occur in other (lower) areas, like the forest of Zarate.

Because of the enigmatic nature of this species, and because of the paucity of information on Andean cotingas in general, I became interested in *Zaratornis* and from 1974 through 1978, while working for the Louisiana State Museum of Zoology, I was able to observe this bird in three of the seven localities where it is now known to occur: Quebrada Tutapac, near Yánac, Dept. Ancash; the upper Santa Eulalia Valley, Dept. Lima; and Pampa Galeras, Dept. Ayacucho. Of the known sites, six are on the western slopes of the Western Andes, and one is on the western flank of the Eastern Andes in the upper Marañón River drainage. The known elevational range of the species is 2700 to 4240 m.

Habitat and food

The habitat of *Zaratornis* is *Polylepis* spp. (Rosaceae) woodland surrounded by shrubbery and grassland. At the northern end of the distributional range of the species these isolated tracts grow on steep, rocky slopes of deep quebradas, often glacial valleys, separated from one another by high puna grasslands and rugged snow-covered mountains. Most of the habitat there is remote and difficult to reach. In the south, *Polylepis* is more accessible. The woodlands at Pampa Galeras occur on moderate slopes that rise above great expanses of level grasslands. At Zarate this bird has been found in a relict Temperate Zone forest of a variety of tree species. On my study sites *Zaratornis* was noted mainly in small groves of stunted trees less than a hectare in extent, separated from each other by grassy and shrub-dotted areas or rockslides.

Of greatest importance to the cotinga is the presence in the *Polylepis* of two conspicuous orange-flowered mistletoes, *Tristerix chodatianus* at Tutapac and Santa Eulalia, and (probably) *Ligaria cuneifolia* at Pampa Galeras. The former was the only fruit-producing plant observed at Tutapac, and certainly the most important one found in the upper Santa Eulalia Valley. In both of these localities, *Zaratornis* was seen to feed solely on the fruits of *Tristerix*. At Pampa Galeras *Ligaria* was the only observed food source for *Zaratornis*. Koepcke (1958) mentioned *Phrygilanthus peruviana* (= *Tristerix secundus*) as an important food item for the cotingas *Zaratornis* and *Ampelion rubrocristatus*. The clumps of both of these mistletoes grow at or near the ends of *Polylepis* branches at all heights in the trees.

During foraging bouts, the cotingas perched on mistletoe clumps and swallowed up to five berries in succession. Within a few minutes individuals flew to another perch site, either an exposed calling perch or a sheltered limb within the foliage of a tree. There, after five to ten minutes more, the sticky seeds were regurgitated, one by one, and wiped onto the surface of the limb. I never saw a seed fall to the ground during this process and assume that a very high percent of all fruits taken are successfully dispersed in this manner. The exposed dead branches of calling perches were thickly covered with regurgitated seeds, and examination of less frequently used perch sites of living branches and limbs also revealed seeds, a few in various stages of germination. The seeds, quite large for mistletoes (A. Gentry, pers. comm.), are apparently always regurgitated.

Zaratornis was the only frugivorous bird observed on my three study sites, and is probably the sole dispersal agent for mistletoes growing above 3000 m. It appears that both species of mistletoes produce fruit throughout the year, though fruit seemed to be less abundant during the dry months August–October. This might account for the post-breeding dispersal of part of the *Zaratornis* population and subsequent appearance of the species in wooded areas at lower elevations (i.e. Zarate).

Behaviour

Almost nothing has been written about the behaviour of *Zaratornis* or its two close relatives *Ampelion rubrocristatus* and *A. rufaxilla*. Farrand (in Snow 1973*b*) wrote: 'In its general behaviour it is very like *Ampelion rubrocristata*. In a manner very reminiscent of that species it often pops up suddenly onto a dead snag and sits upright, looking about rather nervously. The flight of *Zaratornis* is very similar to that of *Ampelion* and both species approach a perch flying low and making a final upward sweep, rather like that of a kestrel or shrike.' As noted by Koepcke (1958), individuals characteristically perch quietly, often for long periods, atop a tree on a favourite exposed branch. This is apparently a part of nesting or feeding territory surveillance, though *Ampelion rubrocristatus* occasionally hawks insects from the air about such perches. Though I have never seen *Zaratornis* take an insect in any manner, I would expect them to do so from time to time.

At seemingly long but regular intervals, loud songs or calls are uttered from the calling perches (see below). When disturbed, a bird perched in the open usually bobbed its head and flicked its wings and tail in a nervous manner. Birds on territory (see under nesting behaviour) often pursued conspecifics that had entered the defended area. Territories of mated pairs at Tutapac were small, averaging about 100 m × 60 m.

Twice I observed a display between members of a mated pair. In both instances this occurred after both birds had been foraging. One individual (the sexes are monomorphic) flew from a mistletoe clump to a conspicuous calling perch where it was soon joined by the second bird. Both faced each other, and, while less than a foot apart, bowed towards each other slightly, and commenced head bobbing and wing flicking. After approximately 30 to 60 seconds, these displaying birds regurgitated *Tristerix* seeds onto the exposed surface of the *Polylepis* branch. During this type of display no vocalizations were uttered. Similar posturing and behaviour were exhibited by members of feeding aggregations (4–10 individuals) noted in August and September in the Santa Eulalia Valley.

Like other cotingas, *Zaratornis* has a rather limited, unmusical repertoire. The primary song of the species, which under normal conditions is repeated three to six times at intervals of 30 to 60 seconds, is a loud, low-pitched series that may be written as: *reh-reh-reh-reh-rrrrrrrrrrr-re-re*. It averages about 4 seconds in length, and falls within a frequency range of 2 to 4 kHz. This vocalization speeds to a roll towards the middle and ends with two or three emphatic notes; it is nasal in quality and sounds rather frog-like at a distance. It is given by both members of territorial pairs, usually from the tip of an exposed calling perch, and also by members of feeding aggregations during the non-breeding season. Calling normally begins in the morning (08.00–09.00) when sunlight first illuminates a woodland. One calling bird is usually answered by several others in adjacent groves. Calling is most frequent during early morning and late afternoon.

A regularly heard disturbance call uttered by incubating birds upon being flushed from a nest and also by adults engaged in intraspecific territorial encounters, is a drawn-out *raaaaaaah*. Contact notes between members of pairs or feeding aggregations are short but similar in quality to other vocalizations. While calling, birds remain upright and almost motionless.

Nesting

Prior to 1976, no definite record of nesting in *Zaratornis* had been obtained. Between 23 and 31 May 1976, I found four active nests of the species in Quebrada Tutapac. A fifth was found in the upper Santa Eulalia Valley on 6 May 1978. All were discovered by locating presumably mated pairs in small, isolated tree groves away from the larger wooded areas that occur in ravines or along the bases of cliffs. In both localities these groves were on the north-facing slopes of the quebrada, and received up to three more hours of sunlight daily than the north slopes. Considering the very low (freezing) night and early morning temperatures of this environment, the added hours of warmth may influence nest-site selection. Though mistletoe was present in trees on the north slopes, few cotingas were seen there, and no nests were found despite diligent searching.

All nests were well hidden within large clumps (0.5–1 m diameter) of *Tristerix* near the ends of tree branches 4–7 m above ground, and within 1–3 m of a trunk. All were fully shaded by surrounding mistletoe branches and foliage of *Polylepis*.

The fifth nest, which resembled the others very closely in overall size and construction, was collected. It was a well-made, rather deep cup of mosses and greenish-grey lichens, the latter being especially concentrated around the perimeter of the cup, which was lined with coarse green and yellow grasses; a few small (15–70 mm) twigs had also been incorporated into that structure. This nest measured: outside diameter 140 × 160 mm, outside depth 83 mm, inside diameter 76 × 80 mm, and inside depth 42 mm. It contained three eggs measuring 32.4 × 21.6, 32.6 × 22.1 and 33.3 × 21.6 mm. These were Greenish Glaucous of Ridgway (1912), with a distinct wreath of brownish and greyish-brown flecks about the larger end, and a few additional flecks of the same colours scattered over the entire egg.

Two of the four Tutapac nests contained two young and one egg, a third held two eggs and one nestling, and a fourth, which definitely contained at least one young bird, could not be reached for closer examination. The nestlings of the three examined nests were well-feathered for their small size, and resembled adults in coloration. All were very quiet in the nest and held their eyes closed even as I lifted them out for closer examination.

Only two adults, presumably a male and female, were observed in the immediate vicinity of each nest site. At nests with eggs one bird appeared to be doing most, if not all, of the incubation. Incubating adults could almost be touched before flushing to a nearby limb. The second adult of a pair usually appeared only after the first had flushed and uttered alarm calls, or when taped songs were played within the nesting area.

Both adults fed nestlings regurgitated fruit; generally only one adult visited the nest at a time. Of each pair, one adult, presumably the male, was definitely more aggressive and vocal in response to playbacks of songs. Due to other commitments I was unable to obtain detailed information on incubation or feeding rates.

Physical characters

A. rubrocristatus

Unfeathered parts
Male and female alike.
Iris: bright red.
Bill: black at tip, base pale grey.
Legs and feet: black or dark grey.

Measurements
♂♂ (35) Wing 107–121, 112.9. Tail 78–93, 85.9. Tarsus 22.3–27, 24.2. Culmen (from anterior edge of nares) 7.7–9.4, 8.7.
♀♀ (17) Wing 104–115, 109.2. Tail 80–88, 84.3. Tarsus 23–25, 23.9. Culmen (from anterior edge of nares) 8.0–9.3, 8.5.
Weights: 12 ♂♂ 51–80, 66.3 g (mean weights and wing-lengths of 9: 65.0 g, 110.9 mm).
9 ♀♀ 45–67, 66.3 g (mean weights and wing-lengths of 7: 60.1 g, 105.6 mm).

A. rufaxilla

Unfeathered parts
Male and female alike.
Iris: bright red.
Bill: blue-grey basally, black distally.
Legs and feet: dark olive or dark grey.

Geographical variation
The Colombian population (*antioquiae*) differs from the Peruvian and Bolivian population (*rufaxilla*) in being larger and having wider, more numerous streaks on the underparts and darker chestnut areas.

Measurements (A. r. rufaxilla)
♂♂ (6) Wing 114–120, 116.0. Tail 80–84, 80.8. Tarsus 20.5–23.1, 21.7. Culmen (from anterior edges of nares) 8.4–9.2, 8.7.
♀♀ (1) Wing 114. Tail 80.
Weights: 4 ♂♂ 71–77, 75.5 g (mean weights and wing-lengths of 2: 74.0, 115.5 mm).
3 ♀♀ 69–74, 71.7 g.

A. sclateri

Unfeathered parts
Male and female alike.
Iris: grey.
Bill: upper mandible black, lower mandible blue-grey with black tip.
Legs and feet: dark grey.

Measurements
♂♂ (7) Wing 101–104, 101.6. Tail 85–96, 91.9. Tarsus 26.2–27.5, 27.0 Culmen (from anterior edge of nares) 7.6–8.5, 8.1.
♀♀ (4) Wing 96–101, 98.5. Tail 86–93, 88.5. Tarsus 26.5–27.4, 26.9. Culmen (from anterior edge of nares) 7.9–8.2, 8.1.
Weights: 5 ♂♂ 54–69, 60.6 g (mean wing-length 101.8 mm).
3 ♀♀ 55–67, 60.3 g (mean wing-length 99.3 mm).

A. stresemanni

Unfeathered parts
Male and female alike.
Iris: red.
Bill: lead blue, paler towards tip.
Legs and feet: dark brown or blackish.

Measurements
♂♂ (5) Wing 110–115, 112.8. Tail 84–89, 86.2. Tarsus 25.5–26.5, 26.0. Culmen (from posterior edge of nares) 11.
♀♀ (6) Wing 111–114, 112.7. Tail 83–90, 86.5. Tarsus 26.5–27.5, 26.9. Culmen (from posterior edge of nares) 9–11, 10.0.
Weights: 4 ♂♂ 46–57, 53.0 g (mean wing-length 112.5 mm).
5 ♀♀ 47–55, 51.6 g (mean weight and wing-length of 4: 52.0 g, 112.5 mm).

Genus Pipreola – Andean fruiteaters

Plates 6, 7 and 8 on pages 68, 72 and 76

Pipreola riefferii – Green-and-black Fruiteater
Pipreola intermedia – Band-tailed Fruiteater
Pipreola arcuata – Barred Fruiteater
Pipreola aureopectus – Golden-breasted Fruiteater
Pipreola jucunda – Orange-breasted Fruiteater

Pipreola lubomirskii – Black-chested Fruiteater
Pipreola pulchra – Masked Fruiteater
Pipreola formosa – Handsome Fruiteater
Pipreola chlorolepidota – Fiery-throated Fruiteater
Pipreola frontalis – Scarlet-breasted Fruiteater

Pipreola whitelyi – Red-banded Fruiteater

The fruiteaters of the genus *Pipreola* consist of 9 to 11 species (depending on taxonomic treatment, which is still debatable) all but one of which are of Andean distribution. The exception is a very distinct species endemic to the Guiana highlands. They form a rather well-defined genus, the only close relative of which is perhaps *Ampelioides* (see p. 79). All are birds of montane forest. They have not been well studied, but such evidence as there is indicates that they are all predominantly frugivorous, that they live in pairs, and that both sexes attend the nest. Sexual dimorphism is well marked, the males being distinguished by some combination of black on the head and/or yellow, orange or red on the throat, neck or breast.

The three species whose altitudinal ranges extend highest, into temperate forest (the first three in the sequence listed above), differ from the other Andean species by having darker, more olive-green (rather than grass-green) upper parts and no orange or red in the plumage. They are also large, *P. arcuata* being easily the largest species in the genus. The smallest species, *P. chlorolepidota* and *P. frontalis*, are found at the lowest altitudes. Differences in food preference are suggested by the considerable differences in bill width between some of the species, but nothing is known about this.

From the taxonomic point of view *Pipreola* is the most difficult genus of the cotingas; it has the largest number of species or well-marked subspecies, and the critical distributional information needed for a sound judgment of the taxonomic status of related populations is in several cases lacking or in some way defective. Hence it is necessary to devote a special section to a discussion of species limits.

The species of *Pipreola*

P. riefferii and *P. intermedia* (Map 9)
These two species are closely related and have been treated by some authors as conspecific. The only striking difference is in the tail feathers, which are white-tipped with a black subterminal band in *intermedia* and plain green in *riefferii*. *Intermedia* is also slightly larger and has more extensive white tips to the wing-feathers. Over most of their range they replace one another geographically, *riefferii* in the northern part of the Andes from Venezuela to northern Peru, and *intermedia* from south-central Peru to Bolivia; but their ranges overlap in central Peru and they are certainly distinct species. This was suspected long ago by Hellmayr (1929) on the basis of specimens of the two species collected near to one another but at different altitudes in the Department of La Libertad, *riefferii* near Nuevo Loreto at 1200 m and *intermedia* near Cumpang at 2400 m. It has since been confirmed by a series of both species collected at Cumpang at altitudes of 2450–2625 m by members of the Louisiana State University Museum of Zoology. In this area both species were seen feeding together at the same fruiting trees. Both species have also been found in the Carpish Mountains, Department of Huánuco, some 250 km to the southeast; here they overlap narrowly in altitude, *riefferii* occurring mainly at 2130–2280 m and *intermedia* at 2280–2430 m (O'Neill & Parker 1981). Altitudinal data from outside the area of overlap indicate that *intermedia* ranges higher than *riefferii*. Thus further north in Peru *riefferii* has been collected at 2300–2800 m, while further south *intermedia* has been recorded mainly at 2500–3000 m.

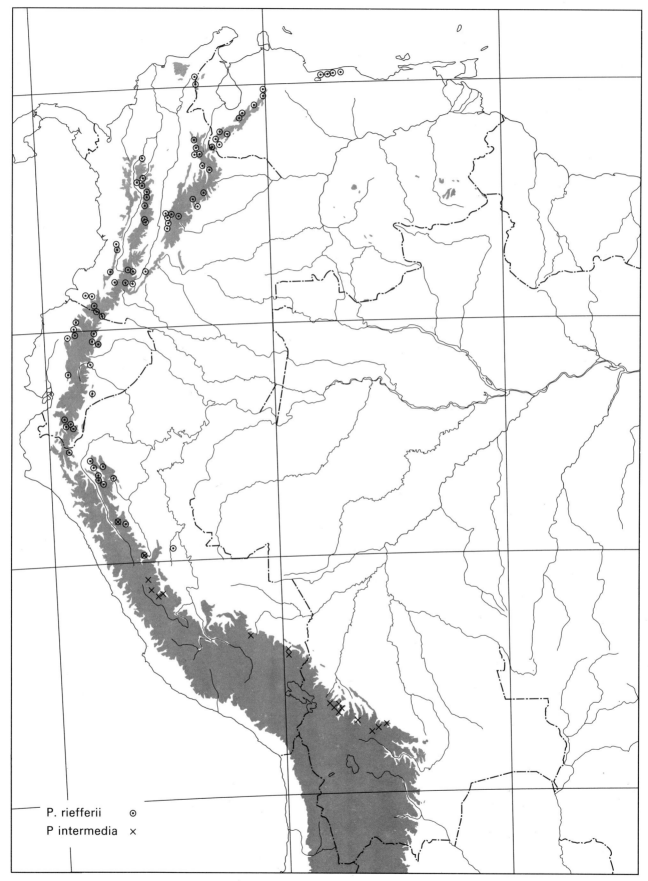

Map 9   Distribution of the Green-and-black Fruiteater (*Pipreola riefferii*) and Band-tailed Fruiteater (*P. intermedia*).

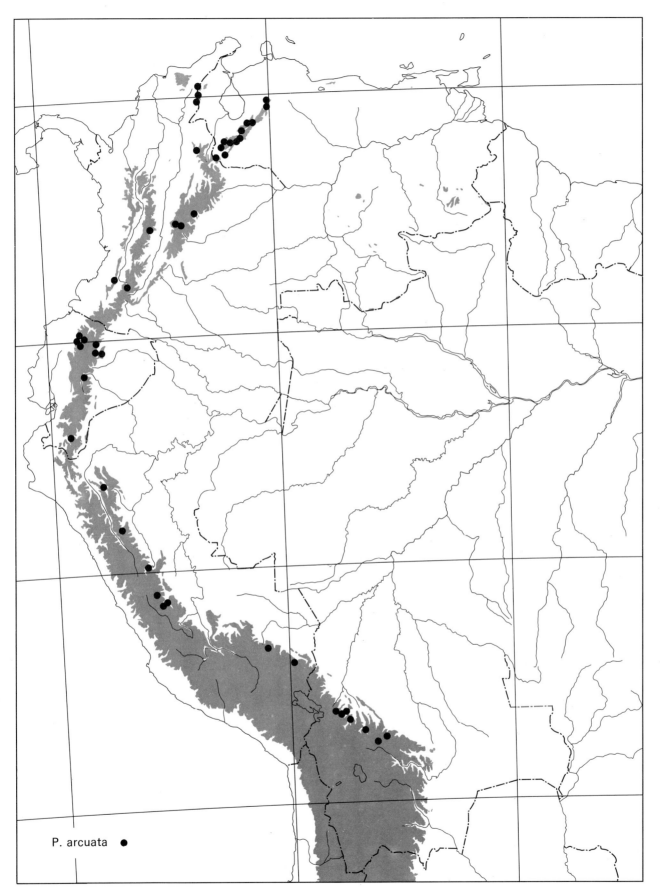

Map 10   Distribution of the Barred Fruiteater (*Pipreola arcuata*).

MWWoodcock

P. arcuata (Map 10)
This very large species seems to be most closely related to *intermedia*; but it differs conspicuously from *intermedia* by the black barring of its underparts. Moreover the pattern of the upper tail-coverts and tail is strikingly like that of *Ampelioides*. It may be that barring is a primitive character that has been lost in the other species or only faintly retained in the underparts of the female plumage.

P. aureopectus and related forms (Map 11)
This is the most difficult group. It consists of four distinct forms, the most widespread of which, *P. aureopectus*, itself shows some geographical variation. Except for overlap between *aureopectus* and *jucunda*, they are almost certainly allopatric; they all have very similar female plumages, streaked below; and all four agree in the combination of colours of the soft parts — yellow iris, orange or red bill, and grey-green feet and legs. The three southern forms, *jucunda*, *lubomirskii* and *pulchra*, are obviously closely related: the males differ only in their head and breast markings, as shown in Plate 7, while the females are extremely similar; and they all have relatively large and broad bills. There is little doubt that they are completely allopatric, but their ranges are certainly not completely known. *Jucunda* is confined to the west slopes of the Western Andes, from southwestern Colombia to southwestern Ecuador. *Lubomirskii* is found from the headwaters of the Rio Magdalena in southern Colombia (near where the Central Andes join the Eastern Andes) south along the eastern slopes of the Eastern Andes of Ecuador to extreme northern Peru west of the Rio Marañón. *Pulchra* has been found in a few localities in Peru east of the Marañón, from Amazonas south to Junín.

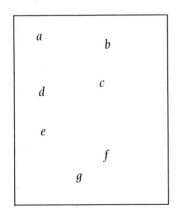

Plate 6
Andean fruiteaters
(*Pipreola* and *Ampelioides*)

a: Band-tailed Fruiteater *P. intermedia signata*, male
b and *c*: Green-and-black Fruiteater *P. riefferii occidentalis*, male and female
d and *e*: Barred Fruiteater *P. arcuata*, male and female
f and *g*: Scaled Fruiteater *A. tschudii*, male and female

Aureopectus is distinct from these three in several respects. It is the only one with white-tipped wing and tail feathers; the yellow underparts (in the male) come up almost to the chin; the rest of the head is the same colour as the upper parts; and the bill is smaller and narrower.

Jucunda, *lubomirskii* and *pulchra* could be treated as well-marked subspecies of a single species, but for the reasons given on p. 12 we prefer to give specific status to each of them. *Aureopectus* must certainly be given specific status. Not only is it the most distinct in plumage, but it overlaps extensively with *jucunda* in the Western Andes of Colombia. (The treatment adopted in Peters' *Check-list*, vol. 8, in which all four were treated as conspecific, following Snow (1973b), was decided before the evidence of extensive sympatry in the Western Andes was available.) It is curious that there is, apparently, a wide gap in the Eastern Andes of Colombia between *aureopectus* in the north and *lubomirskii* in the south. Though they may approach one another closer than has been recorded, the intensive and long-continued collecting that has been carried out in the Bogotá area makes it practically certain that the gap is real.

P. chlorolepidota and *P. frontalis* (Map 12)
The males of these two species at first sight appear very different, since the underparts of *chlorolepidota* are darkish green apart from the throat-patch, and those of *frontalis* are yellow. But the former species retains a small yellow area lateral to the throat-patch, where the feathers are brightest yellow in *frontalis*, and the two species agree in the colour of the soft parts (in the adult male, white or yellow iris, orange or red bill and feet). Moreover, the females are almost identical in plumage. They have probably speciated comparatively recently, but they now overlap extensively in Ecuador and Peru. Available records indicate that the altitudinal range of *frontalis* is higher than that of *chlorolepidota* (Table 5).

P. formosa (Map 12)
This species seems to be closest to *chlorolepidota* and *frontalis*, with which it agrees in having white-tipped secondaries and barred (rather than streaked) underparts in the female plumage. It differs most strikingly in the extensively black head of the male, and less strikingly in the colours of the soft parts (especially in having olive-coloured, not red or orange, legs).

P. whitelyi (Map 12)
This isolated and peculiar species cannot be linked with any other member of the genus. Mayr & Phelps

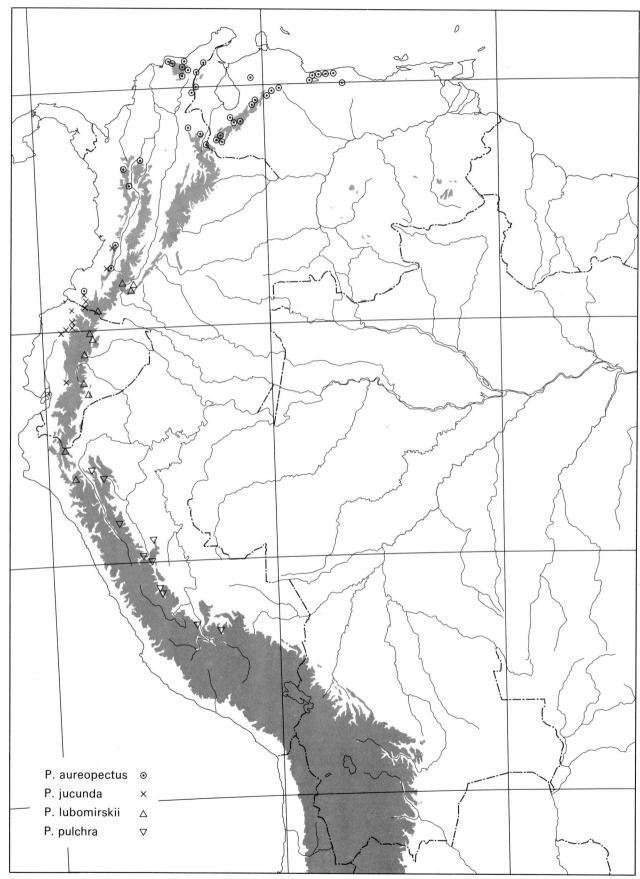

Map 11   Distribution of the Golden-breasted Fruiteater (*Pipreola aureopectus*), Orange-breasted Fruiteater (*P. jucunda*),
Black-chested Fruiteater (*P. lubomirskii*) and Masked Fruiteater (*P. pulchra*).

P. aureopectus   ⊙
P. jucunda   ×
P. lubomirskii   △
P. pulchra   ▽

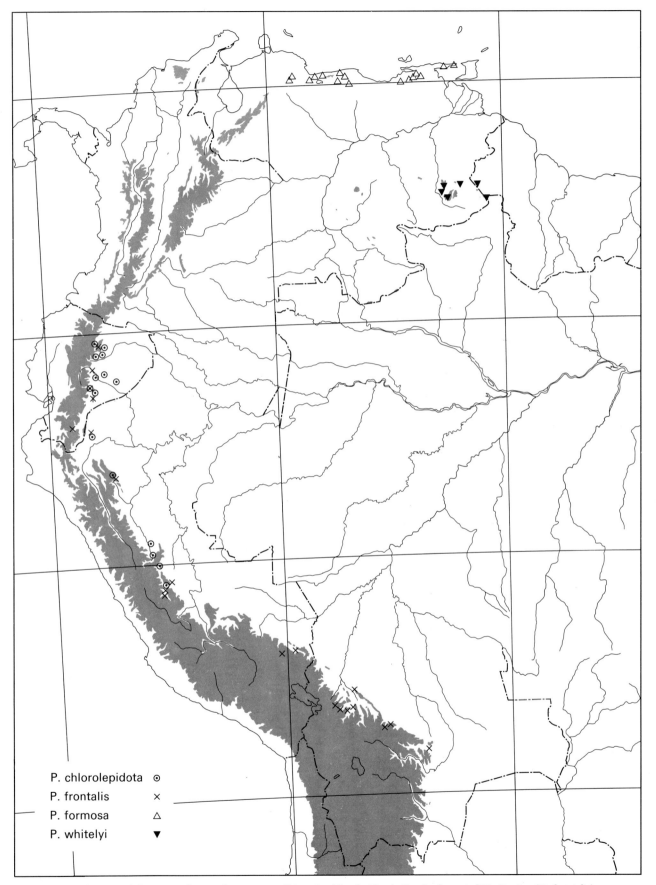

Map 12 Distribution of the Fiery-throated Fruiteater (*Pipreola chlorolepidota*), Scarlet-breasted Fruiteater (*P. frontalis*), Handsome Fruiteater (*P. formosa*) and Red-banded Fruiteater (*P. whitelyi*).

Table 5
Altitudinal zonation of *Pipreola* species (in metres)

	Main altitudinal zone	N. Venezuela	Colombia (E. and C. Andes)	Ecuador (E. Andes)	Peru	Bolivia
arcuata	ST–Te	1800–3100	2200–3200	1200–3350	2200–3350	1670–2700
riefferii	ST–Te	1750–3050	1200–2800	1600–1750	1200–2900	–
intermedia	ST–Te	–	–	–	2400–3100	1100–2800
aureopectus group	ST	800–2300*a*	1250–1850*a* 1200–2150*l*	1500–1850*a* 1000–2300*j*	1850–2300*l* 1820–2250*p*	–
formosa	ST	800–1900	–	–	–	–
frontalis	T–ST	–	–	700–1500	670–1830	1200–2300
chlorolepidota	T	–	–	900–1250	210–1000	–

Notes: Altitudinal ranges indicated are those which embrace the great majority of collected specimens.
Altitudinal zones as follows: T, tropical; ST, subtropical; Te, temperate.
Abbreviations for *aureopectus* group as follows: *a, aureopectus; j, jucunda; l, lubomirskii; p, pulchra.*

(1967) have suggested that the endemic bird species of the 'pantepui' region, of which *P. whitelyi* is one of the most distinctive, mostly colonized the region by long-distance dispersal from the Andes or from the Venezuelan north coastal ranges, and this seems certainly to be the case for *P. whitelyi*, which presumably was one of the earliest of such colonisers.

Habitat and food

Very little is known in detail about the ecology of any of the fruiteaters. They are all forest birds, inhabiting mainly the lower and middle layers of the forest vegetation. They are especially characteristic of very humid cloud forest. Goodfellow (1901) noted that all three of the species which he encountered in Ecuador were found in the thickest part of the forest. Ecological segregation of the sympatric species in partly by altitude (Table 5) and apparently partly by size. Thus Table 5 shows that there is a replacement of species – though with much overlap – from tropical levels (*chlorolepidota* and *frontalis*) through subtropical (*aureopectus* group and *formosa*) to temperate levels (*riefferii* group and *arcuata*). The tropical species are the smallest and *arcuata*, which occurs at the greatest altitudes, is the largest; but over most of its altitudinal range *arcuata* overlaps with the much smaller *riefferii/intermedia* group.

All species, so far as known, feed mainly on fruits which, being rather heavy-bodied birds, they pluck from a perched position or in a clumsy hover. The Green-and-black and Band-tailed Fruiteaters have been reported to take melastome fruits (Stolzmann, in Taczanowski 1884; O'Neill & Parker 1981), and black berries, probably melastome fruits, have been mentioned for other species. Miller (1963) found that the Green-and-black Fruiteater favoured a blue berry which was present in the gut of all the specimens he examined and stained it conspicuously. Insects are also eaten, but apparently in small quantities compared with fruit.

Behaviour

Most observers have reported that fruiteaters are found singly or in pairs. Schaefer & Phelps (1954), however, mention that Golden-breasted Fruiteaters may be found in small groups of 5–10 birds; and Green-and-black Fruiteaters occur in pairs or loose groups of 3–6 birds (Hilty, MS). Most species forage in the lower or middle layers of the forest, or at times visit fruiting trees or bushes in cleared places. The Fiery-throated Fruiteater, the smallest member of the genus, ranges up into the forest canopy. When apparently searching for insects, fruiteaters move

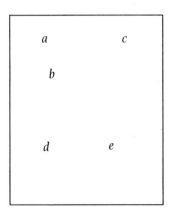

Plate 7
Andean fruiteaters
(*Pipreola*)

a and *b*: Orange-breasted Fruiteater *P. jucunda*, male and female
c: Golden-breasted Fruiteater *P. aureopectus*, male
d: Black-chested Fruiteater *P. lubomirskii*, male
e: Masked Fruiteater *P. pulchra*, male

slowly through the forest, perching for a time motionless and then flying on.

All of their recorded calls are high-pitched. Miller (1963) described the principal note of the Green-and-black Fruiteater as 'a surprisingly high-pitched, but sharp, staccato chatter'. Hilty (MS) describes the same note as 'a very high sibilant *ti-ti-ti-ti-ti* . . . series (up to 5 sec) dying away and descending slightly'. During copulation a rattling *cha-a-a-a-a* is given. O'Neill & Parker (1981) write as follows of the newly described and very distinct subspecies *tallmanorum* of the Green-and-black Fruiteater at the southern extreme of its range in central Peru: 'The song, given by both sexes, consists of several soft, high-pitched notes followed by a very thin, high-pitched *seeee*; this series of notes may be written *ti-ti-ti-seeee*. This vocalization is quite like that of *P. r. chachapoyas*, both north and south of the Río Marañón, and is also reminiscent of vocalizations of *P. intermedia*.' The calls of other species have been described by Hilty as follows. Orange-breasted Fruiteater: an extremely high-pitched (higher than Green-and-black Fruiteater) thin hissing *se-e-e-e-e-e-e-e-e-e* (about 2–2.5 sec) easily overlooked; also a loud high *eeest* repeated at short intervals. Golden-breasted Fruiteater: similar to Orange-breasted Fruiteater, a very high thin *se-e-e-e-e-e-e-e-e-e*, lasting about 2 sec. Barred Fruiteater: an extremely high thin almost hissing *se-e-e-e-e-e-a-a-a-a* (about 2.5 sec), similar to Orange-breasted Fruiteater but longer and descending, in Cauca, Colombia – call shorter in Peru (T. A. Parker).

In the Green-and-black and Orange-breasted Fruiteaters both male and female attend the nest (see next section), and this is probably true for the genus as a whole; but there is no information on whether pairs are permanent.

Breeding and annual cycle

Nesting

Miller (1963) has given what appears to be the only published account of the nesting of any of the fruiteaters in the wild. In cloud forest in the Western Andes of Colombia, at a height of about 6500 feet (1980 m), he found the Green-and-black Fruiteater common, and in the course of a year's field work found two occupied nests, one with eggs and one with young. 'The nest with eggs was situated in wet, thick forest on a steep slope. It was 4 feet up on a leaning tree about 2 inches in diameter and was placed on and held by a vine. The nest was made almost entirely of coarse green moss and thus matched the moss-covered trunks. It was 6 inches across and not bound to the vine. Outside depth was

3 inches; the cup was 3 inches across and $1\frac{1}{2}$ inches deep and was lined completely with black rootlets, so that no moss showed through. The nest with young found on September 16 was in a bush that stood at the edge of the forest wall. It was thus exposed and obvious as a large green ball. It was 5 feet up and constructed like the other nest.

'The eggs of this species are cream colored with sparse, nonaggregated red-brown spots above the equator and a very few on the lower section. They measured 26.1 by 20.0 and 25.1 by 20.3 mm. The young in the nest of September 16 were judged to be about 3 or 4 days old; the eyes were not yet opened. On the 18th the young, still with eyes closed, had pin feathers which showed bright yellowish green areas breaking out at the tips. The mouth lining was red.

'The parent female at the nest with eggs flushed at a distance of 6 feet, returned to stay within 10 feet of me, and scolded with the high-pitched chatter. She had a well-developed edematous brood patch. At the nest with young the female would allow a cautious approach to within 3 feet. On leaving she went into the forest and hopped about silently in the adjoining brush. The male appeared and came to within 15 feet of the nest but did not go to it.'

Additional information on the breeding of the Green-and-black Fruiteater comes from a report on several nestings of two captive females (Everitt 1963). They were paired successively to the same male (the second one after the first had died). The females alone built the open cup nest, the choice of nest-material being dictated by what was available. All clutches were of 2 eggs, laid in two cases on successive days and in two other cases with intervals of 2 and 3 days. The eggs were pale brown, spotted with sepia, most heavily at the thick end; two measured 25×18 mm. Only the female incubated; but the male fed her on the nest, and stood guard on the nest edge when she was away feeding or for any other reason. Two incubation periods were 19 and 20 days. Both parents fed the nestlings, one of which left the nest successfully at the age of 21 days. Once out of the nest, the fledgling was fed only by the male.

To complete the record of nesting data for the Green-and-black Fruiteater, five eggs collected in Antioquia, northern Colombia, by T. K. Salmon, now in the British Museum collection, were described by Sclater & Salvin (1879) as pale salmon-coloured with a few dark red-brown spots. They measure 25.1–27.2 (mean 26.2) × 18.3–20.3 (mean 19.6) mm (Schönwetter 1969).

The only other published account of the nesting of any of the fruiteaters describes the nesting in captivity of a pair of Orange-breasted Fruiteaters (Lint & Dolan 1966). In general, the nesting behaviour of these birds was similar to that of the Green-and-black Fruiteaters. The male fed the female before the eggs were laid as well as when she was incubating. The clutch of 2 eggs, light tan in colour with fine brown flecks, was laid on successive days. The incubation period was 17 days (or 16, the account being discrepant), and the fledging period of the single young that survived was 25 days. Both parents fed the young, both in the nest and after it had fledged.

Annual cycle

Schaefer & Phelps (1954) made the general statements that at Rancho Grande, at about $10\frac{1}{2}°$N in the coastal mountains of northern Venezuela, the Green-and-black Fruiteater nests in June, the Golden-breasted Fruiteater in May, and the Handsome Fruiteater from April to June. Miller (1963) suggested that these periods were too restricted, since in southwestern Colombia at $3\frac{1}{2}°$N he had evidence that the Green-and-black Fruiteater had an extended nesting season. His actual records indicated layings in February, March, May and August. The breeding seasons in Venezuela are almost certainly somewhat longer than Schaefer & Phelps stated, for juvenile specimens of Golden-breasted Fruiteaters indicate laying dates in June and probably July. Nevertheless, the season in Miller's area in western Colombia is undoubtedly more protracted than in the coastal mountains of

Venezuela. There are no other nesting data supporting this conclusion, but the timing of the onset of the post-breeding moult provides clear evidence. Thus 17 of the 21 moult records for northern Venezuela give calculated dates of onset of moult in May–July (the other four being 2 in April and 2 in August); but in southwestern Colombia, between about 1° and 4°N, the 32 moult records give calculated dates of onset of moult in every month of the year, with no obvious peak.

The general pattern of moult seasons for all *Pipreola* species combined (Table 6) shows that reproductive cycles are well synchronized only in the extreme north and the extreme south of the range of the genus. Only in Bolivia, between about 14° and 18°S, is there a degree of synchrony comparable to what is found in north coastal Venezuela, the peak at the southern extreme of the range being in November–December, exactly 6 months different from the peak in the north. It is noteworthy that in the north the synchrony largely breaks down at about 8–9°N in northwestern Venezuela (Mérida and adjacent states), though the May–June peak is still apparent. In northern Colombia there is a peak in May–July, but records are spread through the year. In southern Colombia and Ecuador records are spread out more or less evenly through the year. The southern hemisphere regime that is well-marked in Bolivia is already apparent in Peru south of 10°S. These broad geographical patterns are almost certainly determined by the rainfall regimes in the different areas.

Table 6

Seasonal patterns of moult in *Pipreola*, all species combined

	Month of onset of moult											
	Jan	Feb	Mar	Apr	May	Jun	Jul	Aug	Sep	Oct	Nov	Dec
N. Venezuela coastal mountains				2	6	7	4	2				
Andes of N.W. Venezuela	2	3	2	1	7	5	1	2	3	3	3	1
S.E. Venezuela (*P. whitelyi* only)	2	1	3	3	8	2	2					
N. Colombia, south to c. 4°N	2	2	5	3	6	7	8	3	1	1	1	1
S. Colombia	3	3	3	4	5	3	4	1	1	4	1	4
Ecuador and Peru north of 10°S	6	4	4	5	5	3	3	3		3	12	5
Peru south of 10°S	1	1	2							1		2
Bolivia	2	1							2	2	3	4

Notes: The table shows the numbers of specimens for which the calculated date of onset of moult falls in each month, allowing a total duration of moult of 120 days in the individual (Snow 1976a). The irregularity of the figures for the areas where seasonality is poorly marked is due in part to the fact that specimens have not been evenly collected throughout the year.

M.W.Woodcock

Plumages and moult

P. riefferii
Nestling down sparse, black. Juvenile plumage dark olive-green above (darker and duller than adult), dull olive, streaked yellow, below; feathers of crown and humeral area with yellow apical streaks. Juvenile body plumage and coverts apparently replaced soon after fledging by fully adult plumage (in male reared in captivity, black feathers of throat showing 24 days after leaving nest, and fully adult plumage almost complete at age of 3 months).

Other species
Plumage sequence apparently similar. In juvenile plumage of *P. whitelyi*, spots on upper parts are larger and broader, buff-coloured with blackish terminal fringe, and extend to wing-coverts and sparsely to lower back and rump.

Physical characters

Structure
Bill rather weak, slightly hooked, dorsoventrally compressed, of very variable width in different species (very wide in *jucunda*, narrow in *riefferii*); nostrils exposed, oval; weak bristles round base of both mandibles. Legs and feet moderately strong; tarsus with no scutellation along plantar surface. Wing rounded and rather short, flight feathers not modified. Feathers of back and rump very loosely attached; preen gland very small (*P. formosa*; Wetmore 1939).

Unfeathered parts
Similar in male and female, except as noted.

P. riefferii
Iris: dark red-brown; in some males described as red (*occidentalis*) or dark red (*melanolaema*).

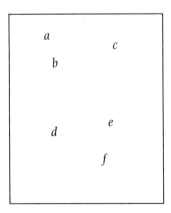

Plate 8
Andean and Guianan fruiteater (*Pipreola*)

a and b: Scarlet-breasted Fruiteater *P. frontalis squamipectus*, male and female
c: Handsome Fruiteater *P. formosa formosa*, male
d: Fiery-throated Fruiteater *P. chlorolepidota*, male
e and f: Red-banded Fruiteater *P. whitelyi*, male and female

Bill: bright red; in some specimens described as black-tipped, probably an age character as juveniles have black bills.
Feet and legs: red or orange-red.

P. intermedia
Iris: brown; in some specimens described as grey.
Bill: crimson; some described as having culmen-ridge black.
Feet and legs: red or orange-red.

P. arcuata
Iris: cream-coloured; some males described as brown, and one female as greenish grey.
Bill: crimson, sometimes with black tip.
Feet and legs: scarlet.

P. aureopectus
Iris: yellow.
Bill: orange.
Feet and legs: greenish grey.

P. jucunda
Iris: light yellow to golden yellow or orange.
Bill: orange to red.
Feet and legs: greenish grey.

P. lubomirskii
Iris: yellow.
Bill: orange red to coral red in male, duller red to reddish brown in female.
Feet and legs: greenish grey to brownish olive.

P. pulchra (male only recorded)
Iris: yellow.
Bill: red.
Feet and legs: greenish.

P. formosa
Iris: orange-yellow.
Bill: reddish orange.
Feet and legs: dull greenish olive or olive-brown.

P. chlorolepidota (male only recorded)
Iris: cream-coloured.
Bill: orange with black tip.
Feet and legs: orange.

P. frontalis
Iris: yellow.
Bill: orange red in male; blackish, yellow at base of lower mandible, in female (based on young bird?).
Feet and legs: orange red to scarlet in male; dull red to brownish yellow in female.

P. whitelyi
Iris: orange in male; light ochre in female.
Bill: dark red in male; dark brown in female.
Feet and legs: bright orange or red in male; brown
   in female.

Geographical variation
Seven species of *Pipreola* show geographical variation that is marked enough for the recognition of
subspecies. They are listed, with a summary of their
characters, on pp. 188–189.

Measurements
P. riefferii melanolaema (Venezuela)
♂♂ (5) Wing 90–97, 92.1. Tail 74–80, 77.3.
   Tarsus 23–23.5, 23.1. Culmen 8.5–9.5, 8.8.
♀♀ (4) Wing 84–92, 89.3. Tail 69–75, 72.5.
   Tarsus 23–24, 23.6. Culmen 8–10, 9.3.

P. riefferii riefferii (E. and C. Andes of Colombia)
♂♂ (5) Wing 91–95, 92.5. Tail 67–75, 70.3.
   Tarsus 22–24, 23.3. Culmen 8.5–9.5, 9.0.
♀♀ (4) Wing 89–94, 90.5. Tail 68–73, 71.3.
   Tarsus 22–22.5, 22.3. Culmen 8.5–9, 8.9.

P. riefferii occidentalis (W. Andes of Colombia)
♂♂ (8) Wing 90–96, 94.1. Tail 68–74, 70.5.
   Tarsus 22–24.5, 23.3. Culmen 9.5–11, 9.9.

P. riefferii chachapoyas (N. Peru)
♂♂ (7) Wing 87–90, 87.8. Tail 65–70, 67.5.
   Tarsus 19.3–23, 21.3. Culmen 8.5–9, 8.8.

P. riefferii tallmanorum (C. Peru – data from O'Neill &
   Parker 1981)
♂♂ (14) Wing, mean 84.0. Tail, mean 68.6.

Weights: 5 ♂♂ (*chachapoyas*) 46–61, 48.6 g (mean
      wing, 87.7 mm).
      5 ♂♂ (*occidentalis*) 49.9–51.6, 51.0 g.
      3 ♀♀ (*occidentalis*) 49.0–50.3, 49.4 g.

P. intermedia intermedia (C. Peru)
♂♂ (5) Wing 87.5–99, 92.7. Tail 68–75.5, 73.4.
   Tarsus 21.4–23.8, 22.3.
♀♀ (3) Wing 87–89, 88.2. Tail 72.5–77, 74.7.
   Tarsus 21.2–24.5, 22.3.

P. intermedia signata (Bolivia)
♂♂ (4) Wing 92–97, 94.8. Tail 73–78, 75.5.
   Tarsus 23–24.5, 23.6. Culmen 9–10, 9.3.

Weights: 4 ♂♂ (*intermedia*) 44–58, 48.8 g (mean wing,
      90.9 mm).
      3 ♀♀ (*intermedia*) 44–51, 46.7 g (mean wing,
      88.2 mm).
      2 ♂♂ (*signata*) 54.3, 58.9 g.
      1 ♀ (*signata*) 50.8 g.

P. arcuata
♂♂ (9) Wing 120–129, 124.3. Tail 85–93, 90.3.
   Tarsus 26.5–29.5, 27.7. Culmen 10–12, 11.3.
♀♀ (7) Wing 114–127, 121.6. Tail 89–95, 93.0.
   Tarsus 26–29, 27.6. Culmen 11–12, 11.5.
Weights: 3 ♂♂ 112–120, 115.0 g.
      3 ♀♀ 120–128, 124.7 g.

P. aureopectus festiva (N. Venezuela)
♂♂ (10) Wing 89–95, 91.9. Tail 65–71, 68.7.
   Tarsus 20.5–23, 21.8. Culmen 8.5–9.5, 9.1.
♀♀ (7) Wing 90–94, 92.1. Tail 64–71, 68.2.
   Tarsus 20.5–23, 21.5. Culmen 8.5–10, 9.4.
Weights: 1 ♂ 46 g.
      2 ♀♀ 46 g (wing 92 mm), 60 g (egg-laying?).

Pipreola jucunda
♂♂ (11) Wing 91–100, 95.4. Tail 58–65, 60.7.
   Tarsus 21–23.5, 22.2. Culmen 10.5–11.5, 11.0.
♀♀ (4) Wing 95–97, 96.0. Tail 59–63, 61.3.
   Tarsus 21.5–23, 22.2. Culmen 11–11.5, 11.2.

P. lubomirskii
♂♂ (7) Wing 90–97, 92.3. Tail 62–68, 65.0.
   Tarsus 20.5–23, 21.7. Culmen 9.5–10.5, 10.4.
♀♀ (4) Wing 90–94, 92.5. Tail 61–67, 64.5.
   Tarsus 21–22.5, 21.6. Culmen 9.5–10.5, 9.9.

P. pulchra
♂♂ (4) Wing 93–101, 95.8. Tail 65–78, 70.0.
   Tarsus 23.0. Culmen 10.5.
♀♀ (2) Wing 92, 93.
Weights: 4 ♂♂ 54–63, 59.0 g.
      2 ♀♀ 42 (abnormally low?), 63 g.

P. formosa formosa
♂♂ (10) Wing 84–90, 87.8. Tail 55–65, 61.4.
   Tarsus 19–21, 20.2. Culmen 8.5–9.5, 9.0.
♀♀ (6) Wing 85–89, 87.0. Tail 63–64, 63.3.
   Tarsus 20–20.5, 20.4. Culmen 8–9.5, 8.8.
Weights: 3 ♂♂ 43–49, 46.3 g.
      2 ♀♀ 41, 45 g.

P. chlorolepidota
♂♂ (9) Wing 73–77, 74.6. Tail 45–47, 45.9.
   Tarsus 17–19, 17.8. Culmen 7.5–9.5, 8.6.
♀♀ (3) Wing 73–75, 74.0. Tail 42–46, 44.3.
   Tarsus 17.5–18, 17.7. Culmen 8–8.5, 8.3.
Weights: 1 ♂ 28 g.
      1 ♀ 31 g.

P. frontalis squamipectus
♂♂ (2) Wing 87, 88. Tail 62, 66. Tarsus 19.5.
   Culmen 10.
♀♀ (4) Wing 83–88, 86.0. Tail 54–58, 57.0.
   Tarsus 18–19.5, 18.5. Culmen 9–9.5, 9.2.
Weights: 4 ♂♂ 40.0–45.3, 43.1 g.
      3 ♀♀ 39.5–44.3, 41.4 g.

P. whitelyi whitelyi
♂♂ (9) Wing 89–95, 92.3. Tail 59–66, 62.4.
   Tarsus 21–22, 21.3. Culmen 8.5–10.5, 9.6.
♀♀ (7) Wing 88–94, 91.4.

Genus *Ampelioides*

Plate 6, page 68

Ampelioides tschudii – Scaled Fruiteater

Ampelioides is probably not very distantly related to *Pipreola*. Both genera are Andean, and both are distinguished from all other cotinga genera, with the exception of the very different *Iodopleura*, by having the planta tarsi (the posterior region of the tarsus) without any kind of scutellation. In some details of its plumage pattern *A. tschudii* bears a striking resemblance to the largest species of *Pipreola*, *P. arcuata*. In both, the middle tail feathers in the male are basally green with a broad subterminal black area and white tips, the outer tail feathers are black with white tips, and the upper tail-coverts green with a subterminal black area and yellow tips. The yellow, black-barred under tail-coverts of *A. tschudii* are very similar to the feathers of the underparts of *P. arcuata*, but the feathers of the rest of the underparts have the bars drawn out to a point, giving a scaly appearance. If these resemblances indicate affinity, the implication is that *A. tschudii* and *P. arcuata* retain a plumage pattern characteristic of the ancestral *Pipreola/Ampelioides* stock, and that the brightly plumaged *Pipreola* species, with spots and bars reduced or absent, are a more recent evolutionary development.

In the details of feather markings, especially the shape and distribution of black bars and pale feather tips and fringes, *A. tschudii* has one of the most complex plumage patterns found in the cotinga family. It is further unusual in one feature of its sexual dimorphism. The most conspicuous difference between the sexes is the much greater extent of glossy black on the upper parts in the male; but on the underparts the reverse is the case, the dark feather markings being black in the female and olive-green in the male.

Distribution (Map 13)

Ampelioides tschudii is widely distributed in the Andes, from the Sierra de Perijá on the border between northern Colombia and Venezuela south through Colombia (with an outlying population on the plateau of the Sierra de Macarena) and Ecuador to about 15° 30'S in Bolivia. Until its recent discovery in Bolivia (Parker *et al.* 1980), the southernmost record was at about 11°S in Peru, some 800 km to the northwest. It is a bird of the upper tropical and subtropical zones, most records coming from altitudes between 1200 and 2000 m. Venezuelan records are all within this range, Colombian records are from 900 to 2150 m, Ecuadorian records 1100–2300 m, Peruvian records 1200–1900 m, and Bolivian records 1650–1675 m.

Habitat and food

The Scaled Fruiteater inhabits thick humid forest, where it keeps mainly to the middle and upper levels of the vegetation. Little has been reported of its ecology; its broad, somewhat flattened bill suggests that it feeds mainly on fruits that are relatively large for its size. This is supported by the limited data available. The two specimens collected in Bolivia had both been feeding on a large red fruit measuring 10×10 mm. Another bird, collected in Peru, had been feeding on purple berries measuring 8 mm at a height of about 10 m.

Behaviour

Only a few scattered observations are available. Goodfellow (1901) wrote that the Scaled Fruiteaters that he saw in Ecuador frequented the higher trees and were more solitary than the Barred Fruiteater *Pipreola arcuata*. Hilty (MS) notes that in Colombia Scaled Fruiteaters are seen singly or in pairs, or less often in groups of 3–4; they hop deliberately along moss- and bromeliad-covered limbs in the middle storey and canopy, and frequently follow bird flocks. Parker *et al.* (1980) wrote of two birds collected in Bolivia: 'These individuals perched motionless for many minutes at a time in the subcanopy 10–20 m above ground, making occasional short, noisy (wing rattle) flights. The female uttered a soft chatter, barely audible, that resembled some calls of *Icterus* spp. (especially *spurius*) or of *Piaya cayana*. The song (male only?) consists of a series of rather loud, mellow, downward inflected, short whistles at 5–10 sec intervals for several minutes at a time. These are reminiscent (to Parker's ear) of calls of *Myiarchus tuberculifer*.'

79

Breeding and annual cycle

The nest is unrecorded, and no very young birds seem to have been collected. Hence nothing is known directly about the breeding season, but some idea of the timing of the annual cycle can be derived from moult records. Five moulting birds from the Sierra de Perijá at the extreme northern end of the range (about 10°N) had all begun to moult about April or May. Further south in Colombia records are few (one each in the months February, March, June and July), while of 11 moult records from Ecuador all but two indicate starting dates in December–April. Three records for Peru are in January and June (2). There seems to be no obvious difference in timing between males and females, but the records are too few and scattered for any firm conclusion.

Plumages and moults

Nestling down and juvenile plumage not seen. Immature plumage apparently extensively pale-tipped, as birds moulting into adult plumage show a variable number of old feathers with yellow-green subterminal spots on the crown and yellow-green tips on the back, wing-coverts and inner secondaries.

Physical characters

Structure

Bill broad at base, upper mandible somewhat swollen laterally; nostrils large, oval, exposed, bristly feathers well developed round base of lower mandible. Tarsus without scutellation along plantar surface. Wing and tail feathers unmodified; tail relatively short.

Unfeathered parts

Iris : Male, golden yellow. Female, apparently duller, described as yellow, lemon yellow, or olive green; also recorded as pale brown (young birds?).

Bill : Both sexes, upper mandible black, lower mandible paler, olive or olive-horn.

Legs and feet: olive-grey or bluish-grey; soles dull yellow.

Measurements

ad ♂♂ (14)   Wing 98–108, 102.6.   Tail 57–65, 61.9.
  Tarsus 21–23, 21.9.   Culmen 12–13.5, 12.8.
subad ♂♂ (5)   Wing 100–104, 102.4.
♀♀ (13)   Wing 96–104, 99.8.   Tail 58–66, 63.0.
  Tarsus 20.5–22, 21.7.   Culmen 12–12.5, 12.3.
Weights: 4 ♂♂ 74–95, 84.0 g.
        3 ♀♀ 71.5–80, 76.5 g.

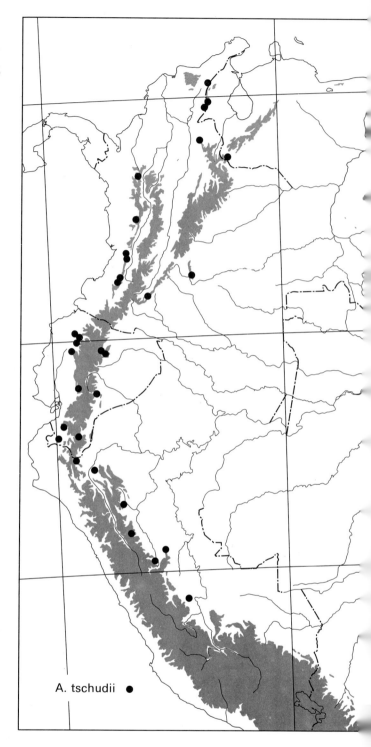

A. tschudii ●

Map 13   Distribution of the Scaled Fruiteater (*Ampelioides tschudii*).

Genus *Cotinga* – the blue cotingas

Plates 9 and 10, pages 86 and 90

Cotinga amabilis – Lovely Cotinga
Cotinga ridgwayi – Ridgway's (or Turquoise) Cotinga
Cotinga nattererii – Natterer's (or Blue) Cotinga
Cotinga cotinga – Purple-breasted Cotinga
Cotinga maculata – Banded Cotinga
Cotinga maynana – Plum-throated Cotinga
Cotinga cayana – Spangled Cotinga

The blue cotingas constitute a distinct and well-defined genus, with no near relatives except perhaps *Porphyrolaema*. Their most striking character is the brilliant blue of the male's plumage, a structural colour not found elsewhere in the family. All the *Cotinga* species are of medium size and stocky build, and have short wide beaks typical of specialised frugivores that take relatively large fruits. They are fairly long-winged and short-tailed, with short legs and small feet. In the adult males, some of the outer primaries are variously modified in the different species (Fig. 5, p. 88), and these modified feathers are almost certainly responsible for the mechanical rattling noises, of unknown function, that the males make in flight. None of the species is at all well known; in particular almost nothing is known of their social organization, except that the female alone attends the nest. They are preeminently birds of the forest canopy, ranging at times into more open areas adjoining forest. As far as the scanty information goes, they seem to be almost wholly frugivorous, plucking fruits in flight and swallowing them whole.

Six of the seven species replace one another geographically (Map 14); the seventh, *C. cayana*, overlaps extensively with *maynana* and *cotinga*. Of the six allopatric species the three westernmost (*amabilis*, *ridgwayi* and *nattererii*) are very similar to one another, and considered in isolation might reasonably be treated as conspecific. The two eastern species (*cotinga* and *maculata*) are also very similar to each other. They differ most conspicuously from the three western species by the deep blue (not turquoise) upper parts in the male and the more extensive purple below. The sixth species, *maynana*, is rather distinct from the others, as is apparent from Table 7, which sets out the main external differences between the species. This table shows that *maynana* has four peculiar characters, while none of the others has any character (except for details of primary modifications) not found in at least one other form. Moreover, *maynana* shares with *cayana*

two of the plumage characters in which it differs from the other five species. It is also unusual in that males are distinctly shorter-winged than females, whereas in the others they are about the same size (western group) or distinctly larger (eastern group). Of the western group of species, *amabilis* resembles the two eastern species in its abbreviated 7th primary, while *ridgwayi* approaches them in the modification of its two outer primaries (but not in its 7th primary, which is normal). Altogether these six species exhibit a mosaic of characters which link one with another in different ways, and the only practical course seems to be to give specific status to each. The three western species may be recognised as constituting a zoogeographical species (Mayr & Short 1970), as may the two eastern species. It does not seem justified to regard all six allopatric species as a single zoogeographical species, still less to give them more formal status as a super-species, since *maynana* may be as closely related to *cayana*, with which it is sympatric, as it is to the others.

Of all the species, *C. maynana* is most unusual in plumage colour, as the concealed basal part of the blue feathers is purple-pink; in the others it is black. This suggests that in the evolution of the genus structural blue has replaced an originally purple plumage. Purplish red is a widespread colour in the family, whereas structural blue is unique to the genus *Cotinga*.

Distribution (Maps 14 and 15)

The genus is confined to lowland tropical forest, except in parts of central America where all three species range up to the lower part of the sub-tropical belt in their respective areas.

Several points concerning the ranges of the six species shown on Map 14 deserve comment. *C. ridgwayi*, confined to a very restricted area of humid forest on the Pacific side of eastern Costa Rica and extreme western Panama, is separated by high mountains from *C. amabilis* on the Caribbean side;

the gap is probably no more than about 30 km. To the east and west, on the Pacific side, its range is bounded by areas of drier forest. The gap between *C. amabilis* and *C. nattererii* on the Caribbean side is, however, less easy to explain, as humid forest extends along the whole of this part of the Caribbean coastal belt. The eastern limit of the range of *C. nattererii* is uncertain, the single Venezuelan record, just south of Lake Maracaibo, perhaps being a straggler. *C. cotinga* seems to have a rather limited range in southern Venezuela, and neither it nor *C. maynana* has been recorded from the forests along the eastern base of the Andes in Colombia north of about 2°N. In both of these areas *C. cayana* is widespread.

The ranges of adjacent members of the six allopatric species shown on Map 14 are separated by areas of unsuitable habitat (mountains or unforested areas), except for *amabilis* and *nattererii*, mentioned above, and *cotinga* and *maynana*. The latter pair approach one another closely in the area of the lower Rio Negro. *C. cotinga* has been collected at Manaus and further upstream at Camanaus, both on the left bank of the Rio Negro, while *C. maynana* has been collected at Joanari, a place not listed in modern gazetteers but said to have been on the right bank at the mouth of the Rio Negro (Pelzeln 1868),

and at Tabatinga a little to the west. Further east, *cotinga* has been collected at Igarape Anibá on the north side of the Amazon, and *maynana* at Rosarinho near the Madeira mouth on the south side. It thus seems that the ranges of these two species are separated by the Rio Negro and Amazon in this area, but records are few.

With the destruction of most of the eastern Brazilian coastal forests the range of *C. maculata* is now much reduced from that shown on the map. In recent years the species has been reported from only three forest areas, in the states of Bahia and Espirito Santo, and Sick & Teixeira (1979) include it among the Brazilian bird species that are threatened with extinction.

Ecology

Little has been recorded for any species in the genus. A synthesis of available information indicates that blue cotingas commonly feed in groups, of males and females mixed, sometimes in company with other species, and that they are seldom noticed except when they visit fruiting trees. In some areas they may undertake seasonal movements. Thus Schomburgk (1848) reported that Spangled Cotingas were met with abundantly in coastal areas

Table 7

Characters of males of *Cotinga* species

	amabilis	ridgwayi	nattererii	maynana	cotinga	maculata	cayana
Shade of blue	turquoise	turquoise	turquoise	turquoise	deep blue	deep blue	turquoise
Distribution of purple	throat and belly (two patches)	throat and belly (two patches)	throat and belly (two patches)	small throat patch	extensive patch, throat to belly	throat and belly (two patches)	throat patch
Colour of feather bases	black	black	black	pinkish purple	black	black	black
Under-wing	black	black	black	extensive white (coverts and inner webs of primaries)	black	black	white on inner webs of primaries
Secondaries and greater coverts	blue-edged	blue-edged	blue-edged	blue	black	black	blue-edged
Wing-tip:							
length of p 7	abbreviated	normal	normal	normal	abbreviated	abbreviated	normal
shape of p 9–10	unmodified	9 attenuated, 10 slightly so	9 with constricted inner web, 8 and 10 slightly so	7 with constricted inner web	9 and 10 attenuated	9 and 10 attenuated	9 and 10 attenuated
Eye colour	brown	brown	brown	yellow	brown	brown	brown
♂ wing-length as % of ♀	102	99	100	95	105	104	102

of Guyana from November to mid-January, and were then absent from March to the end of October. Reports from other areas suggest that occurrence may be erratic, but no definite movements have been documented.

The blue cotingas have been recorded taking fruits of various kinds, but there has been little systematic study. Kantak (1979) watched birds taking fruits from five different kinds of trees over a period of about $2\frac{1}{2}$ months in semi-evergreen seasonal forest in southern Mexico. Lovely Cotingas were recorded visiting one of the trees, the fig *Ficus padifolia*, 27 times, and were never seen to visit the other four kinds of tree (species of *Neea*, *Ehretia*, *Metopium* and *Talisia*). The *Talisia* fruits, 16 mm in diameter, were probably too large for them to swallow, but the other three were comparable in size to the figs and certainly not too large. Natterer's Cotinga has also been recorded eating figs by both Bangs & Barbour (1922) and Wetmore (1972). Possibly, therefore, the blue cotingas show a preference for figs, when they are available, but their diet is by no means restricted to them. Skutch (1969) observed Lovely Cotingas regularly feeding on the fruits of a lauraceous tree, probably *Nectandra* sp. He also recorded Ridgway's Cotinga eating small palm fruits (*Euterpe* sp.), and the fruits of a mistletoe (*Psittacanthus* sp.) and of *Phytolacca*, a weedy plant of forest edge and clearings. Wetmore (1972) observed Ridgway's Cotinga eating fruits of *Cecropia* sp. The only recorded fruits eaten by the Spangled Cotinga were lauraceous (Chubb 1921, Schubart *et al*. 1965); and the only record for the Purple-breasted Cotinga is of *Euterpe* fruits in the stomachs of two collected specimens.

Nothing definite can be said about such differences in ecology as there may be between the different species. In Costa Rica Ridgway's Cotinga, occurring on the Pacific side, is much more abundant than the Lovely Cotinga of the Caribbean side, and ranges from the coastal lowlands to the subtropical zone, up to at least 4500 ft (1400 m), whereas the Lovely Cotinga seems to occur only from about the middle of the tropical to the middle of the subtropical zone (Slud 1964). Natterer's Cotinga has been collected as high as 4000 ft (1250 m) in eastern Panama; but other records are from lowland forest, as are all records of the species occurring in South America.

Behaviour

Little can be said under this heading. Blue cotingas habitually perch on dead tree-tops, sometimes for long periods. They fly strongly, with undulating flight. In flight, adult males make a rattling or tittering noise, presumably produced by their emarginated outer primaries. When feeding, they perch in a fruit tree and make short flight sallies to pluck one fruit at a time. They feed socially, in groups consisting of both males and females. Schomburgk (1848) reported large feeding flocks in coastal Guyana, but most observers refer to small parties. They are generally silent birds, apart from the male's flight rattle; but at least two calls are associated with defence of the nest against predators. Skutch (1969) records screaming calls made by a female when it was mobbing a toucanet that had just attacked its nest (see next section), and the same bird, when it was alarmed by his searching for the fledgling on the ground below the nest, uttered a clear, monosyllabic *ic, ic, ic*.

That the female alone attends the nest is evident from Chapman's and Skutch's observations, which are summarized below. Little appears to be known of the courtship or of other aspects of the relationship between the sexes. Some observations were made on the Plum-throated Cotinga by B. K. Snow in eastern Ecuador during the 1976 Los Tayos Expedition. On several occasions over a period of 15 days (6–21 July) an adult male was seen on a number of leafless tree-top perches around the expedition's camp site, occasionally flying from one exposed perch to another and making a continuous twittering noise (presumably with the wings) as it flew. On one occasion, at 1645 hours on 15 July, it directed a display towards two birds in female plumage that were perched about 25 m away in an adjacent tree and about 5–6 m above him. In the display he faced the other two birds, leant forward on his perch, and puffed out the plum-coloured feathers of his throat. Almost certainly he accompanied this display with a call, which unfortunately could not be heard above the noise of the camp generator.

Obviously no certain generalizations can be made from this observation. It suggests that males display solitarily, that they advertise themselves by flights between tree-top perches and the wing-noise may be part of the advertisement, and that the purple parts of the plumage may be brought into play in the second phase of courtship, when a female has been attracted to a perch in the male's display area. That the male Plum-throated Cotinga's full display repertoire is more elaborate than this is indicated by S. Hilty (MS), who notes that the male's wings whistle in normal flight, but 'much louder in display as male leaves high perch, angles slightly downward, then straight out over open space (often water) for about 40 m, brakes suddenly with loud whistling "whirr", and returns to perch'. Clearly

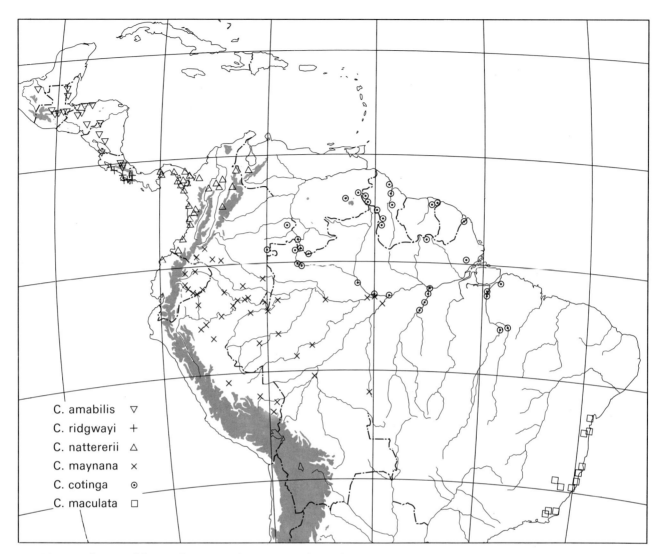

Map 14   Distribution of the Lovely Cotinga (*Cotinga amabilis*), Ridgway's Cotinga (*C. ridgwayi*), Natterer's Cotinga (*C. nattererii*), Plum-throated Cotinga (*C. maynana*), Purple-breasted Cotinga (*C. cotinga*) and Banded Cotinga (*C. maculata*).

there is still almost everything to be learnt about the displays of the blue cotingas.

Breeding and annual cycle

The first record of the breeding of a blue cotinga was obtained in 1924, when a nest and egg of the Spangled Cotinga were collected on 21 August near Belém (Pinto 1953). The nest was 11 m above the ground (nest-site not stated) and was a very summary saucer-shaped construction, $7\frac{1}{2}$ cm in diameter, made of twigs and dry rootlets, all the materials being coated with a white fungal mycelium. The single egg, very large for the size of bird (broken, but not less than 34 × 24 mm), was white in ground colour with a very pale bluish wash, and was covered with abundant rust-

coloured markings, most thickly at the broad end, with pale ash-violet spots in between.

Chapman (1928, 1929) was the first to make field observations on the nesting of any of the blue cotingas. He watched a female Natterer's Cotinga nesting in two successive years (1927 and 1928) on Barro Colorado island, Panama. In both years the bird nested in the same site, about 90 ft (28 m) up in a sandbox tree (*Hura crepitans*), in an angle formed by an orchid growing from the side of a nearly horizontal branch about 5 inches (23 cm) in diameter, about half way between the trunk and the terminal twigs. In 1927, when he first found the nest on 24 March, it contained two nestlings apparently clothed in silvery white down. On 31 March the young were missing, and on 2 April the nest was partly pulled to pieces by the female. In

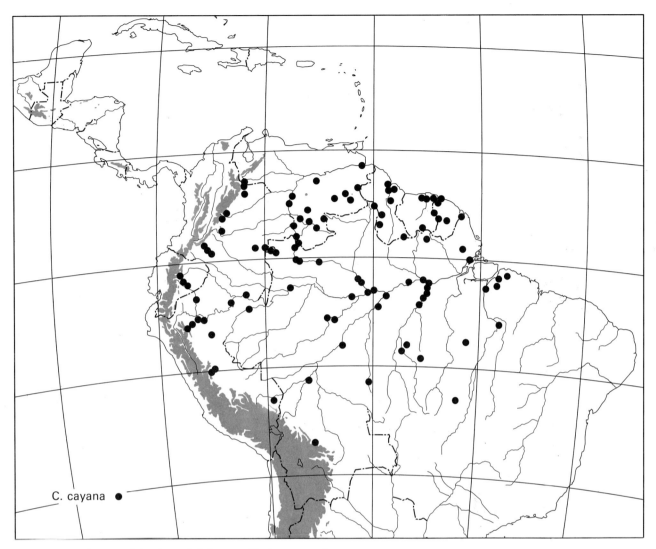

Map 15 Distribution of the Spangled Cotinga (*Cotinga cayana*).

1928, he saw the bird building in the same site between 19 January and 10 February. She laid shortly afterwards, and incubated until 12 March, when the nest was found to be deserted. On 24 March she was building again in the same tree, on the other side of it and a little higher up, but this nest could not be followed.

Skutch (1969) observed a Ridgway's Cotinga building and incubating in Costa Rica. The nest was about 30 ft (9 m) above the ground, on the lowest limb of a tall *Cordia* tree whose crown rose above the surrounding young trees and bushes, in secondary vegetation not far from primary rain forest. It was sited about a yard out from the trunk, at a point where the limb divided into three nearly parallel branches, and rested on the slightly lower central branch supported by the two lateral branches. The nest was 'a slight, shallow cup composed chiefly of coiled tendrils, mixed with which were some long, thin, wiry, gray strands, up to two feet in length, which were apparently the rhizomorphs of fungi'. Building went on for at least 22 days, from 2 to 24 March, and by 27 March the clutch of 2 eggs had been laid. The eggs, buffy in ground colour and speckled all over with brown, most heavily at the broad end, almost filled the nest, which was so small that the female, when incubating, seemed to be sitting on top of it rather than in it. After 7 days of incubation the nest-site was found to be bare except for a few shreds of nest material, the rest being scattered on the ground below.

A Lovely Cotinga's nest, found by Skutch (1969) a few moments after it had been predated, was built in a large yos tree (*Sapium*) standing in a pasture

M W Woodcock

near the forest edge. It was about 100 ft (31 m) up in a fork of a moss-covered branch at the very top of the tree. Skutch's attention was attracted by the calls of the cotinga as she mobbed a Blue-throated Toucanet in the tree top. After the toucanet had flown away the cotinga went to the nest and twice picked up some material in her bill and let it fall to the ground. Skutch later found that one of the nestlings had fallen to the ground, where it was tended for several days by its parent.

The only other published account of the nesting of any of the blue cotingas is a short note by Nicéforo (1947). On 24 February 1946, at Villavicencio at the foot of the Eastern Andes of Colombia, he shot a female Spangled Cotinga which was sitting at the end of a low branch of an isolated tree without foliage. When the dead bird was recovered from the ground below it was noticed that there was something remaining on the branch; it proved to be a downy chick about 10 days old. The chick was covered with abundant ashy white down, and was resting on a small epiphyte, apparently with no trace of any nest material.

From these accounts it appears to be a general rule in the genus that the nest is extremely small and flimsy and is normally placed in a horizontal fork or a niche formed by an epiphyte on a horizontal branch, generally on the middle or outer branches of a more or less isolated tree. The scanty data suggest that the clutch-size is normally 2 in Natterer's and Ridgway's Cotingas, but may be only 1 in the Spangled Cotinga.

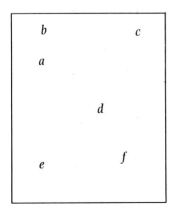

Plate 9
Blue cotingas
(*Cotinga*)

a and b: Lovely Cotinga *C. amabilis*, male and female
c: Natterer's Cotinga *C. nattererii*, male
d: Ridgway's Cotinga *C. ridgwayi*, male
e: Purple-breasted Cotinga *C. cotinga*, male
f: Banded Cotinga *C. maculata*, male

Not much is recorded of the care of the eggs and young. The Ridgway's Cotinga observed by Skutch incubated rather steadily in long spells, those timed being 119, 36, 156 and at least 145 minutes, with long recesses of 37, 44, 35 and 88 minutes (the last of these being the final recess before she returned to the nest for the night). Chapman saw the Natterer's Cotinga feed its young on black berries the size of cherries. Before he had found the Lovely Cotinga's nest, Skutch saw the female fly to the nest tree with the fruit of a laurel (*Ocotea pentagona*) in her bill; and later he saw what was probably the same bird flying with a lizard in her bill. This last observation appears to be the only record of any of the blue cotingas taking any food other than fruit. It is not clear whether the young are normally fed by regurgitation, but Chapman's account suggests that this is so, in which case food seen in the parent's bill may be only the last of several items to be taken before returning to feed the nestlings.

As mentioned above, Chapman saw a Natterer's Cotinga pull to pieces the nest from which the nestlings had disappeared. Skutch watched a Lovely Cotinga do the same after its nest had been raided by a toucanet, and had indirect evidence that a Ridgway's Cotinga also did so after a predator had taken its eggs. The same unusual behaviour has been recorded for the Rufous Piha, and its possible function is discussed in the account of that species (p. 118).

Annual cycle
All of the recorded or calculated egg dates north of the Equator are in the early part of the year, the months of laying being January (*C. cayana*, Colombia), February (both *C. nattererii* records, Panama), March (*C. ridgwayi*, Costa Rica), and March or April (*C. amabilis*, Costa Rica). The postnuptial moult begins soon after (e.g. March and April, *C. nattererii*, Panama; mainly May, *C. amabilis*, Costa Rica and Nicaragua), and lasts about 100 days (Snow 1976a). Calculated dates for the start of the moult are generally in the first half of the year in all areas north of the Equator. A little south of the Equator, in the Belém and Manaus areas, the moult begins mainly in the second half of the year; the single egg record is in August. At the southern extreme of the range of the genus, calculated dates of the onset of the moult of *C. maculata* in southeast Brazil are in November and December.

Plumages

The nestling Lovely Cotinga which Skutch (1969) found after it had fallen from the nest (see above) had tufts of short, dense white down adhering to the tips of its feathers. Nicéforo (1947) described the nestling Spangled Cotinga as covered with abundant ashy white down, and the nestling Natterer's Cotingas which Chapman (1928) watched being fed in Panama appeared to be covered with snowy white down.

The juvenile plumage, as determined from a small number of specimens and from Skutch's description of the nestling Lovely Cotinga, is

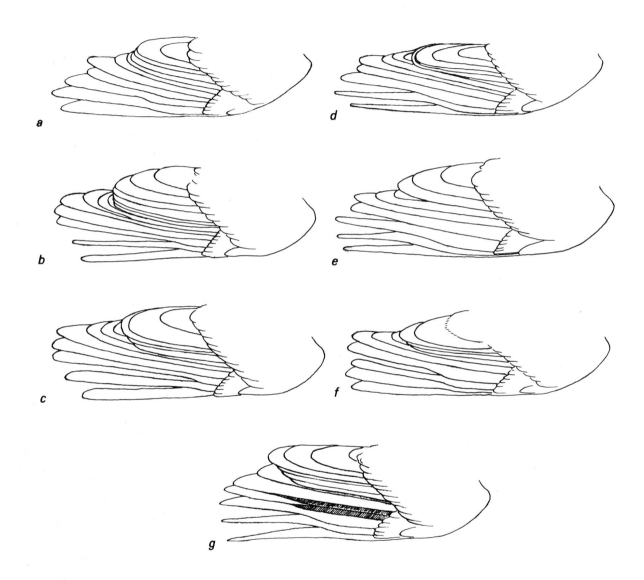

Figure 5 Wings of adult males of the blue cotingas (*Cotinga* spp.):
  (*a*) *C. amabilis*: p 7 short, p 8 and 9 with outer webs sinuated; secondaries short.
  (*b*) *C. ridgwayi*: p 9 and 10 thin and short (p 9 markedly thinner than p 10), somewhat incurved at tip; p 8 and 9 with outer webs sinuated near base.
  (*c*) *C. nattererii*: p 9 thin, slightly expanded at tip; p 10 less modified in same way, and p 8 slightly so ; p 8 and 9 with outer webs sinuated at base.
  (*d*) *C. cotinga*: p 7 short, p 9 and 10 thin and tapering; p 8 and 9 with outer webs sinuated.
  (*e*) *C. maculata*: like *C. cotinga* but p 8 as long as or longer than p 9 and somewhat modified in the same way.
  (*f*) *C. maynana*: p 7–10 with inner webs sinuated; p 7–9 with outer webs sinuated; p 7 expanded at tip, p 8 very slender.
  (*g*) *C. cayana*: p 9 and 10 thin and tapering, slightly recurved; p 6–9 with outer webs sinuated, p 6 and 7 with barbs of outer webs forming a fringe, not interlocking (shaded); inner secondaries very long.

characterized by buff-coloured tips to the primaries, secondaries, greater wing-coverts and tail-feathers. The outer edges of the secondaries are also buff. The feathers of the upper parts have broader whitish edges than in the adult female plumage, especially on the head, and the dark parts of the mantle feathers lack the blue-green wash that is evident in the female plumage. The underparts, especially the throat and upper breast, are much paler than in the adult female. Except for the flight feathers, this plumage is soon replaced in both sexes by a plumage similar to the adult female plumage. As the buff tips tend to wear off the flight feathers, the young bird after a few months is not very different from the adult female.

In the Lovely Cotinga, the adult male plumage is evidently acquired by a full moult when the bird is just over a year old, the moult taking place at about the same time as the adult's post-breeding moult. There is no subadult plumage, as there is in all the larger cotingas that are sexually highly dimorphic; the moult from immature plumage leads directly to the fully adult male plumage, except that the purple of the throat tends at first to be paler, sometimes much paler, than that of older males.

Physical characters

Structure

Bill wide at base, dorsoventrally compressed; nostrils exposed, oval, rather large; rictal bristles moderately developed. Flight-feathers modified in adult males, as shown in Figure 5. Tail short. Legs and feet short and rather weak.

Unfeathered parts

Iris: dark brown in all species except *C. maynana*; pale yellow in *C. maynana*.

Bill: similar in all species: upper mandible mainly black, greyish at base; lower mandible mainly grey, blacker at tip.

Legs and feet: dark grey or blackish in all species.

Measurements

C. amabilis

♂♂ (11) Wing 113–120, 117.0. Tail 63–69, 66.4. Tarsus 20.5–23, 21.5. Culmen 10–11, 10.6.

♀♀ (5) Wing 110–118, 114.6. Tail 66–70, 68.0. Tarsus 22–23, 22.3. Culmen 11.5–12, 11.6.

Weights: 2 ♂♂ 73, 75 g.
3 ♀♀ 66, 70, 73.5 g.

C. ridgwayi (from Wetmore 1972, except for culmen and weights)

♂♂ (10) Wing 100–108, 103.1. Tail 58–63, 60.2. Tarsus 20–21.5, 20.6. Culmen 11, 11.0.

♀♀ (4) Wing 103–106, 104.3. Tail 59–65, 62.1. Tarsus 21–22, 21.4.

Weights: 7 ♂♂ 51.5–54, 53.1 g.
3 ♀♀ 63.2–65.7, 64.6 g.

C. nattererii (from Wetmore 1972, except for culmen)

♂♂ (10) Wing 103–112, 108.8. Tail 65–71, 66.6. Tarsus 20–22, 21.2. Culmen 9–11, 10.2.

♀♀ (10) Wing 106–111, 108.3. Tail 65–70, 66.7. Tarsus 20–21.5, 21.0. Culmen 10–11.5, 10.5.

C. cotinga

♂♂ (14) Wing 103–115, 109.9. Tail 60–65, 62.9. Tarsus 19–21.5, 19.8. Culmen 9.5–11, 10.3.

♀♀ (9) Wing 99–107, 104.5. Tail 65–69, 66.4. Tarsus 19.5–20.5, 19.8. Culmen 10–11, 10.5.

Weights: 1 ♂ 53 g (wing 110 mm).
1 ♀ 55 g (wing 105 mm).

C. maculata

♂♂ (12) Wing 119–124, 120.4. Tail 71–76, 73.7. Tarsus 21–23.5, 22.3. Culmen 10–12, 10.8.

♀♀ (3) Wing 112–120, 116.3. Tail 72–81, 75.7. Tarsus 23–24, 23.7. Culmen 11–11.5, 11.3.

Weights: 1 ♂ 65 g (wing 119 mm).

C. maynana

♂♂ (8) Wing 105–110, 108.1. Tail 67–75, 72.0. Tarsus 20.5–21.5, 20.9. Culmen 10.5–11.5, 11.0.

♀♀ (8) Wing 107–119, 114.0. Tail 73–86, 79.1. Tarsus 21.5–23, 22.4. Culmen 11.5–12.5, 11.9.

C. cayana

♂♂ (14) Wing 109–118, 112.5. Tail 72–79, 75.3. Tarsus 20.5–22, 21.1. Culmen 11–12.5, 11.8 – one exceptionally short (9.5) omitted.

♀♀ (19) Wing 107–115, 110.6. Tail 75–86, 81.0. Tarsus 20–22, 21.3. Culmen 10–12.5, 11.5 – one exceptionally long (14.5) omitted.

Weights: 9 ad ♂♂ 56–72.5, 63.8 g (mean weight and wing of 5: 63.1 g, 110.8 mm).
1 subad ♂ 66 g (wing 110 mm).
5 im ♂♂ 56–67, 60.6 g (mean wing 106.0 mm).
4 ♀♀ 59.5–72.5, 65.5 g (mean weight and wing of 3: 63.2 g, 109.0 mm).

M W Woodcock

Genus *Porphyrolaema*

Porphyrolaema porphyrolaema – Purple-throated Cotinga

The single species constituting this genus is one of the least known members of its family. Confined to the forests of upper Amazonia, it inhabits a wide area but one in which field ornithologists have only recently begun to work. The genus has been supposed to be close to *Cotinga*, the main structural difference being in the form of the bill, which is considerably stouter, not flattened dorsoventrally, with rather small, circular nostrils. The purple throat of the adult male and the brown, barred plumage of the female suggest affinity with *Cotinga*, but the purple throat occurs in a number of cotinga genera which are not closely related, and the barring of the female is in detail quite unlike that of *Cotinga* females, being in fact most similar to the barring seen in parts of the plumage of juvenile Bare-necked Fruit-crows *Gymnoderus foetidus*. Hence there seem no strong grounds for linking *Porphyrolaema* with *Cotinga*, but equally no reason to move it to any other position in the sequence of genera.

The sexes are very unlike, not only in colour but in some details of feather structure. The body feathers of the female (and immature male) are of looser texture than those of the adult male, and the tail-feathers are longer and more pointed at the tip. Were it not for the existence of immature male specimens in intermediate plumages, it would be easy to suppose that male and female belong to different species.

Distribution (Map 16)

The Purple-throated Cotinga is an upper Amazonian species, occurring mainly in lowland forest but recorded also up to 3000 ft (900 m) in the Andean foothills of eastern Peru. It has been found in more different localities in Peru than any other country. There are two records for eastern Ecuador (Limoncocha, Sarayacu), one locality for Colombia (La Morelia, Caquetá), and five known localities for Brazil, on the Rio Negro, Rio Purús, and upper Amazon. The easternmost record (Cacao Pereira) is just west of Manaus on the lower Rio Negro. Altogether it seems that fewer than 50 specimens have been collected, and it is remarkable that 13 of them were taken by S. M. Klages at Arimã on the Rio Purús between 20 September and 4 November 1922. No doubt they were collected while visiting a favourite fruiting tree. The majority of all known specimens (at least 27) were collected between 1922 and 1930, since when only three have been collected, two at Codajáz on the Amazon in 1935 and the last in Colombia in 1941. Recently, however, the intensive field work carried out by American ornithologists in Amazonian Peru has shown that the species is locally not uncommon in that area.

Annual cycle

Twelve dated specimens in wing-moult show a wide scatter in their timing. Assuming that the complete moult lasts about 3 months, as it does in *Cotinga*, the calculated months of onset of moult are in every month except February, March, June and November.

Plumages

Nestling plumage unknown. Juvenile plumage like female, but paler and buffier; edges of back-feathers with buff, not whitish, fringes. Males in transitional

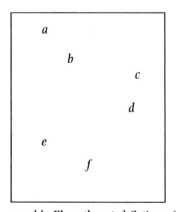

Plate 10
Blue cotingas
(*Cotinga*)
and Purple-throated
Cotinga
(*Porphyrolaema*)

a and b: Plum-throated Cotinga *C. maynana*, male and female
c and d: Spangled Cotinga *C. cayana*, male and female
e and f: Purple-throated Cotinga *P. porphyrolaema*, male and female

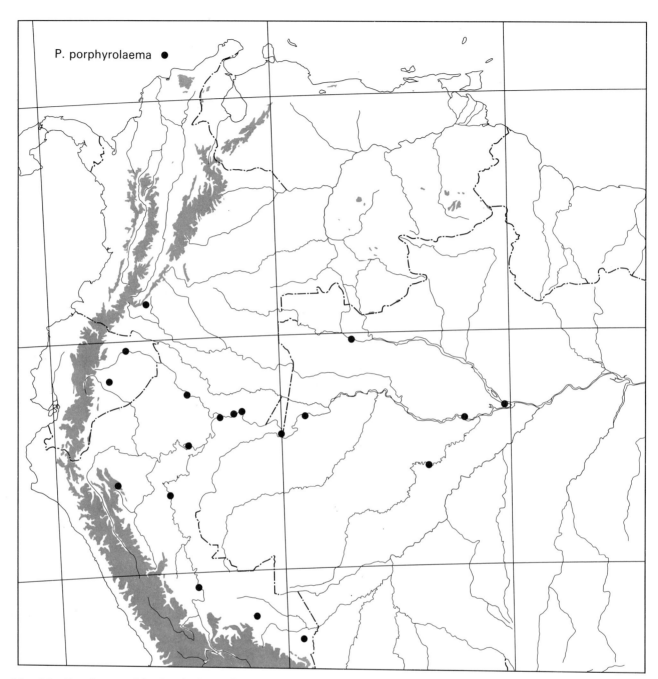

Map 16   Distribution of the Purple-throated Cotinga (*Porphyrolaema porphyrolaema*).

plumage, when moulting tail, have rectrices of markedly different lengths, the old, juvenile feathers (attenuated at tip, brown with blackish spots and subterminal bar) longer than the new black, adult feathers.

Physical characters

Structure
Bill wide basally with strongly arched culmen; nostrils exposed, more or less circular; rictal bristles weakly developed. Flight-feathers unmodified.

Unfeathered parts
Colours unrecorded, but bill and legs apparently blackish.

Measurements
♂♂ (6) Wing 95–100, 97.2. Tail 66–70, 67.2. Tarsus 18–20, 19.0. Culmen 10–11.5, 10.8.
♀♀ (7) Wing 92–97, 94.6. Tail 67–72, 69.9. Tarsus 19.5–21, 20.3. Culmen 11, 11.0.

Genus *Xipholena* – the white-winged cotingas

Plate 11, page 96

Xipholena punicea – Pompadour Cotinga
Xipholena lamellipennis – White-tailed Cotinga
Xipholena atropurpurea – White-winged Cotinga

This is a very distinct genus consisting of three closely related allopatric species. They are medium-sized cotingas, most strikingly distinguished from all others by the male plumage which is deep crimson or purplish black with white flight-feathers. In depth of pigmentation, combined with surface gloss, *Xipholena* represents the extreme in a trend of feather modification seen in several genera of cotingas (*Haematoderus, Querula, Pyroderus* etc.). In two species, *X. punicea* and *X. lamellipennis*, the tips of the major coverts are stiffened and elongated to form spear-like spikes that partially conceal the folded flight-feathers. The drab grey and whitish female plumage is very similar in all three species. In structure and size the three species are broadly similar; *punicea* is the largest of the three, *atropurpurea* the smallest, and *lamellipennis* has a distinctly longer tail than the other two.

Xipholena shares a number of characters with the white cotingas (*Carpodectes*) of Central and trans-Andean South America (p. 99), and it seems likely that the two genera, while not very closely related, are closer to one another than either is to any other genus. Their present distributions suggest an early split of the common ancestral stock into an eastern and a western part, perhaps as a result of the uplifting of the Andes, the eastern section giving rise to *Xipholena* and the western to *Carpodectes*.

Distribution (Map 17)

The genus is restricted to lowland evergreen forest. *X. punicea* and *X. lamellipennis* between them occupy the forests of the Amazon basin and the Guianas, *lamellipennis* replacing *punicea* on the south side of the lower Amazon. Their ranges are incompletely known in the area where they approach one another; *punicea* has been recorded from Borba on the right bank of the lower Rio Madeira, Porto Creputia on the upper R. Cururú, and the Serra do Cachimbo between the upper Xingú and Tapajós. *X. lamellipennis* has been recorded from Parintins, west of the lower Tapajós, the upper Cururú, and the Serra do Cachimbo. Whether both species regularly occur and breed together in the Serra do Cachimbo/Cururú area seems doubtful, especially as there is evidence of some seasonal wandering.

X. atropurpurea is isolated in the lowland coastal forest belt of eastern Brazil. These forests have been so extensively destroyed that its survival must be considered threatened (Sick 1969). The most recent museum specimen dates from 1944, but a small population was extant at least up to 1977 in the Sooretama Forest Reserve in Espirito Santo, where Sick (1979) made the observation quoted below in the section on Breeding and the Annual Cycle.

Haffer (1970) has interpreted the present distribution of *Xipholena* as indicating that it was isolated in three forest refuges during a past arid period, and that each of these isolated populations differentiated to reach specific status: *punicea* in the Guiana refuge, *lamellipennis* in the Belém refuge, and *atropurpurea* in the southeastern Brazilian refuge. When the forests were re-established across the Amazon basin with the onset of a more humid period, *punicea* spread southwest and south and *lamellipennis* spread southwest and west, so that they met on the south side of the Amazon and, being reproductively isolated but still similar enough ecologically to be competitors, remained distinct but were unable to penetrate each other's ranges. If this interpretation is correct, it is puzzling that *punicea* apparently has not yet completed its potential westerly spread; it either has not yet reached the western limit of the Amazonian forest or, if it has, is very scarce in the extreme west. It has not been recorded from Bolivia or Peru, is known from only one locality in eastern Ecuador, and has not been recorded from the eastern base of the Andes in southern Colombia.

Ecology

Although they are widespread and have been extensively collected, extremely little is known of the ecology of any of the white-winged cotingas. They

Map 17 Distribution of the white-winged cotingas (*Xipholena* spp.).

are apparently entirely frugivorous, but the little available information gives no indication that they feed on nutritious drupes of the kinds that are eaten by the larger frugivorous cotingas. According to Schomburgk (1848) the favourite foods of the Pompadour Cotinga are figs (*Ficus* spp.) and the fruits of *Brosimum* spp., both members of the family Moraceae. Possibly the wide gape is adapted for swallowing rather large but soft fruits such as those

of *Brosimum*. Sick (1970) mentions that the White-winged Cotinga is fond of the fruits of *Phytolacca decandra*, a coarse herbaceous plant of wood edges, whose fruits are eaten by many kinds of birds.

Schomburgk, quoted by Chubb (1921), says that in Guyana the Pompadour Cotinga is present in the coastal forests only from December to February, apparently moving further inland in other months. The dates of collected specimens in Guyana and

Surinam do not support this, as there are specimens taken within 50 miles of the coast in almost every month of the year. Nevertheless it may well be that these birds move about to a certain extent in search of suitable trees in fruit, and this would be consistent with the fact that their displays, described in the next section, seem to be appropriate for a bird with a tendency to wander and contrast with the elaborate displays that are centred on a traditional perch.

Behaviour

Haverschmidt (1968) calls the Pompadour Cotinga a noisy bird but gives no details. Its call was described by Beebe (1924) as follows: 'Its note . . . is unmistakable, a sudden loud, ventriloquial, frog-like, rattling croak. The sound seems to come from no direction whatever, and, until the bird flies, is no clue to its whereabouts. Until I had seen the bird utter it, I presumed it only another weird voice of some of the giant, jungle tree-frogs.' There seems to be no further information on this call or its function. The Pompadour Cotinga's flight displays, described below, are silent, or any calls that may accompany the displays are too quiet to be heard at any great distance.

Beebe & Beebe (1910), in their account of an early expedition to Guyana, mentioned a 'quartet' of male Pompadour Cotingas flying silently about together in the tree-tops. This may well have been the ritual chasing which I observed in the Kanuku Mountains of southern Guyana in 1970 (Snow 1971a). On several occasions, over a period of 13 days, two or three males spent up to half an hour chasing each other round a group of tree tops, keeping above the trees so that their white wings, flashing against the dark foliage, were visible for a great distance. The longest sequence, lasting about half an hour and involving three males and two female-plumaged birds, was seen on 7 March. 'The males spent most of this time performing a kind of ritualised chasing with fluttering flight from tree-top to tree-top. They maintained a fixed order of dominance during the spells when all three were in view, and probably this order was maintained throughout. Male A would fly to Male B, who would fly away as Male A approached and similarly displace Male C. This performance was repeated again and again. Sometimes only two males were present, and then the chasing was simplified to Male A again and again flying to Male B, who simply fluttered a short distance and landed. Sometimes one of the displaced birds would fly 100 m or more to a more distant tree-top, in which case the pursuing bird would follow the same course and displace it again. The ritualised nature of the chasing seemed evident from the way in which the displaced bird flew off unhurriedly as the pursuer approached, and the latter made no attempt to do more than simply occupy the other's perch; also the chases revolved round the same group of tree-tops, the same perches often being used several times. The whole of this time, the two female-plumaged birds kept close to the males but took no part in the chasing. The whole performance seemed to be silent; but low calls might not have been heard.'

This display took place near a tree where a female-plumaged bird was seen apparently prospecting for a nest-site. Although the tree was visited at least twice subsequently, probably by the same bird, once accompanied by a male, and contained an old nest that may have been a Pompadour Cotinga's, no further breeding activity was seen. On one occasion, after a bout of ritualised chasing between three males, one of the males returned by himself to a dead tree top about 100 m from the nest tree and spent 17 minutes flying to and fro between this perch and two other tree tops about 20 m away. It did a two-way flight about every 90 seconds, going each time to one of the two other perches and spending about 30 seconds on it before returning to the main perch. This display was also silent.

In November 1972, from the vantage point of a 110-foot tower (the 'Rockefeller tower') used for sampling forest mosquitoes, I had the good fortune to observe a somewhat similar flight display by the White-tailed Cotinga in forest near Belém. Only a single male was involved. 'From the topmost dead branch of a large tree whose leafy crown emerged well above the surrounding treetops, it fluttered steeply upward for about five feet, then turned and fluttered down, with tail fanned, to land a little below its taking-off point. After landing, it hopped up to the topmost point again before its next upward flutter. The flights were repeated about every two minutes. Sometimes it varied this routine by making fluttering flights to another perch about fifteen feet away, on the crown of the same tree. For one long sequence lasting half an hour, it alternated these two kinds of flight with complete regularity, first fluttering up and down, then making a flight to the other perch, spending three to five minutes there, then back to the main perch, an upward flutter, and so on. Between flights the wings were held away from the body feathers and showed up conspicuously white. This was in striking contrast to a male that I saw later perched in normal resting posture; the

M.W.Woodcock

white wings were largely concealed by the coverts and flank feathers. Nothing more happened; the display went on nearly continuously for an hour and a half, and the bird then flew off.

'We returned to the Rockefeller tower on three subsequent days, and twice, each time in the afternoon, saw what was presumably the same bird displaying from the same tree or from one nearby. The routine was the same; sometimes the jumps were repeated with intervals as short as a minute, sometimes they were a little more spaced out, but the timing was surprisingly regular, with an average interval of about two minutes. During one display bout, the bird made a number of flights of an intermediate kind, flying up and then fluttering down to land on a perch several yards to the side. As a rule, however, they were of two clearly distinct types: the up-and-down flutter, and the sideways flight to a neighboring perch. I saw no female visit him. Only once did I see another male in the area, and that was in the morning when no display was taking place' (Snow 1977).

These display flights of the White-tailed Cotinga are probably homologous with the Pompadour Cotinga's flight to and fro between adjacent tree tops. Further than this one can only speculate. It seems that males have two kinds of display, a ritualized chasing within a group which may be associated with the establishment of a dominance order, and a solitary display which may advertise a male's local dominance and may be associated with the presence of a breeding female. The main features of the male's plumage, especially the white wings contrasting with the dark body plumage, seem to be adapted to making these flight displays visually striking. It is significant that the extra element that distinguishes the White-tailed Cotinga's flight-display from the Pompadour's, the upward flutter and downward glide, displays the pure white tail to full effect.

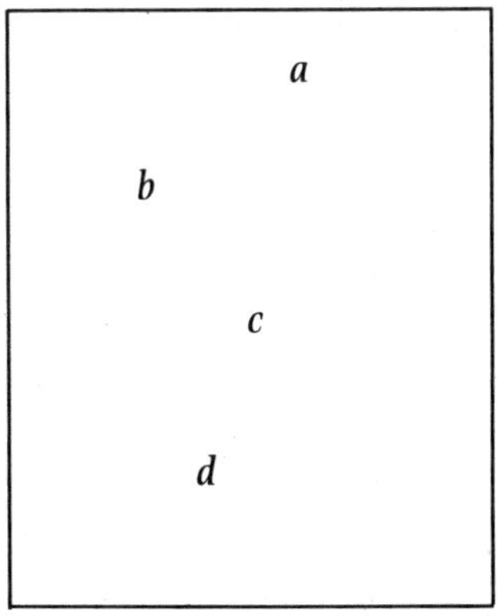

Plate 11

a and *b*: Pompadour Cotinga *X. punicea*, male and female
c: White-tailed Cotinga *X. lamellipennis*, male
d: White-winged Cotinga *X. atropurpurea*, male

Probably the finer details of the plumage, including the modified spear-like wing coverts, are conspicuously deployed during the later stages of display that lead up to copulation.

Breeding and annual cycle

The only occupied nest of any *Xipholena* species to be seen by an ornithologist was the Pompadour Cotinga's nest reported by Beebe (1924) from Kartabo, Guyana. It was a minute but deep openwork cup composed of a few curly woody tendrils, and was placed some 60 feet up in the crotch of a bamboo between a main stem and a side shoot. The incubating female was collected. The single egg, which just fitted the nest cup, measured 30.8 × 22.2 mm (weight 7.9 g) and was 'very pale, light greenish grey, thickly spotted and blotched with intermingling patches of drab', the markings being denser and more confluent at the large end.

Knowledge of the breeding of the White-tailed Cotinga is based on a single nest, also containing one egg, collected near Belém on 6 November 1925 (Pinto 1953). The nest (not described) was 5 m up in a rubber tree, and the egg measured 29 × 21 mm and was pale bluish in ground colour, spotted with ashy violet, most thickly at one end.

The nesting of the White-winged Cotinga in the wild is still unknown, but an egg laid by a female in captivity in the Rio de Janeiro Zoo was blue-green in ground colour, thickly covered by sepia spots and flecks of various sizes (Sick 1970). There was no nest and the egg was too badly broken to be measured. More recently, Sick (1979) reported seeing a female disappear into a huge bromeliad clump about 18 m up in a tree on the edge of a forest on 26 September 1977. Some time later it came out from the same place, and doubtless had a nest.

These records provide little information on any of the species' annual cycles. Probably the breeding season is prolonged in the Pompadour and White-tailed Cotingas, whose ranges lie entirely within 10° of the Equator. Calculated dates of onset of the complete moult, which is presumably a post-breeding moult as in other cotingas, are in every month of the year in the Pompadour Cotinga and in all months except March and November in the White-tailed. Only two moult records are available for the White-winged Cotinga (March and April), both from the north of its range. The complete moult is estimated to take about 125 days (Snow 1976a).

Plumages and moults

Juvenile plumage (only one example seen (*lamellipennis*) out of about 350 specimens examined) like female but head and body plumage paler, browner and fluffier; lower back especially pale, feathers with pale bases and brown tips; lesser wing-coverts extensively white with dark fringes (instead of all dark) and major coverts with broader white margins and tips. Contour feathers soon replaced (beginning before flight-feathers are full-grown) by immature plumage, resembling adult female plumage except for more extensive white on wing-coverts.

Immature plumage (distinguishable only in males) variable. In *punicea* remiges and rectrices replaced at first wing and tail moult by feathers still of immature type, and at next moult by feathers of subadult type (white with variable dark markings); adult male head and body plumage develops variably through this period, modified major coverts of fully adult type sometimes preceded by semi-modified feathers, elongated and pink-edged; traces of immature plumage usually persist longest on upper parts. At third wing moult remiges replaced by feathers of fully adult type. In *lamellipennis* immature remiges may be replaced (probably at second wing moult) by feathers either of subadult or of fully adult type; thus adult male plumage apparently acquired after three wing moults in *punicea* and after either two or three in *lamellipennis*.

Physical characters

Structure

Bill wide at base, rather flattened dorsoventrally, slightly hooked at tip. Rictal bristles absent. Legs and feet moderately strong. Flight-feathers rounded at tip, primaries unmodified, similar in male and female. Male plumage characterised by very heavy deposition of carotenoids combined with structural modification of the barbs, producing a hard glossy surface, transversely barred in *lamellipennis* (Brush 1969, Olson 1970). Secondary major coverts elongated and stiffened in *punicea* and *lamellipennis*, pointed at tips but otherwise unmodified in *atropurpurea*.

Unfeathered parts

Iris: pale yellow in adults of all three species, dark brown in immatures (some apparently adult females also described as having brown eyes, but age not determinable from plumage and these may be young birds).

Bill: dark brownish horn.

Legs and feet: dark brownish black, soles buff-coloured.

Geographical variation

None reported in *punicea* or *atropurpurea*. Females of *lamellipennis* from Santarem have been described as being paler on the underparts than females of the typical form (Belém area), the males being indistinguishable (Griscom & Greenway 1937). Santarem is near the inland extreme of the range of *lamellipennis* and has a less humid climate than Belém, hence a slight decrease in pigmentation would not be unexpected; but the difference is very slight and this race is not recognized in Peters' *Check-list*.

Measurements

X. *punicea*
♂♂ (8)   Wing 121–128, 124.4.   Tail 65–72, 68.4.
    Tarsus 22.5–24, 23.1.   Culmen 12–13, 12.3.
♀♀ (8)   Wing 113–121, 117.6.   Tail 63–68, 66.1.
    Tarsus 21–23, 21.6.   Culmen 11.5–12, 11.7.
Weights: 8 ♂♂ 68–72, 70.0 g.
       7 ♀♀ 58–76, 66.0 g.

X. *lamellipennis*
♂♂ (14)   Wing 111–119, 115.4.   Tail 74–80, 76.9.
    Tarsus 20–21.5, 20.5.   Culmen 10.5–12.5, 11.8.
♀♀ (11)   Wing 108–117, 111.5.   Tail 67–77, 71.8.
    Tarsus 18.5–22, 20.9.   Culmen 11–12.5, 12.0.

X. *atropurpurea*
♂♂ (12)   Wing 108–122, 112.5.   Tail 61–70, 64.5.
    Tarsus 21.5–24, 22.6.   Culmen 10.5–12, 11.6.
♀♀ (6)   Wing 104–116, 107.8.   Tail 61–69, 64.3.
    Tarsus 21.5–22.5, 21.9.   Culmen 11–12, 11.4.

Genus *Carpodectes* – the white cotingas

Plate 12, page 100

Carpodectes nitidus – Snowy Cotinga
Carpodectes antoniae – Antonia's Cotinga
Carpodectes hopkei – White Cotinga

Like *Xipholena*, which appears to be its nearest relative, this genus consists of three closely related allopatric species. They are medium-sized cotingas of plump build, most notable for the white plumage of the males. Their soft plumage, high foreheads, and strong flight give them a superficially pigeon-like appearance; hence the local Panamanian name 'Paloma del espiritu santo' for the Snowy Cotinga. The female plumage is very like that of *Xipholena*, and there are other similarities between the two genera, in particular the white wings of the males and what little is known of the courtship behaviour. These resemblances, between genera that are still very little known, should not be overemphasized, but added to the fact that they replace one another geographically they suggest that *Carpodectes* and *Xipholena* may be the products of early divergence of an ancestral stock following isolation of the two sections east and west of the Andes. It should be noted, however, that Ames (1971) placed the two genera in different sections of the family on the basis of syringeal structure (see p. 11). His grouping of *Carpodectes* with *Querula* seems unlikely to reflect affinity, and it seems more probable that syringeal structure has been subject to relatively rapid modification in the course of the family's evolutionary diversification.

C. nitidus and *C. antoniae* are very similar, differing chiefly in bill colour, and some authors have treated them as only subspecifically distinct. *C. hopkei* is a larger species with more distinct male plumage (pure white without any grey, and black tips to the outer primaries). The recognition of three species rather than two obscures their probable degree of relatedness one to another, but is adopted for reasons that have been discussed earlier (p. 12).

Distribution (Map 18)

The genus is restricted to areas of evergreen tropical forest. Between them the three species range from Honduras south to northwestern Ecuador, but their distributions are patchy and there

is a major gap, covering most of Panama, where none occurs. *C. nitidus* occurs on the Caribbean slopes of Honduras, Nicaragua and Costa Rica, just entering western Panama in the Almirante area. According to Slud (1964) it is characteristic of the lower hills of the Caribbean slope of Costa Rica, avoiding the flat coastal lowlands. *C. antoniae*, on the other hand, seems to be associated with coastal mangroves on the Pacific side of Costa Rica; like *nitidus* it just enters extreme western Panama, but on the other coast. The third species, *C. hopkei*, has been recorded in three localities in hill forest in Darien in the extreme east of Panama, and thence southward through the Pacific coastal area of western Colombia to northwestern Ecuador.

From the very little that is known of these birds in life it is impossible to guess what ecological

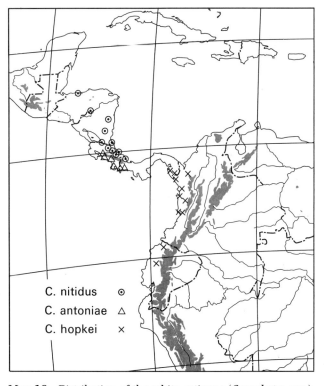

Map 18 Distribution of the white cotingas (*Carpodectes* spp.).

99

MWWoodcock

factors confine them to their present ranges; but it is clear that the ranges of all three are effectively separated by wide tracts of country where none occurs.

Ecology

Very little can be said about any aspect of the ecology of any of the white cotingas. They all appear to be primarily fruit-eaters, but there is no information on the fruits that they eat, except that Ridgway (1905) reported a flock of Snowy Cotingas alighting in 'laurel' trees in Costa Rica, presumably to feed, Howe (1977) recorded two instances of Snowy Cotingas taking the fruit of *Casearia corymbosa* (Flacourtiaceae), also in Costa Rica, and Hilty (MS) notes that White Cotingas are often seen at *Cecropia* trees. Several reports mention their feeding in small flocks, e.g. 15 or more Snowy Cotingas at one tree in Nicaragua (Richmond 1893). Slud (1964), writing of the Snowy Cotinga, mentions that a bird may 'lean down nonchalantly to pluck food from the foliage', suggesting that insects are occasionally taken.

As mentioned in the previous section, while the Snowy Cotinga is a bird of evergreen forest, preferring hilly country, Antonia's Cotinga has most often been found near coastal mangroves, either in the mangroves or in adjacent woodland. Skutch's observations on territorial and courtship behaviour, made well inland at a height of about 2500 feet above sea level, show that this species is not confined to the coastal lowlands, though it is evidently rare so high up. Possibly there is some seasonal migration from the coast to the hills inland, perhaps for the breeding season.

Behaviour

The few observers who have reported on the white cotingas agree in stressing their social feeding

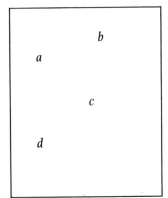

Plate 12
The white cotingas
(*Carpodectes*)
a and *b*: Snowy Cotinga *C. nitidus*, male and female
c: Antonia's Cotinga *C. antoniae*, male
d: White Cotinga *C. hopkei*, male

behaviour, strong flight and generally pigeon-like appearance. Slud (1964) writes of the Snowy Cotinga in Costa Rica as follows: 'The bird flies well, in the direct manner of an arboreal pigeon, usually towards a lofty perch; occasionally it is seen in high, rapid, and, so to speak, purposefully sustained flight, when it is quickly lost from sight. Sitting quietly on a bare branch or screened by foliage, the bird can often be approached closely. The high forehead imparts a gentle, dovelike, dreamy expression to this cotinga, which has the habit of looking around slowly by means of a deliberate, lethargic head turning.' He also mentions seeing 'a flock of up to 10 or more birds (all males) exploding parrot-like' out of the crown of a tree. Of Antonia's Cotinga he writes: 'In the mangroves individuals are almost constantly flying about and may be seen actively fluttering up and down between the higher and lower branches. The bird flies easily and well, either in the direct, flowing manner of a pigeon or in long and shallow, tityra-like dips.'

Skutch (1970) gives the only account of territorial behaviour and what appears to be the male's courtship display. His observations were made on Antonia's Cotinga in southern Costa Rica. 'In 1940, while engaged in field work near Santa Rosa at the head of the Térraba Valley, about 2,500 ft. a.s.l., I saw a good deal of a male Yellow-billed [= Antonia's] Cotinga and frequently watched what was evidently his simple courtship display. This bird had several favourite stations: the dead top of a great living tree just within the edge of the forest on the ridge behind my cabin; a tall, slender, dead tree in the clearing close to this forest; and another dead tree at the edge of the forest far across the cleared valley of the Río Pacuar. In March and April, he was usually to be found during the early morning on one or another of these trees. I often watched him fly conspicuously from one to another; and I never noticed a white cotinga in two of these trees simultaneously.

'In sharp contrast to such noisy cotingas as bellbirds *Procnias* and pihas *Lipaugus*, this Yellow-billed Cotinga was always silent. If he had any note, I failed to detect it during the four months when we were neighbours. As he perched on some slender bare branch projecting above the roof of the forest, his pure white form was conspicuous against the blue sky at so great a distance that the utterance of a sound to advertise his presence might have been a superfluous waste of energy. Usually he rested in his high treetops in silent inactivity, but from time to time he would suddenly fly in a deep catenary loop from one dead branch to another in the same treetop. Sometimes he would sidle a short distance along his perch. Then of a sudden he would fly several hundred yards across the clearing to another of his stations, there to repeat his display; or else he would fly beyond sight over the undulating green roof of the forest. His flight was swift and direct. As May advanced, he displayed more seldom.

'The arrival of a second male Yellow-billed Cotinga on 3 April provided further evidence that the first claimed as his display territory trees hundreds of yards apart. I watched one male, doubtless the resident bird, chase the other swiftly from the ridge behind the cabin, where two of the display trees were situated, to the forest on the steep slope across the valley of the Pacuar, where the third display tree stood. Here the pursuit continued back and forth above the treetops, so far away that an eight-inch bird with less gleaming plumage might have been invisible. Finally both cotingas vanished behind the ridge . . .

'I saw no female until 27 April, after which she was sighted repeatedly; but no evidence of nesting was noticed. This locality at the northern foot of the coastal range is the only spot where I have seen Yellow-billed Cotingas during my 30 years in El General, as the mountain-rimmed basin at the head of the Río Térraba is called. Mostly they live at lower altitudes.'

Skutch stressed the silence of the birds that he watched. Slud mentions that Antonia's Cotinga calls seldom, its note being 'a dovelike or trogon-like "cah" or "cow", ending in a throaty scrape. When repeated several times, it forms a not un-musical call reminiscent of that of *nitidus*.' Of the latter he writes: 'The seldom-heard call consists of two to six rapidly repeated, short-voweled notes, between "chü" and "chee", having the quality of the call of an oriole.'

Breeding and annual cycle

No nest of any of the white cotingas has yet been seen by an ornithologist, unless C. F. Underwood found the nest containing the nestling Snowy Cotinga that he collected at San Carlos, Costa Rica, on 21 March 1891. The specimen, in the AMNH, is so young that it could not have been ready to leave the nest (see next section). It almost certainly came from an egg laid in February. Another Underwood specimen, collected on 30 November 1898 at Carrillo, Costa Rica, appears to be a young bird still mainly in juvenile plumage; but, puzzlingly, it seems to be just completing a wing-moult, the outermost primary in each wing being about half-grown and the others full-grown and new. It does not seem possible to base a breeding date on this specimen with any confidence.

For Antonia's Cotinga the only evidence of breeding activity is Skutch's observation of court-ship display, quoted above. For the White Cotinga, the only evidence is a female specimen with enlarged ovary collected at Nuqui, northwestern Colombia, on 23 February. All this evidence, such as it is, suggests that breeding takes place mainly in the first four months of the year.

Almost certainly the breeding season is pro-gressively earlier from north to south through the range of the three species. This is strongly suggested by the moult records. Thus males of the Snowy Cotinga in Costa Rica and Nicaragua mostly begin to moult in April–July (7 out of 8 records), and in Panama in March and April (8 records). Male Antonia's Cotingas, whose range is mainly a little to the south of the Snowy's, begin to moult in March–June (10 records); while male White Cotingas, further south still, begin to moult in January–April (6 records). In all three species, females begin to moult on average later than males, but there is much overlap and the smaller number of records for females (14 against 32 for males) makes it impossible to determine how much later.

The complete moult of the wing and tail feathers takes about 140 days in the individual.

Plumages and moults

Nestling: white down above and below (one specimen only, AMNH 494659, still with nestling down, juvenile plumage growing, wing 77 mm). Juvenile plumage: contour feathers notably fluffy, feathers of upper parts white with brown fringes, those of underparts white; flight-feathers dark. Juvenile contour feathers replaced by immature plumage, resembling adult female plumage. Further plumage changes distinguishable only in males.

Male immature plumage replaced by subadult plumage, resembling adult male plumage but primaries dark, secondaries with dark markings especially on inner webs, tail and rump with tendency to grey wash (*nitidus* and *antoniae*) or tail with most or all feathers black-tipped (*hopkei*). This somewhat variable plumage replaced by fully adult male plumage.

Physical characters

Structure

Bill wide at base but not flattened dorso-ventrally, depth about equal to width at level of nostrils. Culmen ridged, regularly decurved; tip of maxilla notched, distinctly uncinate. Nostrils large, oval, partly covered at rear by dense latero-frontal feathering. Rictal bristles absent in male, slightly developed in female. Tarsus rather short, fairly stout, pycnaspidean. Flight-feathers broad, rounded at tip; none with marked structural modifications, but secondaries notably broader in males than in females, and in *C. hopkei* there is a sharp break in length between primaries 1–4 (unspotted) and primaries 5–10 (black-tipped) instead of a more or less even gradation in length as in the other two species. Tail short.

Unfeathered parts

Iris: dark brown in *C. nitidus* and *C. antoniae*, orange in *C. hopkei*; sexes similar.

Bill: *C. nitidus* – neutral grey, darker along culmen; sexes similar.

    C. antoniae – male: wax yellow with blackish line along culmen; female: brownish yellow, blackish along culmen.

    C. hopkei – black in both sexes.

Legs and feet: blackish with dull brown pads in all species.

Measurements

C. nitidus

♂♂ (9) Wing 136–142, 139.9.   Tail 64–73, 67.1. Tarsus 23.5–25.5, 24.3. Culmen 13.5–14.5, 13.9.

♀♀ (6) Wing 128–132, 129.7.   Tail 60–65, 63.8. Tarsus 23.5–25, 24.3. Culmen 13–14, 13.6.

C. antoniae (from Wetmore 1972, except for culmen)

♂♂ (6) Wing 130–145, 137.8.   Tail 60–68, 64.1. Tarsus 24–26, 25.0. Culmen 12.5–14.5, 13.5.

♀♀ (5) Wing 123–131, 127.1.   Tail 56–64, 59.5. Tarsus 23–24, 23.5. Culmen 12–13, 12.5.

C. hopkei (from Wetmore 1972, except for culmen)

♂♂ (10) Wing 153–169, 162.1.   Tail 80–95, 89.1. Tarsus 24.5–25.5, 24.9. Culmen 14–15.5, 14.7.

♀♀ (8) Wing 137–150, 144.3.   Tail 75–88, 80.9. Tarsus 23–25.5, 24.2. Culmen 14, 14.0.

MWWoodcock

Genus *Tijuca*

Tijuca atra – Black-and-gold Cotinga
Tijuca condita – Grey-winged Cotinga

Until the discovery that a cotinga specimen in a Brazilian museum represented a new species, probably referable to *Tijuca* (Snow 1980), this genus was thought to be monotypic. *Tijuca atra* has been known from specimens for a long time, but is not well known in life; its generic status has not been questioned. *Tijuca condita*, however, the new species, seems to be a link between *T. atra* and *Lipaugus*, and further study may indicate that it is closer to *Lipaugus* than to *T. atra*. Analysis of feather proteins suggests that in any case *Tijuca* and *Lipaugus* are quite closely related. These points are discussed in more detail in the account of *T. condita* that follows. Here we maintain the separation of *Tijuca* and *Lipaugus*, indicating their relationship by moving *Tijuca* from its traditional place next to *Carpornis* (Hellmayr 1929, and subsequent authors) and placing it next to *Lipaugus*. Structural characters of the genus, which are similar in both species (and also similar to those of *Lipaugus*), are summarised under *T. atra*.

Tijuca atra – Black-and-gold Cotinga

A southeastern Brazilian endemic of very limited distribution, the Black-and-gold Cotinga is notable for its remarkable voice and for a group display apparently of a unique kind. It is a medium-large cotinga of the size and much the same build as a large thrush. Males are all black in plumage, except for a patch of pure yellow on the flight feathers; females are olive-green all over. They are tree-top birds of steep forested mountains, and consequently have remained little known although the mountains where they live are within a short distance of the two cities of Rio de Janeiro and São Paulo. The following account is based very largely on a brief study that Derek Goodwin and I were able to make in the Serra dos Orgãos, not far from Rio de Janeiro, in 1972 (Snow & Goodwin 1974).

Distribution

Tijuca atra is found only in the highest mountains of the state of Rio de Janeiro and neighbouring parts of São Paulo and Minas Gerais. Specifically, it is recorded from the Serra dos Orgãos (Rio de Janeiro), the Serra da Bocaina and adjacent Serra do Bananal (extreme eastern São Paulo), and the higher parts of

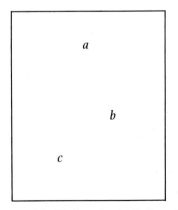

Plate 13

a and *b*: Black-and-gold Cotinga *Tijuca atra*, male and female
c: Grey-winged Cotinga *T. condita*, female

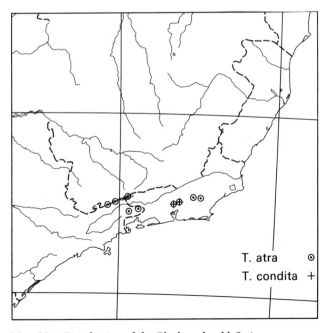

Map 19 Distribution of the Black-and-gold Cotinga (*Tijuca atra*) and Grey-winged Cotinga (*T. condita*).

T. atra ⊙
T. condita +

the Serra da Mantiqueira (including the Itatiaia massif) on the borders of Rio de Janeiro, São Paulo and Minas Gerais. All records are from an area measuring some 230 km from east to west and 60 km from north to south.

Ecology

Black-and-gold Cotingas are birds of the upper forest zone. Holt (1928) noted that in the Serra do Itatiaia most of his records were from the upper limit of heavy forest, at 5500–6800 ft (1700–2050 m). In the Serra dos Orgãos, a lower range, we also found them mainly near the upper level of heavy forest, at heights of 1200–1500 m. Occasional birds were found feeding down to about 1150 m. They are not known to make regular vertical migrations, but apparently there is some wandering to lower altitudes in the off-season. Thus Mitchell (1957) saw one in the Itatiaia area in July with a 'winter association' of birds foraging at a height of 3800 ft (1150 m), some 600 m below the usual level.

They are predominantly frugivorous. In the Serra dos Orgãos we saw Black-and-gold Cotingas feeding on the fruits of four lauraceous trees and one tree of another family, *Oreopanax fulvus* (Araliaceae). Three of the lauraceous trees had dense canopies, and the cotingas typically perched on the outside of the foliage, stretching to take a fruit and then fluttering to a new position. Those watched feeding in the more open tree perched on the inner branches within the canopy, looking about for the rather sparse ripe fruits, tugging at many that would not come off and occasionally fluttering to pull at a fruit in flight.

Males which we watched at their calling posts (see below) occasionally made short sallies to seize prey, probably insects, from the foliage near their perches, and sometimes a bird fluttered apparently to take something in the air.

Behaviour

In his account of the first thorough ornithological survey of the Itatiaia massif, in 1921–22, Ernest G. Holt included the following memorable account of his experience of the Black-and-gold Cotinga (Holt 1928).

'My acquaintance with the Saudade* was

---

*'The word *saudade* is a poetic Portuguese term signifying memory imbued with longing. Its application to *Tijuca nigra* [= *T. atra*] is evidence of the impression made upon the Brazilians by this bird's remarkable song' (Holt). It also has the more prosaic Brazilian name *Sobiador* or *Assubiador*, 'the whistler'.

considerable before I had actually seen the bird. My notebook contains altitudinal records based on song alone, but these are as sure as if the birds had been in hand, for that song once heard is not soon forgotten. In my experience it is unique, and to have heard it delivered amidst the full wealth of its lonely forest setting was one of the greatest privileges of my work upon Itatiaya. My first audience was impressive.

'I had been long hours in the saddle. Now, amid lengthening shadows, I was traversing the upper reaches of the forest zone . . . Unexpectedly there floated out upon the thin, clear air a vibrant note, a long-drawn plaintive whistle that rose in pitch and intensity, and then faded away in a mere thread of sound — withal so sad, so mournful, that it seemed the cry of some languishing wood sprite rather than a vibration of purely organic origin. With every sense alive, I craned my neck to see the tallest tree tops. Nothing moved except a great sparkling drop which fell from a rosette of bromeliads high overhead to splash into a puddle in the trail. After a tense moment, the disembodied voice drifted again through the trees, this time joined by another, the two singing in unison. I turned in my saddle then, and looked back and down as well as up, for the air seemed filled with sound, but the notes died away, leaving on every hand only silent green gloom. It was not until weeks after, when I trudged those high trails day after day, that I stumbled by chance upon the owner of that wonderful voice.'

In the Serra dos Orgãos we made most of our observations in a steep-sided forested valley at a height of about 1400 m. Here a group of males was to be found day after day calling from the tops of a number of large trees whose crowns rose above the general level of the tree tops. Another group of males called in an adjoining valley 2–300 m higher. Holt's evocative description of the call was probably written some time after he had heard it and is not quite accurate. The fully developed call has a characteristic form, which is not always evident when a bird is heard at a distance, especially if it is turning its head so that the volume reaching the hearer fluctuates. It is an extremely pure whistle, starting at a frequency of about 3.1 kHz and increasing very gradually to about 3.15 kHz. After a little over 2 seconds there is a short break, and the whistle is then continued for about $\frac{3}{4}$ second at a pitch of about 3.2 kHz. The total duration of the call is about 3 seconds. Heard at a distance it sometimes seems to die away, but in fact there is a gradual increase in volume throughout the first part of the call to a peak just before the break, and the volume of the short terminal note is also high. Not infrequently the terminal note is omitted. The normal interval between calls is about 2 seconds. A male calling uninterruptedly repeats the call at a maximum rate of 12–13 per minute.

Because the interval between calls is shorter than the duration of the call itself, when two males call at the same time they can produce continuous sound, as long as they more or less alternate their calling. This is in fact the normal pattern. We regularly heard continuous, sustained calling in chorus, especially when females were known or suspected to be present.

Whenever we were able to keep the birds in view for long it was apparent that most of the calling was done by one male. As this bird tended to occupy the same favoured perches in a large emergent tree on different days, we thought that the same individual was involved, and concluded that he was the dominant male of the group. From time to time this male was joined by one or two other adult males. Many times three adult males were in sight together, but never more. Often the other male or males would perch silently in the same tree as the calling male or in an adjacent tree, but at times they would call in chorus with him. Sometimes, at least, calling in chorus was stimulated by the presence of a female, but we could not be certain that this was always the case. Nor could we be certain whether one of the other males ever called sustainedly while the dominant male was silent, but it was certain that the other males were very often silent for long periods while the dominant male was calling. It also seemed certain that the subordinate males were often near by, but out of sight, while the dominant male was calling, as several times when a female was seen to fly to the calling area one or two additional males were at once in evidence, but they were never seen flying in from a distance as the females were.

Several times birds in female plumage were seen to visit the calling area, sometimes flying directly in from a distance of a few hundred metres. On some occasions the presence of these birds seemed to cause no special activity by the adult males, but merely some aggression, and it may have been that the visitor was a young male or a female who showed by her behaviour that she was not interested in mating. On other occasions the visits were accompanied by greatly increased calling and other activity by the males, and it seemed probable that the visitor was a breeding female. The sequence of events was variable. Sometimes the female flew directly to a perch low in the trees below the calling male, nearly always out of sight. One or more of the males at once flew down after her, and continuous

calling in chorus began from the place where the birds had gone. On two occasions when the female landed on a low perch that was in view, two males at once flew down to perches below her and started to call in chorus, and on one of these occasions a third male joined them half a minute later. It is probable that all three males called in chorus on this and other occasions, but it is hardly possible to tell how many birds are contributing to the continuous, fluctuating whistle of birds calling in chorus.

On other occasions the female flew to a high perch, and a chorus at once developed. The dominant male then flew down out of sight into the trees below, and the female followed. Several times also, when no female was in view, the calling male dived steeply down from his high perch into the lower trees. No chorus developed, and the male returned to a high perch after a minute or two, so that it seemed probable that the dive to a lower perch was spontaneous behaviour occurring in the absence of a female.

As the males always flew down out of sight on these occasions, and the terrain was so steep and matted with vegetation that observation from close at hand was impossible, we could find out nothing about the later stages of courtship, except that it must begin, at least, with a sustained chorus from the males, who probably maintain positions below the female. Probably the wings are spread to display the brilliant yellow patch to better advantage. Several times males in the higher trees were seen to crouch and half-spread their wings, but it was not clear in what circumstances this was done.

The daily output of calling by the group of males was most remarkable. A dawn watch showed that calling began at 05.05 (local time). On three days when we left the calling area between 16.45 and 17.00 hours, in order to get down the valley before dark, calling was still in progress although the valley was in deep shadow. Throughout the 12 intervening hours sustained calling continued almost the whole time. Thus during long watches of over 4 hours each on five different days the combined periods of silence, nearly all between 2 and 8 minutes in length, lasted only 8–16% of the total time, with periods of continuous calling lasting for up to an hour or more. Usually during long watches it was impossible to follow individual males for very long periods, but during one 75-minute watch a single male that was in view all the time called continuously. One day, when we climbed to a ridge high above the calling area, the more or less continuous thin whistling, attenuated by the distance, was constantly to be heard from the birds far below.

In the very early morning the birds called from exposed tree tops. Later, after the sun had entered the valley, they seldom appeared on exposed perches but called from high in the canopy where they were sometimes difficult or impossible to see. At about 16.00 the sun was cut off from the calling area by the steep mountain side, and within a few minutes the birds were again calling from exposed perches. On one very dull day, with thick hill fog, they called from exposed perches in the middle of the day.

Breeding and the annual cycle

Goeldi (1894–1900) mentioned, without any details, that he found a nest of a Black-and-gold Cotinga in November in a patch of forest that had been cut. There is no other record of a nest. November is the height of the general breeding season in southeastern Brazil. The considerable activity of the calling males and the visits by females that we saw in October suggested that breeding was in progress or was about to begin.

Seven adults collected in the months January–March were all in wing-moult. One of ten collected in April was in the final stage of wing-moult, the others being in fresh plumage; and not one of 13 collected in the months May–August was in wing-moult. If the wing-moult takes about 150 days to complete, as it does in other cotingas of comparable size, extrapolation from the observed stages of moult indicates that the five males must have started to moult in the second half of October and the first half of November, and the three females all in December. In several other cotinga species, especially those in which the males have conspicuous displays and take no part in nesting, the males begin to moult some weeks before the females, apparently at about the time that the females are beginning to nest (see p. 27). The moult records for *Tijuca* suggest that it follows a similar regime, and that the events of the annual cycle are well synchronized in the population as a whole.

Plumages

Nestling and juvenile plumages not seen. Immature male plumage similar to adult female; replaced after complete moult by subadult plumage in which a variable number of contour feathers are of immature type, especially on belly. This plumage probably replaced at the following moult by fully adult plumage.

Physical characters

Structure

General proportions thrush-like. Bill slightly hooked, notched near tip; bristles weakly developed at rictus, nostrils and base of mandible. Wings rather short, rounded at tip; tail moderately long. Flight-feathers unmodified.

Unfeathered parts

Iris: red brown.
Bill: brilliant orange in male; dull brown or orange-brown in females.
Feet and legs: dark brown.

Measurements

ad ♂♂ (20)   Wing 141–152, 147.0.   Tail 111–120, 115.4.   Tarsus 27–30, 28.5.   Culmen 15.5–17.5, 16.1.
im ♂♂ (7)   Wing 142–147, 144.0.
♀♀ (10)   Wing 140–146, 143.4.   Tail 114–119, 116.0.   Tarsus 29–30, 29.3.   Culmen 15.5–18, 16.4.

Tijuca condita – Grey-winged Cotinga

The English name, proposed above, for this newly recognized species is based on the most distinctive feature of what is a generally unremarkable plumage. The species was first collected in 1942 in the Serra dos Orgãos in the course of field studies on the epidemiology of yellow fever in the coastal zone of southeastern Brazil. The single specimen, a female, was identified as *T. atra*, and was placed with that species in the collection of the Department of Zoology of the University of São Paulo. In November 1972 Derek Goodwin and I noticed the specimen in the São Paulo collection, and later drew attention to its main peculiarities in our account of *Tijuca atra* (Snow & Goodwin 1974). Seven years later I was able to re-examine the specimen, and through the kindness of Dr H. F. de A. Camargo I was allowed to cut off the end of one of its secondary feathers for analysis of its feather proteins and comparison with *T. atra* and other cotingas. The result of this analysis, carried out by Dr Alan Knox of Aberdeen University, showed that the specimen without any reasonable doubt represented a new species, as indeed was practically certain from its external characters.

Tijuca condita is a smaller bird than *T. atra*, with a smaller, more delicate bill and markedly more delicate legs and feet. In plumage the female resembles the female of *T. atra*, but the body plumage has a stronger suffusion of yellow, especially on the rump, under wing-coverts and underparts, the wing-feathers are grey with pale blue-grey edges, and the tail is also mainly grey. In the female of *T. atra* both wings and tail are olive-green.

The feather protein analysis gave 'electrophoretic similarity values' of 0.76 between *T. condita* and *T.*

atra, and 0.65 between *T. condita* and *Lipaugus vociferans*. Between *T. atra* and *L. vociferans* the value was 0.77. (Values vary from 1 (electrophoretic patterns identical) to 0 (patterns totally different).) In other words, while it was reasonable on this evidence, combined with the general resemblance in structure and proportions and in the female plumage, to place the new species in *Tijuca*, *Tijuca* itself appears to be quite close to *Lipaugus*. The plumage of the unknown male remained a matter for speculation.

Almost exactly at the time of publication of the description of *T. condita*, Drs D. A. Scott and M. de L. Brooke, in the course of a survey of the montane forest avifauna of southeastern Brazil, rediscovered the species at high altitude in the Serra dos Orgãos. They were able to make limited field observations on it, as described below, from which two points emerged that are relevant to its systematic position: first, it is practically certain that the adult male's plumage is essentially the same as the female's, but somewhat brighter; and second, in its voice and calling behaviour it is not unlike some *Lipaugus* species. Both of these points strengthen the suggestion of a close relationship to *Lipaugus*.

Distribution

The Grey-winged Cotinga occurs, as far as known, only in the Serra dos Orgãos, northeast of and only 40–50 km from Rio de Janeiro. The altitude at which the type specimen was collected was not recorded, but there was reason to suppose that it was either collected at high altitude or, if not, that it was a straggler from a higher level (Snow 1980). This was confirmed by Drs Scott and Brooke, who in November 1980 mist-netted a bird at about 4500 ft (1370 m) in elfin cloud forest near the summit of the range above Tingua and later, in early December, found several birds calling at 6000–6500 ft (1830–1980 m), also in elfin forest, above Teresópolis. The bird caught at 4500 ft, on 15 November, was a female with a well-developed brood patch, which indicates that the species breeds at that level and at the same time provides the only information on its breeding season.

Ecology and behaviour (by Derek A. Scott & Michael de L. Brooke)

A total of six birds were located in November and December 1980: a female mist-netted in the Serra do Tingua, and five males found calling in the Serra dos Orgãos National Park near Teresópolis. All were in small patches of extremely humid elfin cloud forest rich in bromeliads and with a rather even canopy at 5–10 metres above ground level. The three birds found at the lowest elevations, 4500, 6000 and 6200 ft respectively (1370–1890 m), were in exposed ridge-top situations, while the other three were located in small isolated patches of forest on sheltered slopes in an otherwise rather open area of bamboo and tussock grass at 6500 ft (1980 m), above the main tree-line. The main altitudinal ranges of the Grey-winged and Black-and-gold Cotingas appear to be largely non-overlapping. In the Serra dos Orgãos National Park, the Black-and-gold was found commonly to 5500 ft (1680 m), and on one occasion a wandering band of 3 males and 1 female was watched for some 25 minutes moving through the territory of a calling Grey-winged Cotinga at 6000 ft (1830 m). In the Tingua area, there was an active lek of Black-and-gold Cotingas about 400 ft below the site where the female Grey-winged was netted, and on several occasions Black-and-gold Cotingas were seen moving over the ridge at 4500 ft (1370 m).

No field observations were made on the female caught in the Tingua area. The bird was first found hanging in a mist-net, and when released flew off rapidly into thick forest. Despite subsequent intensive searches in the area, no Grey-winged Cotingas were seen or heard. It is possible that the netted bird was a foraging bird which had moved unusually far down from a larger area of suitable habitat near the main summit of the Tingua range (1520 m).

All five birds found in the Serra dos Orgãos National Park were located from their calls. The call, although bearing a slight resemblance to that of the Black-and-gold Cotinga, was quite distinctive, being of much shorter duration, more explosive, and disyllabic, with emphasis on the second syllable. A possible rendering would be *sooee-wheee*. At any great distance, only the second syllable was audible, as a short plaintive *wheee*.

Calling Grey-winged Cotingas were extremely wary and elusive. Only three of the five birds were ever seen, and one of these was only observed on one occasion. There was no indication of any lekking behaviour; three of the five birds were at least 1 km from their nearest calling neighbour, while the two closest together were some 500 m apart. Calling occurred sporadically throughout the day (05.30 to 17.30 hrs), but was most frequent in the morning between 07.00 and 10.30 hours, and again in the afternoon between 15.00 and 17.00 hours. Calling was heard under a variety of weather conditions — bright sunlight, strong winds, heavy rain and thick mist — but was most frequent during periods of calm with low overcast. Undisturbed birds at the height of their calling uttered one call every 1 to 2 minutes, although occasionally a sequence of four or five calls was given with gaps of only 25–40 seconds between calls. Calling birds were continually on the move within a clearly defined patch of forest, uttering several calls from one perch, then moving on to another. Calling almost invariably occurred from a hidden perch within the dense forest canopy, and at the slightest disturbance, the bird would fly off quickly to a similar perch at some distance. On only two occasions was a male seen calling from an exposed perch on top of the canopy: once during a period of low mist and heavy rain at 17.30 hrs, and once in fine weather conditions, as the bird was feeding on berries exposed above the canopy.

Calling birds held the body in an upright position. with the wings slightly spread and drooping, the tail slightly spread and pointing almost vertically downwards, and the feathers of the lower back and rump puffed out. On uttering the call, the head was thrown back quickly into the vertical position, with the bill wide open, this motion occurring during the utterance of the first syllable of the call. Then, without pause, the head was brought back down again more slowly, as the second syllable was uttered. This head movement resembles rather closely that of calling pihas (*Lipaugus*), and contrasts with the stationary head posture of a calling Black-and-gold Cotinga.

Because of their wariness it was seldom possible to obtain more than fleeting glimpses of calling or foraging birds, and little information was obtained on general behaviour. On one occasion, however, a male was watched for over ten minutes, initially exposed on the top of the canopy, delicately plucking small red berries and swallowing them whole and occasionally calling, and later perched just below the top of the canopy, calling and preening.

Only two of the calling birds were seen sufficiently well for a detailed description of their plumage to be taken. They were identical to one another, and resembled the mist-netted female closely, although their plumage was distinctly brighter. There was a more pronounced greyish suffusion on the lores, chin and upper throat, and below the eye; the silver-grey edges to the flight and tail feathers were obvious even in flight and contrasted strongly with the bright yellowish-olive wing coverts and rump; and the breast and belly were a noticeably brighter olive-yellow than in the female, and had a distinctly apricot tinge in bright light.

Physical characters

Unfeathered parts
Iris: brown.
Bill: dark greyish with yellow-olive lower mandible.
Legs and feet: dark horn.
[Data from the mist-netted bird mentioned above, superseding less accurate information from label of type specimen quoted by Snow (1980).]

Measurements
♀ (type) Wing 122.   Tail 106.   Tarsus 26.5.   Culmen 14.5.
Measurements of mist-netted ♀   Wing 129.   Tail 107.   Tarsus 26.   Bill, from tip to feathering 21.5, to skull 24.
Weight: ♀ (mist-netted) 80 g.

Genus Lipaugus – the pihas

Plate 14 and 15, pages 112 and 116

Lipaugus vociferans – Screaming Piha (Greenheart Bird)

Lipaugus unirufus – Rufous Piha	*Lipaugus streptophorus* – Rose-collared Piha
Lipaugus lanioides – Cinnamon-vented Piha	*Lipaugus cryptolophus* – Olivaceous Piha
Lipaugus fuscocinereus – Dusky Piha	*Lipaugus subalaris* – Grey-tailed Piha

The seven species of *Lipaugus* are medium-sized or fairly large cotingas with mainly grey, brown or olive-green plumage. Only one species shows striking sexual dimorphism in colour. Proportions are rather thrush-like, except that the tail is relatively long in two species; the bill is wide and somewhat hooked at the tip. To compensate for their dull plumage several, perhaps all, of the species have very loud, piercing calls, and this outstanding feature has given them their common name. The genus is probably quite closely related to *Tijuca*, and perhaps to *Chirocylla*. The recently discovered *Tijuca condita* may indeed be more correctly placed in *Lipaugus*, as discussed on p. 109. *Tijuca* and *Chirocylla* may be regarded as early derivatives of *Lipaugus* stock with relict distributions respectively in the southeast Brazilian coastal mountains and the Bolivian Andes.

The wider relationships of *Lipaugus* within the Cotingidae are uncertain. Evidence from syringeal structure gives no guidance, as *vociferans* and *unirufus*, the only species examined (with inadequate material), are unlike any other genus (Ames 1971). In skull structure, however, *Lipaugus* most resembles the fruit-crows, and on this basis Warter (1965) places the genus in the subfamily Querulinae (see p. 12).

Characters of plumage and behaviour also link the genus with other members of the family, though none is very convincing in isolation. Two species, *cryptolophus* and *subalaris*, have mainly olive-green plumage with black head markings. In this they show some resemblance to other montane genera with ranges peripheral to the Amazonian forest region. One species, *streptophorus*, has a bright magenta collar in the male, thus providing a link with cotinga genera that have brilliant red and mauve areas of plumage. Finally, the lek behaviour of *vociferans* suggests affinity with the other lek-forming cotingas; but this argument is not strong, as many manakins, *Pipromorpha* among the tyrant-flycatchers, and probably some other tyrannid genera, show similar behaviour (Snow & Snow 1979).

The genus comprises a superspecies consisting of two species, *vociferans* (Amazonian) and *unirufus* (Central and northwest South American), which between them range over most lowland forest areas of both South and Central America; three species which seem to be most closely related to *vociferans* and occupy widely disjunct, restricted ranges in mountains peripheral to the Amazon basin; and two closely related Andean species whose ranges overlap one another broadly (*cryptolophus* and *subalaris*). Possibly these two latter species are only distantly related to the other members of the genus.

The wide-ranging Screaming Piha *L. vociferans* is a lek bird, famous for its extraordinarily loud, piercing call which is one of the most characteristic sounds of lowland South American forests. Even so, its natural history remains little known. Dr Skutch's studies in Costa Rica have made the nesting habits of the Rufous Piha *L. unirufus* better known than those of most cotingas, but in other respects it is no better known than the Screaming Piha. All the montane species remain very poorly known.

Structural characters of *Lipaugus*

Bill wide at base (less so in *cryptolophus* than other species) and markedly hooked at tip. Tarsus rather short (mostly 16–18% of wing-length, somewhat longer in *cryptolophus*). Wing-feathers unmodified except that in males of *lanioides* primary 9 is distinctly long, projecting beyond the otherwise curved outline of the spread wing. Tail of variable length proportionally to wing, from 75% in *streptophorus* to 92% in *fuscocinereus*.

MWWoodcock

Lipaugus vociferans – Screaming Piha (Greenheart Bird)
Lipaugus unirufus – Rufous Piha

These two species resemble one another closely in all respects except the colour of their plumage: uniform grey in the Screaming Piha, uniform rufous brown in the Rufous Piha. In this they show a curious parallelism to what is found in two other species-pairs, the mourners *Rhytipterna simplex* and *R. holerythra* and *Laniocera hypopyrrha* and *L. rufescens*. The mourners also consist of a grey species widespread in tropical forest east of the Andes, including the southeast Brazilian coastal forest, and a rufous species west of the Andes and in Central America, the distributional pattern being remarkably similar in all three pairs. *Rhytipterna* and *Laniocera* were formerly placed in the Cotingidae, but are now, on anatomical grounds, considered to be members of the Tyrannidae. The two *Rhytipterna* species are superficially very like smaller versions of the two *Lipaugus* species; the two *Laniocera* species, having some spotting on the wing-coverts and underparts, are more distinct. It is hard to avoid the suspicion that the regional colour differences in these three pairs have not been independently evolved.

Distribution (Map 20)

Lipaugus vociferans and *L. unirufus* replace one another geographically in lowland forest areas of South America and Central and northwestern South America respectively, but their ranges do not abut; there is an extensive gap in northeastern Colombia and northern Venezuela where neither occurs. This area lacks many other lowland forest bird species, though it seems suitable for at least some of them (see discussion on p. 13–14). In eastern Venezuela,

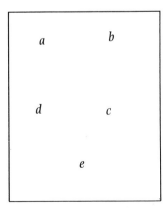

Plate 14
Screaming Piha and allies
(*Lipaugus*)

a: Rufous Piha *L. unirufus*
b and *c*: Rose-collared Piha *L. streptophorus*, male and female
d: Cinnamon-vented Piha *L. lanioides*
e: Screaming Piha *L. vociferans*

vociferans is found north of the Orinoco along the coast through Delta Amacuro (the Orinoco delta) to Guanoco in the State of Sucre, an extension from its main range that parallels what is found in the manakin *Chiroxiphia pareola* and some other forest species. In Colombia it extends north along the base of the Eastern Andes to about latitude 5°N. Elsewhere its range is more or less co-extensive with the Amazonian and Guianan forest region, with the addition of a narrow strip in the coastal forests of eastern Brazil. The isolated eastern Brazilian population is not subspecifically differentiated from the Amazonian population, suggesting that its isolation is not of very long standing.

Ecology

Apart from the fact that the Screaming and Rufous Pihas inhabit evergreen tropical forest, little is known of their ecology. Screaming Pihas eat fruit and insects, apparently showing a tendency to concentrate temporarily on one or the other since reports of stomach contents mostly indicate either fruit or insects, not both (Burmeister 1856, Snethlage 1908, Olivares & Hernandez 1962, Schubart *et al.* 1965). In the foothills of the Kanuku Mountains of southern Guyana we saw Screaming Pihas taking the fruit of a small melastomataceous and a large lauraceous tree. The Rufous Piha seems to have very similar feeding habits. Skutch (1969) mentions insects and scorpions taken in flight from the foliage, palm fruits, and hard green fruits, probably lauraceous.

Behaviour

Screaming Piha. The Screaming Piha is a lek bird that, as indicated by its scientific and English names (see p. 192), makes itself conspicuous by its voice and not by its appearance. Indeed, the almost uniformly grey birds are not at all easy to see as they call at middle levels in fairly thick forest. Leks may consist of up to 30 birds, spaced over several hectares of forest, but most are smaller. Reports indicate that groups of 4 to 10 birds are more usual; doubtless the size is very variable and depends on the local abundance of the species. Within the lek area, birds are typically spaced some 40 to 60 m apart.

The main call (variously rendered as *pi-pi-yo, cri-cri-ó*, etc.), which seems to be essentially the same all over the species' range, is one of the most distinctive sounds of the forests where these birds occur, its ringing, somewhat ventriloquial quality seeming to lure the traveller ever onwards into the woods. Thus in Guyana it used to be known as the 'gold-bird', as its calls, if followed, were supposed to

Map 20   Distribution of the Screaming Piha (*Lipaugus vociferans*), Rufous Piha (*L. unirufus*), Cinnamon-vented Piha (*L. lanioides*) and Dusky Piha (*L. fuscocinereus*). The Rufous Piha's range extends west in southern Mexico to just off the map.

lead to places where gold could be found, while in Bolivia it was the 'seringuero', the bird that led one to rubber trees. In spite of the fact that the call must be familiar to all ornithologists who have visited the forests of Amazonia and the Guianas, the difficulty of watching the calling birds, and even more of trapping them for marking, seems to have discouraged detailed investigation, and the only published study of the birds' behaviour at their leks is that made by B. K. Snow in Guyana in 1960 (Snow 1961). The following paragraphs are quoted from her account.

'All the calling birds of which a good view was obtained lacked the chestnut markings, and it seems probable that it is only the males that hold territories in the calling grounds and give the *pi, pi, y-o* call [this refers to the fact that birds with chestnut-tinged wing and tail feathers have been supposed to be females, but they are in fact young birds – see p. 119]. This call is extremely loud and audible through approximately 300–400 meters of forest... Close at hand, the call seems to be more nearly described as *qui, qui, y-o*. While calling, the bird has the feathers of the head erected to form a slight crest, and the pale-grey flank feathers puffed out covering part of the wing. As a preliminary to the call, the bird leans forward, opens the bill slightly and at the same time utters two somewhat dovelike notes, *groo groo*, audible for about 100 meters. The first note is slightly lower pitched than the second. From the forward position held in the *groo* call, the bird suddenly jerks its head back so that it almost rests on its scapulars. At the same time the beak is opened very wide, displaying an orange gape, and the first *qui* note is uttered. With the beak still open, the bird gives another jerk back for the second *qui* and then relaxes forward and closes the bill with the *y-o* note. This final note has an indescribable ringing quality and carries further than the more-piercing *qui* notes. When watching a bird call one morning against the early-morning light, it was evident that much air was expelled with the *qui, qui, y-o* but not with the *groo groo* notes, when probably air is inhaled. The quite violent and ritualized bodily movements involved in the call give the impression of being physically essential to the production of the call, but are probably really a visual display, as the bird occasionally makes another equally loud call without any movement. . .

'The number of calls per minute varies greatly, from one or two per minute, when the bird may also be occupied with preening, to eight per minute. On one occasion 12 per minute were witnessed. The bird was very excited, and this rapid calling was followed by a different call and behavior, described below, which possibly heralded the approach of a female.

'One individual, A, watched for $16\frac{1}{2}$ hours at the Wineperu calling ground, had a territory approximately 75 meters by 35 meters. It was seen in this territory on six successive days. Fortunately, this individual had the tip of the right, outer tail feather missing, so it was possible to check its identity. It was not seen calling outside its territory. The $16\frac{1}{2}$ hours spent watching this individual covered the whole of a day from 0645 to 1645 and duplicated many of the hours. Seventy-seven percent of this time was spent calling in the territory; the remainder of the time the bird was silent, and I usually lost sight of it. The silent periods recorded usually lasted for from 5 to 10 minutes, but a period of 23 minutes was once recorded.

'Very occasionally, while calling, the bird would flutter up to a nearby leaf and take an insect. But judging from the short times taken to feed, fruit must be its main diet. Like the Bellbirds and Calfbirds, it was frequently seen regurgitating fruit seeds. Twice it was seen taking fruit, once from a melastomaceous tree of about 13 meters and from an unidentified tree of about 32 meters. Most of the fruit must have come from high up, as usually after a spell of calling, the bird would disappear into the upper canopy, where it would be silent and was presumably feeding.

'There appears to be a strong social bond between neighboring birds. Thus the individual A had two neighbors, B and C, with which it synchronized its day so that all three birds, but more particularly A and B, would tend to have their silent periods and period of high- and low-tempo calling at the same time. When all three birds were calling at a fairly high tempo, such as six calls a minute, the calls were timed to follow each other and not overlap. A and B, timing their calls alternately, would reach a tempo of eight per minute. As the full call of *groo groo, qui, qui, y-o* took approximately four seconds, careful timing was required, and it could only be accomplished by one bird starting its *groo groo* call when the other was terminating with its *y-o*. These bouts of alternate calling were made when the two or three neighbors were calling near each other, probably not more than 100 meters apart.

'The bird usually calls from below the canopy, perching on fairly thin, horizontal branches 6 to 16 meters up. Occasionally, it will call from higher perches. It moves its perch rather frequently, calling from all parts of its territory with no apparent preference for any particular perch. When excited, A was seen on several occasions to fly down to perches 4 to 5 meters above the ground, where it hopped about from perch to perch while calling at a very high tempo . . . Although I saw no other bird when A flew to these low perches, it seems probable that one may have been present and visible to A . . .

'Another call made very occasionally by the calling birds holding territories was a loud, whistling *wee-oo* repeated several times. This call was usually made before or after a silence of five or more minutes. It was also made early in the morning and in the evening. In the Kanakus, where we camped in the middle of a calling ground, the *qui, qui, y-o* calling started around 0645 hours and continued until about 1715 hours in the evening. But each morning, sometimes as much as 20 minutes before the day's calling started, a few *wee-oo* calls would be heard, and the same would happen in the evening after the calling had finished for the day. There was no special body movement made with this call, although it was equally as loud as the *qui, qui, y-o* call. It seems likely that this is a preliminary contact call between neighbors who have temporarily lost contact through silence. From the following incident, it looks as if it may also be a contact call between the sexes. The individual A flew from the borders of its territory, where it had been calling, into the lower branches of a sapling in the center of the territory. Here it called *qui, qui, y-o* at the rate of 12 per minute, evidently excited, moving from branch to branch, and frequently turning on the branch to call in the opposite direction. It suddenly stopped calling and hopped up the sapling, giving a low, whistling *queue queue*, probably not audible for more than 15 meters. At about 10 meters, it stopped and called *wee-oo*, which another bird, somewhere above,

M W Woodcock

answered with a *wee* call. This calling and answering was repeated two or three times before A flew off and there was silence. It seems possible that the answering bird was a female, although unfortunately I never saw it.'

Rufous Piha. Surprisingly, there seems to be little evidence that the Rufous Piha, so similar to the Screaming Piha in other ways, is a true lek bird at all, at least in the Central American part of its range. All the evidence suggests that single birds, presumably males, occupy calling territories well separated from one another, though they may be concentrated in certain areas of forest. Hilty (MS), however, refers to 'scattered leks' in Colombia. Moreover their calling seems to be always more or less sporadic, and is often elicited by some extraneous loud noise. Thus Tashian (1952) reports that they respond 'instantly to any loud noise such as thunder or a gun shot', and other accounts agree. The call is described as 'a sharp explosive cry with a downward inflection' (Tashian), 'a very loud, emphatic, whistled chu-weé-oo, repeated from time to time' (Eisenmann), and 'a staccato, explosive *see-you, I see-you,* a long silvery whistle' (Chapman). Skutch (1969) has given the fullest account, from his observations in Costa Rica, from which it is clear that the Rufous Piha's vocal repertoire is more varied than the Screaming Piha's.

'As one wanders through the forests of southwestern Costa Rica, he hears from time to time a clear whistle, so sharp and loud that, if a newcomer to this region, he may look around for the man who is trying to attract his attention . . . Even if the silence is so prolonged that one may doubt that any bird is within hearing, a sudden loud sound, such as a sneeze, a shout, a hand-clap, may elicit the clear whistle. When a Great Tinamou, alarmed where it

forages unseen amid the ferny ground cover, rises abruptly with loudly whirring wings, the piha often calls out far above, as though exclaiming at the occurrence . . .

'Sometimes the piha's whistle consists of a single note, loud, shrill, and far-carrying: *peer*. At other times the whistle consists of two softer, less insistent notes: *wheer-weet* . . . More seldom the whistle consists of three notes, of which the first is long, the second short and contrasting in tone: *whee-er-wit*. Again, the whistle may be prolonged into a short, loud trill, or a longer, very musical trill, both of which are difficult to paraphrase. Each bird seems to have its particular part of the forest, where it is heard day after day over a long period. Early in April, I watched a piha which for over half an hour remained unusually low, from 20 to 30 feet up, in the same small area on a forested ridge. The bird rested quietly for many seconds on a slender branch; then it suddenly flew to another perch. Sometimes it whistled twice in the course of a minute, but more often only once. At times the utterances were still more widely spaced. If I made a noise, as by calling out or breaking a dry twig, the bird answered immediately. But even with this stimulation, I could not greatly increase the rate of calling . . .'

Breeding and annual cycle

Breeding

Skutch (1969), in the only full account of the nesting of any species of *Lipaugus*, has described five nests of the Rufous Piha from Costa Rica. Russell (1964) has given a short description of a nest found in British Honduras (now Belize) which he attributed to the same species. Dr E. O. Willis (pers. comm.) found a nest of a Screaming Piha near Manaus in Brazil. These appear to be the only records of the nesting of any of the pihas.

Four of the nests found by Skutch were on his farm in the valley of El General, in a restricted area of well-grown secondary forest adjoining a large tract of primary forest. The fifth was in fairly open forest on a ridge in the Sarapiquí lowlands of northeastern Costa Rica. They were most diminutive structures, about 3 inches across, formed mainly of curled tendrils, so loose and open that in one case it was possible to read a printed page through the middle of the nest. Of the first nest that he found, Skutch wrote: 'The most meager arboreal nest that I had seen, this unbelievably slight structure seemed to contain the irreducible minimum of material that would suffice to support an egg in the air.' All five nests were on branches of small trees well out from the main trunk and at heights of from 17 to about

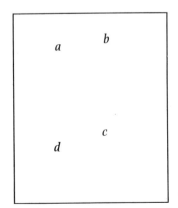

Plate 15
Andean pihas
(*Lipaugus* and *Chirocylla*)

a: Olivaceous Piha *L. cryptolophus*
b: Grey-tailed Piha *L. subalaris*
c: Dusky Piha *L. fuscocinereus*
d: Scimitar-winged Piha *C. uropygialis*

35 feet, either at the fork of a branch or supported by two close parallel branches. The nest reported by Russell was rather different: it apparently consisted simply of a shallow depression beside an epiphytic bromeliad in a crotch 10 feet up in a large tree. Furthermore it contained 2 eggs, whereas all of the clutches found by Skutch consisted of a single egg. Hence there must be some doubt as to the identity of the British Honduras nest.

Three of Skutch's nests contained single eggs, 'smoky gray, or grayish brown, heavily blotched and mottled all over with darker brown, which on the thick end nearly masked the ground color'. One egg measured about 31 × 22 mm. At one nest, the incubation period was between 24 days 20 hours and 25 days 23 hours. On hatching, the nestling was sparsely covered with grey down; at the age of 17 days it was feathered, and it left the nest at the age of 28 or 29 days. It received an unusually large amount of brooding, being covered for 64% of the time during a watch when it was 11 days old, and 47% of the time when it was 19 days old. It was fed on insects, spiders, fruits, and an occasional small scorpion, feeds being at the rate of one per hour or less in the first week and increasing to nearly two per hour at the end of the nestling period. At all stages, only one parent attended the nest.

Skutch watched a Rufous Piha, accompanied by a fledgling which had evidently just flown, tear apart a nest, not using the material to build another but simply dropping it at random; and he had evidence that other nests were dismantled after they had come to an unsuccessful end. Natterer's Cotingas and Lovely Cotingas behave in the same way (pp. 85 and 87). For birds that rely on inconspicuousness for the safety of their nests, as these species clearly do, it may be advantageous to destroy unused nests so that potential predators can less easily acquire the 'search image'.

The only recorded nest of the Screaming Piha was found by Dr E. O. Willis in September 1972 at the edge of forest by a partly cleared tree plantation in the Reserva Ducke, near Manaus. It was a thin stick nest, like a dove's but even thinner, and was 7 metres up in a small tree, supported by a branch and one of its side twigs about 15 cm out from the main stem. The nest was so small that it was quite concealed by the sitting bird; it was revisited occasionally over a period of 7 days, but its contents were never seen.

Annual cycles
Rufous piha. The laying dates for the five Rufous Piha nests found by Skutch in Costa Rica, at about 10°N, ranged from 4 March to 3 or 4 August, the months of laying being March (2 nests), May (2) and August (1). No doubt individual females regularly make more than one nesting attempt in the course of this fairly long season; the female that laid on 3 or 4 August was accompanied by a juvenile with a half-length tail when she was building in late July.

The moult records, when set beside the breeding records, strongly suggest that breeding and moult overlap. Males begin to moult on average well before females, as is the case in other cotinga species in which males take no part in nesting duties (see, e.g. Cock-of-the-rock, p. 183). Thus in Costa Rica and neighbouring Nicaragua males begin to moult in the months February–May (10 records), and females in the months April–August (14 records). Some males at least must continue to mate after they have begun to moult; females may perhaps not begin to moult until they have finished their last nesting attempt, but if so, some of them must give up nesting very early in the breeding season. This question is discussed for the family as a whole on p. 27. The duration of the moult in the individual bird, from the dropping of the innermost primary to the completion of growth of the outermost, is about 150 days.

The Rufous Piha maintains quite well-marked moulting seasons throughout its range, which extends nearly to the Equator west of the Andes. The season shifts progressively earlier towards the south, presumably reflecting a progressively earlier breeding season. Thus in western Colombia and Ecuador males begin to moult in the months November–March (25 records), and females in the months February–August (10 records).

Screaming Piha. The Screaming Piha has well-marked moulting seasons in the north of its range, in Surinam, Guyana and adjacent parts of Venezuela (males begin mainly February–May), but to the south, in the extensive area of the middle to lower Amazon valley, seasonality seems to be poorly marked. The records from Belém, at the mouth of the Amazon, suggest why this may be so. Large samples of moult records are available from this area for the years 1959 and 1960, and indicate that the main time of onset of moult was in the months April–July and January–April respectively. The records for other years, however, suggest that October–February is the main period of onset of moult, as it is for other frugivorous cotingas in the Belém area. The rainfall was abnormally heavy and prolonged in the Belém area in 1959, and it is probable that this affected the timing and extent of the 1959 and 1960 breeding seasons, and in consequence the following moults (Snow 1976a). In an area where seasonal changes in day-length are negligible, annual differences in rainfall pattern may be expected to have overriding effects.

In upper Amazonia the records, though not numerous, indicate that moult seasons are better defined than on the middle and lower Amazon. Here a southern hemisphere moult regime is evident almost on the Equator (males begin July–December), and this regime is maintained to the south, through Peru to Bolivia. A well-marked southern regime is also evident, as would be expected, in the records for the isolated eastern Brazilian population, between about 9° and 20°S (most males begin September–December).

Plumages and moults

Screaming Piha. Nestling unknown. Juvenile (only one specimen seen in fully juvenile plumage, out of several hundred examined) entirely rufous brown on head and body, paler below than above, feathers whitish at base giving a patchy appearance; flight-feathers dull dark brown shading to rufous at tips and along outer edges of wing-feathers. Most contour feathers replaced, presumably soon after fledging, by grey feathers of adult type, but rufous feathers often persist on throat, upper breast, nape and round vent. Juvenile (rufous) wing-coverts and (rufous-tipped) flight-feathers are retained until first complete moult, when fully adult plumage is acquired.

Rufous Piha. Nestling down sparse, light grey (Skutch). Juvenile plumage like that of adult.

Physical characters

Unfeathered parts
Iris: brown, with some individual variation towards a more grey colouration in *vociferans*.
Bill: dark brown or blackish brown, paler at base of lower mandible (pale flesh in *unirufus*, greyish in *vociferans*).
Legs and feet: dark grey, with some individual variation towards pale green in *vociferans* and olive in *unirufus*.

Geographical variation
There is slight geographical variation in both species.
  L. vociferans. The birds occurring in the extreme south of the range, in Bolivia and the Andean foothills of Peru, are larger than those from lowland Amazonia and the Guianas. Bolivian birds have been separated by Todd (1950) as subspecies *dispar*

(wing-lengths of 3 males 136–141, cf. 116–128 for 9 males from Guyana). Geographical variation in plumage colour, if it exists, must be extremely slight.
  L. unirufus. Variation affects the depth and brightness of the rufous colouration. Birds from the extreme south of the range, in the very humid coastal areas of western Colombia and north-western Ecuador, are deepest in colour (subspecies *castaneotinctus*). Birds from northern parts of the range, approximately from Costa Rica northwards, are dullest (nominate subspecies); while those from intermediate areas are intermediate (*clarus*). Opinion has been divided as to the number of subspecies worth recognizing and also the limits of each, variation apparently being to some extent clinal. We recognize only two (p. 189).

Measurements

L. vociferans
♂♂ (10, Belém area) Wing 118–123, 120.6. Tail 101–110, 106.0. Tarsus 20.5–22, 21.8. Culmen 14.5–16.5, 15.6.
♀♀ (10, Belém area) Wing 112–123, 116.6. Tail 95–105, 102.6. Tarsus 21–22.5, 21.8. Culmen 14.5–17, 15.9.
Wing-lengths of other populations:
Eastern Brazil (Pernambuco-E. Santo) 16 ♂♂ 121–130, 124.5. 5 ♀♀ 119–121, 120.0.
Guyana 9 ♂♂ 119–128, 123.9. 5 ♀♀ 114–121, 118.0.
Eastern Peru (Huánuco) 8 ♂♂ 126–131, 128.4. 5 ♀♀ 123–128, 125.2.
Northern Bolivia 5 ♂♂ 128–141, 134.0.
Weights:
Surinam 5 ♂♂ 71–74, 72.6 g.
        5 ♀♀ 68–74, 71.8 g.
Peru (Huánuco) 7 ♂♂ 77–85, 81.9 g (mean wing 128.4 mm).
              5 ♀♀ 78–87, 82.6 g (mean wing 125.2 mm).
Bolivia 2 ♂♂ 80, 83.4 g (wings 128, 129 mm).

L. unirufus
Nicaragua and Costa Rica 6 ♂♂ Wing 125–139, 132.5. Tail 100–108, 105.0. Tarsus 20–22, 21.2. Culmen 14.5–16, 15.3.
5 ♀♀ Wing 125–134, 130.0. Tail 99–108, 104.2. Tarsus 21–23, 21.8. Culmen 15.5–16, 15.8.
Panama (Wetmore 1972) 10 ♂♂ Wing 125–133, 128.8. Tail 96–104, 100.8. Tarsus 20–22.5, 21.1.
10 ♀♀ Wing 122–128, 124.4. Tail 94–104, 98.0. Tarsus 20.5–22.5, 21.1.
Weights: 6 ♂♂ 79–87, 83.7 g.
        3 ♀♀ 69, 80.3; 87.2 (ovary enlarged).

Lipaugus lanioides – **Cinnamon-vented Piha**
Lipaugus fuscocinereus – **Dusky Piha**
Lipaugus streptophorus – **Rose-collared Piha**

These three species, which at least superficially seem closest to the Screaming Piha *L. vociferans*, have limited, mainly montane distributions peripheral to the range of *vociferans* (Maps 20, 21). *L. lanioides* replaces *vociferans* in eastern Brazil, from Espirito Santo southwards to Santa Catarina. In central Espirito Santo, where *lanioides* reaches its northern and *vociferans* its southern limit, the former occurs in montane forest and the latter in lowland forest. Further south, *lanioides* occurs in both lowland and montane forest. This might suggest that the two species are competitors and each limits the other's range; but such a conclusion may not be justified, as they are probably adapted to forests of rather different types, *vociferans* to lowland tropical forest that is quite strongly seasonal, and *lanioides* to humid subtropical forest. *L. fuscocinereus* is found in subtropical and temperate forests between about 1700 and 3000 m in the Andes of Colombia, Ecuador and extreme northern Peru, its northeastern limit being set by the comparatively low-lying area between the headwaters of the Río Zulia and Río Uribante, and its southern limit (so far as known) being in the Peruvian Department of Cajamarca. *L. streptophorus* occurs in montane forests at 1000–1800 m on a few of the isolated tepuis of southeastern Venezuela and adjacent Guyana and Brazil, where it may be found in close proximity to, but altitudinally isolated from, *vociferans*. These three species are thus all spatially segregated from the centrally placed *vociferans*.

Ecology and behaviour

Practically nothing has been recorded of their ecology. There are several records of stomach contents of the Cinnamon-vented Piha, one containing a mantid and a beetle, another vegetable remains (Schubart *et al.* 1965), and five containing 'large fruits' or simply 'fruits'. Brief observations that I have been able to make on the Rose-collared Piha (see below) suggest that it may be mainly insectivorous. Their behaviour also remains very little known; the following accounts indicate that the Dusky Piha is a lek bird, perhaps not unlike the Screaming Piha in its social organization, whereas the Rose-collared Piha, the only member of the genus with marked sexual dimorphism and bright male plumage, has a fundamentally different organization.

Dusky Piha. Dr Steven Hilty has observed what was apparently a lek of Dusky Pihas in mountain forest above Bucaramanga in northern Colombia, at a height of 2400 m. A number of birds were calling in a group from tree-tops or exposed high branches, with much flying back and forth between trees. The call was a loud *pee-a-weeee*, or *pee-a-weeee-a-weeee*, the last syllable slurring down the scale and the whole reminiscent of the Screaming Piha. The major differences from the behaviour of the Screaming Piha that Dr Hilty noticed (from his observation point a considerable distance away) were that the Dusky Pihas stayed in the tree-tops and flew about between the trees, unlike Screaming Pihas which keep to the middle levels of the forest and usually move relatively little when calling.

Rose-collared Piha. In April 1976 I camped for a few days in thick forest at 1700 m on the slopes of Ptari-tepui in southeastern Venezuela. In the area of the camp the Rose-collared Piha was a tree-top bird, apparently not very abundant and tantalisingly difficult to see. Two or three males appeared to hold territories within a radius of a few hundred metres round the camp. All the foraging that I saw appeared to be for insects, mostly 60–70 feet up in the main canopy. As they moved from tree to tree, foraging males infrequently uttered a sharp, monosyllabic *weee* or *weest*. Once, during several hours of recording, this call was repeated after only 30 seconds; several times it was repeated after an interval of about one minute, but more often the intervals between calls were of 2 to 5 minutes. Much less often, a lower-pitched *weeoo* was heard, which may have been uttered by females. The birds appeared to be in pairs. On one occasion two birds were seen keeping together while foraging; on another occasion I saw a male accompanying a female who was collecting nest-material. She picked a fine branched twig from a tree and flew off with it, and the male at once flew off after her. Disappointingly, the pair did not return to the tree in the course of the following two hours. These fragmentary observations suggest that the Rose-collared Piha is a predominantly insectivorous bird, that it forms pairs, and that the infrequent calls of the male serve to advertise his ownership of a territory. If this is correct, it is curious that sexual dimorphism in plumage colour should be pronounced in the Rose-collared Piha and absent in the lek-forming pihas.

Annual cycle

The nests of all three species are unrecorded. Moult records, however, give some idea of the annual cycle (Snow 1976a). The Cinnamon-vented Piha, of the eastern Brazilian coastal mountains between about

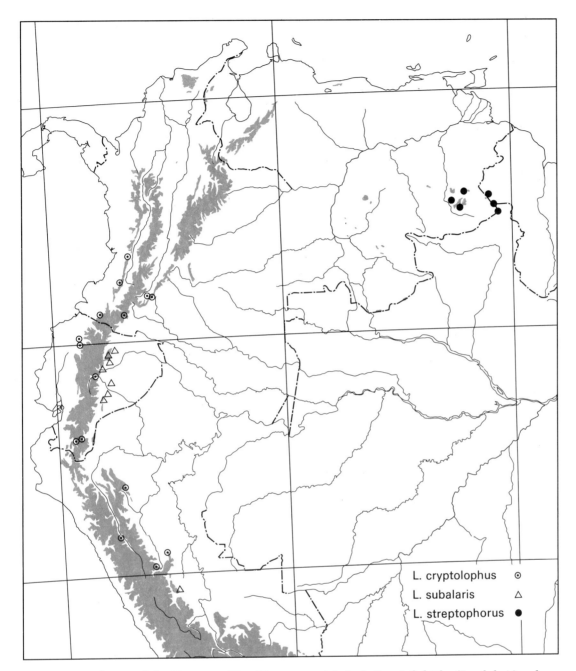

Map 21   Distribution of the Olivaceous Piha (*Lipaugus cryptolophus*), Grey-tailed Piha (*L. subalaris*) and Rose-collared Piha (*L. streptophorus*).

20° and 26°S, begins to moult mainly in October and November, with no clear difference between the sexes. This is well in line with the seasons of other frugivorous cotingas in this region. Moult records for the Dusky Piha, all from within a few degrees of the Equator, are rather evenly spread throughout the year. The Rose-collared Piha, confined to a restricted area between 4° and 6°N in the Guiana highlands, has an extended but definite moulting season, 32 of 35 records indicating a start in the months December–May. The records do not suggest any difference between the sexes.

Plumage sequence

The Dusky Piha probably has a rufous juvenile plumage, like the Screaming Piha, as presumed young birds retain rufous-tipped greater wing-coverts and some lesser coverts. Juvenile plumages of the other two species not seen, and apparently unrecorded.

Physical characters

Unfeathered parts
Similar in all three species, and in both sexes.
Iris: dark brown.
Bill: dark brown or blackish brown, paler at base of
 lower mandible.
Legs and feet: grey.

Measurements
L. lanioides
♂♂ (13) Wing 131–140, 135.5. Tail 113–125,
 119.0. Tarsus 22–25, 23.7. Culmen 14.5–16.5,
 15.7.
♀♀ (12) Wing 127–140, 133.2. Tail 111–128,
 117.5. Tarsus 23.5–26, 24.2. Culmen 15–17.5,
 16.2.
Weights: 8 ♂♂ 85–105, 92.6 g (mean wing 136.1).
  4 ♀♀ 92.7–110, 99.3 g (mean wing 137.0
  mm); some probably breeding.

L. fuscocinereus
♂♂ (7) Wing 172–188, 179.0. ♀♀ (8) Wing
 171–187, 178.9. ♂♀ (9) Tail 158–169, 163.6.
 Tarsus 27.5–29, 28.1 Culmen 17–19, 18.5.

L. streptophorus
♂♂ (8) Wing 121–130, 123.9. Tail 91–95, 93.3.
 Tarsus 20.5–21, 20.7. Culmen 14.5.
♀♀ (6) Wing 119–126, 122.2.

Lipaugus cryptolophus – Olivaceous Piha
Lipaugus subalaris – Grey-tailed Piha

These two Andean species are very alike in
appearance and overlap broadly in their ranges
(Map 21). *L. subalaris* has a grey tail and bright
yellow under-wing coverts, *L. cryptolophus* a green-
edged tail and duller under-wing coverts. Both
sexes of *cryptolophus* have the semi-concealed black
crown-patch, but only the male of *subalaris*. The two
species are very similar in size, but *cryptolophus* has
relatively long legs compared with *subalaris* and
other *Lipaugus* species. It also has a somewhat
narrower bill, so that one may suspect that it has
different feeding behaviour; but nothing has been
recorded of their food or feeding habits. They are
very little known birds, living in the humid upper
tropical and subtropical zones of the Andean forests
where observation is especially difficult.

 L. cryptolophus has much the more extensive
range, occurring in both the Eastern and the
Western Andes of Colombia and Ecuador and south
to about 10°S in Peru. *L. subalaris* has been found
only in the Eastern Andes of Ecuador and in one
locality in Peru at about 10° 40'S. Its range thus
lies, as far as known, largely within that of
cryptolophus, but it is unlikely that the range of either

is at all completely known. Information on the
altitudes at which they are found is scanty, records
being as follows:

L. cryptolophus	Head of Magdalena Valley, Colombia	2000–2300 m
	Western Andes, Colombia	570–2000 m
	Western Andes, Ecuador	1230–1700 m
	Southern Ecuador	620–1750 m
	Peru	1540 m
L. subalaris	Eastern Andes, Ecuador	850–1350 m

 Little can be said of the behaviour of either species.
Dr Steven Hilty has observed the Olivaceous Piha on
a number of occasions in the Andes of Colombia,
but has seen nothing to suggest that this species
displays in leks. 'All observations of this bird have
been of singles, although I have suspected pairs, and
have seen 2–3 birds at fruiting trees.'

Physical characters

Unfeathered parts
Similar in both species, and in both sexes.
Iris: dark brown.
Bill: dark horn, paler at base of lower mandible.
Legs and feet: grey.

Geographical variation
Reported only in *L. cryptolophus*. Birds from the west
slopes of the western Andes of Ecuador and Colombia
(*mindoensis*) may be slightly smaller than other
populations (wing-lengths of males 125–126 mm,
cf. 130–132 mm for other populations according to
Hellmayr (1929); but larger series show that
measurements range up to 130 mm), and the
concealed bases of the black crest feathers are
extensively creamy white (brown in other populations).

Measurements
L. cryptolophus
L. c. mindoensis ♂♂ (6) Wing 125–130, 127.7.
 Tail 97–100, 98.8 Tarsus 24.5–25, 24.8. Cul-
 men 15–15.5, 15.3.
L. c. cryptolophus (from Hellmayr 1929) ♂♀ Wing
 130–132. Tail 105–113.
L. subalaris
♂♂ (5) Wing 124–133, 128.0. Tail 98–101, 99.5.
 Tarsus 21–22, 21.3. Culmen 14–15.5, 14.9.
♀♀ (4) Wing 124–133, 129.0. Tail 96–109, 102.8.
 Tarsus 21–22, 21.5. Culmen 13–15, 14.3.
Weights: 1 ♂ 86.3 g.
  2 ♀♀ 82.0, 81.8 g (wings 129, 130 mm).

Genus Chirocylla

Plate 15, page 116

Chirocylla uropygialis – Scimitar-winged Piha

When Sclater & Salvin (1876) described this still almost unknown bird, they placed it in the genus *Lathria* (= *Lipaugus*), suggesting that its uniquely modified primaries entitle it to rank as a subgenus, for which they proposed the name *Chirocylla*. Later Sclater elevated it to a genus and this treatment, which has been generally followed, is justified by the fact that far too little is known about it to give confidence that it is really close to *Lipaugus*, though certainly it superficially resembles the Dusky Piha *Lipaugus fuscocinereus* in colour, size and general proportions.

The outstanding character of this bird is the modification of the primaries in the male, which are attenuated, strongly recurved terminally, and unusually graduated in length. They are described in more detail below, under Structure. In the female, the modifications are only slightly developed.

Distribution (Map 22)

Chirocylla uropygialis appears to be confined to Bolivia, where it has been found in a few localities in the 'Yungas', the humid, heavily forested subtropical eastern slopes of the Andes. Recorded altitudes are all between 2000 and 2500 m.

Habitat and food

Almost nothing is known. Niethammer (1956), in the most recent report of the species, wrote that it was local and uncommon, and was found singly in the rain forest. The stomach contents of the only bird collected consisted of berries and tree fruits.

Breeding and annual cycle

Nothing is known, except that two males have been collected in wing-moult, one on 27 July in a late stage of moult (primaries 9 and 10 old, rest new) and the other on 23 November in an early stage (primaries 1–3 new and growing, rest old).

Plumages and moults

Nothing is known of the succession of plumages.

Physical characters

Structure
Bill similar to *Lipaugus*; rictal bristles well developed. Legs and feet rather slender, tarsus short. Primaries as follows: p 1 unmodified; p 2–4 nearly equal in length, pointed at extremity and slightly recurved; p 5–8 each progressively shorter than the preceding one, 6–8 strikingly attenuated, 5 intermediate in form between 4 and 6; p. 9 and 10 longest of the series (9 about 12 mm longer than 8), attenuated and recurved as shown in Fig. 6.

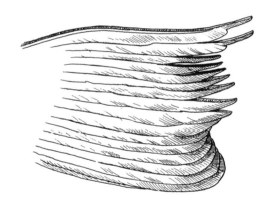

Figure 6 Wing of *Chirocylla uropygialis*, from below (redrawn from Sclater & Salvin 1876).

Unfeathered parts
Sexes similar.
Iris: red-brown.
Bill: black, dark horn below.
Legs and feet: plumbeous.

Measurements
♂♂ (2)   Wing 141, 145.
♀ (1)   Wing 153.
Unsexed, probably ♂♂ (3)   Wing 137–139, 138.0.
    Tail 137–143, 140.0.   Tarsus 18–19, 18.7.   Culmen 31–31.5, 31.2.
Weight: 1 ♂ 116 g (wing 145 mm).

MWWoodcock

Genus Conioptilon

Conioptilon mcilhennyi – Black-faced Cotinga

(by John W. Fitzpatrick)

The single member of this, the most recently described cotingid genus escaped discovery by ornithologists until 1965, and continues to be known only from two localities in the Amazonian forests of southeastern Peru. In size and general conformation, *Conioptilon* most closely resembles *Carpodectes*, but it differs from this and nearly all other cotingid genera in possessing abundant patches of powderdown distributed over much of the body between contour feather tracts. A powdery white bloom also appears on the pale grey to whitish contour feathers themselves, and on the otherwise black remiges and rectrices (as in *Gymnoderus*). The jet-black throat, face and crown includes numerous elongate feathers on which the rachis tip is shiny, hardened and free of barbs. Females are slightly smaller than males, but otherwise the sexes are identical. The genus seems to represent an ancient phylogenetic link between *Carpodectes* and *Gymnoderus* (Snow 1973a), and is now almost certainly restricted to extreme southwestern Amazonia near the Andean foothills.

Distribution (Map 22)

Conioptilon mcilhennyi has been collected only at the type locality (Balta), on the Río Curanja in extreme southern Depto. Loreto, Peru, where parties from Louisiana State University collected fifteen specimens on two separate trips in 1964 and 1965 (Lowery & O'Neill 1966). The only other known locality is the vicinity of the upper Manu River, Depto. Madre de Dios, Peru, about 210 km due south of Balta. At this second locality researchers from Princeton University and the Field Museum of Natural History have found the bird to be rather common and easily seen. Based on habitat distribution and the known ranges of other southern Peruvian endemics, *Conioptilon* most likely occurs throughout the lowland tropical forests of southeastern Peru and immediately adjacent Brazil and possibly into Bolivia, where appropriate premontane Amazonian habitat exists.

Ecology and behaviour

Along the Río Manu, the Black-faced Cotinga is invariably found high in the forest canopy. It appears to favour swampy and seasonally inundated

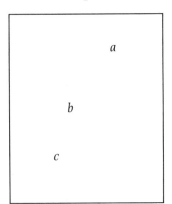

Plate 16
a: Black-faced Cotinga *Conioptilon mcilhennyi*
b and c: Bare-necked Fruit-crow *Gymnoderus foetidus*, male and female

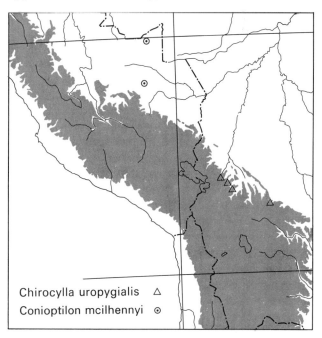

Chirocylla uropygialis △
Conioptilon mcilhennyi ⊙

Map 22 Distribution of the Scimitar-winged Piha (*Chirocylla uropygialis*) and Black-faced Cotinga (*Conioptilon mcilhennyi*).

125

forest habitats, to the virtual exclusion of high-ground forest. I encountered the bird most frequently in portions of the forest or forest edge where floods and swampy undergrowth result in a shorter, broken and somewhat more open canopy than is typical of forest on dry ground. During a two month period in October and November, 1976, I noted each sighting of *Conioptilon* during my daily routines, which included intensive study in all habitats characteristic of this river-bottom locality. Of 39 different encounters, all were in the canopy. These encounters broke down as follows: 8 (21%) sightings in low, *Cecropia*-dominated river margin habitat, 9 (23%) in the adjacent and taller, *Ficus*-dominated forest zone, 11 (28%) in open, seasonally inundated older forest, 9 (23%) along the open, broken canopy of an oxbow lake margin, and only 2 (5%) in true high-ground forest sites.

Although swampy lake and river margins are preferred along the upper Manu, the Black-faced Cotinga appears to be absent from the vast expanses of this habitat along the flood plains of larger, faster flowing rivers in southeastern Peru. Many ornithologists have explored the forested banks of the Río Madre de Dios, from near its headwaters downstream 180 km to the vicinity of Puerto Maldonado. Even those familiar with its distinctive call around the Río Manu fail to find the species along the Alto Madre de Dios only 60 km away. It seems likely, therefore, that the Black-faced Cotinga is restricted to river margin habitats along small, meandering tributaries, quite upstream from the larger rivers. This may explain why the bird escaped collectors for so many years.

Fruit seems to comprise the greater part of the diet of the Black-faced Cotinga, although the only stomach content record is one individual full of winged myrmecine ants, presumably taken during a reproductive swarm (Lowery & O'Neill 1966).

At both known localities, *Conioptilon* is a regular member of mixed species assemblages around fruiting trees, especially the large *Ficus* spp. Lowery and O'Neill (1966) report seeing it 'associated in the same trees with *Gymnoderus foetidus*, *Gymnostinops yuracares*, *Selenidera reinwardtii langsdorfii*, *Capito niger*, and various tanagers and parakeets.' Along the Manu, in the large fruiting trees, we find it associating with *Cotinga maynana*, *Porphyrolaema porphyrolaema*, *Querula purpurata*, three species of *Tityra*, and a host of Psittacidae, Ramphastidae, Capitonidae, Turdidae, and Thraupidae (Terborgh, Fitzpatrick & Emmons, *in press*). I once watched a pair of Black-faced Cotingas consuming portions of large red flowers on an emergent tree near the margin of the river. Rarely, possibly only acci-dentally, it can be heard amongst the roving, tightly organized canopy flocks of small Tyrannidae, Vireonidae, and Thraupidae. Most frequently, however, *Conioptilon* travels in pairs or trios away from mixed species assemblages. In these situations the birds betray their presence with noisy calling as they fly from tree to tree overhead. In this respect, and even in the quality of the calls, the behaviour of *Conioptilon* resembles that of *Querula purpurata*.

The most frequently heard and easily recognized call of the Black-faced Cotinga bears a remarkable similarity to the common, ascending whistle given by the Smooth-billed Ani *Crotophaga ani*. Although we even confused the two voices for a time, that of *Conioptilon* actually is a more ringing and prolonged version, usually with a distinct vibrato in the accented, rising note: *whil-déeeee-e-e* or *who, méee-ee?* Several birds frequently give this call simultaneously. During typical calling bouts, this loud, ringing call is given every 15 to 20 seconds, and they are interspersed with numerous, softly whistled, two-syllable contact notes: *purr-o . . . purr-o, purr-o . . .*

Breeding and annual cycle

No evidence as to courtship display or nesting behaviour has yet been found. The strongly seasonal climate of the southern Peruvian Amazon suggests a breeding season from September to December. This is the peak nesting period for most forest passerines around the Río Manu, and also corresponds to a strong peak in fruit abundance within the forest (unpubl. data).

Plumages and moults

One specimen among the paratypes appears to be a subadult female. 'In this specimen the black feathers of the head, the feathers of the upper breast, the upper tail coverts, and the greater secondary coverts are narrowly tipped with white; the basal halves of the inner webs of the secondaries, both above and below, are broadly edged with white, and the under tail coverts are noticeably barred subterminally with pale gray' (Lowery & O'Neill 1966, pp. 5–6).

Physical characters

Structure

Bill wide at base, culmen rounded, slightly hooked at tip. Rictal and interramal bristles well developed. Legs and feet moderately strong. White powderdown abundant throughout all apteria of body, lacking on head; remiges and rectrices also showing powdery bloom on dorsal surfaces, also present on contour feathers. Scattered feathers on chin and crown with hardened, shiny carotenous tips to the rachis.

Unfeathered parts
Iris: dark reddish brown in adults.
Bill: dark, greyish brown.
Legs and feet: olive grey (Lowery & O'Neill 1966).

Measurements (from Lowery & O'Neill 1966)
♂♂ (3)   Wing chord 146–153, 148.7.   Tail 93–96, 94.5.   Tarsus 23.4–25.8, 25.1.   Culmen (exposed) 16.5–18.3, 17.2.
♀♀ (9)   Wing chord 139–143, 141.0.   Tail 90–96, 91.8.   Tarsus 23.3–24.8, 24.1.   Culmen (exposed) 16.0–17.6, 16.8.

Genus *Gymnoderus*

Plate 16, page 124

Gymnoderus foetidus – Bare-necked Fruit-crow

The Bare-necked Fruit-crow, the only member of its genus, is very distinct from all other members of its family. It is a large cotinga, most strikingly distinguished by the extensive bare areas on its head and neck which grade in colour from white to cobalt blue, the feathered parts of the head being covered with short velvety black plumage. In life the dark parts of the body plumage have a grey bloom derived from patches of powder-down on the flanks. The female is considerably smaller than the male and has the secondaries and upper wing-coverts concolorous with the rest of the upper plumage instead of pale grey.

The genus appears to be very isolated. Warter (1965) placed it in a subfamily of its own, Gymnoderinae (following Salvin & Godman (1891)), largely on the basis of its aberrant plumage characters; in skull structure he found it to be closer to *Cotinga* than to the other large fruit-crows. Its closest relative is perhaps *Conioptilon*, which was undiscovered when Warter wrote (Lowery & O'Neill 1966). Powder-down is also developed extensively in *Conioptilon* (and to a lesser extent also in a few other cotinga genera). In syringeal structure *Gymnoderus* is similar to *Conioptilon* and the other large fruit-crows (Ames 1971).

Distribution (Map 23)

The species is widespread in the lowland forests of Amazonia, extending in the north to the upper Orinoco and the Guiana forests, and in the south to the upper Paraguai drainage in central Mato Grosso. It appears not to be generally distributed in the forests but to be found mainly along rivers and lake edges. Locally at least it is of seasonal occurrence, apparently being present when the fruits on which it feeds are available. In the Napo region of eastern Ecuador the Indians call it the 'para-anera' (the guan which appears every year) and it is said to migrate in enormous flocks, flying high. For Amazonian Colombia, Hilty (MS) notes that it is most often seen flying very high across large rivers or other large open spaces. In Surinam it appears during the long dry season (August–October) in coastal areas where it is absent at other times (Haverschmidt 1968).

Ecology

Almost nothing is known of the Bare-necked Fruit-crow's ecology. Several collectors and observers in Amazonia have reported that it is found along the forested banks of rivers and lakes, where it may be plentiful, and from this it seems likely that its chief food may be the fruit of some kind of waterside tree. The observation by Novaes (1980) of a single bird eating the fruit of a 'bacaba' palm (*Oenocarpus* sp., probably *O. baccaba*) seems to be the only record of the identity of the fruits that it feeds on. Schubart *et al.* (1965) record that the stomach of a specimen contained three seeds each weighing 13 g; data accompanying museum specimens include references to fruit and seeds in stomach contents. In addition to fruits, large insects are taken — Haverschmidt records Mantidae and Locustidae. The species is thoroughly arboreal, usually keeping high in the trees, but Naumburg (1930) reported that a specimen collected in Mato Grosso was flushed from the ground beneath a tree bearing a berry-like fruit.

Behaviour

Little of significance seems to have been recorded. Haverschmidt (1968) writes that the Bare-necked Fruit-crow lives in small flocks high up in trees, and runs over thick branches like a rail. Added to the fact that its beak does not seem well adapted to plucking fruits in flight, this suggests that fruits are taken from a perched position and not in flight as they are by most other cotingas.

Penard & Penard (1910), the only authors to mention the bird's voice, describe its call as *moe, moe*.

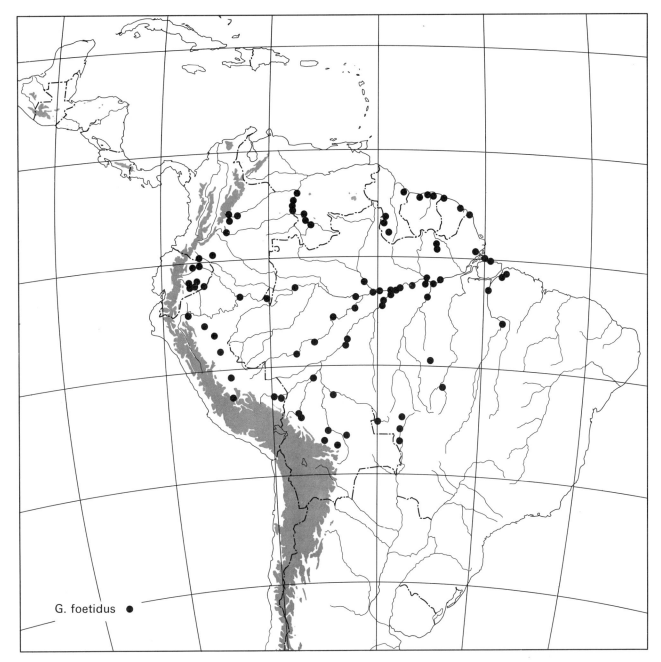

Map 23   Distribution of the Bare-necked Fruit-crow (*Gymnoderus foetidus*).

Breeding and annual cycle

Sick (1957) mentions seeing a Bare-necked Fruit-crow on a nest in the crown of a *Caryocar brasiliensis* tree (Butter Nut or Souari Nut), in the source region of the upper Xingú in October 1947. No details of the nest are given, except that nest material that had fallen to the ground included a few dry twigs strikingly coated with a white fungus.

The only other record of nesting is by Béraut (1970), who found two nests in northern Mato Grosso, of which one was being built at the end of January and the other had a chick which hatched on 2 December. 'The nest, which is placed on a thick horizontal branch (of about 15 cm diameter) at a height of 6–10 m, is very small for a bird the size of *Gymnoderus*. Its diameter does not exceed 10 cm and its height 3 cm, and it is in the form of a loose cup, the bottom of the nest being formed by the branch itself. It is entirely composed of lichens and the fine tendrils of some climbing plant which is white, probably because of a fungal growth. But what is most interesting is that the nest could not possibly hold more than a single chick, and it seems impossible for the female to cover the egg with her feet inside the nest. She must place them at either side. When she is incubating she appears to be perched on the branch, and the nest is invisible.' Béraut further reports that he never noted the presence of a male near the nest.

The three records cited above, all from the southern extreme of the range of the species, suggest that egg-laying takes place from September or October to February, which coincides well with the general breeding season in Mato Grosso given by Allen (1891) as September–March. It seems that the onset of the moult takes place at the same time: for all but 3 of 26 specimens in wing moult from the southern part of the range (southern Peru, Bolivia, Mato Grosso) the calculated dates of onset of moult are from October to March, the dates for the two sexes being similar.

The moult data from elsewhere suggest that the annual cycle becomes progressively later as one moves to the north, as is general in the family. Thus in the middle and lower Amazon valley, from Manaus to the Belém area, the calculated dates of onset of moult for 55 out of 70 specimens are in the months December–May, and for 7 of the rather small sample of 10 moulting specimens from the Guianas and Venezuela the calculated dates are in the months February–May.

The complete moult probably takes about 190 days in the individual (Snow 1976a). With such a protracted moult a random sample of specimens would be expected to contain just over half in wing-moult, and this expectation is fulfilled almost exactly: out of 229 adult specimens examined, 118 were undergoing a wing-moult.

Plumages and moults

Béraut (1970) hand-reared a young bird which he obtained from one of the nests mentioned above, and describes the nestling as follows: 'The nestling is most remarkable, as it is invisible in the nest, and appears to be made of lichens. The skin is a violaceous grey-black, but as early as the fourth day it is covered with very short tufts of pale grey-green curly down which exactly resembles lichen.'

The nestling down is replaced by a juvenile plumage which must be almost as striking when fully developed, but it too is apparently soon replaced, on the head and body, by a darker, predominantly grey-black immature plumage. This, at least, seems the most likely explanation of the

fact that I have examined a considerable number of specimens partly in juvenile plumage but none entirely in juvenile plumage; in all, the juvenile head and body plumage had been superseded partly or entirely by feathers of the next generation. The juvenile feathers are mainly or entirely white (body feathers and coverts) or grey with white tips (secondaries and rectrices), with one to three narrow and somewhat irregular subterminal dark bands and (on the larger feathers) a variable amount of dark speckling. These feathers are looser in texture than the darker feathers that supersede them.

The predominantly white juvenile plumage is replaced on the head and body by a sooty immature plumage, uniform above and with whitish feather edges below. A few juvenile upper tail-coverts tend to persist, and the juvenile upper wing-coverts are retained longer still. The first moult of the flight feathers leads to a more advanced immature plumage in which the secondaries are dark grey with broad pale edges and the rectrices blackish. The replacement of the juvenile wing-coverts by all-dark feathers begins at about this time but seems to be variable.

The second moult of the flight feathers leads to a plumage which, in the female, is hardly distinct from the adult; in the male it leads to a subadult plumage in which the grey of the secondaries and upper wing coverts is darker than in the adults and peppered with dusky speckling. At the third wing moult these feathers are replaced by pale, clear grey feathers of fully adult type.

Physical characters

Structure
Beak of moderate size, less stout and more flattened dorso-ventrally than in other large fruit-crows. Rictal bristles absent. Feet and legs strong; legs relatively short. Flight feathers unmodified, secondaries relatively long and broad. Large powderdown patches on flanks. Parts of sides of head and most of neck unfeathered, bare skin at sides of neck extended into elaborate folds in adult male (Goodfellow 1901). Feathering of feathered parts of head dense, short and velvet-like.

Unfeathered parts
Descriptions of the adult's eye colour are discrepant. Several collectors give it as grey or plumbeous, and one as greyish cream. Goodfellow (1901), however, specifically stated that the eye colour of an adult male from eastern Ecuador, which he described in detail and figured, was 'dark crimson', and the eye colours of two specimens that he collected on a later

expedition, in Bolivia, are given on his labels as 'deep red' (a subadult male) and 'dark red' (a female). This might suggest geographical variation in eye colour, since most other records are from more easterly parts of the species' range; but the eye of a female from Madre de Dios in Peru (between Ecuador and Bolivia) is recorded as greyish cream. The eye colour of a juvenile collected in Bolivia is given as dark brown ('cafe obscuro'). More data are needed to resolve this discrepancy.

Bill basally grey, black at tip. Legs and feet leaden grey. Skin of nestling violaceous grey-black (Béraut, *loc. cit.*). Bare skin of adult (including abdominal skin) mainly cobalt blue, grading to grey or whitish — degree of development of blue perhaps dependent on age and sex.

Geographical variation
None substantiated. Friedmann (1948) noted that a subadult male from the upper Orinoco had a shorter wing than a male from the Amazon and another from eastern Peru, but such a difference might be attributable to age. Measurements of adult males from Peru, Ecuador, the lower Amazon and the Guianas indicate no consistent geographical differences. (The wing measurements given by Haverschmidt (1968) — 187–196 mm — refer to females only (Haverschmidt, pers. comm.).)

Measurements
♂♂ (10) Wing 205–223, 211.7. Tail 125–140, 133.6. Tarsus 18–20.5, 19.3. Culmen 32–34, 32.7.
♀♀ (13) Wing 185–198, 192.1. Tail 119–130, 124.5. Tarsus 18–20, 18.8. Culmen 28.5–30, 29.4.
Weights: 3 ♂♂ 331–359, 343.3 g (mean wing-length 212.7 mm).

Genus Querula

Plate 17, page 142

Querula purpurata – Purple-throated Fruit-crow

The affinities of this genus are obscure. The black plumage, relieved only by the crimson throat (not purple, in spite of its name), suggests a relationship to *Pyroderus*, but the resemblance is almost certainly misleading; *Pyroderus* is without doubt more closely related to *Cephalopterus*. On the basis of syringeal structure Ames (1971) links *Querula* and *Carpodectes*, but these two genera differ markedly in most other respects and *Carpodectes* is much more likely to be related to *Xipholena* (see p. 99). *Querula* thus remains, like so many others in the family, an isolated genus of uncertain systematic position.

Purple-throated Fruit-crows are rather large cotingas, agile in flight and highly social. They are forest birds, living in closely knit groups with a social organization that seems to be unique in the family. Although the species is geographically one of the most widespread of the family and in some areas is quite common, it remains little known. Much of what follows is derived from a 3-month study made in southern Guyana in 1970 (Snow 1971c).

Distribution (Map 24)

The species ranges throughout much of the tropical forest zone of South America, extending into Central America as far as Costa Rica.

In Costa Rica it occurs only in the humid forests of the Caribbean slope, not quite reaching the Nicaraguan border. In Panama it is found along the whole length of the Caribbean side, but on the Pacific side only from the Canal Zone eastward, being absent from the drier forests to the west. In adjacent parts of Colombia it extends throughout the humid forested parts of the middle Cauca and Magdalena valleys and down the Pacific coast into northwestern Ecuador. This western section of the species is totally isolated from the main South American populations, which extend through most of the Amazonian and Guianan forest region, south in the west to northern Bolivia and in the east to the middle reaches of the great southern tributaries of the Amazon.

As Purple-throated Fruit-crows are fairly conspicuous birds and have been collected in considerable numbers, the lack of any records from a large area in northwestern Brazil, eastern Colombia and southern Venezuela seems to indicate a major gap in its range, for which there is no obvious explanation. The area in question embraces the Rio Negro, the upper Orinoco, and the forests along the eastern base of the Andes from the Sierra Macarena northwards. On the other hand, the absence of this species from the forests of northern Venezuela is less surprising, as these forests lack many other typically Amazonian species.

Ecology

Purple-throated Fruit-crows are birds of the tree-tops and the middle levels of the forest, seldom coming to less than about 10 m from the ground. In the area where I studied them, in the Kanuku Mountains of southern Guyana, the group of birds with which I became most familiar, consisting of four individuals, ranged over a strip of forest about 250 m long, mainly along a stream where the vegetation was luxuriant. They seemed not to move far up the slopes on either side of the narrow valley, where the forest was drier and poorer. A neighbouring group, consisting of three birds, occupied a stretch of valley at least 350 m long. We never saw any interaction between these two groups, which most of the time stayed well apart from each other. On a 4-km walk through valley-bottom forest, most of which seemed to be suitable for fruit-crows, I regularly passed within sight or sound of four or five groups. These groups, which were only casually watched, also consisted of 3–4 birds, but in other areas groups are larger. Chapman (1929) reported parties of 6–8 birds in Panama, and Olivares (1958) mentioned bands of 4–6 birds in Colombia.

Purple-throated Fruit-crows usually feed in the manner typical of cotingas – by seizing their food, both fruits and insects, in flight; but those that I watched in Guyana regularly perched to pluck the

Map 24   Distribution of the Purple-throated Fruit-crow (*Querula purpurata*).

fruits of two trees, *Didymopanax morototoni* and *Guarea trichilioides*, both of which bear their fruits in large bunches on strong stalks that afford a foothold. They search for insects also in typical cotinga fashion, by perching quietly and scanning the vegetation around them, often bending low, twisting the neck, and turning the head. In 81 observations of fruit-crows taking food in Guyana the fruit-eating records were 2½ times as numerous as the insect-eating; but these figures are undoubtedly biased, as fruit-eating was much easier to see and record once we had got to know the main fruit trees in the area. They took fruits most often round the middle of the day, perhaps because they needed liquid at this time.

We saw fruit-crows eating eight different kinds of fruits during an 11-week period (17 January to 3

April). These eight were certainly the main ones taken at this time in our study area, since all but three of the many regurgitated seeds collected in a tray placed beneath a nest (see below) were from trees at which we saw the birds feeding. Four main fruits together accounted for 90% of the fruit-eating records: *Didymopanax morototoni* (Araliaceae), *Guarea trichilioides* (Meliaceae), *Hirtella* sp. (Chrysobalanaceae) and a species of Lauraceae. In addition they fed on the fruit of another species of Lauraceae, *Cecropia* sp. (Urticaceae), and two unidentified trees. The largest fruits recorded were lauraceous, measuring 27 × 15 mm.

Other published information on identified food of this species is as follows. Of six stomach contents recorded by Schubart *et al.* (1965) from Brazil, all contained both fruit and insect remains except one which contained only a quantity of beetles (Melolonthidae). The insects in the other stomachs included Orthoptera, Hemiptera, Lepidoptera (imagines), Coleoptera (Chrysomelidae, Curculionidae) and ants (Formicidae); also a spider. The only fruit identified was *Cecropia* sp. For Surinam, Haverschmidt (1968) mentions Orthoptera (Gryllidae) and a species of ant, *Cephalotes atratus*. In Panama, Howe & De Steven (1979) and Howe (1980) report that Purple-throated Fruit-crows eat the arillate fruit of *Guarea glabra*, the seeds being defaecated intact, and the fruit of *Heisteria costaricensis* (Olacaceae).

Behaviour

Groups of Purple-throated Fruit-crows are closely integrated social units which not only move around, feed, and rest together, but also jointly attend a single nest. That they also spend the night together is indicated by an observation by F. Gary Stiles, who found a group of them in Costa Rica roosting side by side in close contact with one another. The group consisted of five birds, one adult male (purple-throated) and four females or young males (black-throated). Over a period of four days (19–22 July) they roosted on a thin horizontal branch of a small *Compsoneura* tree, about 30 feet up; on 24 July and subsequent nights they were not present, having apparently changed their roost.

The only other information on the composition of these social units comes from our Guyana study. The group that I watched in most detail consisted of four birds: two adult males, a female (which was nesting) and a bird of unknown sex. This last bird was in female plumage except for two red feathers on one side of its throat. The neighbouring group consisted of a male and two females. A third group

consisted of two males and one or two females. Members of a group maintain contact with one another by frequent, at times almost continuous, calling which normally ceases only when all members of the group perch close together, resting. The social bonds between individuals in a group are extremely close, and there is almost no aggression between them. In the group that was watched most closely, the two males maintained a stronger social bond with each other than with the nesting female. They often perched side by side, sometimes almost touching, and occasionally preened each other. One of the males (Male A) was the dominant bird, or more appropriately, as there was no aggression, the 'leader' of the group. When the group moved from place to place it was this bird that initiated the move. He associated with the nesting female more closely than did the other male (Male B), and he attended the nest more assiduously. The fourth bird, of unknown sex, was the most detached of the group. It nearly always trailed behind the others when the group moved, and tended to perch a little apart from the others. Its unobtrusive behaviour may have been partly due to the fact that it was in wing moult during nearly the whole of the period of observation.

The usual call, uttered repeatedly whenever the birds are active, is a mellow, disyllabic *oo-waa*, delivered with the beak closed and the throat feathers more or less fanned. This is the call that gives the bird its many local names — 'ter-wo' in the Kanuku Mountains and 'cuaba' in western Colombia (Olivares 1958). When uttering this call, the bird typically leans forward nearly horizontally and shivers its partly fanned tail with a curious side-to-side movement which, as Chapman (1929) remarked, gives the impression that it is shaking water out of its tail feathers. It frequently intersperses the disyllabic call with a monosyllabic, more drawn-out *wooo* with an upward inflection.

The vocal repertoire also includes a variety of harsher calls uttered with the beak open. Frequently, when the birds are feeding or moving about together, one of the group gives a sharp *wak* or *wak-wak*, apparently a signal serving to alert the other birds but not in a situation of serious alarm. When truly alarmed, they call with a considerably louder, harsher and more arresting version of the *wak-wak*, usually of several syllables.

We saw courtship display on only one occasion, when Male A began to try to entice the female away from the nest which she was building to a new nest site which he had chosen. He followed her persistently in short flights among the tree tops, calling repeatedly, spreading his throat-fan widely and shivering his tail. Later when showing the female the new site that he had chosen, he behaved in the same way. The only copulation we saw occurred on a different occasion, almost certainly involved other birds, and was preceded by no special ceremony.

Breeding and annual cycle

Breeding

There are few published references to nests of the Purple-throated Fruit-crow. Ellis (1952) watched a male and female cooperating in building a nest about 75 feet (23 m) up in a tree at the edge of a clearing on Barro Colorado Island, Panama. Later a female was seen incubating, but no further details could be obtained. Haverschmidt (1968) found a bird sitting on a nest 20 m up in a leafless tree on the edge of a forest in Surinam, and on another occasion watched a male building. The nests described by both Ellis and Haverschmidt were insubstantial, open cups. The reference by Olivares (1958) to the nest of this species seems to be based on a mis-identification; he states that the nest is built at no great height and that two whitish eggs are laid (in fact all undoubted nests have been high, and the egg is extremely dark). Merizalde de Abuja (1975), writing of the species in western Ecuador, gives no details of the nest but reports an incubation period of 17 days and a fledging period of 16 days — both much too short — and implies that the family size is at least two, which is also questionable. Here too a misidentification must be suspected.

Nests and nest building. We found two nests in our Guyana study area. The first was 35 feet (11 m) up, very near the top of a slender tree beside a forest trail. It was a loose cup, consisting partly of twigs and partly of dry fruiting panicles of a vine (*Sparattanthelium wonotoboense*) which hung down in sprays from the top of a neighbouring tree. These had been incorporated into the nest in such a way that the seed-heads hung down in a fringe around the bottom of the nest. The fork, from which several fine branches grew obliquely upwards, afforded good support for the apparently rather weak nest structure. When first found, on 19 January, the main structure of the nest was complete but the lining was unfinished. Nest-building continued intermittently for 26 days. Only the female brought material, but Male A was seen to sit in the nest and shape it several times; once he stayed on it for 4 minutes. I never saw him bring material to the nest, but once he picked a twig from a tree near by and dropped it. Once Male B also picked and dropped a piece of the fruiting vine that was such a conspicuous part of the nest structure. I never saw Male B on the

nest, but he often perched near it; and I never saw the fourth bird of the group do any building, but once it pecked at the material hanging below the nest and then perched just above the nest, looking down into it, while the female, just returned with nest material, waited on a perch near by. I saw no aggression between any of the members of the group at the nest; on every occasion, if one was there first, the other simply waited quietly not far away. The material brought to the nest for the lining consisted mainly of the very fine terminal twigs of an abundant under-storey tree (Myrtaceae sp.), with a smaller proportion of fine terminal twigs of another abundant small tree (*Rinorea brevipes*). The twigs of the myrtaceous tree, which are very fine, tough and springy, and branch obliquely at short intervals, were also used in the lining of the second nest.

There was a long delay between the finding of the nest and the laying of the egg. For a few days the female appeared to lose interest in it, and then she began to visit other possible sites, including a fork in a high branch of a huge mora tree (*Mora excelsa*) about 100 m away. Male A always took the initiative, flying to the mora branch and calling from it. The female followed, alighting in a particular fork where she sat, calling and making settling movements. It appeared that the male was dis-satisfied with the original nest-site; possibly the mora site, about 75 feet (23 m) up, was nearer the preferred height. Eventually, however, the female began to take material again to her original nest, and she laid a single egg in the early morning of 17 February or during the preceding night. The egg was visible through the bottom of the nest cup, which after four weeks of desultory lining still let through chinks of light.

Our observations at the second nest (which failed soon after incubation began) were less com-plete. This nest we found by following the group (a male and two females) when they were building. We had seen the two females collecting twigs from a tree — the same myrtaceous tree that was used for the lining of the first nest — about 100 m from their nest site. We saw only one female, however, go to the nest with material, and it seemed probable that the other was picking material and dropping it. The male went regularly onto the nest and on one occasion sat for 2 minutes while the female waited on a perch just below. This second nest was about 70 feet (22 m) up in a tree about 30 m high, on sloping ground in forest where there was no closed canopy but a rather open growth of large but mainly slender trees. It was similar to the first nest except that it had no hanging fringe of *Sparattanthelium* panicles, and was placed in the same kind of fork.

These observations on nest-building differ slightly from the reports of Ellis (1952) and Haverschmidt (1968). At the nest watched by Ellis the male brought material and the female did the building; the details of their co-operation are not described. Haverschmidt briefly mentioned a male building a nest, without further details. All the observations agree, however, in showing that the male is actively concerned in the building of the nest. His exact role may well be variable. Since we did not see the building of the main structure of either of our nests it may be that the males built or helped to build the outer cup, leaving the females to do the lining.

Incubation and fledging. As mentioned above, the egg was laid in our first nest in the early morning of 17 February (or during the preceding night). The female left the nest at 07.00 hours; 15 minutes later all four birds came to the nest, and in the minute that elapsed before the female settled onto the egg both males looked into the nest while the fourth bird perched above it in a position from which the egg must have been visible. Thus within a short time of the egg being laid all members of the group almost certainly saw it.

The routine of incubation remained much the same throughout the period. Only the female incubated, sitting on the nest for about two-thirds of the time between her first departure from the nest in the morning (at 06.50–07.12 hours) and her final return to the nest in the late afternoon (at 17.18–17.45 hours, once 16.35). Her absences from the nest were of rather uniform duration, half of them being for 12–17 minutes (maximum 31, minimum 4); her sessions on varied from $\frac{1}{2}$ minute to 75 minutes. Early in the incubation period, the female's departures from the nest were usually stimulated by the other fruit-crows in the group. After a period of perching quietly near the nest they would grow restless, begin to call, and then fly off to feed, whereupon the female would leave the nest and join them. Later, her departures seemed more often spontaneous in that she left when the others were silent or out of sight. Several times she left the nest to join the others in mobbing an intruder. Just as during nest-building, all four birds normally returned to the nest together, Male A leading.

Throughout the incubation period, we could see the egg against the sky through the bottom of the nest cup when the female was off. The first sign of hatching was on the afternoon of 11 March, when she appeared very restless. She left the nest and returned to it at short intervals, and at times stood looking down into it and turning her head sideways.

Later events suggested that she was beginning to hear the chick call inside the shell. On 12 and 13 March, she was more settled and the egg was still visible in the nest. Then at 06.45 on 14 March, after 25 days of incubation, half the eggshell was lying beneath the nest. It was exceedingly dark, with a deep olive ground colour thickly covered with blackish-brown markings.

On the day it hatched, the female brooded the chick for over 90% of the time during the morning, but for only 38% of an hour's watch in the late afternoon. Over the next three weeks she spent increasingly less time on the nest. Morning watches of 2 hours or more, when the chick was aged, 2, 6, 9, 12, 14, 17 and 21 days gave the following percentages of time on the nest: 77, 60, 30, 18, 16, 9 and 3. She spent less time on the nest in the afternoons. After the chick was a few days old it was regularly left uncovered during light or moderate rain.

All four adults brought food to the nest, but in unequal amounts. From 20 March, when the chick was 6 days old, until observations finished on 4 April, I recorded 78 visits with food by the two males, and 16 by the female. I saw the fourth bird of the group go to the nest with food only once. In the course of watches when a special effort was made to distinguish the males at all their visits to the nest (Male B had lost a central tail feather and the gap could be seen from below), Male A made 36 and Male B 13 visits. The following routine was usually maintained. Just as Male A flew in with food, followed by the two other members of the group, the female left the nest. Male A then went to the nest, while the other two birds perched near by. When Male A left the nest, Male B, if he had food as he did on a minority of occasions, flew to the nest and delivered it, and then all four birds flew off together, Male A leading. One or both of the males sometimes returned again with food while the female was still off the nest; then after a few minutes the female returned, perhaps fed the chick herself, and settled down to brood again.

The chick was fed almost entirely on insects. Cicadas, katydids, mantids and moths were recognisable, together with many other adult, winged insects and small numbers of insect larvae. All the large insects were held with the head pointing forward and the wings, and sometimes the legs, sticking out to the sides. On the 12th day an adult brought a fruit to the chick, and over the next 9 days I saw them bring three more fruits, one of which was probably from a matchwood tree (*Didymopanax*) about 100 m away. Altogether, of 76 feedings which were recognizable only four consisted of fruit. The female regularly fed on fruits at this time, the seeds of which we collected on a sheet slung beneath the nest.

During morning watches of two hours or more, the adults fed the chick at the rate of 2 to 7 times each hour, and exactly 4 times an hour during the longest watch of six hours, from 06.30 to 12.30. Although three of the adults regularly fed the chick, Male A alone contributed 60% of all the food, and he evidently had no difficulty in increasing his rate. He regularly brought food to the nest at short intervals (6 minutes or less), especially in the early morning. The adults regularly offered the chick more than it could take. It refused the food offered on 10 out of 95 occasions on days 6 to 21; earlier, when it was 2 days old, it refused three of 11 offerings of food.

The nestling was covered in buff-coloured down, which by day 12 appeared speckled with black from the feathers growing beneath it. When it was 17 days old, it still appeared buffy with black patches, and the wing and tail feathers seemed to be about one-third grown. The long quills, terminating in the expanded black vanes, gave the wings and tail the appearance of a Chinese fan. At the age of 20 days, the head and wing-coverts appeared black with scattered buffy spots. My observations ceased when the nestling was 21 days old, but William Clements, our camp helper, visited the nest regularly until the young bird left when it was 32 or 33 days old.

Defence of the nest. Neither the location of the nests nor the behaviour of the birds suggested that in this species it can be at all important for the safety of the nest that it should be inconspicuous, as are so many nests in tropical forest; but it is certainly significant that both nest trees, along their entire length, were growing clear of other trees. Once a group of Capuchin monkeys passed close to our main nest, and once a troupe of squirrel monkeys passed through trees adjacent to the other nest. In neither case did the monkeys climb the nest tree, which they could not have reached without first descending to the ground.

It soon became clear that the fruit-crows' method of ensuring the safety of the nest against avian predators is to establish a zone around it in which they are dominant and from which they persistently chase most other birds. They regularly mobbed intruders near the nest during nest-building and on through the nesting cycle until our observations ceased, shortly before the young bird flew. On some days mobbing took up a considerable part of their time. They occasionally mobbed toucans at distances of up to 200 m from the nest, but mostly they mobbed birds that came within about 50 m. All members of the group spent much of their time within 100 m of the nest, returning to its vicinity at intervals after they had fed farther afield, and resting and preening on high perches within sight of the nest.

When mobbing an intruder, fruit-crows utter the *oo-waa* call repeatedly, occasionally varying it with the drawn-out, upwardly inflected *wooo*. They face the intruder, lower the head, and while calling fan out the throat-ruff and shiver the tail. Sometimes they snap the beak several times in quick succession. If the intruder is in an accessible position, they dive at it repeatedly, one after the other, coming to within a few inches of it and then swerving away at great speed. At the closest point, they utter a curious rasping call not heard on other occasions. An intruding bird may enjoy a degree of immunity if it perches quietly in thick cover where the fruit-crows cannot dive at it; but as soon as it flies they are after it at once, often in a close pack, pursuing it closely and harrying it until it is well away from the nest area.

Altogether, we saw the fruit-crows mob 13 species of birds. Toucans *Ramphastos vitellinus* and *R. tucanus* and Cayenne Jays *Cyanocorax cayanus* were the species most frequently mobbed. The other species included three kinds of hawks, three icterids, a cock-of-the-rock, and a small flycatcher. Once they mobbed a troupe of monkeys. Those birds that were not potential nest predators were mobbed rather half-heartedly or even ignored, unless they happened to come very close to the nest, in which case they were driven away vigorously. Mobbing nearly always succeeded in causing the intruder to leave the nest area, except in the case of a Black-faced Hawk *Leucopternis melanops*. This bird, certainly the same individual on the four occasions recorded, stolidly perched in a tree near the nest, taking little notice of the succession of diving fruit-crows that passed within inches of its head and only occasionally raising a foot to ward them off.

At the nest in which a young one was reared, intruders became less frequent as the nesting cycle progressed, presumably because they learned to avoid the constant harrying to which they were subjected in the area. I recorded 12 mobbing incidents in 19 hours 20 minutes of observation during the nest-building period; 10 in 37 hours 20 minutes during the incubation period; and only five in 28 hours 20 minutes during the nestling period – a decline from one incident about every 40 minutes to one about every 6 hours.

Annual cycle
Very few dated breeding records are available either

from direct observation or by calculation from the dates of juvenile specimens, which are very rare in collections. The moult season can, however, be calculated with some accuracy from the large number of adult specimens available in museums. The duration of the moult in an individual bird is estimated at about 200 days (Snow 1976*a*).

For Panama, at 8–9°N, the two known or calculated months of egg-laying are July (Ellis 1952) and October (barely fledged juvenile specimen, December). This indication that breeding takes place in the second half of the year (the wet season) is supported by moult records, the great majority of which indicate the onset of moult in the months January–April (36 out of 41 records, the others being May–September). In adjacent Costa Rica the onset of moult seems to be a little later (February–June, 16 out of 19 records). The annual cycle in Guyana and Surinam, at 3–7°N, appears to be less well-defined. Our two Guyana egg-laying records were in February, and Haverschmidt (1968) observed a nest in which egg-laying must have been in early April, but these alone are probably not a reliable guide to the extent of the breeding season. The 23 moult records are spread throughout the year, with no indication of a peak. Little or no seasonality is evident in the moult records from the Amazon basin within 5° of the Equator, but south of 6°S, in Peru and Bolivia, the records indicate that moult begins mainly in May–November (32 out of 37 records). The data, though very inadequate, thus suggest that breeding takes place mainly in the wet season and the moult mainly in the dry season.

Plumages

Nestling down buff-coloured (see Incubation and fledging, above). Juvenile plumage dull black (feathers sooty, with blacker fringes). This plumage succeeded by all-black plumage, similar in male and female. Crimson throat-feathers of adult male appear gradually, not closely linked with wing-moult, the first to appear sometimes crimson with black tips. If reliance can be placed on sexed museum specimens, females rarely have a few crimson throat-feathers.

Physical characters

Structure
Bill strong, hooked at tip, somewhat flattened dorso-ventrally and broad at base; nostrils ovoid, half covered by feathers of forehead; rictal bristles well developed. Wings long for body-size, with relatively very long secondaries (see p. 16); flight feathers unmodified. Legs short. Crimson throat-feathers of adult male highly modified, barbs flattened and lacking barbules (Strong 1952).

Unfeathered parts
Iris: dark brown.
Bill: blue-grey.
Legs and feet: black.

Geographical variation
None reported, but there is some variation in size. As indicated by their wing-lengths and weights (next section), birds from the Andean foothills of Peru are considerably larger, and birds from Central America somewhat larger, than those from lower Amazonia and the Guianas.

Measurements
♂♂ (8, Guianas) Wing 176–185, 180.3. Tail 108–123, 115.9. Tarsus 23–25.5, 23.9. Culmen 20.5–23, 22.1.
♀♀ (8, Guianas) Wing 165–174, 169.9. Tail 108–118, 112.9. Tarsus 23.5–25, 24.2. Culmen 20–23, 21.4.
Wing-lengths of adult males from other areas: Panama (10) 179.5–185.5, 183.0 (Wetmore 1972); lower Amazonia (8) 175–185, 179.8. Rio Pachitea, Peru (6) 182–195, 191.0.
Weights:
Guianas: 10 ♂♂ 91–112, 102.1 g.
            5 ♀♀ 91–105, 97.6 g.
Central America: 4 ♂♂ 105–122, 112.5 g.
            4 ♀♀ 93–101, 95.5 g.
Peru: 5 ♂♂ 112–133, 119.8 g.
        6 ♀♀ 100–114, 109.2 g.

Genus Pyroderus

Plate 17, page 142

Pyroderus scutatus – Red-ruffed Fruit-crow

The Red-ruffed Fruit-crow is a very large and strikingly ornamented cotinga. Its most distinctive feature is its brilliant throat and upper breast patch, the feathers of which are glossy, orange red with darker red edges, and somewhat crimped. It is unusual among the large and spectacular cotingas in that the plumage of males and females is similar, the only difference being that males, which are considerably larger, have longer feathers on the nape. Placed in a monotypic genus, like so many of the larger cotingas, it is almost certainly most closely related to the umbrellabirds (*Cephalopterus*). In both, the trachea has two expanded portions and the males make a booming sound in display, inflating a distensible throat pouch. It is noteworthy that the inflated throat, which in the Red-ruffed Fruit-crow is made conspicuous by the brilliant red feathering, is similarly made conspicuous in the Bare-necked Umbrellabird *C. glabricollis* by its bare scarlet skin. The red throat patch, setting off an otherwise mainly black plumage, suggests affinity with the smaller Purple-throated Fruit-crow *Querula purpurata*. On the basis of syringeal structure, however, Ames (1971) places *Querula* in a group separate from the large fruit-crows, linking it with *Carpodectes*.

Although it is widespread, the Red-ruffed Fruit-crow is generally a rather uncommon and local bird, and in consequence has remained little known. What seem to have been the only detailed observations of its communal display associated with the booming call – apparently a form of lek behaviour – were made by Paul Schwartz in Venezuela. He was to have written the appropriate sections of this account, but died suddenly just as he was about to do so. The account that follows is based on the tape-recordings which he made, and the editing sheets that accompany them.

Distribution (Map 25)

The Red-ruffed Fruit-crow's range is peripheral to the Amazonian basin. It is widespread in the Andes (but does not extend so far south as most widespread Andean cotingas), curiously local in the forests of the Guiana region, and widespread in the east Brazilian forest belt from Bahia south to Rio Grande do Sul, extending inland to Goias, parts of northern Argentina, and eastern Paraguay. In some areas its range has undoubtedly been fragmented by recent destruction of forest, especially the subtropical Andean forests which were its headquarters in the western part of its range. Even before this, however, it seems that it was divided into a number of isolated populations, corresponding to the subspecies currently recognized.

Habitat and food

In the Andes the Red-ruffed Fruit-crow ranges from the upper tropical zone through the subtropical to the lower part of the temperate zone, most records being concentrated in the subtropical zone. The great majority of all recorded altitudes fall between the following limits:

Venezuela	1200–2000 m
Colombia, Eastern and Central Andes	2100–2700 m
Colombia, Western Andes	650–2700 m
Peru	1400–2200 m

The small Guiana population, by contrast, is found at tropical levels, in fairly low hill forest or even in lowland forest not far above sea level. Somewhat surprisingly, in view of the altitudinal preferences of the Andean populations, it is absent from the montane forests of the Guiana highlands (the tepui region), where many other montane forest birds are found. The eastern population also occurs in low-level forests, extending up into montane forest but not, apparently, to the higher forests where the specifically montane avifauna occurs.

Nothing is known of the ecology of the species which could explain these different altitudinal preferences. Like other fruit-crows, the Red-ruffed feeds on fruits and large insects. Fruits of palms, Laura-

139

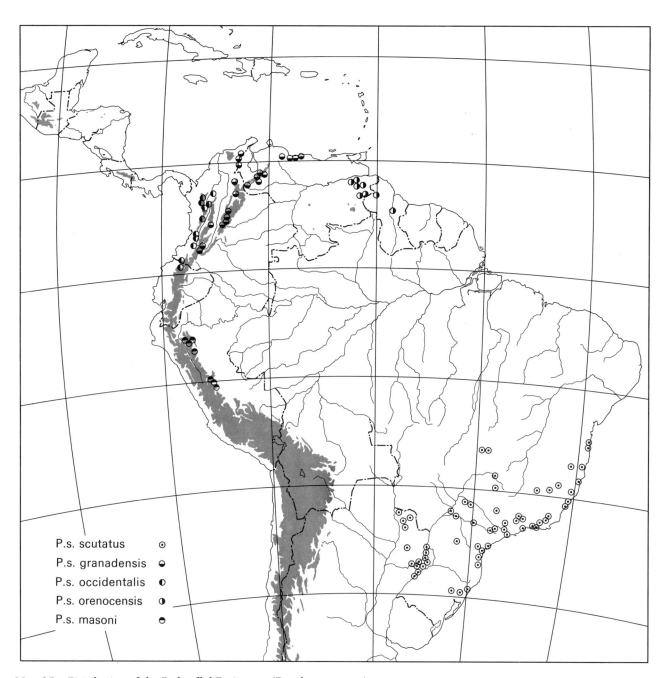

Map 25   Distribution of the Red-ruffed Fruit-crow (*Pyroderus scutatus*).

ceae, nutmegs (*Virola* sp., Myristicaceae), Melastomataceae and Myrtaceae have been recorded in its diet (Descourlitz 1852, Burmeister 1856, Schubart *et al*. 1965). In the Serra do Mar of southeastern Brazil, in October 1979, Dante Teixeira and I found it feeding on the fruits of a species of *Pisonia* (Nyctaginaceae), which seemed too small to be a very suitable food for such a large bird but were the only tree-fruits available at the time in the very humid forest at the crest of the serra at about 900 m. Wyatt (1871) wrote that in northern Colombia, in oak woods at about 6000 feet (1800 m), Red-ruffed Fruit-crows came apparently to feed on the acorns; but it may be suspected that they were in fact taking some other fruits. Insects recorded in stomach contents include beetles (Tenebrionidae, Curculionidae and others), and there is one record of the bones of a small bird (Reinhardt 1870).

Behaviour

It is impossible to give anything more than a most incomplete account of the behaviour of the Red-ruffed Fruit-crow, and especially of its remarkable courtship behaviour. It is certainly a lek bird, but apparently only one ornithologist, the late Paul Schwartz, has had the opportunity to make careful observations at a lek in the wild; his observations could not be continued for long, and he died before writing them up for publication. His tape-recordings and accompanying notes have been used in the account that follows. Some observations have also been made of courtship behaviour in captivity. The significance of observations made at leks without individually marked birds that have been followed over a long period is hard to assess, especially if, as in this species, the two sexes are alike in plumage.

Olalla (1943) reported that in eastern Brazil (Espirito Santo) ten or more males may display together, activity being concentrated in the early morning (before 09.00 hours) and the afternoon (after 16.00 hours). He described the birds as flying around, making short flights, occasionally stopping and uttering hollow bellowing calls. At one display ground he killed six males. According to the natives, display grounds are occupied for years. Olalla's very summary account of the display behaviour of the Brazilian subspecies (*scutatus*) is consistent with what was found in the Venezuelan population (*orenocensis*) studied by Paul Schwartz, the emphasis on flying around perhaps reflecting a higher level of disturbance by the observer.

The lek studied by Paul Schwartz was in deciduous forest near Upata in the State of Bolívar, Venezuela, at a height of about 250 m above sea level. Observations were made from 4 to 23 May 1966, activity being much less on the last date than in the first five days of the period. The trees in the general area were almost completely leafless in early May (end of the dry season), but those in the immediate lek area had a fair profusion of green leaves. Activity began before sunrise, at about 05.25 hours, while it was still almost dark, and continued at a high level until about 06.20 hours, after which it fell off markedly. (It was not recorded whether there was a period of activity in the afternoon.)

Seven or eight males regularly displayed at the lek, each apparently having its favourite display perch. Display perches were quite low, the highest being about 6 m above ground. The perches were about 3 m apart from each other, but evidently the birds adjusted their positions to some extent, as two birds, calling at the same time, regularly came within about 1 m of each other.

The main display consists of a booming call, accompanied by a special posture and movement. The 'boom' is in fact a double call, consisting of two brief, but intense, hollow-sounding pulses of sound, the second of which is always louder than the first. When booming, the bird bends forward, with the red ruff extended, then bobs up and down. During the upper part of the movement the wings may be 'wiggled' while being held close to the body. When the bird bends down the red ruff hangs down like a bib, falling away from the body, and when the bird is upright the ruff sticks straight out clear of the body (apparently pushed out by the inflation of the throat-pouch). A single bird may utter the booming call by itself at the lek, and when it does so it usually at once attracts others to come to their perches, and a chorus of booms takes place. Similarly, if the birds are silent at the lek, booming is stimulated by the arrival of a newcomer. Booming is, in fact, very much a communal activity. Listening to the tape-recordings, it is difficult to tell if there is any synchronization of calls when several birds are booming together; the impression is that two individuals tend to time their calls to some extent so that they call successively, but that when more birds join in this pattern quickly breaks down. In any case, when two or more birds are booming together a continuous, but somewhat irregular and fluctuating, volume of sound is produced which may go on for minutes on end.

There was also a good deal of chasing between the males. In particular, a male would sometimes fly and drive from its perch another bird 6 or 8 m away, ignoring males perched much closer. This behaviour suggests that established males are aggressive to subordinate or unestablished males (with peripheral perches at the lek?), but tolerate their established neighbours, and is very similar to the behaviour of male Calfbirds at their lek.

Paul Schwartz's vocal comments on the tape emphasize that the males, when not booming, spend a lot of time looking downward, with body horizontal. This is apparently not a special posture with significance in display, but the birds are simply on the watch for something below them. He thought that they were in fact watching for the arrival of females, and particularly noted that they always fly low through the forest, just above the level of the undergrowth.

On several occasions during his periods of observation and recording, birds that he took to be females visited the lek. These birds came and perched near or within the main lek area but remained silent and did not display. (The possibility cannot of course be excluded that some at least of

MWWoodcock

these birds were males, perhaps young unestablished males.) When one of these visitors was present, the displaying males would all turn and boom facing it. On at least two occasions a visiting, non-displaying bird perched close to a displaying male, who at once began vigorous, presumably ritualized preening of the wings, first one wing then the other. On one occasion the male is described as 'having real fits, nearly turning upside down'. P.S. evidently thought that the visitor on these occasions was a female, but in Calfbirds display-preening is aggressive and directed towards rival males, and it is perhaps more likely that in the Red-ruffed Fruit-crow too it is directed towards males that intrude onto another male's display perch.

At times when display is slack, and also apparently when a bird is 'working up' towards a bout of booming, more or less abrupt, low-pitched twanging calls may be given. These calls are rather variable in form; they may be short and abrupt, or more drawn-out, and uttered singly or in pairs. Occasionally they lengthen out and pass into the typical boom. They were the only calls recorded apart from the booming.

Incomplete as it is, this account indicates that in its display organization the Red-ruffed Fruit-crow has several points in common with the Calfbird. In both, groups of males gather at traditional display grounds at which individual birds have their special perches; there is a good deal of aggressive behaviour between them; and they advertise themselves, and presumably attract females, by joining in producing loud and more or less continuous lowing or booming sounds. It is interesting that in both species the male and female plumage is similar and that, by inference, it is the difference in vocal behaviour and the accompanying displays that acts as the main signal identifying the sexes at the display ground.

The display of a single male of the Brazilian subspecies, *scutatus*, to a female in the Berlin Zoo has been described by Wünschmann (1966). The male is described as quivering his wings and snapping his bill, and hopping with sideways jumps up to the female. When close to her, he ruffled his feathers, especially the red throat feathers, and quivered his half-opened wings. He then lowered his head and shook it, puffing out the throat pouch so that the spread ruff swung to and fro. He then drew himself up suddenly upright, threw back the head, so that the blown-up pouch protruded like a goitre, and with closed bill and half-opened wings uttered two short, hollow notes sounding as if someone was blowing jerkily across the neck of a bottle. Then he made a little bow forward, smoothed down his feathers and deflated his throat, and the ceremony, which altogether lasted about 10 seconds, was over. Wünschmann notes that this display is very like that of the Umbrellabird (see p. 151), and it supports the suggestion, made above, that the preening displays seen by Paul Schwartz in Venezuela were aggressive displays to other males and not courtship. Wünschmann's bird sometimes did the full display when the female was not present. When threatened, it uttered, with the bill closed and the throat pouch somewhat inflated, a nasal croaking call, much less loud than the display call.

Breeding and the annual cycle

T. K. Salmon, who collected birds and eggs and made many new observations in northern Colombia in the 1870s, was apparently the first ornithologist to find the nest of a Red-ruffed Fruit-crow. Sclater & Salvin (1879) quote him as follows: 'The nest, composed of sticks, is generally built rather high in the fork of a slender branch, and is exceedingly slight and small, not much larger than the nest of the Common Ring-Dove [*Columba palumbus*]. By frightening the bird from her nest, I have caused the eggs to fall to the ground. The bird is exceedingly fierce in defending its nest from hawks. I found the first nest I ever saw entirely from seeing a Red-necked Fruit-Crow fly out at a passing hawk.' Two eggs collected by Salmon are in the British Museum collection. They are, respectively, very pale buff and deeper buff in ground colour, and both are marked with spots and blotches of pale lilac overlaid by similar markings of sepia brown. They measure 47.6 × 33.6 and 45.8 × 33.2 mm. Another egg, also from Colombia but with no exact locality, measures 46.6 × 33.3 mm and is similarly coloured. Salmon's account suggests that the clutch consists of more

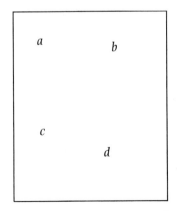

Plate 17

a: Red-ruffed Fruit-crow *Pyroderus scutatus*, northwestern race (*occidentalis*)
b: Red-ruffed Fruit-crow, southeastern race (*scutatus*)
c and *d*: Purple-throated Fruit-crow *Querula purpurata*, male and female

than one egg, but this is open to doubt. The two eggs collected by him are so different in ground colour that they almost certainly came from different nests; the third British Museum egg is also single. All other large cotingas that build nests of the type Salmon described lay one-egg clutches.

Nothing else seems to be known of the nesting of this species, but moult records give some information on the annual cycle. The complete moult apparently takes about 6 months in the individual (Snow 1976a). Males appear to moult on average a month or two in advance of females, as suggested by the calculated dates of onset of moult in the coastal cordillera of northern Venezuela:

Month of onset	♂	♀
March	3	—
April	1	2
May	1	1
June	1	3

Eastern Brazilian populations begin to moult mainly in September and October (19 out of 26 records, the other 7 being in November and December), and those of northern Venezuela and northern Colombia in March–June, exactly six months different. Records from intermediate latitudes are fewer but indicate a less well synchronized annual cycle. Schaefer & Phelps (1954) state that at Rancho Grande in northern Venezuela the Red-ruffed Fruit-crow nests at the beginning of the wet season (i.e. about May). This statement was apparently not based on nests actually found; if true, it indicates that many males must begin to moult before nesting begins.

Plumages and moults

Nestling not seen. Juvenile plumage dull black, variably brown below (probably according to subspecies). Plumage in area of ruff soon replaced (at least in some individuals before wings are full-grown) by red feathers of adult type but less bright and glossy; rest of body plumage also replaced by feathers of adult type. Juvenile tail-feathers (with primaries and secondaries, not replaced until first complete moult) not only more pointed than adult tail-feathers (as is general in the family) but sometimes distinctly longer than adult tail-feathers.

Physical characters

Structure
Bill strong, crow-like; oval nostrils almost concealed by forwardly directed feathers of forehead. Rictal bristles wiry and recurved (3–4 strong ones, a few shorter and weaker). Trachea with two expanded portions. Feathers of ruff with distal ends of barbs conspicuously flattened (Olson 1970), feather-tips tending to be crimped or crinkled. Wing-feathers unmodified. Legs and feet strong.

Unfeathered parts
Iris: blue in some adult males; perhaps an age character, as described as brown, grey-brown or grey in others: brown or grey-brown in females.

Bill: apparently variable; described as pale grey or grey-blue in some adult males, black or blackish in others; apparently normally dark (blackish or greyish) in females, lower mandible paler than upper.

Feet and legs: black or blue-black, soles yellow-green.

Geographical variation
The Red-ruffed Fruit-crow shows conspicuous geographical variation in the extent of brown on the underparts posterior to the ruff, and less conspicuous variation in some other plumage characters and in size. Five subspecies are usually recognized, the ranges of which are shown in Map 25. Their main characters are summarized in Table 8. This table presents the general picture, but there are some complications and uncertainties. Within each subspecies, size probably varies to some extent. Thus specimens of *granadensis* from 9500 ft (2900 m) are larger than those from 5000 ft (1500 m), and this and similar local differences undoubtedly account for part of the size ranges shown in the table. Birds from the north coastal ranges of Venezuela (Carabobo to Distrito Federal) tend to have more extensive brown on the underparts than those to the west, and thus in this character tend towards *orenocensis*, from which, however, they are geographically isolated. Also within the range of *granadensis* a more striking divergence from the typical colouration is shown by two specimens collected by T. H. Wheeler in the last century and labelled 'Soledad, Magdalena Valley, 3000 ft'. They have extensively brown underparts, exactly matching *occidentalis* to the west. Soledad unfortunately cannot be located, but other specimens collected there by Wheeler suggest that it must be on the western slopes of the Eastern Andes. Its altitude, if correct, is lower than any others recorded for the species in the Eastern Andes of Colombia. These two puzzling specimens raise the question whether there is (or was, as deforestation may well have extirpated it) a population of *occidentalis* type at low altitudes in some part of the Magdalena Valley.

Table 8
Characters of the subspecies of *Pyroderus scutatus*

	Wing of adult ♂♂ (N, range and mean)	Brown of under parts	Ruff	Other characters
scutatus	(15) 220–263, *246.7*	spots (brown feather tips), mostly in centre of breast	feathers with broad red fringes	upper parts glossed
orenocensis	(2) 238, *242*	most extensive, covering all under parts	feathers with narrow red fringes	upper parts dull lustreless black; frontal feathers rather stiff, tending to produce a median crest
granadensis	(8) 225–240, *233.3*	spots, paler than in *scutatus*, variable in extent but mainly in centre of breast.	as *orenocensis*	upper parts glossed
occidentalis	(8) 230–254, *245.7*	darker than in *orenocensis*; extensive, but not extending to abdomen and under tail-coverts	feather fringes less bright than in other subspp.	upper parts glossed
masoni	(6) 228–240, *236.4*	dullest in tone; moderate in extent, typically leaving black band across lower breast	deepest in colour; fringes dark red, approaching crimson	upper parts dull, lacking iridescence

Note: Measurements for *granadensis* include some unsexed adults, apparently male.

Measurements

P. s. scutatus
♂♂ (15)   Wing 220 (young?), 236–263, 246.7.   Tail 154–179, 165.7.   Tarsus 41–45, 43.4.   Culmen 29.5–33, 31.6.
♀♀ (16)   Wing 213–241, 233.4.   Tail 153–175, 164.6.   Tarsus 38.5–42, 40.6.   Culmen 27.5–31.5, 29.7.
Weights: 3 ♂♂ 418.6, 413, 313 g (wings resp. 255, 245, 220 mm).
1 ♀ 350.3 g (wing 242 mm).
2 unsexed 393, 293 g (wings resp. 233, 226 mm).

P. s. orenocensis
♂♂ (2)   Wing 238, 242 mm.

P. s. granadensis
♂♂♀♀ (15)   Wing 207–240, 227.2.   Tail 136–150, 144.4.   Tarsus 37–43, 40.4.   Culmen 25–28, 26.3.
Weight: 2 ♀♀ 375, 300 g (wings resp. 227, 219 mm).

P. s. occidentalis
♂♂ (8)   Wing 230–254, 245.7.   Tail 149–158, 152.7.   Tarsus 42–46, 44.3.   Culmen 29–31.5, 30.5.
♀♀ (7)   Wing 225–235, 227.1.   Tail 144–160, 150.4.   Tarsus 38–43, 39.8.   Culmen 27–30, 28.3.

P. s. masoni
♂♂ (6)   Wing 228–240, 236.4.

MWWoodcock

Genus Cephalopterus – the umbrellabirds

Cephalopterus ornatus – Amazonian Umbrellabird
Cephalopterus penduliger – Long-wattled Umbrellabird
Cephalopterus glabricollis – Bare-necked Umbrellabird

The three umbrellabirds are closely related to one another, have no other close relatives, and replace one another geographically. They thus present the same problem as several other cotinga genera, whether they should be treated as three subspecies of a single species as Hellmayr (1929) did, or as three separate species. For reasons that have been discussed earlier (p. 12), we treat them as separate species, while recognizing that the decision is to some extent arbitrary.

They are the largest of the cotingas, approached in size only by the Red-ruffed Fruit-crow and the Calfbird, which are almost certainly their closest relatives. The males are distinguished by two unique secondary sexual characters, an umbrella-like tuft of modified feathers on the crown, and an extensible throat wattle. The trachea is also modified, having two expanded portions whose function is probably to produce the booming call made during courtship. All these modifications are much reduced in the considerably smaller females.

As is usual in the cotingas, the most conspicuous differences between the species involve the secondary sexual characters. The most strikingly distinct species is *C. glabricollis*, in which the wattle is much reduced and is merely an appendage of a brilliant

scarlet inflatable throat pouch that has no counterpart in the other species. There are some other less obvious differences. *C. ornatus* is larger than the other two species and has a relatively longer tail; its plumage, in the male, is more strongly glossed with blue, and the crest feathers have conspicuous white shafts (blackish in the other two). In *C. penduliger* the underside of the wing is extensively white, whereas in *ornatus* it is dark grey and in *glabricollis* mainly grey with only a little white near the bend of the wing. Finally, the eye is very pale blue-grey, almost white, in *ornatus* and dark brown in the other species. Superficially, because of its similar wattle, *penduliger* looks more like *ornatus* than glabricollis, but in the other characters it is more like *glabricollis*. Their distribution suggests that *penduliger* and *glabricollis* may have a more recent common ancestry than *penduliger* and *ornatus*, since many Central American forest birds have close relatives in South America west of the Andes.

Distribution (Map 26)

C. ornatus, much the most widespread of the three species, ranges over the greater part of the Amazon basin and the upper drainage of the Orinoco. In the extreme south it just extends into the area of the headwaters of the Rio Paraguai. It is, however, by no means uniformly distributed over this vast area, and in particular is absent from the main course of the lower Amazon. Long ago Wallace (1850) noted that, in ascending the Amazon, he first met it opposite the mouth of the Rio Madeira. In his experience its headquarters were the many islands that fill the course of the lower Rio Negro; he noted that he found it only on islands in the rivers. Hagmann's (1907) record of a specimen collected on Mexiana Island at the mouth of the Amazon was the first, and apparently is still the only, record for the lower Amazon. Although this species is closely associated with islands in the great rivers it is by no means confined to them, as Wallace supposed. In the west of its range, along the eastern Andean foothills, it has been recorded up to about 1400 m

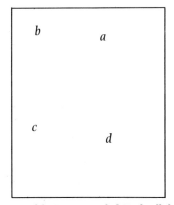

Plate 18
The umbrellabirds
(*Cephalopterus*)

a and *b*: Long-wattled Umbrellabird *C. penduliger*, male and female
c: Amazonian Umbrellabird *C. ornatus*, male
d: Bare-necked Umbrellabird *C. glabricollis*, male

Map 26   Distribution of the umbrellabirds (*Cephalopterus* spp.).

C. ornatus   ×
C. penduliger   ⊙
C. glabricollis △

in Colombia, 2000 m in Peru, and 1350 m in Bolivia. In all areas it is dependent on virgin forest.

C. penduliger is a bird of the lower forested slopes of the western flanks of the Andes of Colombia and Ecuador, in the upper tropical and subtropical zones (mainly 800–1400 m). The San Juan river forms its northern boundary. Thus it is absent from the swampy forests of the Chocó region of northwestern Colombia (which would seem to be suitable habitat for *ornatus*).

C. glabricollis, of Costa Rica and western Panama, is an even more markedly montane bird than *penduliger*. It is reported to occur up to 3000 m, but is probably exceptional at such a height. In Costa Rica it appears to breed in the humid subtropical belt, mainly on the Caribbean slopes of the country's mountain backbone, moving to low altitudes in the off-season. Seasonal vertical migrations have not been reported from Panama, where the species has been found comparatively seldom.

Ecology

As already mentioned, Wallace's experience was that the Amazonian Umbrellabird was strictly associated with islands in the middle and upper Amazon and lower Rio Negro. Sick (1954, 1955), who studied the bird in the region of the upper Rio Xingú, found it mainly along river banks, on islands in the river, and in swampy areas with small patches or narrow tongues of forest. In eastern Ecuador, Goodfellow (1901) found it only on the banks of the Río Cosanga, below Baeza. Whether the forest in such areas is especially favourable for their feeding is not clear from published accounts. The diet consists of large insects and fruits. There is agreement in the several available lists of stomach contents (Pelzeln 1868, Sick 1954, Schubart *et al.* 1965, specimens in S. Paulo Mus.) that the insect food consists mainly of large Orthoptera and Coleoptera; such prey is snatched from the foliage and branches of trees, usually in flight, and beaten against the perch.

T. A. Parker watched an immature male for half an hour on 10 October 1974 as it foraged at the forest edge along the road between Quincemil and Puerto Maldonado in southeastern Peru; either it was very tame or it was unaware of the observer's presence, the latter being unlikely since he was in clear view much of the time. The bird was moving from tree to tree through the middle storey 5 to 7 m up, perching on horizontal branches in the open, peering up and down, and making short forward flights into denser clumps of leaves, where after a few seconds it would emerge and return to a horizontal branch in the open. On two such flights the bird captured a large (5 cm) green caterpillar, and an *Anolis* lizard about 13 cm long.

Few of the fruits eaten have been identified. Sick mentions several species of dicotyledons with angular seeds about the size of cherry stones, only one of which (*Byrsonima*, fam. Malpighiaceae) could be identified. Of six specimens from the Serra do Cachimbo in southwestern Pará (S. Paulo Mus.), two contained only large palm fruits, the other four a mixture of fruits and animal matter.

Goodfellow's (1901) account of the Long-wattled Umbrellabird in western Ecuador suggests that palm fruits are an important part of its diet. He mentioned that the birds generally kept to the tops of the highest trees, but came down to feed on the large fruits of a species of palm, at no great height. 'The fruits, which they swallowed whole, resembled a hard green date and were quite two inches in length.' Von Hagen (1938) also mentions palm fruits as an important part of the diet of this species in Ecuador.

Nothing specific seems to have been recorded of the diet of the Bare-necked Umbrellabird since Cordier's observations that it feeds on palm fruits and Cecropia fruits, the latter being apparently of lesser importance (Cordier 1943, Todd *et al.* 1972).

If palm fruits are a staple food of the umbrellabirds, as seems likely, this may explain the birds' association with swampy forest and river edges in Amazonia, since palms tend to be numerous in such places. Palms are also richly represented in the forests on the humid lower slopes of the eastern Andes, the other main home of the Amazonian Umbrellabird, as they are too on the slopes of the western Andes where the Long-wattled Umbrellabird is found. Future observers should miss no opportunity of finding out exactly what fruits the umbrellabirds eat, as this will be one of the keys to a better understanding of their ecology.

Behaviour

Sick (1954, 1955), who studied the Amazonian Umbrellabird in the upper Xingú region, has given the most thorough account of any of the umbrellabirds in the wild. He describes it as somewhat crow-like not only in form but also in its movements. Among tree branches it moves with long springing jumps and flutters; it tends to be noisy as it works through the trees, often landing on thin branches that give beneath its weight. In flight the crest is laid back and the wings, which are not very long for the size of the bird, are broadly spread. On longer flights both male and female make a loud wing-noise, but shorter flights are nearly silent. The bird is not an especially good flier, but may nevertheless make flights of several hundred metres across rivers, flying at a height of 50–80 metres.

Males advertise themselves with a deep, melodious, far-carrying call which they utter from the tops of the tallest trees, at a distance reminiscent of the lowing of a bull. Bates (1863) described it as a 'deep, loud, and long-sustained fluty note'. At the beginning of the breeding season (apparently June–July in the upper Xingú region), this call is heard from first dawn onwards throughout the morning, and then again shortly before sunset. Each male has its favourite calling tree. In his study area Sick found that these were well separated from those of other males, at such distances that two birds, or under favourable conditions three, might be heard from one place. He reported that a female was regularly associated with each calling male, so that they seemed to be in pairs. It seems likely, however, that these were temporary associations and that females visit the males only for mating, as in other cotingas with striking sexual dimorphism and highly developed courtship displays.

Sick was only once able to make exact observations on a calling male. He described three phases in the uttering of the call. (1) The bird leans forwards and downwards; the crest falls forward and at the same time is spread laterally, and the lappet hangs free of the neck with its feathers conspicuously ruffed out. (2) The anterior part of the body is stretched forward, accompanied by a choking or shaking action and a grating sound. This and the first phase apparently serve to fill the bird's air-sacs, the grating sound being a by-product of the process. (3) The head and neck are thrust forward, and at the same moment the boom is produced.

In addition to the boom, which is given only by the male, both sexes utter deep, but not loud, ventriloquial calls. Sick mentions a churring or growling note, and from a female a combination of calls that he transcribes as goh-ahk, go-uh gogogo, goh-akh goh-akh goh-goh goh-ahk etc., the last syllable of the goh-ahk being often prolonged for some seconds.

Nothing comparable has been recorded of the Long-wattled Umbrellabird. It too utters a loud booming call, which has given it the same local name in western Ecuador, Vaca del monte, as is given to the Bare-necked Umbrellabird in Central America (Todd *et al.* 1972). Knowledge of the Bare-necked Umbrellabird is based very largely on the field observations made by Charles Cordier (1943), who captured three birds for the Bronx Zoo in the mountains of Costa Rica, supplemented by subsequent observations on the display of one of the captive males (Crandall 1945, Delacour 1945). From these accounts it is clear that the Amazonian and Central American species have many similarities of behaviour; but visually, owing to the great development of the bare inflatable throat-pouch in the latter species, they differ most strikingly. Cordier studied four males which had taken up display territories on a heavily wooded ridge. Each bird had from one to three branches, 15 to 30 feet above the ground, where it could always be found except when feeding. He gave the following outline of the daily activity of a male Bare-necked Umbrellabird.

'Half an hour before it is completely daylight the bird greets the new day by his resounding boomings, first in the highest branches of the tallest trees. . . After this early calling he makes a dive and alights on the lowest branch where he is accustomed to passing most of the daylight hours — figuratively speaking, his armchair. There he lets forth a further series of his calls and then in the twinkling of an eye he is again a hundred feet above ground, feeding on the fruit of the sloth tree [*Cecropia*] which grows very tall in this area.

'Having fortified himself, he notices his rivals, who are making a similar din. Wrathfully he alights on his rivals' trees, fifty to a hundred yards distant, and tries to chase them off, all the time giving out his calls. A third and a fourth bird or maybe more — to this day, I do not know how many — are attracted by this commotion, and join the chase. Black shapes flit back and forth, up and down, in the dim light. The noise is terrific. Twenty to thirty minutes later it is suddenly quiet. The birds have disappeared to feed off something more fanciful than the seeds of the sloth tree.

'It is now around 6 o'clock. By 7 o'clock, the bird is back, very quiet, chockful of fruit, and he remains absolutely motionless for 40 minutes to an hour. From time to time he expels the pits of the fruit he is digesting. He feels contented, blows out the airsack on his throat and gives forth a long-drawn, low mooooh. Occasionally he notices a leaf, breaks it off, and after a time lets it fall. He goes off again to feed, this time darting through the tree top and vanishing in a straight, rapid flight above the highest trees. Usually, however, he flies between the tree tops with consummate skill and great speed, making sudden turns, never touching an obstacle.

'Between 9 and 10 o'clock, *Cephalopterus* is back again. He decides to visit his rivals once more, but this time the fieryness of his temper is gone. Three, four birds are in a single tree, chasing each other mildly. A few carry small dead sticks in their beaks and from time to time utter low chuckling sounds. Sometimes they quarrel and voice their protests with a throaty *oooaaahh*, repeated over and over.

'Feeding and digesting take up the rest of the day. Sometimes late in the afternoon the bird will give another booming session. He has his days of activity and his days of comparative quiet — influenced by the weather, perhaps. I noticed that all of the Umbrella Birds behaved more or less the same way at the same time.

'In order to produce his resounding call the bird fills out his airsack, which is bright scarlet, to the size of a big tomato, the feather-tipped fleshy wattle attached to the airsack becoming greatly extended and hanging down 3 or 4 inches. When the airsack is distended the boom is produced. Then he suddenly throws his head violently back, far back, and quickly forward again, expelling the air with a swishing sound closely resembling the spitting of a big cat. He immediately fills his airsack again and lets forth another boom, but now he expels the air without going through any contortion or sound. At a certain distance only the two resounding boom notes can be heard.'

Two significant points emerge from Cordier's account. First, the males were organized in what was clearly a small lek. This is not apparent, and perhaps was not true, for the more widely spaced male Amazonian Umbrellabirds described by Sick. Second, in addition to the high tree-top calling posts the Bare-necked Umbrellabirds had much lower display perches beneath the canopy. In this they resemble the better known bellbirds (p. 167). Indeed, the general picture, as given by Cordier, suggests that the umbrellabirds and bellbirds may be rather similar in their display behaviour and social organization.

Crandall's (1945) observations on the display of the male Bare-necked Umbrellabird in captivity add to Cordier's account. 'There are two distinct display forms', Crandall wrote. 'In the first, the bird turns his head forward and down, gasps, and distends his air sack to the size and shape of a scarlet goose egg, big end down. The fleshy tassel, tipped with scraggly feathers and ordinarily about three-quarters of an inch in length, is seen to have lengthened to quite three inches, although its diameter is hardly greater. Then the head is moved rapidly from side to side, making the tassel gyrate wildly, like a pendulum out of time with its clock. During this performance, the bird utters a soft "br-r-r-r". . . In the second form of display, the force of the expansion is forward rather than downward. There is the same pigeon's egg at the bottom to begin with, but this time the bird stands upright, his crest doing a tight pompadour. Suddenly, he snaps his head forward, dropping the spread umbrella so that the bill is entirely covered. He then jerks upright again and extends his air sac until he looks like a brilliant toy balloon and nearly as perfectly spherical. Now he throws his head sharply backward, making the tassel fly violently in and out, in the axis of his body. At the same time, he gives forth a loud "plunk" – which Cordier calls a boom. After several of these violent convulsions, the air is expelled with no sound.' It seems clear that the first of the two displays described here corresponds to phases 1 and 2 of the display described by Sick (the filling of the air sacs), and the second form of display corresponds to Sick's phase 3 (the uttering of the boom).

Breeding and the annual cycle

The first undoubted nest of an umbrellabird of which there is a record was found by Sick (1951, 1954) in the upper Xingú region of Mato Grosso, Brazil. The nest, placed at a height of about 12 m in the crown of a tree in a small forest patch bordering a swamp, was a very open structure of twigs, so thin that the egg could be seen from below. The female was first seen with nest-material on 2 July, when the nest was already almost complete, and the single egg that constituted the clutch was first seen on the 15th. Sick began to watch the incubating female from a hide; but as she proved to be extremely suspicious, and the hide threatened to betray the nest site to passing Indians, he later collected the egg.

The egg was khaki-coloured, spotted with light chocolate and purplish brown and lightly stippled with dark brown; it was rather pointed and measured 56.0 × 35.8 mm. The nest was a rather flat structure, about 19 cm in diameter (not counting projecting twigs), built of twigs of various sizes up to 65 cm long and 1.5 cm thick. Although of very open construction it was strong, as it was supported by several forked stems and its constituent twigs interlocked firmly.

On 12 October 1974 T. A. Parker observed a female Amazonian Umbrellabird building a nest in a slender tree about 8 m tall, in high tropical forest about 600 m above sea level east of Quincemil, Depto. Cuzco, southeastern Peru. The nest was a flimsy structure of long slender twigs set on a fork of several branches about 6 m up. The bird was picking up nest material from the ground, and from low bushes, within 30 m of the nest site.

In view of the fact that both of these nests were thin structures of twigs, of essentially the same type as those of other large cotingas whose nests are known, some doubt must attach to the reports of the nests of the two other umbrellabird species. Goodfellow (1901) was told by the local people in western Ecuador that the Long-wattled Umbrellabird nests in tree holes, and von Hagen (1938), also in western Ecuador, described how he took an adult male at night from a small hollow in a tree about 6 feet above the ground. He mentioned that 'the hole seemed to have been enlarged a little by the bird itself, and the characteristic black feathers inside the nest gave us a definite clue to its nesting habits'. There are several puzzling aspects to his account, not least the site of the 'nest' and the fact that the bird was a male. No nest contents are mentioned. The 'nest' was found by von Hagen and an Indian, apparently quite by accident, some days before it contained the bird. One cannot help suspecting that the Indian in fact captured the bird elsewhere and planted it in the hole; von Hagen's account does not exclude this possibility.

Almost equally doubtful is the identity of the three nests shown to Cordier in Costa Rica and said to have been built by Bare-necked Umbrellabirds. He described them as like over-sized thrush nests, each one being 4–6 feet from the ground between the trunk of a medium-sized tree and a branch.

Little can be said about the annual cycles of any of the umbrellabirds, except that the Central American species probably breeds about May in the highlands (the month when Cordier was told that the males' calling is most persistent) and descends to lowland forests in the off-season. Slud (1960) recorded that it was absent from the lowland forest of Finca La Selva on the Caribbean side of Costa Rica from March to late July, and reappeared in August. Sick (1954) had evidence that in the two years of his field study on the upper Xingú, at 11–12°S, the Amazonian Umbrellabird had two breeding periods, in June–July and in December. There is, however, no reason to conclude that these are the regular times of breeding in this area, and Sick commented on the fact that breeding seemed independent of the seasons. The only very young bird that has been collected, in Bolivia at about 17°S (see next section), must have come from an egg laid about January.

Moult records show no well-marked seasonal pattern in any of the species. This is probably due in part to the very long duration of moult in the individual – about 300 days (Snow 1976a), and probably individually variable. Probably, too, there is a difference in moult regimes between the sexes, as there is in the other cotingas whose social organization is similar to the umbrellabirds'.

Plumages and moults

There seems to be only a single very young specimen of umbrellabird in any museum collection, a just-fledged juvenile from Bajo Palmar, Prov. Chapare, Cochabamba, Bolivia, collected on 20 March 1958 (Paris Mus. 1959/1301). The plumage of this bird, which was not fully grown (bill still small, tail very short, wing 195 mm), is dull black all over, and the remnants of the nestling down are also black.

The fully adult male plumage is certainly acquired in stages, with at least one subadult plumage intervening between the juvenile and fully adult state; but available specimens are inadequate for working out the details and timing of these stages.

Physical characters

Structure

Bill strong, crow-like, with large, exposed (except when concealed by crest), elongated nostrils; rictal bristles well developed. Trachea with two expanded portions, the anterior one larger. Crest of male (less developed in female) umbrella-like, feathers outwardly curving and terminating in a brush of hair-like barbs. Throat and breast ornamentation of male (much reduced in female) as follows: *ornatus*, fleshy wattle, flattened dorso-ventrally, densely feathered on both sides, up to 150 mm long (including feathers); *penduliger*, wattle similar to *ornatus* but much longer, up to 350 mm; *glabricollis*, skin of throat and upper breast bare, inflatable, with thin central tassle tipped with elongated feathers. Wing-feathers unmodified. Legs and feet strong.

Unfeathered parts

Iris: very pale blue-grey or pearl-grey, almost white, in *ornatus*; dark brown in *penduliger* and *glabricollis*.

Bill: maxilla black; mandible plumbeous, paler at tip, in *ornatus* and *glabricollis*, slate-grey to bluish in *penduliger*.

Feet and legs: black or very dark plumbeous grey.

Bare skin: throat and breast skin scarlet in *glabricollis*; skin in these areas (not bare) dark in the other two species.

Measurements

C. ornatus

♂♂ (15) Wing 268–295, 281.1. Tail 165–192, 172.8. Tarsus 51–54, 52.7. Culmen 44–52, 49.2.

♀♀ (9) Wing 216–250, 238.9. Tail 144–156, 152.0. Tarsus 41.5–47, 43.2. Culmen 41–44, 42.7.

Weight: 1 ♀ 380 g (wing 236 mm).

C. penduliger

♂♂ (5) Wing 249–259, 255.4. Tail 125–133, 128.8. Tarsus 40–43, 42.0. Culmen 47–49, 48.2.

♀♀ (3) Wing 226–240, 233.0. Tail 121–127, 124.0. Tarsus 44–47, 45.5. Culmen 37.5–44, 40.8.

C. glabricollis

♂♂ (6) Wing 241–255, 251.2. Tail 119–125, 120.7. Tarsus 45–48, 46.7. Culmen 36.5–38.5, 37.2.

♀♀ (4) Wing 212–235, 222.5. Tail 112–127, 116.0. Tarsus 38.5–45, 43.9. Culmen 33–36, 34.3.

Genus *Perissocephalus*

Plate 19, page 154

Perissocephalus tricolor — Calfbird, Capuchinbird

One of the largest of the cotingas, and certainly the most grotesque, the Calfbird has always been placed in a monotypic genus. Its affinities with the other large fruit-crows are, however, clear. It is similar to *Cephalopterus* and *Pyroderus* in syringeal structure, and like them has the anterior part of the trachea dilated, a modification that presumably helps in the production of the remarkable bellowing calls for which these birds are so notable. The Calfbird's social organization and displays are also remarkable, but further field research is needed to clarify the function of the displays, which have so far been studied only by Barbara K. Snow who contributes the relevant sections of this account.

Calfbirds are very large, crow-sized cotingas with long powerful bills, short tails, and strong legs. They give a superficial appearance of clumsiness but in fact are quite agile in flight. The predominantly coffee-brown plumage, contrasted with the bare blue-grey skin of the head, produces a colour scheme altogether different from that of any other cotinga. Males are somewhat larger than females, but in plumage they are identical except that males are apparently more likely than females to have a dark patch on the white under wing-coverts (Snow 1972: 139, footnote).

Distribution (Map 27)

The Calfbird is restricted to the heavy tropical forests of the north-central part of South America, north of the Amazon and west to the Rio Negro and upper Orinoco. That these rivers mark the western limit is strongly suggested by the absence of any record from Colombia. Moreover, in the western part of its range the Calfbird seems to be rather rare, or perhaps local. The centre of abundance of the species seems certainly to be the lowland forest of the Guianas and adjacent Amapá in northern Brazil. Whether there is, on a local scale or even over wider areas, competitive exclusion between *Perissocephalus* and the other large fruit-crows would be worth investigating. As Maps 26 and 27 show, the ranges of *Perissocephalus* and *Cephalopterus* are to a large extent mutually exclusive.

Ecology (by B. K. Snow)

Like the other large fruit-crows, the Calfbird is a forest species feeding largely on fruit supplemented with insects. Fruit is taken mostly at canopy level, but only brief periods are spent collecting it and the greater part of a Calfbird's day is spent in the middle to lower layers of the forest; it is at these levels that it nests, attends the communal leks, and does most of its insect foraging.

The fruits taken by Calfbirds are mostly large single-seeded drupes or berries with dense thin pericarps rich in fat and protein. They are swallowed whole, the pericarp is digested off and the seed regurgitated. In my study of the Calfbird in the Kanuku Mountains of southern Guyana (Snow 1972), most of the information on its fruit diet was acquired by daily collection of the regurgitated seeds from beneath the lek perches of three different males. Between 26 January and 5 April, seeds representing 2516 fruits of 37 species were collected beneath these perches. The laurels (Lauraceae) were the most important family, accounting for 37% of the regurgitated seeds; second in importance was the Burseraceae. Although only a few palm seeds (*Euterpe* sp.) were taken by the Calfbirds during the months we were there, large numbers of old *Euterpe* seeds were found beneath the lek perches, so at other times of year this palm must be important. Gilliard (1938) reported a large palm seed in the stomach of a bird collected in Venezuela, and Schubart *et al.* (1965) recorded 6 fruits of a palm, 18 mm in diameter, in the stomach of a specimen collected in Brazil. These results indicate that the same tree families are important in the diet of the Calfbird as in other large frugivorous cotingas such as the bellbirds, and the entirely frugivorous but unrelated Oilbird *Steatornis caripensis*.

Like many other cotingas, the Calfbird takes lauraceous fruits in flight, snatching one fruit at each sally. The fruits of many Lauraceae are pendent at the end of long pedicels, with the basal portion enclosed in a cupule, so are probably not available to birds from a perched position unless they have particularly long beaks. The Calfbird also

MWWoodcock

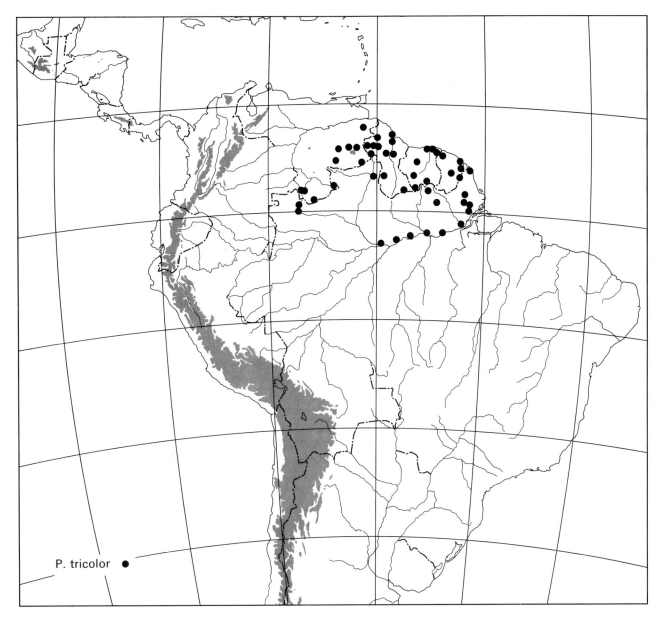

Map 27   Distribution of the Calfbird (*Perissocephalus tricolor*).

P. tricolor ●

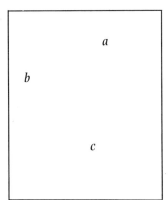

Plate 19

a and b: Crimson Fruit-crow *Haematoderus militaris*, male and female

c: Calfbird *Perissocephalus tricolor*

takes fruits of Burseraceae in flight, but those of *Didymopanax morototoni*, which grow in bunches, while perched.

The insect food taken by Calfbirds is diverse and includes grasshoppers (Tettigoniidae), stick insects (Phasmida), cicadas, moths, caterpillars, cockroaches (Blattidae), beetles, ants and wasps. The hard parts of insects may be regurgitated as pellets; four such pellets were found beneath lek perches. During the dry season in the Kanukus of Guyana, Orthoptera were the insects most frequently taken, particularly large grasshoppers 5–8 cm long. A Calfbird's insect-searching technique consists of moving slowly along in the understorey. Between flights it perches motionless except for the movement of its eyes, while searching the surrounding vegetation. If it spots an insect, either nearby or as far away as 11 m, it makes a winged foray to snatch it from foliage or twig.

Behaviour (by B. K. Snow)

Only the female Calfbird builds and attends the nest. The males spend most of the day at a lek, or calling ground, where they advertise their presence by loud mooing calls and visual displays.

The only two leks observed, both at the foot of the Kanuku mountains, were in flat areas of forest with small trees, either second-growth trees or understorey trees beneath a canopy of much larger ones. A lek studied for three months was attended by four adult males, each of which owned a perch where it called and displayed. Lek perches were the bare horizontal branches of understorey trees; sited 9–11 m above the ground, they were within view of each other and 0.5–15 m apart. While the four adult males were present at the lek for an average of 65% of the daylight hours, four other males, judged to be immatures or sub-adults from their calls and behaviour, came to the lek at dawn and dusk but only intermittently throughout the day.

The male Calfbird has three different calls. The 'moo' call, usually adjusted in its timing so that individuals moo one after the other, is the main advertising call and is accompanied by a spectacular display. Both call and display serve to indicate a male's possession of his lek perch. A male on its own at the lek never utters a complete moo call, only the first half of it, the 'half-moo' (*grr-aaa* – see below), which acts as a contact call and frequently summons the other males back to the lek. Another common but much quieter call, a monosyllabic *wark*, usually repeated at 2 to 3 second intervals, is uttered by a male at the lek before leaving to feed, so is a non-aggressive flight-intention call. An alarm call, a sharp *kack*, was heard only twice from males diving down off their lek perches when attacked by other males.

When uttering the moo call, which in its complete form may be written *grr-aaa-oooo*, the Calfbird first leans slightly forward while it inhales air and utters the *grr*, then while uttering the *aaa* it raises itself on its tarsi and at the same time raises the tail and fluffs out the under tail-coverts and all the feathers of the anterior half of the body so that they form a cowl round the bare facial skin (Fig. 7a). With the final bellowing *ooo* it sinks back on its tarsi until it is leaning backwards at an angle of 15° from the vertical. At the same time it depresses the tail so that the curved orange under tail-coverts are displayed like two bright globes on the black dorsal surface of the tail. When adult males moo near to each other they normally do so back to back; when both are on the same perch they face the same way but twist their bodies during the moo-call so that they look in opposite directions. The adult males that I observed during my study uttered the moo call less often than the sub-adults, and the dominant males slightly less often than subordinate males.

The most important display performed by males in asserting their claims to a lek perch is the Motionless posture (Fig. 7b). In this posture, usually held for 5–10 minutes but occasionally as long as 40–50 minutes, all body feathers are flattened except the curved under tail-coverts displayed on the dorsal surface of the tail. The body, including the neck and head, is held in a horizontal position, the tail is slightly raised and the wings drooped. This posture is assumed (from a normal perched position) by very slow, imperceptible movements. A male in the Motionless posture keeps his eye on his rival, which frequently involves twisting or tilting his head. A male only assumes the Motionless posture when his lek perch is threatened by a rival male trying to establish ownership of a perch nearby. Then the threatened male spends long periods in the Motionless posture, both on his own lek perch and on the perch of his rival; on the latter, both males may spend long periods motionless within 2 or 3 feet of each other.

In the lek area aggressive attacks and chases between male Calfbirds are frequent, and occasionally fights occur. In addition the Calfbird has two ritualized aggressive postures. At lower levels of aggression the Pouter Pigeon posture (Fig. 7d) is assumed. In this posture the upper breast feathers are puffed out while the feathers of the posterior part of the body are flattened and the tail is tucked back between the legs. While in the Pouter Pigeon posture, a male usually hops about his lek perch or nearby perches. With an increased level of aggression he may do some cursory display preening to the under wing-coverts, or pluck and pull at nearby twigs or leaves.

With a further increase in the level of aggression a male may assume the Fluffed-up posture (Fig. 7c). In this posture all the body feathers are raised but the tail continues to be tucked between the legs. The wings are held slightly away from the body or, at a higher level of aggression, opened and held out. Quite frequently there is display-preening of the under coverts of the opened wing. When the latter occurs, it is usually the wing nearest the object of aggression which is raised and preened. Males, both adult and immature, may wrench at and pull off twigs and leaves during and immediately after aggressive chasing or the ritualized agonistic displays. Frequently both contenders in an encounter will do so. After twig-plucking, males occasionally carry them around from tree to tree.

Because Calfbirds are sexually monomorphic, interpreting the situation at the lek is difficult. Females were tentatively identified by their nervous behaviour and silence at the lek. Twice apparent females visited the lek and came to the perch of the same male, judged to be the dominant male in the hierarchy. On each occasion all the other males at the lek also came into or near the dominant male's lek tree. One male, no. 2 in the hierarchy, also landed on the lek perch so that the female was sandwiched between the two males, who then edged towards her. On one occasion the dominant male briefly mounted the female, on the other occasion the female left, apparently nervous. Similar invasive behaviour, but with no female visible, was seen four times at the dominant male's lek perch and once at the perch of male no. 2. It seems reasonable to presume that a fairly typical sequence of mating behaviour was witnessed and probably all the invasions were potentially occasions for mating. An inactive female in the surrounding canopy would be difficult to detect, and may well have been present on each occasion.

There was no evidence that females uttered the moo call with its accompanying display, or participated in any of the agonistic displays. But females do utter a rasping *waaaaaaa* sometimes followed by a short *aw*, somewhat similar to the half-moo. This call was largely used as an alarm call near the nest. In addition females use a quiet version of the *wark* as a contact call. There was evidence that a social bond may exist between two females, so that they may nest near each other, visit the lek together and at times keep company while feeding, particularly when insect-searching.

Breeding and annual cycle

Breeding (by B. K. Snow)

During my study in the Kanukus, three nests with eggs were found and two similar nests, probably 6–12 months old, were also found. These are the only Calfbird's nests known. All the nests were less than 800 m from the lek; two of the occupied nests were 70 m from it.

The nests were thin light open structures made entirely of bifurcating twigs. Slightly larger twigs were used for the base of the nest, while the cup was formed from the slender resilient twigs of a common understorey tree, a species of *Eugenia*. The four nests examined closely had their cups formed entirely from these *Eugenia* twigs, suggesting that this tree may be an important feature of a Calfbird's breeding habitat. Nests are small for the size of the bird; the two cups measured were 115 and 135 mm in diameter. The five nests were all in understorey trees and 4–6 m above the ground. Two of the nests with eggs were only 5 m apart in adjacent trees.

Like many other cotingas, the Calfbird's complete clutch consists of only one egg. Two eggs measured 47 × 32 mm and 46 × 32 mm and their average weight, adjusted for weight loss during incubation, was 25.7 g. The egg has a pale khaki ground colour, overlaid with spots and blotches in two shades of brown. The incubation period, ascertained from one nest, was between 26 and 27 days. On the 19th day of incubation, continuous observations at this nest throughout the day showed the female incubating for 78% of the time, with five recesses varying between 18 and 39 minutes and averaging 30

Figure 7 Display postures of male Calfbirds: (*a*) half way through the 'moo' call; (*b*) two views of a bird in the Motionless posture; (*c*) the Fluffed-up posture; (*d*) the Pouter Pigeon posture. (Redrawn from B. K. Snow (1972).)

minutes. Earlier in the incubation period the female's attendance was lower.

The chick, which hatched overnight or early on the morning of 19 March, was covered in long bright orange-chestnut down and weighed 22.9 g on hatching. At 8 days old it was still covered with down but pin feathers were appearing beneath. At 16 days old the feathers of the body were out of their sheaths; the growing plumage was the same as the adult's and the forehead was largely bare, as in the adult. We had to leave the area when the chick was 16 days old, but a local assistant checked its presence up until it was 25 days old; by the 27th day it had gone. Apparently it had looked full-grown when last seen, but as a fledging period this should probably be treated with reservation as it is considerably shorter than would be expected from the Calfbird's size compared with other cotingas.

Throughout incubation and fledging there was evidence of only the one female attending the nest. Her visits to and from the nest were silent and inconspicuous and the chick kept still and silent in the nest. When the female returned with food for the chick the latter opened its gape wide without any other head movement and without making any noise.

The female brought food for the chick in her beak and did not regurgitate food at the nest. Of the 20 items brought to the chick which were identified, two were fruit, one was a lizard and 17 were insects including grasshoppers, stick insects, cicadas and moths. The female came with food rather seldom, on average 1.5 visits per hour when the chick was under 7 days old and a slightly lower rate when it was older. There was no indication that the female was in any way hard-pressed to find the necessary food for the chick; when it was under a week old she normally brooded it after returning with food but when it was 10 days old or more she briefly brooded it and then often spent between 10 and 20 minutes perched beside the nest. She carried away the chick's faecal sacs and occasionally preened it while perched on the edge of the nest.

Annual cycle
The eggs in the three nests recorded in the Kanuku Mountains of southern Guyana were laid in late February, March and early April, i.e. late in the dry season and at the beginning of the wet season. On the basis of a total period of moult of 220 days in

the individual (Snow 1976a), the calculated dates of onset of moult in 16 specimens from Guyana are all from March to July, which suggests a well defined annual cycle. There is little evidence of any difference in the timing of moult between the sexes. Elsewhere in the range of the species, on the basis of moult records, the annual cycle seems to be less well defined. Thus in the lower and middle Amazon basin, within 3° of the Equator, the 13 records of moult are spread out through the year, with calculated dates of onset of moult in all except five of the months.

Plumages and moults

Nestling down orange. Apparently no distinct juvenile plumage, the feathers that succeed the nestling down being of adult type (see above, under Breeding), but young birds have sparse downy (not bristly) feathers on the bare skin of the head.

Physical characters

Structure
Bill long and strong, hooked at tip; nostrils oval, exposed; rictal bristles well developed. Anterior portion of trachea dilated. Wings long, flight-feathers unmodified; tail short. Crown bare, except for sparse hair-like feathers; feathers at back of head dense and upstanding. Under tail-coverts curled, forming during display (see above, Behaviour) two 'globes' of feathers. Legs and feet strong, claws strongly hooked.

Unfeathered parts
Iris: dark brown.
Bill: upper mandible black, grey at base; lower mandible grey.
Legs and feet: dark blue-grey.

Measurements
♂♂ (16) Wing 210–232, 217.3. Tail 100–107, 103.2. Tarsus 41–45, 43.1. Culmen 32–38, 35.7.
♀♀ (10) Wing 197–210, 203.1. Tail 96–104, 100.2. Tarsus 38–42, 40.0. Culmen 31–33, 32.3.
Weights: 5 ♂♂ 320–395, 360.0 g (mean wing-length 225.0 mm).
6 ♀♀ 267–367, 319.0 g (mean wing-length 212.5 mm).

Genus *Haematoderus*

Plate 19, page 154

Haematoderus militaris — Crimson Fruit-crow

This, the most spectacular of the very large cotingas, is also the least known. Its social behaviour and displays are unknown and its anatomy has not been studied, so nothing can be said about its relationships within the family. Its restricted distribution in lower and middle Amazonia and the Guianas is unlike that of any other cotinga, and suggests the possibility of ecological competition with *Pyroderus* and *Cephalopterus*, with which it seems not to overlap. The male's courtship must be one of the most brilliant displays of all tropical American birds; to see it and describe it is a prize awaiting some future ornithologist.

Distribution and ecology (Map 28)

The known range comprises all three of the Guianas, adjacent parts of Brazil north of the Amazon (west to the Manaus area), and a limited area around Belém and south to Cametá on the left bank of the lower Tocantins. At the northwestern extremity of its range, Schomburgk (1848) reported it as a migrant in the Kanuku Mountains of southern Guyana, occurring only in June and July (the wet season) when the fruits that it eats are ripe. It has never been seen there since, although a fair number of ornithologists have visited the area. At the eastern extremity of its range, in the Belém area, the months of collection of specimens are April (end of wet season) and August–September (dry season); specimens collected in gardens of the city itself in two different years suggest seasonal movements. It seems that the species is generally rare, but possibly local concentrations occur in some areas at times. Thus S. M. Klages collected four specimens at Obidos in January and February 1921. He recorded in his manuscript notes that he met with it in the depths of the primeval forest, where it lives in the tree-tops. Although it was wary, he found that it could be decoyed by imitating its call (which unfortunately

he did not describe). His impression was that it was by no means a common bird, and he never encountered it before or afterwards. Haverschmidt (1977) saw it five times in Surinam between 1946 and 1968, and reports three subsequent sight records by other observers. All those seen by Haverschmidt were perched on the tops of huge trees.

There seem to be only two records of its food, both from stomach contents of specimens. Haverschmidt (*loc. cit.*) recorded Colcoptera, and Novaes (1978) a species of Buprestidae (Coleoptera) 3.5 cm long. Undoubtedly Crimson Fruit-crows are also fruit-eaters.

Annual cycle

The nest is unknown, and the only very young specimen that has been collected (in the British Museum (Natural History)) is undated. The majority of dated adult specimens examined (7 out of 9) are in wing-moult, showing no obvious seasonal pattern.

Plumages

Juvenile plumage dull brown above, with pink centres to feathers of forehead and mid-crown, pale outer edges to primaries and secondaries (the latter vermiculated towards the tip), and pale tips to tail-feathers; underparts pale pink with dark brown edges to feathers of throat, sides of neck and upper breast. This plumage replaced by immature plumage in which back, wings and tail are uniform blackish brown, and whole of head and underparts red. Adult female plumage essentially the same, but some tendency for feathers of crown and breast to be modified as in adult male. In males, immature plumage replaced by adult plumage which is totally deep crimson except for dark brown wings and tail, the feathers especially of the crown, upper back and breast highly modified and glossy (see Structure, below).

159

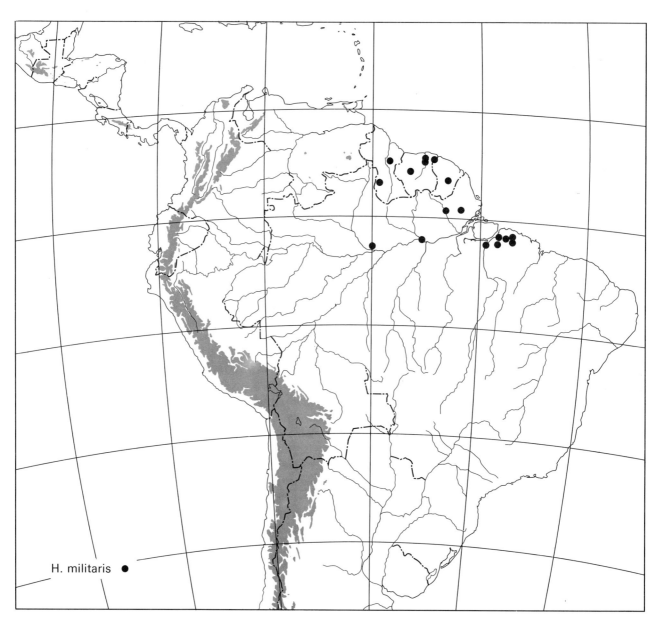

Map 28   Distribution of the Crimson Fruit-crow (*Haematoderus militaris*).

Physical characters

Structure

Bill strong, hooked at tip and wide basally, with ovoid nostrils nearly covered by forwardly directed feathers of sides of forehead; rictal bristles well developed, and long forwardly directed bristles from base of upper mandible. Wing feathers unmodified. Legs relatively short, feet small. In adult male, feathers of crown, upper back and breast highly modified: narrow and much elongated (breast feathers up to at least 105 mm long), darker crimson than rest of plumage and very glossy towards tip.

Unfeathered parts

Iris: dark brown.

Bill: upper mandible dark reddish or reddish-brown; lower mandible pale reddish-brown, darker along sides.

Feet and legs: blackish.

Measurements

ad ♂♂ (6)   Wing 213–225, 217.5.   Tail 121–137, 130.2.   Tarsus 26–30, 28.2.   Culmen 23–28, 25.7.

im ♂♂ (3)   Wing 208–225, 218.7.

♀♀ (4)   Wing 209–214, 211.3.   Tail 125–133, 129.8.   Tarsus 26–29, 27.5.   Culmen 23–26, 24.3.

Genus *Procnias* – the bellbirds

Plate 20, page 164

Procnias averano – Bearded Bellbird
Procnias nudicollis – Bare-throated Bellbird
Procnias alba – White Bellbird
Procnias tricarunculata – Three-wattled Bellbird

The four species of bellbirds constitute a very well-defined genus. They show in extreme form the wide gape which is characteristic of the most specialized frugivorous cotingas; the associated modifications of the skull are so marked that Warter (1965) placed *Procnias* in a subfamily of its own, Procniatinae, within the Cotingidae. In previous subfamilial classifications *Procnias* had been placed with the fruit-crows (Gymnoderinae) or with the typical cotingas (Cotinginae). Warter concluded that the skull of *Procnias* is probably derived from and represents an extreme modification of the cotingine type of skull. He further suggested that the very wide bill might be adapted to enhance the visual effect of the open gape during display, but this seems to have been on a misunderstanding of the male's courtship behaviour and it is more reasonable to suppose that the wide gape is an adaptation to swallow large fruits, as discussed below. Whether the great lateral expansion of the base of the bill during the evolution of the genus may have led to structural modifications that increased the ancestral bellbird's ability to make very loud, explosive calls is a possibility worth investigating.

Another supposed anatomical peculiarity of *Procnias*, the absence of a bifurcation to the manubrium (spina externa) of the sternum, was later found to be invalid as a character separating the bellbirds from the rest of the family (Olson 1971). The degree of bifurcation varies from well-forked in *P. tricarunculata* (which thus agrees with other cotingas) to completely unforked in *P. nudicollis*.

Apart from their anatomy, the most striking feature of the bellbirds is their voice. Displaying males utter what are probably the loudest of all bird calls; the females appear to be silent. The highly muscular syrinx has been described most recently by Ames (1971), who concluded that 'the syringeal cartilages and muscles are so specialized that they tell us little about the relationships of *Procnias*'.

Sexual dimorphism in plumage and ornamentation, and also in size, is very well marked in the genus. The males of each of the four species are adorned with some form of wattle or bare skin in the area of the bill or throat – each quite different from the others and of a peculiarly 'arbitrary' kind, as so often is the case with the secondary sexual characters of closely related species. The males of two of the species are among the very few land birds with wholly white plumage. In contrast to the very distinct males, the females of all four species are very similar and give evidence of a rather close relationship.

On the basis of the male characters the four species fall into two pairs, *P. averano* and *P. nudicollis* on the one hand and *P. alba* and *P. tricarunculata* on the other. Each of these pairs has a number of characters in common, and there is little doubt that the genus in its present state has arisen from an original splitting of an ancestral form into two species, followed by a further splitting of each.

In adult males of *P. averano* and *P. nudicollis* the throat is bare or furnished with rudimentary black feathers; there is a bare patch of skin on the side of the tibia; and the modified tips of the outer primaries (Fig. 11) are similar. In the juvenile male, the crown passes through an intermediate sooty-black stage before it acquires the adult colour. In the adult female, the crown is darker than the back and the throat feathers are mainly dark. These two species are almost exactly the same size, and a little smaller than the other two.

In adult males of *P. alba* and *P. tricarunculata* there is an elongated wattle springing from the base of the upper mandible (*P. tricarunculata* also has two similar wattles arising from the corners of the gape); the throat is feathered; there is no bare patch on the tibia; and the modified tips of the outer primaries are much alike in shape. The juvenile male does not develop a dark crown at any stage. In the adult female, the crown is the same green as the back and the throat is pale.

Map 29   Distribution of the bellbirds (*Procnias* spp.).

Distribution

As Map 29 shows, the four bellbirds replace one another geographically except in a limited area in southeastern Venezuela, and probably adjacent parts of Brazil, where *P. averano* and *P. alba* overlap. At least in the breeding season, all are essentially birds of montane forest; outside the breeding season, Bare-throated and Three-wattled Bellbirds, and probably some populations of Bearded Bellbirds, move down to lower forests. Although White Bellbirds are not known to make regular vertical migrations they too tend to wander, stragglers having been recorded several hundred miles from their normal range (see p. 195).

The distributional and altitudinal relationships between the Bearded and White Bellbirds in their area of overlap are not well known, as this area has been little visited by ornithologists. Recorded altitudes are as follows (from specimens in the

Phelps collection, American Museum of Natural History, and personal observations from the Kavanayén/Ptari-tepui area):

Bearded Bellbird *P. averano*

Kavanayén/Ptari-tepui area	950–1000, 1700–1900 m
Roraima	1070–1280 m
Acopan-tepui	1200–1600 m
Venezuelan-Brazilian frontier	800–1365 m
Uei-tepui	1300 m
Headwaters of Caura River	700 m

White bellbird *P. alba*

Kavanayén/Ptari-tepui area	1100–1250 m
Auyan-tepui	1100–1500 m
Cerro Tomasote	500–600 m
Altiplanicie de Nuria	460 m

In the Kavanayén/Ptari-tepui area in April 1976, I found White Bellbirds calling in the forest on the lower slopes of Ptari-tepui at 1100–1250 m, and Bearded Bellbirds calling higher up on the same mountain, at 1700–1900 m. Some 20 km away, in forest below the mission station of Kavanayén at an altitude of about 1000 m, a small group of Bearded Bellbirds was established and calling. This seems to be the only recorded instance of both species being apparently resident very close to one another. The fact that White Bellbirds occur widely in Guyana at lower altitudes than those listed above, while the Bearded Bellbird has been recorded only twice from Guyana but has been found in more localities and at higher altitudes than the White in southeastern Venezuela, suggests that there is a gradual replacement, with some interdigitation, of the White Bellbird by the Bearded as one moves from the lower mountains of the Guianas westwards to the more lofty highlands (the 'pantepui' region) of Venezuela.

From the present distribution, and apparent relationships between the four species, a tentative distributional history of the genus can be constructed (Snow 1973a). The montane distribution, and the complete absence of the genus from the main part of the Andes, strongly suggest that the genus originated in the highland forest of the Guiana shield or some part of eastern Brazil. It is likely that the first split was into an eastern and a western form, giving rise to the forms ancestral to *averano-nudicollis* and *alba-tricarunculata* respectively. The eastern form probably split into two – *averano* in the north and *nudicollis* in the south – during a period of aridity, when the highland forests of northeastern Brazil were isolated (as they now are) from those of eastern coastal Brazil. The western form probably split into two by establishing an isolated offshoot in

Central America by long-range dispersal. According to this reconstruction, *P. averano* must also have established an isolated population in Venezuela by long-range dispersal from the east, leap-frogging over *P. alba* in the process. In view of the known ability of bellbirds to wander widely, the present allopatric distribution of all four species must be due primarily to interspecific competition between these ecologically very similar species.

Habitat and movements

The bellbirds are essentially birds of montane forest in the breeding season. (It should be stressed that statements about breeding are largely inferential, as few actual nests have been found.) Probably all of them tend to make vertical migrations – not necessarily of any great length – from their breeding area down to lower-lying forest in the off-season. In Costa Rica the Three-wattled Bellbird breeds, apparently from February to July, in highland forest above about 1400 m, and moves down after breeding to lower montane forests, where the bulk of the population probably winters, and in small numbers even to sea level (Slud 1964). Skutch's (1969) records from the valley of El General, at 600–900 m, were mainly in the months January–March and July–September, suggesting birds on upward and downward pre- and post-breeding passage. For Panama, however, Wetmore (1972) found that there was insufficient evidence for any definite conclusion.

The seasonal movements of the Bare-throated Bellbird are apparently regular and extensive, but less well documented. In cloud forest at about 1000 m in the Serra do Mar near São Paulo, in November 1972, calling became more frequent and the birds more in evidence over an 11-day period (3–14 November). In 1979, at 1000 m in another part of the Serra do Mar no birds were seen or heard in the period 25–31 October, but they were calling in the Serra dos Orgãos at about the same altitude in the second half of November. The records of Bare-throated Bellbirds at lower altitudes, which account for a good deal of the spread in the range shown in Map 29, are no doubt largely from birds collected during their off-season wanderings, but too few specimens are accompanied by a record of altitude for any precise statement. In the extreme south of the range, in Rio Grande do Sul, the Bare-throated Bellbird is known only as a breeding migrant, the earliest recorded date being 3 October and the latest 13 March (W. Belton, pers. comm.).

In the Northern Range of Trinidad, where the Bearded Bellbird has been studied most thoroughly

MWWoodcock

(B. K. Snow 1970), the preferred breeding habitat is primary forest on the lower slopes of the mountains, between about 150 m and 460 m, with a preference for the lower levels within this range. Here, in an area where the wet and dry seasons are well-marked but the dry season is not usually very severe, there was no evidence of vertical migration. In northern Venezuela, in the Henri Pittier National park near the north coast, the Bearded Bellbird generally occurs only on the northern (the more humid) side of the mountains, between 200 and 500 m (Schaefer & Phelps 1954). At this level the forest is of a drier type than the forest at similar levels in the Northern Range of Trinidad, and is largely deciduous. There seems to be some vertical movement that is seasonal: in April and May (the beginning of the breeding season) some ascend as high as the Portachuelo Pass (1136 m) and cross over into the valleys on the south side.

Evidence for seasonal movements is slightest in the White Bellbird. In a three-month study of this species in the Kanuku Mountains of southern Guyana, B. K. Snow (1973) found that there was some movement from the lowest slopes of the foothills (some 200 m above sea level) up to the higher mountain slopes, perhaps connected with a scarcity of suitable fruits at the lower levels as the dry season neared its end.

It seems probable that the bellbirds' preference for montane forest is related to the abundance of suitable fruit-trees, especially of the laurel family (Lauraceae). Laurels are found at all levels in neotropical forests, but they are numerically most important in montane forest. For example, a recent monograph of the lauraceous genus *Persea* (Kopp 1966) shows that in Central America, where the genus is strongly represented, the majority of the species have been recorded between 1000 and 2000

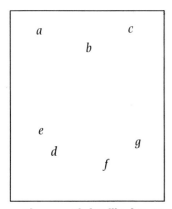

Plate 20
The bellbirds
(*Procnias*)

a: Three-wattled Bellbird *P. tricarunculata,* male
b and *c:* White Bellbird *P. alba,* male and female
d and *e:* Bearded Bellbird *P. averano,* male and female
f and *g:* Bare-throated Bellbird *P. nudicollis,* male and female

m above sea level, and rather few below 1000 m. Dr Skutch has more than once drawn attention to the confusing variety of species of Lauraceae in the montane forests of Costa Rica. By contrast, only two species of *Persea* are recorded by Kopp for the whole of the vast lowland Brazilian State of Amazonas. To what extent the bellbirds' seasonal movements are related to the fruiting seasons of their food trees must await future investigation.

Ecology and behaviour (by B. K. Snow)
Food
Apart from an early record of a female Bare-throated Bellbird with a snail in its stomach (Pelzeln 1868), all the evidence indicates that the bellbirds are entirely frugivorous. They usually pluck fruit on the wing, taking one at each flight and then landing. The Bearded Bellbird takes nearly all its fruit in this way, and so too, as far as known, does the White Bellbird; but the Three-wattled, while also using this method, takes much of its fruit while perched.

I studied the diet of the Bearded Bellbird for $2\frac{1}{2}$ years in the Northern Range of Trinidad. Most of the fruits that it takes are large drupes or berries, each containing a single large seed which is regurgitated. Although many direct observations were made of bellbirds feeding at different trees, a more unbiased record was obtained by spreading sacks to collect regurgitated seeds beneath the chief calling perches of some adult males. Adult males spend the greater part of every day at one or two calling perches beneath the canopy, except during the period of moult from August to the middle of October. In addition, sacks were spread beneath the four nests found. Over 2000 fruits belonging to 45 species were collected by these means. Of the 1777 fruits taken by adult birds, 33% belonged to the family Lauraceae and a further 11% to the Burseraceae. The fruits of both these families have a dense nutritious pericarp rich in fat and protein. Of the 350 regurgitated seeds collected beneath the one nest where the chick fledged, 74% were Lauraceae and 15% Burseraceae, suggesting a positive selection of these nutritious fruits for feeding the chick.

There are no comparable data on the food of the White Bellbird. A few personal observations on this species in the Kanuku mountains of Guyana were all of its feeding on species of Lauraceae.

A 2-month study between April and June of the Three-wattled Bellbird at Monteverde, Costa Rica, again showed the importance of lauraceous fruits in the diet, as two-thirds of the 307 fruits recorded (by direct observation of birds feeding and by collecting regurgitated seeds below calling perches) were from four tree species belonging to this family.

Social organization

Only the female bellbird attends the nest. The male devotes his time to advertising himself with very loud calls from one or two perches in his calling territory, where the female visits him in order to mate. Long-term observations on which this statement is based have been undertaken only on the Bearded Bellbird in Trinidad (B. K. Snow 1970), but shorter periods of observation on the Three-wattled and White Bellbirds (B. K. Snow 1973, 1977) fully support this conclusion. The Bare-throated Bellbird's behaviour has been studied only in captivity (B. K. Snow 1978). The main findings are summarised in the following sections.

Voice

Only the male bellbird calls; females are entirely voiceless. All four species have in their repertoires very loud elements which when delivered from above the canopy can be heard from at least a kilometre away. In three species, the Bearded, Bare-throated and Three-wattled Bellbirds, this loud element is an explosive single syllable, *bock*, uttered with the beak widely opened and lasting about half a second. While the *bock* shows distinctive variations between species and also between some populations of the same species, it has a fundamentally similar function in the three species. Its primary function is long-range advertising, both to females and to other males who are potential rivals for the calling territory. In all three species the *bock* is also incorporated into the climax of the display to visiting bellbirds, which results either in mating (seen only in the Bearded Bellbird) on in the ejection of visiting males.

The White Bellbird's loudest call is a sharp bell-like *ding ding*, which may be uttered while the bird is stationary, or one *ding* may be uttered while it leans to the right and the second after a rapid swing of the head and body through about 100° to the left. The elongated wattle always hangs on the right-hand side of the beak when the call is made with a swing, so that it flies out behind as the head swings suddenly to the left. The *ding ding* accompanied by a swing is audibly different from the call without a swing and louder, and is functionally similar to the *bock* of the other three species.

The Bearded Bellbird has two other calls: a repeated *tonk-tonk-tonk* . . ., delivered at rates of up to 2.5 per second, and a more slowly repeated disyllabic call. The *tonk* is typically repeated between 25 and 50 times and is a much quieter call than the *bock*; the beak remains wide open during the sequence of calls and the lower mandible moves slightly with each syllable. This call is characteristic

of a male calling beneath the canopy at his display sapling. The disyllabic call has been lost by the Trinidad population some time after it was first described by Brewster and Chapman in 1895. In the coastal range of northern Venezuela it is a resonant *kay-kong*, more musical than the *tonk*. In the Kavanayén/Ptari-tepui area of southern Venezuela it is a very different, unmusical call with a slightly hissing quality, transcribed as *bisset, bisset* . . . (D. W. Snow).

The Bare-throated Bellbird has two repeated calls, a loud and a quiet one. The loud call is delivered with the beak widely opened and only the lower mandible moved with each note; it is repeated at a rate of approximately 2 notes per second. This call, which has been likened to the sound of a hammer striking an anvil, consists of a less loud *bock* combined and overlapping with a pure high-pitched note; it is probably homologous with the *tonk* of the Bearded Bellbird. The quiet repeated call is delivered with the beak only just open and the colourful skin of the throat pulsating with each note; its volume is approximately a quarter of that of the loud version. It has probably evolved to display the blue-green skin of the throat, as all other known calls of the four *Procnias* species are uttered with the beak very wide open.

My observations on the voice of the Three-wattled Bellbird were made at Monteverde in the Cordillera de Tilarán of Costa Rica, where there were 13 adult male territory-holders during May–June 1974. Eleven of these males had repertoires of the same three songs, except for slight individual variations and innovations. In addition to the monosyllabic *bock* they had two multiple calls which included elements of the *bock*, a sharp squeak, and several muted notes, the whole sequence lasting about 5 seconds. The two multiple calls were frequently, but not always, followed by particular display movements, and from their contexts were dubbed the flight-display call and the changing-place call.

Of the two remaining males, one uttered songs similar to a recording of the species from Volcán de Chiriquí in Panama, but very different from other Monteverde birds. It, too, had a repertoire of three songs: a monosyllabic *yock*, lacking the harmonics of the *bock* and so sounding much harsher; a *yock-ack*, which preceded the flight display; and an *ack-ick*, followed by some extremely quiet sounds, which preceded the changing-place display. The other male had the normal repertoire of the Monteverde birds and in addition, at intervals of about half an hour, it uttered a loud melodious double whistle. The function of this whistle was not determined, but it was evidently the same note as that described by Wetmore (1972) from observations in Panama, and by Ridgway (1905) and Skutch (1969) from other parts of Costa Rica. It seems that there is much regional variation in the vocalizations of the Three-wattled Bellbird, probably related to its regular vertical migrations from scattered lowland forests up to montane forests 1300–1600 m above sea level. These montane areas are physically well separated and so are likely to foster the development of dialects, as young bellbirds appear to learn the calls of their species.

Of the four species, the White Bellbird produces the most musical sounds. Besides the bell call, described above, it utters a very musical disyllabic *doing doing*, delivered while stationary with a single opening of the beak. It is not so loud as the bell call and is probably analogous to the repeated or multiple calls of the other three species.

Young male bellbirds start to learn the calls of their species when approximately 1¼ years old. First the loudest call (the *bock* or, in the White Bell-bird, the bell call) is learnt. Initially young males of all four species utter a very similar harsh squawk which slowly becomes recognizable as the call of their species. A ringed Bearded Bellbird perfected its *bock* call after 5 months of practice, but had still not perfected the repeated *tonk-tonk-tonk . . .* after 7 months of practising. A captive young Bare-throated

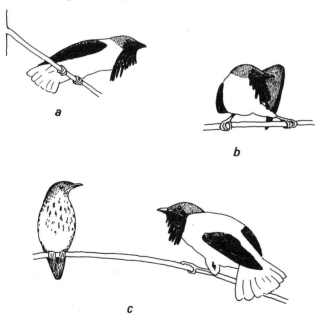

Figure 8 Display postures of the Bearded Bellbird:
  (a) posture held by male after display jump;
  (b) display-preening, with wing held up and bare thigh patch exhibited;
  (c) position of male and female on mating branch just prior to mating. (Redrawn from B. K. Snow 1970.)

Bellbird housed next to an adult male had not perfected his repeated call after 10 months of practice.

The displays of males
Adult male bellbirds that own a calling territory spend practically all the daylight hours there. Observations on a Bearded Bellbird in Trinidad throughout a day in April (a month when display is at a high level) showed it to be present for 87% of the day; it left its calling territory to feed 25 times, usually for 2–3 minutes. Similar day-long observations on a Three-wattled Bellbird in May showed an equally high level of attendance in the calling territory and short periods spent feeding. Shorter periods of observation on White Bellbirds in Guyana indicated a similar level of attendance. The males call continuously in their territories, except when visited by other bellbirds. They then display silently except for occasional loud calls which are part of the displays directed at visitors. Three-wattled and White Bellbirds have their wattles elongated while calling, and retract them when they leave their calling territories to feed.

All four species of bellbirds call from high song-posts above the canopy, usually dead branches without leaves or the topmost branches of thin-foliaged trees. In addition, in the three species studied in the wild the males have a special perch beneath the canopy to which they lead visiting bellbirds, both male and female. On this 'visiting perch' the male displays and may mate. Mating has been seen only in the Bearded Bellbird, but male Three-wattled and White Bellbirds have been seen doing similar pre-mating displays to visiting females on their perches.

All four species have a flight-display or a display-jump. In the Bearded Bellbird it is a silent jump between the visiting perch and an adjacent perch on the same level and about 4 feet (1.2 m) away. It lands from the jump in a crouched position with the tail spread and may turn its head to eye the visitor (Fig. 8a). Display-jumps between the same two perches may be repeated a number of times. The same posture on landing is characteristic of the displays of the other three species. Within the limitations of a cage the Bare-throated Bellbird's display-jump looks extremely similar. The equivalent display of the Three-wattled and White Bellbirds differs in being a flight between two perches 7 to 15 feet (2–5 m) apart, one of the perches being either the high song-post, above the canopy, or the visiting perch. In the Three-wattled Bellbird the flight display is always preceded by the multiple call described above. In all species the arrival of a visitor triggers the display, but flight-displays above the canopy may also be practised when no visitor is in evidence.

When a visitor is at close quarters the male's display is largely silent in all four species. It includes gazing intently at the visitor, with occasional head movements that shake or move the wattles. The same movements are made by the Bare-throated Bellbird although it lacks wattles.

The Three-wattled Bellbird has, in addition, a display that has no equivalent in the three other species, the 'changing-place' display (Fig. 9). It is always preceded by a particular multiple call, described above, and is performed either at the visiting perch or at the high song-post. The male flutters up 1 or 1½ feet (30–45 cm) above the perch and lands back on it in a crouched position with tail spread. The visiting perch of this species is a

Figure 9 The Three-wattled Bellbird's 'changing-place' display:
    (*a*) male uttering the changing-place call at the outer position on his visiting perch, visiting female at inner position;
    (*b*) male changing place with female by flying over her as she moves to outer position;
    (*c*) male uttering a close-up call into the female's ear. (From B. K. Snow 1977.)

broken-off branch growing upwards at an angle of 10–15° above the horizontal. If a visiting bellbird lands on the perch at the inner position, the owning male changes places with it during the display, and then hops up to the visitor and utters close into its ear the changing-place call followed by an extremely loud *bock*. Normally this causes a male visitor to fall or fly off the end of the visiting perch, although it often returns and the sequence is repeated. Once in an encounter between closely matched adult males, the visiting male, having stood its ground when the owner called in its ear, then took up the role of owning male, changed places with the erstwhile owner and dislodged him with a close-up call. During this encounter the owner of the perch, while uttering his calls, had his wattles extended while those of the visitor were retracted, and when the roles were reversed so was the length of the wattles.

Although I witnessed many visits made by females to males on their visiting perches, only once did a female remain throughout the close-up call — at which the male fluttered away from her with a shortened flight-display call, then crouched and with a loud *bock* fluttered back towards her. I believe that this was the mounting movement as it was similar to the Bearded Bellbird's mating leap.

I saw the Bearded Bellbird mating on four occasions, each time at the same place on the visiting perch. In this species the visiting or mating perch is the lowest branch of an under-storey sapling; typically the branch is slender, curves downward, and is uncluttered for 2 to 3 feet (60–90 cm) from its point of attachment to the trunk.

When a female Bearded Bellbird visits a male she first perches above the display sapling and looks down at him. He stops calling the moment he is aware of her presence and silently display-jumps. The female may then fly down to the upper branches of the display sapling, whereupon the male immediately moves to the outer end of the mating branch and display-preens (Fig. 8b). In a crouched position he thrusts forward one of his legs towards the visitor and displays the bare patch of skin on the side of the tibia. The closed wing on the same side is held up and he makes frequent brief preening movements at the under-wing coverts or at the contour feathers beneath it. Between each preening movement he raises his head and looks at the female. If the visit is to culminate in mating, the female now comes down to the inner end of the mating branch. In this event the male slowly stops display-preening and remains motionless in the crouched position with his eye fixed on the female (Fig. 8c). From this position he leaps with a particularly loud *bock* on to the female's back and

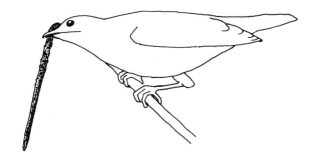

Figure 10 Adult male White Bellbird in the silent wattle-
displaying posture.

mates. It is usual for the female to retire many times in the face of this mating leap before finally remaining and allowing the male to mount.

The White Bellbird's visiting perch is a horizontal uncluttered branch or liana. When the male is visited here by a female he initially crouches over his right leg while he silently shakes his single wattle, which is always kept hanging on the right of the beak (Fig. 10). While he does this the female slowly edges along the perch towards his left flank. When she is a few feet away the male utters the bell call with a swing from the right to his left where the female is perched. Once, as he swung, a male was seen to jump with a flutter. On this and every other occasion witnessed, the female retired. The bell call with a swing and a flutter-jump to the left is fairly certainly the male's mounting movement, and therefore homologous to the Bearded Bellbird's *bock* with a leap and the Three-wattled Bellbird's *bock* with a flutter.

Breeding and annual cycle

Nesting (by B. K. Snow)
The first reliable reference to a bellbird's nest was given by von Ihering (1914), who described the Bare-throated Bellbird's nest as a shallow bowl with a diameter of about 16 cm, looking like the nest of a pigeon. No further information on the nest of any of the bellbirds was forthcoming (Pereyra's (1951) account being clearly based on a misidentification) until Beebe (1954) described two nests of the Bearded Bellbird from Trinidad. Since then eight more nests have been found in the Northern Range of the island. All further details in this section refer to the Bearded Bellbird in Trinidad unless otherwise specified.

All the Trinidad nests were in cultivated land with cocoa and other trees but close to forest. They were sited in crotches of small or medium-sized trees, mostly in the outer branches, from 8 to 50 ft (2.4–15 m) up. The nest is an extremely light construction about 18 cm across, made of fine twigs and so thin

that the egg is visible through it. The female is highly selective about the twigs used; the three nests examined after use had the cups entirely composed of fine twigs from one species of forest tree (*Maprounea guianensis*), while all but 11 of the basal twigs came from another tree species (*Terminalia obovata*). The twigs from both trees have characteristics which make them particularly suitable for interlocking into a resilient strong platform with a shallow cup.

Little is known of the nests of the other bellbirds. For the Bare-throated, in addition to von Ihering's description, Sick (1979) mentions that the nest may be placed on an epiphytic bromeliad. A Three-wattled Bellbird's nest found while being built at Monteverde, Costa Rica, was a slight structure of loosely woven twigs sited 6½ m up in a crotch of an under-storey tree at the edge of the forest. The White Bellbird's nest has never been found, but a female was watched collecting fine twigs from an under-storey tree (*Eugenia* sp.), which suggests that its nest is like the others'.

The female breaks twigs from the living tree, carries them to the chosen nest-site and lays them there with her beak, but after that builds entirely with her breast and feet, by gripping the twigs with her feet and pressing into the nest with her breast. The nest takes four or five days to build, and there is then a pause of three to four days before laying.

A single egg is laid (data from five nests with eggs and two with nestlings). One egg measured 40.3 × 28.4 mm and weighed 17.9 g (about 13% of the female's weight). In colour the eggs are light tan, mottled with brown. Of the five nests found at or before the egg stage four were lost during incubation, three probably to predators and one apparently destroyed by wind. There were records of eggs being laid in all months from April to November inclusive, except September; but in fact breeding ceased for about 2½ months, from early August to mid-October (see next section).

The female incubates very closely, particularly in the second half of the incubation period. During a day-long watch of 12¼ hours at the only successful nest on the 10th day of incubation, the female left the nest five times, her absences totalling 13% of the watch. On the 21st day of incubation she remained on the nest from 14.05 hrs until dark. As she first left the nest in the morning at about 05.45 hrs, she was incubating for nearly 16 hours without a break. The incubation period determined at this nest was 23 (± ½) days.

On hatching the chick was thickly covered in a grey-white hair-like down about 10 mm in length. For the first 12 days when disturbed or handled at the nest, the chick would roll up into a ball so that from above neither eyes, beak nor legs were visible, making it look more like a small mammal or hairy caterpillar than a nestling. The begging behaviour of the chick was striking for its silence and motionlessness: at the approach of the female it silently turned its head towards her and partially opened its beak. The chick gained weight steadily except between the 17th and 21st day, when the unsheathed feathers became visible all over the body and its weight diminished slightly. It left the nest at 33 days, its weight and measurements at 30 days indicating that a substantial amount of growth was still to take place.

The nestling was fed solely on fruit, which the female regurgitated in an unaltered state. It was fed at approximately hourly intervals, the female staying very briefly at the nest to deliver the food, and eat the faecal sac and any regurgitated seeds lodged in the nest. Brooding, except at night, ceased early, at least by the 6th day if not earlier. The female was entirely silent at the nest and made no attempt to defend or protect her chick from intruders. For the last four nights before the chick left the nest, female and chick roosted side by side near it.

Annual cycle

There are no detailed breeding data for any bellbird except the Bearded Bellbird in Trinidad. In spite of this, it is fairly certain that the two species which breed at the highest latitudes, the Three-wattled in the north (about 9–14°N) and the Bare-throated Bellbird in the south (about 12–26°S), follow the spring/summer breeding regimes that are prevalent in Central America and eastern Brazil. The available moult records indicate that females begin to moult immediately after breeding, that the males begin to moult on average considerably earlier than the females, and that young males begin to moult earlier than old males. The moult is slow and appears to take about 160 days in the individual (Snow 1976a). The data for the Three-wattled Bellbird suggest that young males must begin to moult before the breeding season begins and that adult males begin in the course of the breeding season. The calculated dates for the onset of moult in the two age classes are as follows:

	adult ♂♂	immature ♂♂
March	–	4
April (1st half)	–	1
April (2nd half)	1	–
June	1	–
July	2	–
August (1st half)	1	–

The White and Bearded Bellbirds, living mainly within 10° of the Equator, have less clearly defined seasons of moult, and probably also of breeding, over most of their ranges than the other two species. The moult records for the White Bellbird show no clear seasonal pattern. The Bearded Bellbird, in the centre of the Northern Range of Trinidad, at the northern limit of the species' range, has a main egg-laying season in April–July and a minor season in the second half of October and November. The few records suggest that females begin to moult during the first nesting season and so are at the height of their moult between the two nesting seasons. Adult males in the same area are also evidently at the height of their moult in August and September, as shown by detailed field study over three seasons; but records from specimens show a greater spread, with calculated dates of onset of moult from late April to September. As in the Three-wattled Bellbird, immature males moult earlier than adults; thus four records for young males in their first wing-moult indicate starting dates in February and March, while seven records for older birds, probably in their second wing-moult, indicate starting dates in April, May and June.

Plumage sequences and development of wattles

Male bellbirds take a long time to acquire fully adult plumage, and in the course of acquiring it pass through a succession of individually highly variable plumage stages. Presumably because the moulting process is slow, it is often found that the colour of the newly acquired flight or tail-feathers changes progressively along the row, showing progressively more adult characters. Often too the base of a feather is markedly more adult in colour than the tip. There is a tendency for wing-feathers, especially secondaries, to be replaced haphazardly, out of the normal sequence. Furthermore, it is not uncommon for the wing moult to be arrested before it is complete, and it sometimes begins (or is resumed after being arrested) at some intermediate point in the normal sequence. Feathers or parts of feathers that are transitional between juvenile and adult type, especially those transitional to white, tend to show a 'peppered' effect, being finely spotted with the remnants of the dark colour that is being lost.

Because of their more synchronized annual cycle, it is much easier to work out the timing of the plumage changes in Three-wattled and Bare-throated Bellbirds than in the other two species. Young males undergo a succession of complete annual moults, beginning when they are a little under a year old. At the first complete moult the wing and tail are replaced again by juvenile feathers;

the head and body feathers are replaced, variably and perhaps more gradually than the wing and tail, by feathers of more adult type. In some birds, the last wing and tail feathers to be replaced also show a tendency towards adult colouration. When the bird is a little under two years old another complete moult leads to the assumption of wing and tail feathers of adult or nearly adult type, and the head and body also become nearly adult in colour. In some individuals completely adult body plumage is acquired without a further wing moult, presumably by gradual replacement; in others, the fully adult plumage is not acquired until after the third complete moult. The replacement of odd wing and tail feathers between these complete moults may result in irregularities, with a few feathers of more adult type than the rest.

In the Three-wattled Bellbird, the wattles begin to grow when the male is between six months and a year old (assuming hatching in June), and they evidently grow fast, those at the gape much faster than the central one, since by the end of the first year they may be up to 20 mm long. They do not then grow much more during the following year. In the Bare-throated Bellbird the male's throat becomes bare in the course of the first year.

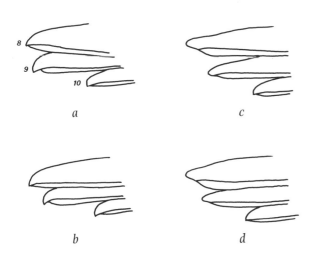

Figure 11   Shapes of the outer primary feathers in adult males of the four species of *Procnias*. a, *P. tricarunculata*; b, *P. alba*; c, *P. averano*; d, *P. nudicollis*. The three outermost primaries of the left wing are shown. Note that not only does the shape of the feather tip agree in *P. tricarunculata* and *P. alba*, and in *P. averano* and *P. nudicollis*, but also the ninth primary is the most modified in the first pair, and the eighth primary in the second pair. There is some individual variation in the degree of modification of the feathers.

In the Bearded and White Bellbirds the less well-synchronized annual cycle and more frequent irregularities of moult sequence make a reconstruction of plumage changes more difficult; but the observed changes in plumage in a male Bearded Bellbird in Trinidad, of known age (B. K. Snow 1970), provide a useful time-scale for part of the juvenile period. It seems that the plumage sequence and timing are very much the same as in the Three-wattled and Bare-throated Bellbirds. There is a succession of full moults, apparently starting when the bird is nearly a year old. After the first, the wing and tail are still of juvenile type, after the second they are sub-adult, and after the third fully adult in colour. In the Bearded Bellbird an early moult, probably of the whole head and body, leads to the assumption of a sooty crown, and this is replaced by the brown crown of the adult during the second year. After the first full moult the back also becomes sooty in colour rather than green, and later often grey-brown, before the very pale grey adult colour is acquired. The change is variable and probably depends on the relative timing of hormonal changes and of moults.

In the Bearded Bellbird the pale juvenile throat feathers are replaced by sooty feathers at about the same time as the sooty crown is acquired. The wattles probably develop at the age of about a year; in the Trinidad juvenile they were just visible, in the field, at the age of 16 months. In the only specimen of the White Bellbird examined at the appropriate stage, the wattle was present but short when the bird was half-way through its first wing moult, presumably at an age of just over a year.

Physical characters

Structure
Bill weak, very wide and much depressed basally; nostrils rather large, oval. Rictal bristles absent. Wings long and broad; tarsus rather short. Adult males with elongated wattles springing from base of bill or throat (for wattle structure see Burton 1976), or with throat and sides of face bare; and with tips of outer primaries modified (Fig. 11). Adult males of *P. averano* and *P. nudicollis* with bare patch on outer side of tibia.

Unfeathered parts
Iris: very dark; described as black in *P. averano* and *P. alba*, as brown or sooty in *P. nudicollis*, and as dark brown in *P. tricarunculata*.
Bill: generally described as black in all species, but lower mandible of female *P. tricarunculata* mainly dull greenish grey, black at tip (Wetmore 1972).

Legs and feet: black or dark grey in all species; pads of toes yellowish in *P. tricarunculata* (Wetmore).

Geographical variation

Reported only in *P. averano*. Adult males from northeastern Brazil (*P. a. averano*) have almost white body plumage, those from Venezuela and Trinidad (*P. a. carnobarba*) pale grey body plumage. Northeastern Brazilian birds are probably a little smaller (see below).

Measurements

P. averano carnobarba

ad ♂♂ (10)   Wing 150–166, 157.9.   Tail 75–90, 82.3.   Tarsus 27–30, 28.3.   Culmen 15–16.5, 15.8.

im ♂♂ (9)   Wing 146–161, 155.0.

♀♀ (6)   Wing 133–142, 138.3.   Tail 81–85, 83.7.   Tarsus 26–27, 26.8.   Culmen 13.5–14, 13.8.

Weights: ad ♂ 178 g (wing 166 mm).

3 ♀♀ 127–135, 130.7 g (mean weights and wings of 2: 132.5 g, 140.0 mm).

5 unsexed (♀ or immature plumage) 110–130, 119.9 g (ffrench 1973).

P. averano averano

ad ♂♂ (5)   Wing 152–155, 152.8.

♀♀ (2)   Wing 130, 136.

P. nudicollis

ad ♂♂ (24)   Wing 151–164, 156.7.   Tail 81–88, 84.1.   Tarsus 27.5–31, 29.2.   Culmen 13–15, 14.0.

im ♂♂ (51)   Wing 144–162, 154.0.

♀♀ (41)   Wing 130–149, 139.1.   Tail 83–92, 86.9.   Tarsus 25.5–29, 26.9.   Culmen 12–13.5, 12.9.

Weights: 4 ad ♂♂ 177–225, 200.5 g (mean weights and wings of 3: 208.3 g, 158.7 mm).

6 im ♂♂ 168–200, 186.3 g (mean weights and wings of 4: 193.8 g, 156.3 mm).

5 ♀♀ 140–150, 148.0 g (mean weights and wings of 4: 150.0 g, 139.8 mm).

P. alba

ad ♂♂ (13)   Wing 155–170, 160.8.   Tail 94–100, 96.9.   Tarsus 27–29, 28.1.   Culmen 14–17, 15.2.

im ♂♂ (6)   Wing 156–163, 160.0.

♀♀ (11)   Wing 131–140, 136.4.   Tail 83–84, 83.3.   Culmen 12–13.5, 12.8.

Weights: 1 ad ♂ 210 g.

2 im ♂♂ 210, 215 g.

P. tricarunculata

ad ♂♂ (39)   Wing 160–175, 165.5.   Tail 101–112, 107.4.   Tarsus 27–31, 29.0.   Culmen 16–18, 16.7.

im ♂♂ (16)   Wing 155–171, 163.4.

♀♀ (13)   Wing 136–152, 145.1.   Tail 95–109, 101.0.   Tarsus 25–30.5, 27.9.   Culmen 15–16.5, 15.8.

Weights: 6 ad ♂♂ 193.5–233, 210.1 g.

Genus *Rupicola* — cocks-of-the-rock

Plate 21, page 180

Rupicola rupicola — Guianan Cock-of-the-rock
Rupicola peruviana — Andean Cock-of-the-rock

Because the main artery of the thigh is the sciatic in *Rupicola* and the femoral in all other cotinga genera that have been examined, *Rupicola* has been placed in a separate family by some authors. It is now usually included in the Cotingidae, but it is certainly a very isolated genus and this is indicated by placing it last in the sequence. In addition to its arterial peculiarity it is unique among cotingas in its nesting habits.

The adult males of both species are among the most brilliantly coloured of the cotingas and indeed of all birds. In its combination of brilliance of colour and fantastic, delicately elaborated feather structure, the Guianan species is second only to the most spectacular of the birds of paradise. Not surprisingly, the skins of adult males have long been famous as collectors' items, but field studies of their displays and other aspects of their life histories have only recently been carried out. Indeed it is only in the last few years that any proper study has been made of the Andean species.

The two species share a number of external characters: a strong, hooked bill; powerful legs with very sharp claws; predominantly orange or red plumage (in the adult male); a crest of upstanding modified feathers running along the centre line of the crown and (in the adult male) almost concealing the bill; and similarly modified outer primaries. They differ most strikingly in some of the details of the male's display plumage, especially the completely different modifications of the secondary feathers, the modification of the long rump feathers and upper tail-coverts in *rupicola* (structurally unmodified and unusually short in *peruviana*), the presence of a white wing speculum in *rupicola*, and in the detailed form of the crest. There are also differences in size and proportions: *rupicola* is a smaller species than *peruviana* and has a relatively shorter tail. Warter (1965) has drawn attention to a striking skeletal difference between the two species, in the ossification of the skull in the nasal region.

Most notably, the display behaviour of the two species is completely different. I am indebted to Sr and Sra Benalcazar, whose summary of their unpublished study of the display of *R. peruviana* (pp. 178–181) makes it possible for the first time to compare the behaviour of this remarkable pair of species.

Distribution (Map 30)

As a consequence of its specialized nesting habits *Rupicola* is confined to mountainous areas, *peruviana* to the Andes and *rupicola* to the mountains of the much more ancient, eroded Guiana shield. At the local level, the distribution of each is dependent on suitable rocky areas in forested country. The physiography of the two mountain massifs is such that, at the altitudinal levels where suitable forest occurs, *rupicola* is associated with cliffs, boulders and rocky clefts, and *peruviana* with steep-sided river gorges.

R. rupicola is widespread in southern Venezuela, the Guianas, and adjacent parts of Brazil. It also occurs to a limited extent to the west of the upper Orinoco and upper Rio Negro, in the low table-mountains of southeastern Colombia that are structurally similar to but geologically much younger than the table-mountains of the Guiana shield (Haffer 1974). It is found at relatively low elevations, between about 150 and 1500 m above sea level.

R. peruviana occurs in suitable areas on the slopes of the Andes from Norte de Santander in Colombia to northern Bolivia. Its occurrence in Venezuela was for long based on a single female collected by A. Goering in 1873 at San Cristobal in southwestern Táchira near the Colombian border (Sclater & Salvin 1875), and (more doubtfully) on two males labelled 'Merida', obtained from the nineteenth century commercial collector S. Briceño Gabaldon of Mérida (specimens in BMNH). Its presence in southwestern Táchira was recently confirmed by Paul Schwartz, who recorded birds calling at 1100 m on Cerro El

Map 30   Distribution of the cocks-of-the-rock (*Rupicola* spp.).

Teteo in March 1969. This is a low altitude for the species; it is mainly a bird of the upper tropical and subtropical zones (about 1500–2500 m), even ascending locally to 3000 m or a little higher.

Habitat and food

The habitat requirements of both species of cock-of-the-rock are more obvious than is usual in the cotingas, for in addition to the evergreen forest that supplies their food they need rock faces for nesting.

As mentioned in the previous section, there is a difference in nesting habitat between the two species: the Guianan Cock-of-the-rock nests in caves, on the sides of great boulders, or in cracks among broken masses of rock, whereas the Andean species nests on rock faces in gorges beside mountain streams. Clearly their nest-sites are determined by the kind of rock faces that are available in, respectively, an ancient, eroded massif and a young, deeply dissected mountain range. Both species keep mainly to the lower levels of the forest in all their activities.

Both species feed mainly on fruit, which they usually pluck in flight. In captivity they have been reported to take insects as well as fruit. Olalla & Magalhães (1956) say that the Guianan Cock-of-the-rock takes insects, seizing them in flight, and lizards, which it catches in the trees. The only systematic study of the food of this species in the wild provided no supporting evidence. Regular collections of food remains from below a nest over an 11-week period spanning the start of the breeding season, and occasional collections from below other nests and from the courts at a display ground, gave evidence of nothing except fruit (Snow 1971*b*). Altogether the seeds of some 26 different plants were collected. Analysed by families, the composition of the fruits was as follows: Araliaceae 40% (*Didymopanax morototoni* only); Burseraceae 22% (*Protium neglectum*, *Protium* sp., *Trattinickia rhoifolia*); Meliaceae 12% (*Guarea trichilioides* only); Palmae 5% (*Astrocaryum* sp., *Euterpe* sp.); Lauraceae 4% (several species, unidentified); others 17%. Of the five main families, all except the Meliaceae are of outstanding importance in the diet of other specialised frugivorous birds in the New World tropics and are characterised by pericarps rich in fat and protein. The high place taken by the Meliaceae in the sample may have been attributable to the presence of two *Guarea* trees with abundant fruit near the nesting cave where most of the samples were taken; but the Meliaceae too is a family whose fruits are regularly eaten by specialised neotropical frugivores, though not so generally important as the other five.

There have been no other detailed studies of the food or feeding habits of the Guianan Cock-of-the-rock. There are references to fruits of palms, probably *Oenocarpus* (Lloyd 1895), Lauraceae (Olalla & Magalhães 1956) and *Miconia*, Melastomataceae (Carvalho & Kloss 1950).

For the Andean species, the only previously published reference to an identified fruit appears to be that of Stolzmann (in Taczanowski 1884), who reported that the favourite food in northern Peru was the fruit of a species of *Nectandra* (Lauraceae). Sr and Sra Benalcazar's study of this species in the mountains west of Cali in Colombia provides much new information, and in particular shows that small vertebrates constitute a significant part of the diet of the young. The remainder of this section summarizes their findings. Analysed by weight, 88.5% of the food brought to the nestlings was fruit pulp and 11.5% vertebrates. Among the latter an arboreal lizard, *Anolis eulaemus*, and a terrestrial frog, *Eleutherodactylus w-nigrum*, were identified.

Probably the calcium content of the bones as well as the high protein content of this vertebrate food is important for the growing nestlings. Arthropods were never seen to be brought to the nestlings, nor were their remains found in the faeces. Based on 71 samples totalling 3317 seeds, collected at seven nests, and analysed by the calculated weight of the fruit pulp, the three most important plant families were the Lauraceae (21.6%), Annonaceae (17.0%) and Rubiaceae (13.9%), with seven other families contributing less than 10% each (Musaceae, Solanaceae, Cucurbitaceae, Myrtaceae, Palmae, Myrsinaceae and Araliaceae).

When a female captures a vertebrate for its young, it seizes it in the beak, kills it by beating it against a branch, and then macerates it in the bill. It always presents the morsel head first to the nestling. Adults and young both regurgitate large seeds, such as those of the fruits of Lauraceae and Cucurbitaceae, so that quantities of them are found around and below the nests.

Behaviour

Although they are rather heavily built birds, the cock-of-the-rocks' broad and powerful wings give them great manoeuvrability. They can fly with rapid, twisting flight through thick undergrowth, and the females fly to and from their nests, if necessary negotiating narrow rock clefts, with speed and agility. Males of the Guianan Cock-of-the-rock can rise swiftly from their display courts on the ground if danger threatens. Sr and Sra Benalcazar report that the Andean Cock-of-the-rock comes down to the banks of streams to bathe. Males of this species forage together in pairs, presumably the same pairs as display together at the lek (p. 178), since they tend to leave the display area, and return to it, together. At night the males roost singly, generally on a low branch overhanging a stream among thick vegetation.

In both species the males display at leks and take no part in nesting. Their displays are so different, in almost all respects, that they need separate treatment. They are discussed in an evolutionary context on p. 181.

Display of the Guianan Cock-of-the-rock

Early accounts of the display behaviour of the Guianan Cock-of-the-rock, especially that by Robert Schomburgk which Darwin quoted in *The Descent of Man*, gave the misleading impression that the males collect in groups and take turns at dancing on a sort of communal dance-floor, while the rest watch from the side-lines. Gilliard's (1962) thorough study, however, made it clear that each male owns, and displays on, its own cleared area or 'court' within the general area of the lek. Gilliard's observations clarified many of the details of the displays, and my supplementary notes (Snow 1971*b*, 1976*b*) added some further points.

Only two display grounds were studied in any detail, both in the Kanuku Mountains of southern Guyana, at altitudes of about 140 and 600 m. Both were situated on forested ridges, the lower one in old secondary forest and the higher one in primary forest. A third display ground, briefly visited by Gilliard, was at a height of about 1000 m near the summit of a rocky peak. Display grounds are apparently traditional, being used for year after year as long as the forest remains suitable. The two that were studied were apparently used by 5–10 adult males, in addition to which a number of immature and sub-adult males were present at times. Gilliard's main lek measured about 12×22 m in total extent; the one that I watched, on rougher and steeper ground, was considerably larger but difficult to determine accurately. Within the general area of the lek the spacing of the courts of individual males varies widely; they may be nearly contiguous or up to 10 m or more apart. Large courts, typically more or less oval in shape, may measure as much as 1.5×2 m across; small ones, in less active use, may be only some 0.5 m across. Courts that are in active use are kept clear of dead leaves, twigs and other debris. The males do not, however, remove such debris from their courts, as some manakins do, but it is simply blown away by the powerful beating of the wings when the birds land on the courts and when they fly from them.

The males which own courts at a display ground also dominate the perches immediately above their courts. Much of their time is spent on these perches, or on perches at the periphery of the display ground. The males are mutually aggressive to one another, but aggressive behaviour is usually limited to ritualized posturing and jockeying for position. Dominance hierarchies within the group of established males are probably the rule, and would-be intruders are attacked. Gilliard observed on one occasion a band of seven presumed young males which invaded a display ground; the owning males repeatedly attacked them when they came down near the courts, and they eventually withdrew.

The males' display repertoire is very varied; some displays are vocal but most are visually striking. Two are accompanied by mechanical sounds.

Vocalizations. On first arrival at the lek, if it is unoccupied, males may utter a loud, bugle-like

ka-wasooh or *ka-haaow*, which Gilliard called the 'assembly call'. Possibly this serves to attract the other court-owners. Males also utter a variety of monosyllabic squawks, and 'wavering caws and muted, gabbling, fowl-like chatter' (Gilliard), the latter especially when they are interacting with others aggressively on the perches above their courts.

Head-bobbing with click. This is a common display, performed in a variety of contexts, apparently often in situations involving some sort of conflict. The bird hops (if on a perch) or raises its body by straightening the legs; at the same time the head is thrust upward and forward, and then jerked sharply down to the level of the perch or a bit below it. Then without a pause it is jerked up again, producing a sharp click, apparently as the opened bill snaps shut. As the bill is almost completely covered by the crest, the manner in which the sound is made must be inferred, but Gilliard produced a typical click by manipulating the bill of a freshly dead bird.

Wing-noise. During aggressive interactions, especially when the males are chasing one another in rapid flight, the wing-actions are accompanied by what Gilliard described as 'a low, undulating sound (a kind of whinnying whistle)', apparently produced by the attenuated end of the modified 10th primary.

Other displays associated with interactions between males. During aggressive interactions, males often fan out their modified rump feathers and under tail-converts, and depress their tail, in the same manner as they do when displaying on the ground. Often the wings are partially spread, so that the white speculum is visible. Usually, when displaying thus, they cling to vertical perches (Fig. 12), often beating their wings and accompanying their display with the calls described above. When several birds are displaying thus, jockeying for position and chasing one another, the general impression is of confusion and is in striking contrast to the calmness of the terrestrial display described below.

Displays on the court. When a female appears at the lek the males at once fly down to the ground, each to his own court. Sometimes they go down to the courts when no female appears to be present (though it is never possible to be sure of this under the conditions of observation). Gilliard noted that males were stimulated to go down to their courts when the sunlight struck them, but I never saw this. Typically, the method of landing on the court is conspicuous; the male lands with a loud squawk, with wings rapidly beating and held up above the back for much longer than would be required merely by the mechanics of landing. The combination of the loud call with the whirring wings, exposing the white speculum, makes the bird extremely conspicuous and probably functions to draw the female's attention to him. Once on the ground, the displaying male crouches and freezes, often for minutes on end (Fig. 12). Typically, the legs are flexed, the rear end of the body is elevated so that the upper surface of the back is more or less horizontal, the rump feathers and upper tail coverts are flared out, and the tail is depressed. The head may be held in normal position or it may be tilted sideways so that the crest lies in a horizontal plane, one eye looking directly upwards. Other orientations of the head may be adopted, probably depending on the position of the female to which the male is displaying; his aim seems to be to present her with his head in side view, thus showing to the full the spectacular crest.

Changes in the static posture are made gradually, probably determined, at least in part, by the need to present the head and body to best advantage to the female as she moves about in the trees above. Occasionally more sudden movements are made. The male may hitch itself forward a little and then return to its former position; it may bob its head with a click; or it may make a sudden jump into the air, with a squawk and conspicuously fanning wings, to land back in the same crouching position again. Gilliard noted that when a court was partially in sunlight a male might shift its position so as to move into the sun.

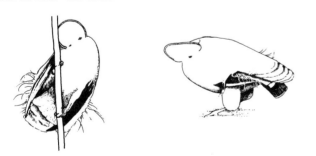

Figure 12 Display postures of the Guyanan Cock-of-the-rock. *Left:* male clinging to vertical perch; wing-feathers partly spread, showing white speculum. *Right:* male crouching on his court, with head turned, eyeing female in the trees above.

Interactions between males and females. Copulation, the culmination of these courtship activities, has not been seen. Females tend to be shy and unwilling to go to the ground if there is any possibility of disturbance. During my study at the higher of the two display grounds in the Kanuku Mountains in 1970, I witnessed what was almost certainly pre-copulatory behaviour. 'At 12.50 hours on 4th March, there was an obvious increase in excitement among the males at the display ground, and the two males under observation simultaneously came down to their courts. Shortly afterwards a female landed on the court of the nearer of the two males, both of which were motionless on their courts in the usual squatting posture. The female landed behind the male and hopped up to him until she almost touched him, then leant forward and began to nibble the long silky fringes of the male's modified secondary feathers. She was nervous, apparently of my hide, and moved away after about 10 seconds; then she approached again and began to nibble again at the secondaries of the male, who remained motionless. Unluckily at this point the female was alarmed at the noise of my camera shutter and flew off. . . She remained near by, calling occasionally, and the males remained frozen on their courts for several minutes; but she did not come down again. There was then a general scare and all the birds flew off.

'While the female was down on the court, a curious whining squawking went on continuously in the trees overhead, and contrasting with the silence of the displaying males gave an impression of tense excitement to the whole scene. Later, when the female had flown up from the court and was calling near by, with the usual monosyllabic crowing squawk, another bird was calling in the same way from the other end of the display ground. It seemed probable that two females had visited the display ground together, one of which had uttered the whining squawking while watching the other's approaches to the male on his court.'

If this behaviour was typical, it throws light on the extraordinary development of the fringes on the adult male's secondary feathers, since they play a direct part in the sequence of mating behaviour and presumably are sexually stimulating for the female.

Display of the Andean Cock-of-the-rock (by Cesar E. Benalcazar & Fabiola Silva de Benalcazar)*
Our study was carried out at Peñas Blancas, 28 km west of Cali, at an altitude of 1800 m, and lasted for 15 months, from April 1977 to July 1978. We made regular and intensive observations throughout this period, and individually marked a number of adults and juveniles. Our observations were concentrated principally on breeding activities at eight nests, feeding habits, and sexual behaviour.

A display area was found on sloping ground 60 m from the river along which the females nested, in the interior of the forest and distant 80 and 200 m, respectively, from two groups of nests. This was the only display area discovered in the whole region, and according to the local people it has persisted in the same place for many years.

The males concentrate their communal activity into two main periods per day, each of 2–3 hours' duration, the first from a little before 06.00 hours until 08.00–09.00 hours and the second from 15.00–16.00 hours until about 18.00 hours. Regular photometric measurements at the display area suggested a relationship between the birds' activity and light intensity. Thus the period of morning activity terminates when the light intensity is similar to that at the commencement of the afternoon activity. It may well be that confining the display activity to the times of day when light levels are low serves to reduce the risk of predation, as the displaying males are extremely conspicuous, and perhaps especially vulnerable.

Six males were regularly present at the display area, and were divided into three pairs. Within the area there were a number of display perches ('courts'), each of which was owned by an individual male. The members of the group could thus be clearly distinguished from one another by their positions. The area occupied by the group of display perches was 20–25 m across, and the distance between the pairs of males varied from 6 to 9 m. The courts of each pair of males were adjacent to one another. Except for the court of the dominant male, which was considerably larger, each court consisted of one, or at most, two branches or lianas 4–6 m above the ground, and occupied an area about 1 m across.

Within the group of males there was a hierarchy, the outstanding feature of which was that one male (male A) was dominant over all the others. His dominance was expressed in the following ways:

1. His court was larger than those of the other males. It was situated in a tree about 7 m high (of the genus *Vochysia*), the branches of which were horizontal. These branches remained practically devoid of leaves, as the male plucked them in the course of his display activity, using both bill and claws.
2. He was the only male to copulate with the females that visited the display area. Furthermore, it was clear that all the females went almost exclusively to his court.
3. He always took it upon himself to attack and evict strange males and juveniles which from time to time appeared in the neighbourhood of the display area.
4. He spent more time than the other males in the display area, and he usually arrived earliest and departed latest.
5. He made sporadic attacks on his partner (male B). When male B resisted the attack, they would grapple with interlocking claws and fall to the ground, remain there for some moments and then fly back to their respective perches and continue their displays.

The commencement of a period of display was generally signalled by the arrival of male A, who would go directly to his court. Sometimes males A and B appeared almost simultaneously. Generally the whole group of males were assembled in a few minutes. When male A arrived, he would announce his presence by uttering a loud call accompanied by a bowing movement of the head and body. This call might be repeated several times. He would also make a number of upward jumps, with the wings half opened, landing back in the same place, and would frequently make a mechanical sound by snapping the bill together. When his partner, male B, arrived at his court, both birds would approach each other at the boundary between their courts and would regularly perform a display which we have called the 'confrontation display' (Fig. 13). This display, which is the most conspicuous and the most frequently performed of the displays between the members of the male pairs, consists of several simultaneous movements: the head and tail are depressed so that the bird's upper surface forms a regular curve, the wings are slowly flapped, the tail fanned, and a call is uttered beginning as the curved posture is assumed and ending when the head reaches its lowest point. Onomatopoeically the call may be written as *youii*, which is the name given to

*Our thanks are due to the following bodies who financed our study: Fondo Colombiano de Investigaciones Cientificas "Francisco José de Caldas"; Fundación para la Educación Superior (FES) de Colombia; Smithsonian Tropical Research Institute.

the Andean Cock-of-the-rock by the Quechua-speaking peoples of upper Amazonia (Olalla & Magalhães 1956).

The members of each pair perform this display facing one another and practically simultaneously. Once it has begun, it may be repeated again and again, with brief intervals, for the whole period of activity. Each pair of males performs the display at the boundary between their courts and the displays of the different pairs tend to be synchronized. The resulting sound can be clearly heard at a distance of some hundreds of metres. When the level of excitement is increasing, the males begin to utter a brief croaking call, which is repeated continuously and finally ends suddenly with the confrontation display and its characteristic call. Occasionally a male may perform the confrontation display in the absence of his partner.

These communal activities of the males may continue for the whole of the time that they are present at their courts, without any female being present. Periodically they stop displaying and move away to forage in the neighbourhood of the display ground, returning a few minutes later. Occasionally they regurgitate seeds at the display area.

Females visited the display area singly or in small groups, and were much quieter than the males. Their presence raised the level of excitement among the males, stimulating them to utter loud calls and to increase the frequency of their confrontation displays. On those occasions when copulation did not occur male A and one or more of the 'females' (in these cases the possibility that they were immature males could not be excluded) performed one or more of the following five displays: (1) the confrontation display, as described above. (2) The two birds approach one another on the same perch, with short hops, fluttering their wings and brushing them against each other. (3) The two birds move to and fro between two perches, remaining always face to face; this may be repeated many times without interruption. (4) The two birds perch close together on the same branch, but look fixedly in opposite directions. (5) The male clings obliquely to the vertical stem of the tree. All these movements are accompanied by continuous and monotonous short croaking notes on the part of both birds, the female's voice being noticeably more subdued than that of the male. The joint display may continue for periods of 10–20 minutes before the female departs; but generally females remain for relatively short periods at the display area.

On occasions when copulation occurred the course of events was generally different. On their arrival the females, from one to five in number, flew directly to male A's court (Fig. 14), then made short flights between the various perches in the court, briefly fluttering their wings between flights, making little vertical jumps on the perch, and uttering brief subdued calls. Male A would make abrupt, apparently aggressive movements towards them and thus drive some of them from the court. One female, however, might remain and it was generally with this one that the male copulated. The sequence of events is as follows. The male chases the female from perch to perch within his court, continually performing the confrontation display towards her. He then suddenly begins a continuous series of brief, sharp calls and takes a position face to face with the female and about one metre away; she remains still and silent, with her body inclined forward. The male then stops calling and flies directly onto the female. Copulation takes place silently, the male half-opening his wings, arching his body over the female and opening his tail into a fan.

On the occasions when we observed copulation male B remained still and silent or displayed alone in his court. Copulation was recorded only in the morning, mainly before 06.00 hours, although females also came to the display area in the afternoon.

Olalla & Magalhães (1956) mention that in Ecuador they found a group of some dozens of

Figure 13 The 'confrontation display' performed by two male Andean Cocks-of-the-rock. Drawn from a photographic sequence of male A (left) and male B (right) – see text.

MWWoodcock

males. Hence it is possible that our findings are not quite typical but illustrate the simpler conditions obtaining in a small population. Nevertheless they probably indicate the basic organization and relationships within a group.

Evolution of courtship displays in *Rupicola*

Apart from the spectacular nature of the displays themselves perhaps the most striking thing about the courtship behaviour of the cocks-of-the-rock is that it differs so completely in the two species. The differences presumably began to evolve when the two stocks were first separated, at which time two of the special features of the male's display plumage must have been at least partly developed: the peculiarly shaped crest and the conspicuously modified inner secondaries. The subsequent differentiation of these characters must have occurred in step with the differentiation of the courtship behaviour, as structure and behaviour are so well matched together.

Thus in the Guianan Cock-of-the-rock the crest is laterally very compressed and, seen from the side, has an almost perfectly semicircular outline set off by a narrow dark line just in from the edge. It is, as it were, designed to be seen from the side, and this is how the male, displaying on the ground, presents it to the female in the trees above. In the Andean Cock-of-the-rock the crest is bushier and much less compressed, and no less conspicuous when seen from the front than seen from the side; in the main display, the confrontation display, it is presented frontally to the female. The inner secondaries of the Guianan Cock-of-the-rock not only are greatly broadened but have long silky fringes and, together with the crest and modified rump feathers, provide

the main visual impact for a bird looking down at the male squatting in flattened posture on his court. In the Andean Cock-of-the-rock the inner secondaries are broad and rather square-ended but not otherwise structurally modified. Their pale grey colour, however, contrasts strikingly with the red or orange of the body plumage on one side and the black wing-feathers on the other side, and this contrast is conspicuously presented to the female when the male bows before her in the confrontation display. Finally, the white wing speculum enhances the effect of the male Guianan Cock-of-the-rock's conspicuous landing on his court, and the fluttering jump which he occasionally makes when down on his court. These elements are absent from the display of the Andean species, whose wings have no speculum.

Why the displays, and the display organization, of the two species should have diverged in this way must remain a matter for speculation. It is noteworthy, however, that the manakins provide parallels to both of them in the organization (but not the details) of their displays, the White-bearded Manakin *Manacus manacus* with the Guianan Cock-of-the-rock (cleared courts on the ground, each owned by one male – Snow 1962a) and some *Pipra* species with the Andean Cock-of-the-rock (horizontal display perches in small trees; regular ritualized display between pairs of males – Schwartz & Snow 1979). The existence of these parallels suggests that the two kinds of display organization represent alternative stable strategies evolved under the interacting demands of sexual selection, inter-male competition, the needs of foraging, safety from predators, and all the other requisites for survival and reproduction.

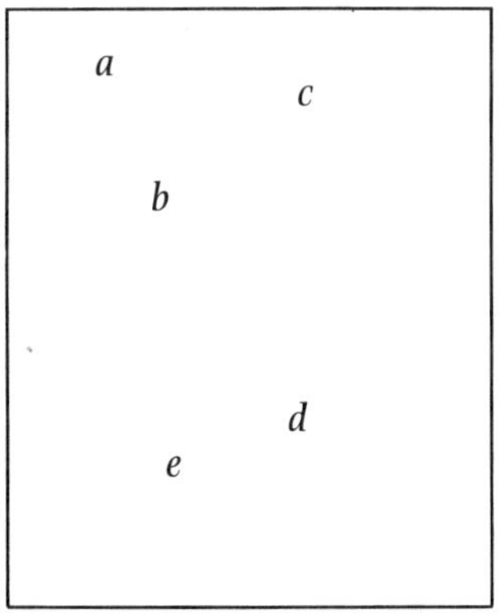

Breeding and annual cycle

Breeding

All observations that have been made indicate that only the female attends the nest. Nesting is often semi-colonial, in that several nests may be found in close proximity; but this is probably a consequence of the shortage of suitable nest-sites and indicates tolerance of near neighbours rather than a positive tendency to social breeding. At sites which do not provide more than one good nest-site, single nests may be found. Semi-colonial nesting is probably facilitated by the fact that nests are inaccessible to predators, so that there is no disadvantage in their being grouped close together.

Guianan Cock-of-the-rock

The nest consists of a solid bracket of mud and plant material fixed to a vertical rock face, usually in a

Plate 21
The cocks-of-the-rock
(*Rupicola*)

a and b: Andean Cock-of-the-rock *R. peruviana sanguinolenta*, male and female
c: Andean Cock-of-the-rock *R. peruviana aequatorialis*, male
d and e: Guianan Cock-of-the-rock *R. rupicola*, male and female

cave or crevice. Being sheltered from the weather, nests may persist from year to year, but in the weeks preceding breeding the females extensively repair the old structures. The female brings in her bill either a lump of mud (in the one case observed, collected from a streamside about 70 m away) or a mixture of mud and rootlets, which she wipes off against the nest-edge, securing the rootlets in place by pressing them against the rim of the nest, with a vibratory movement so that they acquire a sticky coating and eventually adhere. Loose pieces of rootlet are pulled in with the beak and pressed into the nest structure. The female also shapes the nest by pressing her tail against the outside of the rim. Cohesion is apparently given to the whole structure by a salivary secretion, which shows as a glistening coat on the outside of freshly built nests.

The clutch consists of 2 eggs, laid with an interval of about 48 hours. Eggs are pale buffish brown to very pale buff, almost white, in ground colour, with spots and blotches of pale lilac-grey, overlaid with dark olive-brown, the markings sparse over most of the surface but concentrated in a loose wreath round the blunt end. Measurements of

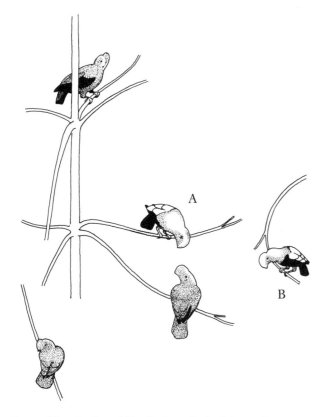

Figure 14 Display of the Andean Cock-of-the-rock. Position of females on arrival at the court of male A; male B on smaller court adjacent – see text. Drawn from a photographic sequence.

5 eggs are as follows: length 40.4–44.0, mean 41.6 mm; width 30.4–31.1, mean 30.7 mm; weight of two fresh eggs, 22.4 and 20.6 g. Observations at one nest during incubation showed that the female's spells on the eggs varied from $12\frac{1}{2}$ to 125 minutes, her absences (doubtless to feed) varied from 6 to $35\frac{1}{2}$ minutes, most being 6–10 minutes, and that she was on the nest altogether for 76% of the daylight hours. Incubation periods, determined at two nests, were 28 and 27–28 days. The nestling period has not been determined; in fact no observations seem to have been made on any aspect of the care of the young.

Andean Cock-of-the-rock (by Cesar E. Benalcazar & Fabiola Silva de Benalcazar)
Nest-building was not studied in detail, but we observed a female carrying a mixture of mud and fern rootlets which she used to repair an old nest. Nests in our study area were in groups of from three to nine, and were at heights of 3–12 m, attached to irregularities on rock faces adjacent to the river or to its affluents in humid, shady places. The nest is generally in the form of a truncated cone, with a concave nest-cup 11.2–16 cm in diameter and 5.5–7 cm deep. The external dimensions vary according to the shape of the rock to which it is attached. Externally it is made of mud, the interior of the cup being lined with a layer of coarse vegetable fibres.

Females roost on their nests outside the breeding season. Sometimes a female has to defend her nest from other females, or she may usurp another bird's nest before the nesting season begins. The nest may also be taken over by birds of other species which share the cock-of-the-rock's habitat, for instance the Torrent Duck *Merganetta armata*, a pair of which may use a nest as a roosting place, or the Glossy-black Thrush *Turdus serranus*, which may give it a moss lining and nest successfully in it.

The clutch is of 2 eggs [in colour similar to those of the Guianan Cock-of-the-rock] laid with an interval of about 24 hours. Measurements of 8 eggs are as follows: length 44.5–49.0, mean 46.7 mm; width 32.6–33.7, mean 33.1 mm; weight of 6 fresh eggs, 25.4–29.0, mean 27.3 g. Incubation begins with the laying of the first egg and hatching occurs 28 days later, in the same order as the eggs were laid. Most of the active nests were recorded between May and July, just after the main rainy season and at a time when the fruiting of forest plants is at its height.

During 61 hours of observation at three nests during incubation, the females were on the nest for 93.6% of the time, with a maximum period on the nest of 306 minutes and a minimum period of 45 minutes. Periods of absence varied from $2\frac{1}{2}$ to 20 minutes. At night the female remains on the nest the whole time.

Recently hatched nestlings weigh about 23.9 g (two weighed), that is, about 88% of the weight of the fresh egg. The nestling period varied from 42 to 44 days at three nests, and appeared to be independent of the number of young reared (2 in two nests, 1 in the other). Feeding visits were at the rate of 1.5 and 2.0 per hour, respectively, at two nests. Based on the average visitation rate and the mean weight of food brought at each visit, it may be calculated that two young received a total of about 9.5 kg of food up to the moment when they left the nest. Surprisingly large food items may be given to the nestlings. For instance, a chick only a few days old was fed a lizard of about its own length which it took several hours to swallow, the tail and hind legs projecting from its bill while the front parts were being digested. Females continue to feed their young for some time after they have left the nest.

Annual cycle

The Guianan Cock-of-the-rock has a well-defined breeding season and annual cycle. All exactly recorded laying dates (mostly from Guyana) have been in March and April (2 March–25 April), but laying apparently continues into May and occasional replacement clutches may be laid even later. Further west, in the Venezuelan and Brazilian states of Amazonas, breeding is probably a little earlier, to judge from the somewhat earlier moult dates.

The moult lasts about $5\frac{1}{2}$ months in the individual. Its timing differs markedly in the two sexes. In Guyana and adjacent parts of southeastern Venezuela males begin to moult in February (3 records) and March (5 records), and females in April–July (8 records). Further west, in Amazonas, males begin to moult a little earlier, in January (2), February (11) and March (4 records) – a general difference between this area and the Guiana area to the east (Snow 1976a).

The Guiana records indicate that some males at least must begin to moult actually before the females begin egg-laying, and others at about the time that egg-laying begins. It is not possible to tell from the records whether females wait until they have finished their nesting before they begin to moult; but those that begin to moult in June and July have probably finished nesting, while those that begin to moult in April cannot have nested successfully in that season. This question is discussed in more detail on pp. 27–28.

For the Andean Cock-of-the-rock, which has a much greater latitudinal range than the Guianan species, few generalisations can be made about the annual cycle. As mentioned above, Sr and Sra Benalcazar found that most nesting activity in the Western Andes of Colombia, at 3° 24'N, was in the months May–July. Of four breeding females which they examined, two that were incubating were in very fresh plumage, one that was feeding young was finishing a moult and another was in rather worn plumage. This indicates a lack of any very precise synchronisation between breeding and the moult. Moult records for males from this part of Colombia indicate a wide spread of dates of onset, from January to August, 6 being in the months January–March, 3 in April–May, and 3 in July–August. This strongly suggests that, as in the Guianan species, males regularly begin their moult before the females begin egg-laying. Widely spread moulting dates appear to be usual in all low-latitude populations of the Andean Cock-of-the-rock; at the extreme south of the range, south of 10°S, they tend to be more synchronized with a concentration of moult-onset (in males) in the months October–January, the usual southern-hemisphere pattern.

Plumages and moults

Nestling (*R. peruviana*) with long grey down above, bare below; down feathers 30–32 mm long.

Juvenile (*R. rupicola*, aviary-bred) predominantly dull grey-brown (colour of female) above; whitish below, washed with straw-colour; whitish feathers in two tracts above and behind eye; secondaries with long whitish to straw-coloured fringes and extensive whitish on inner webs (much longer fringes than in adult female and more white on inner webs).

Immature plumage (apparently acquired soon after juvenile plumage): female like adult female; male like adult female but redder or more orange according to species/subspecies. In males immature plumage is gradually replaced on head, body and coverts by adult plumage; inner secondaries also replaced by feathers approaching adult male type. Moult of flight-feathers and tail-feathers to adult type begins when head and body are at least half in adult plumage, and adult head and body plumage is almost fully acquired by the time wing and tail moult is complete. A bird bred in captivity (*R. peruviana*) acquired adult male plumage at the age of 15 months (C. E. Benalcazar, pers. comm.). In *R. peruviana* (not seen in *R. rupicola*) some individuals acquire a subadult plumage in which body feathers are washed with olive and the modified secondaries are not of fully adult type.

Physical characters

Structure

Bill strong, wide at base becoming laterally compressed towards the tip; nostrils large, oval in *peruviana*, more elongated in *rupicola*. Rictal bristles absent. Legs and feet very strong, stout, claws large and well hooked. Modifications of plumage of adult males as follows: 10th primary with long, slender tip, deeply notched where tip joins expanded portion of inner vane (modification most marked in *rupicola*; Fig. 15). Innermost secondaries very broad and square-ended in *peruviana*; broad, angular at end, and with long silky fringes in *rupicola*. Feathers of back and upper tail-coverts modified similarly to secondaries in *rupicola*, degree of modification increasing towards tail; these feathers unmodified and unusually short in *peruviana*. Crest formed of two rows of feathers, their ventral surfaces meeting along the mid-line to form a semi-circular casque; the feathers flattened and the two rows closely adpressed in *rupicola*, looser, fluffier and less closely adpressed in *peruviana*. Feather modifications all present to a much smaller degree in females.

Unfeathered parts

R. rupicola

Iris: adult male: orange, yellower towards the outside.

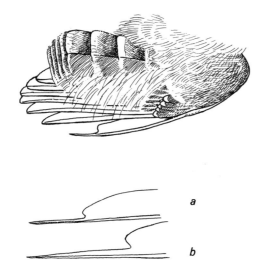

Figure 15 Wing of adult male *Rupicola rupicola*; below, tip of 10th primary of (*a*) *R. rupicola*, (*b*) *R. peruviana*.

female: paler, duller orange, greyer towards the outside.

Bill: adult male: basal half deep orange, distal half yellow.

female: blackish horn, ridge of culmen and tip yellow.

Legs and feet: adult male: yellowish orange, interscutal skin paler; claws pale yellow with blackish dorsal ridges.

female: legs dark brownish horn, paler and yellower at sides and back; feet dark horn.

R. peruviana

Iris: adult male: varies geographically; bright yellow in *aequatorialis*; red in *sanguinolenta* (sometimes with grey outer rim, or with yellow next to the pupil); usually white in *saturata* (also recorded as pale blue or pale yellow).

female: varies geographically in the same way as in adult male, but colours more variable; from white to brown in *aequatorialis*; light red with grey next to pupil, or pinkish grey-brown in *sanguinolenta*; usually pale blue, sometimes brown, in *saturata*.

Bill: adult male: intense golden yellow in all populations (but a specimen of *sanguinolenta* from W. Ecuador was described by Goodfellow, who collected it, as having the bill (and feet) 'red — both only a shade lighter than the feathers').

female: blackish with pale yellow tip.

Legs and feet: male: yellow or orange-yellow (but see above, under Bill).

female: generally recorded as dark brown or black, in some cases with mixture of yellow.

Geographical variation

None reported in *R. rupicola*. *R. peruviana* shows considerable geographical variation, four subspecies being distinguishable. Variation affects mainly the depth and shade of pigmentation of the orange or red parts of the male's plumage, the extent of grey on the three inner secondaries, and eye colour (see above). The general colour of the female's head and body plumage varies in parallel. In the populations of the Eastern and Central Andes of Colombia, of eastern Ecuador, and of Peru south to Cajamarca and northern San Martín (subspecies *aequatorialis*), the colour is bright orange (somewhat variable), and the grey of the inner secondaries is restricted, the black basal area being exposed. In the other three subspecies the grey of the inner secondaries extends over the whole of the exposed area and part of the concealed area. In populations to the south, from southern San Martín to Junín (subspecies *peruviana*), the orange is paler. Further south, from Cuzco in Peru to northwestern Bolivia, a very deeply pigmented orange-red form occurs (subspecies *saturata*). Finally, the population of the Western Andes of Colombia and Ecuador, in the northwest of the species' range, is the deepest coloured of all, with blood red plumage in the male (subspecies *sanguinolenta*).

Measurements

R. rupicola
ad ♂♂ (10)   Wing 172–181, 176.8.   Tail 82–91, 86.9.   Tarsus 34–36, 34.9.   Culmen 20.5–22.5, 21.3.
♀♀ (8)   Wing 164–175, 169.1.   Tail 89–97, 93.3.   Tarsus 33–35, 34.2.   Culmen 20.5–22, 21.2.
Weight: 1 ♀ 140 g.

R. peruviana aequatorialis
ad ♂♂ (10)   Wing 182–196, 189.6.   Tail 113–131, 120.2.   Tarsus 37–39, 38.1.   Culmen 17–19, 18.2.
♀♀ (5)   Wing 174–184, 180.0.   Tail 116–124, 118.6.   Tarsus 36–37, 36.8.   Culmen 18–19, 18.4.

R. peruviana saturata
ad ♂♂ (11)   Wing 179–193, 187.4.   Tail 110–124, 118.4.   Tarsus 38–41, 39.6.   Culmen 17.5–19, 18.2.
♀♀ (3)   Wing 176–179, 177.3.   Tail 115–116, 115.3.   Tarsus 38.   Culmen 17–18.5, 17.7.
Weight: 1 ♀ 216 g.

R. peruviana sanguinolenta
ad ♂♂ (8)   Wing 183–188, 186.0.   Tail 110–120, 113.3.   Tarsus 38–39, 38.6.   Culmen 17–18, 17.4.
Weights: 1 ♂ 266 g.
3 ♀♀ 226, 223 and 213 g.

Note: the difference in culmen length between *R. rupicola* and *R. peruviana* is largely due to the different shape of the nares in the two species (the measurement being taken from the posterior edge of the nares to the bill-tip). In *rupicola* the nostril opening is prolonged backward as a slit.

Appendix 1

Taxonomic summary of the Cotingidae

It does not seem necessary to repeat here the full citations and synonymy of the scientific names of the cotingas, which are given in volume 8 of Peters' *Check-list of birds of the world* (1979). Readers may, however, find it useful to have for reference a list of the species and subspecies, with brief citations, type localities (either original or by later designation), and notes on the characters of subspecies. Ranges of species are not given, as they are more satisfactorily shown in the distribution maps; ranges of subspecies are given briefly, and can be determined more fully by reference to the maps of the species concerned.

A few of the names are substitutions for earlier names that were found to be invalid. These earlier names are given in brackets, with author and date. The reader can thus find out when each species and subspecies of cotinga was first formally named, and by whom.

Phoenicircus carnifex (Linnaeus) 1758, *Syst. Nat.*, ed. 10, **1**, p. 94.—Surinam.

Phoenicircus nigricollis Swainson 1832, *in* Swainson & Richardson, *Faun. Bor.-Amer.*, **2**(1831), p. 491. —Rio Negro near Barcelos, Brazil.

Laniisoma elegans (Thunberg) 1823, *Dissert. Tullberg.*, Nov. Spec. Ampelis, p. 2.—Mountains of Rio de Janeiro.

Subspecies:

L. e. elegans. Larger than the Andean subspecies, and the female with crown sooty (concolorous with the back in Andean subspecies).

L. e. venezuelensis Phelps & Gilliard 1941, *Am. Mus. Novit.* no. 1153, p. 9.—Santa Barbara, Barinas, Venezuela. Described as similar to *cadwaladeri* but with slightly brighter upperparts and flanks less heavily barred.

L. e. buckleyi (Sclater & Salvin) 1880, *Proc. zool. Soc. Lond.*, p. 158.—Pindo, Pastaza, Ecuador. Smaller than nominate *elegans*, and with less barring on the underparts.

L. e. cadwaladeri Carriker 1935, *Proc. Acad. nat. Sci. Philad.* **87**, p. 329.—Santa Ana, Rio Coroico, La Paz, Bolivia. Described from a single male, with almost immaculate yellow underparts. The validity of this subspecies needs confirmation.

Geographical variation in the Andes is not properly understood, and ranges cannot be given for the subspecies.

Calyptura cristata (Vieillot) 1818, *Nouv. Dict. Hist. nat.*, new ed., **24**, p. 528.—Rio de Janeiro.

Iodopleura pipra (Lesson) 1831, *Cent. Zool.*, p. 81.—Rio de Janeiro.

Subspecies:

I. p. pipra.—Range as shown on Map 4.

I. p. leucopygia Salvin 1885, *Ibis*, p. 305.—British Guiana. Smaller than *pipra*, with a broad white rump-band (lacking or barely present in *pipra*) and with a more extensive and purer buff throat. The provenance of the two specimens on which this subspecies is based is problematical (see p. 41).

Iodopleura fusca (Vieillot) 1817, *Nouv. Dict. Hist. nat.*, new ed. **8**, p. 162.—Cayenne.

Iodopleura isabellae Parzudaki 1847, *Rev. Zool.*, **10**, p. 186. —San Carlos, Amazonas, Venezuela.

Subspecies:

I. i. isabellae. Range of the species, except for the extreme east.

I. i. paraensis Todd 1950, *Proc. biol. Soc. Wash.* **63**, p. 6.—Benevides, Pará, Brazil. Belém area and along the Tocantins; a slightly marked subspecies, with less white below and browner flanks.

Phibalura flavirostris Vieillot 1816, *Analyse*, p. 68.—Rio de Janeiro.

Subspecies:

P. flavirostris flavirostris. Range of the species, except Bolivia.

P. flavirostris boliviana Chapman 1930, *Auk.* **47**, p. 88.—near Atén, Apolobamba, La Paz, Bolivia. Longer-tailed than *flavirostris* and with fewer dark markings on underparts. For further details, see p. 49. Known only from the type locality.

Carpornis cucullatus (Swainson) 1821, *Zool. Illus.* **1**, pl. 37.—Rio de Janeiro, Brazil.

Carpornis melanocephalus (Wied) 1820, *Reis. Brasilien* **1**, p. 168.—Quartel de Barreiras, Espirito Santo, Brazil.

Ampelion rubrocristatus (d'Orbigny & Lafresnaye) 1837, *Mag. Zool.* **7**, p. 39.—Ayopayo, Cochabamba, Bolivia.

Ampelion rufaxilla (Tschudi) 1844, *Archiv f. Naturg.* **10**(1), p. 270.—Vitoc Valley, Junín, Peru.

Subspecies:

A. r. rufaxilla. The Peruvian and Bolivian part of the range of the species.

A. r. antioquiae Chapman 1924, *Am. Mus. Novit.* no. 138, p. 8.—Santa Elena, Antioquia, Colombia. The Colombian part of the range of the species.

Larger than *rufaxilla*, streaks on underparts wider and more numerous, and chestnut areas averaging darker.

Ampelion sclateri (Taczanowski) 1874, *Proc. zool. Soc. Lond.*, p. 136.—Maraynioc, Peru.

Ampelion stresemanni (Koepcke) 1954, *Publ. Mus. Hist. nat. Javier Prado*, ser. A, zool., no. 16, p. 3.—Zárate, Rio Rimac, Lima, Peru.

Pipreola riefferii (Boissonneau) 1840, *Rev. Zool.* 3, p. 3.—Bogotá, Colombia.

Subspecies:

P. r. riefferii. Extreme western Venezuela, and the Eastern and Central Andes of Colombia, except the extreme south of these ranges. Male with head and breast blackish green.

P. r. melanolaema Sclater 1856, *Ann. Mag. nat. Hist.*, ser. 2, 17, p. 469.—Caracas, Venezuela. Venezuela, except extreme western Táchira and the Sierra de Perijá. Male with head and breast glossy black, no greenish wash.

P. r. occidentalis (Chapman) 1914, *Bull. Am. Mus. nat. Hist.* 33, p. 630.—San Antonio, Western Andes, Colombia. Western Andes of Colombia, extreme south of Central Andes, and western slopes of the Andes of Ecuador. Males with head and throat black, similar to *melanolaema* but throat and breast washed greenish, and wing-coverts and tertials less conspicuously tipped.

P. r. confusa Zimmer 1936, *Am. Mus. Novit.* no. 893, p. 2.—Upper Volcán Sumaco, Napo, Ecuador. Eastern slopes of the Andes of Ecuador, just extending into northern Peru. Like *chachapoyas*, but head and upper breast more greenish, and lower breast and belly more strongly marked. A doubtful subspecies, perhaps not distinct from *chachapoyas*.

P. r. chachapoyas (Hellmayr) 1915, *Verh. Orn. Ges. Bayern* 12, p. 206.—Chachapoyas, northern Peru. Northern Peru east of the Marañón, in Amazonas and San Martín. Male like *occidentalis* but smaller, darker above and more spotted below.

P. r. tallmanorum O'Neill & Parker 1981, *Bull. Br. Orn. Club* 101, p. 294.—N.E. of Carpish Pass, Huánuco, Peru. Known only from the Carpish Mountains and the Cerros de Sira, Huánuco, Peru. Male differs from all other subspecies in combination of small size, shiny black head and throat and nearly unmarked lemon yellow lower breast and belly. Very distinct from *chachapoyas* to the north.

Pipreola intermedia Taczanowski 1884, *Orn. Pérou*, 2, p. 376.—Maraynioc, mountains of central Peru.

Subspecies:

P. i. intermedia. Mountains of central Peru from southern San Martín to Junín.

P. i. signata Hellmayr 1917, *Verh. Orn. Ges. Bayern* 13, p. 199.—Chulumani, Yungas of La Paz, Bolivia. Male differs from *intermedia* by having a post-auricular band of yellow across sides of neck, and middle of breast and abdomen extensively unmarked bright yellow.

Pipreola arcuata (Lafresnaye) 1843, *Rev. Zool.* 6, p. 98.—Bogotá, Colombia.

Subspecies:

P. a. arcuata. Northern part of the range of the species, south to central Peru.

P. a. viridicauda de Schauensee 1953, *Proc. Acad. nat. Sci. Philad.* 105, p. 37.—Incachaca, Cochabamba, Bolivia. Peru from Junín southwards, and Bolivia. Differs from *arcuata* by having considerably more green on the four outermost tail-feathers.

Pipreola aureopectus (Lafresnaye) 1843, *Rev. Zool.* 6, p. 68.—'Bogotá', Colombia (almost certainly erroneous, as the species is not known to occur in the Bogotá area).

Subspecies:

P. a. aureopectus. Northeastern Colombia, except the Santa Marta area, and western Venezuela.

P. a. festiva (Todd) 1912, *Ann. Carnegie Mus.* 8, p. 211.—Cumbre de Valencia, Carabobo, Venezuela. Coastal mountains of central Venezuela. Male similar to *aureopectus*, but yellow area of underparts much more extensive.

P. a. decora Bangs 1899, *Proc. biol. Soc. Wash.* 13, p. 98.—Santa Marta, Colombia. The Santa Marta region of Colombia. Similar to *aureopectus* but smaller; male with a distinct post-auricular band of bright yellow across sides of neck.

Pipreola jucunda Sclater 1860, *Proc. zool. Soc. Lond.* 28, p. 89.—Cachillacta, Pichincha, Ecuador.

Pipreola lubomirskii Taczanowski 1879, *Proc. zool. Soc. Lond.*, p. 236.—Tambillo, Peru.

Pipreola pulchra (Hellmayr) 1917, *Archiv f. Naturg.* 9(1), p. 385 (new name for *Ampelis elegans* Tschudi 1843).—River Tullumayo, Junín, Peru.

Pipreola frontalis (Sclater) 1858, *Proc. zool. Soc. Lond.* 26, p. 446.—Samaipata, Santa Cruz, Bolivia.

Subspecies:

P. f. frontalis. Southern part of the range of the species, from central Peru (Junín) south to Bolivia.

P. f. squamipectus (Chapman) 1925, *Am. Mus. Novit.* no. 187, p. 5.—Zamora, eastern Ecuador. Northern part of the range of the species, in Ecuador and northern Peru. Differs from *frontalis* by wider bill, male with darker head and less red on throat, female with entire underparts barred with dark green (unbarred in *frontalis*), and in other details of colouration.

Pipreola chlorolepidota Swainson 1837, *Anim. Menag.*, p. 357.—Moyobamba, Peru.

Pipreola formosa (Hartlaub) 1849, *Rev. Mag. Zool.*, ser. 2, 1, p. 275.—Caracas, Venezuela.

Subspecies:

P. formosa formosa. Western part of the range of the species, east to Miranda (about 66°W).

P. f. rubidior (Chapman) 1925, *Am. Mus. Novit.* no. 191, p. 10.—La Trinidad, near Carapas, Sucre, Venezuela. East-central part of the range of the species, in the mountains south of the Gulf of Cariaco. Like *formosa*, but white markings on tertials much more restricted, chest spot of male generally redder, less suffused with orange; female with throat yellowish, spotted or barred with dusky greenish (instead of wholly green).

P. f. pariae Phelps & Phelps 1949, *Proc. biol. Soc. Wash.* **62**, p. 38.—Cerro Azul, Paria Peninsula, Venezuela. Mountains of Paria Peninsula. Similar to *rubidior*, but red chest spot brighter and more extensive.

Pipreola whitelyi Salvin & Godman 1884, *Ibis*, pp 449.—Cerro Roraima, Venezuela.

Subspecies:

P. w. whitelyi. Extreme southeastern Venezuela and adjacent Guyana, on Mts. Roraima and Twek-quay.
P. w. kathleenae Zimmer & Phelps 1944, *Am. Mus. Novit.* no. 1270, p. 10.—Remainder of the range of the species, west of *whitelyi*. Differs from *whitelyi* in having more extensive yellowish on forehead, and (in the female) blacker stripes on underparts.

Ampelioides tschudii (Gray) 1846, *Genera Birds* 1, p. 279 (new name for *Ampelis cincta* Tschudi 1843).—Pangos, east of Tarma, Peru.

Cotinga amabilis Gould 1857, *Proc. zool. Soc. Lond.* **25**, p. 64.—Verapaz, Guatemala.

Cotinga ridgwayi Ridgway (ex Zeledon MS) 1887, *Proc. U.S. natn. Mus.* **10**, p. 1.—Pozo Azul, Costa Rica.

Cotinga nattererii (Boissonneau) 1840, *Rev. Zool.* **3**, p. 2.—'Bogotá', Colombia.

Cotinga maynana (Linnaeus) 1766, *Syst. Nat.*, ed. 12, **1**, p. 298.—Maynas, Peru.

Cotinga cotinga (Linnaeus) 1766, *Syst. Nat.*, ed. 12, **1**, p. 298.—Belém, Brazil.

Cotinga maculata (Müller) 1776, *Natursyst.*, suppl., p. 147.—Rio de Janeiro, Brazil.

Cotinga cayana (Linnaeus) 1766, *Syst. Nat.*, ed. 12, **1**, p. 298.—Cayenne.

Porphyrolaema porphyrolaema (Deville & Sclater) 1852, *Rev. Mag. Zool.*, ser. 2, **4**, p. 226.—Sarayacu, Río Ucayali, Peru.

Xipholena punicea (Pallas) 1764, in *Vroeg, Catalogue, Adumbrat.*, p. 2.—Surinam.

Xipholena lamellipennis (Lafresnaye) 1839, *Mag. Zool.* **1**, cl. 2, pl. 9.—Belém, Brazil.

Xipholena atropurpurea (Wied) 1820, *Reise Brasilien*, 1, p. 262.—Rio Mucuri, Espirito Santo, Brazil.

Carpodectes nitidus Salvin 1865, *Proc. zool. Soc. Lond.* **1864**, p. 583.—Tucurriquí, Costa Rica.

Carpodectes antoniae Ridgway (ex Zeledon MS) 1884, *Ibis*, p. 27.—Pirris, southwestern Costa Rica.

Carpodectes hopkei Berlepsch 1897, *Orn. Monatsb.* **5**, p. 174.—San José, Río Dagua, Colombia.

Tijuca atra Férussac 1829, *Bull. Sci. nat.* **19**, p. 324.—Serra do Mar, Rio de Janeiro, Brazil.

Tijuca condita Snow 1980, *Bull. Br. Orn. Club* **100**, p. 213.—near Teresópolis, Rio de Janeiro, Brazil.

Lipaugus subalaris Sclater 1861, *Proc. zool. Soc. Lond.*, p. 210.—Rio Napo, Ecuador.

Lipaugus cryptolophus (Sclater & Salvin) 1877, *Proc. zool. Soc. Lond.*, p. 522.—Monji, Ecuador.

Subspecies:

L. c. cryptolophus. Eastern slopes of the Andes.

L. c. mindoensis (Hellmayr & Seilern) 1914, *Verh. Orn. Ges. Bayern* **12**, p. 89.—Mindo, western Ecuador. Western slopes of the Andes in Ecuador and Colombia. Concealed bases of the black crest-feathers extensively creamy white (brown in *cryptolophus*), and perhaps smaller than *cryptolophus* (see p. 122).

Lipaugus fuscocinereus (Lafresnaye) 1843, *Rev. Zool.* **6**, p. 291.—'Bogotá', Colombia.

Lipaugus vociferans (Wied) 1820, *Reise Brasilien*, **1**, p. 242 (replaces *Ampelis cinerea* Vieillot 1817).—Faz. Pindoba, north of Caravellos, Bahia, Brazil.

Lipaugus unirufus Sclater 1859, *Proc. zool. Soc. Lond.* **27**, p. 385.—Playa Vicente, Oaxaca, Mexico.

Subspecies:

L. u. unirufus. Range of the species, except extreme southwestern Colombia and northwestern Ecuador.
L. u. castaneotinctus (Hartert) 1902, *Novit. zool.* **9**, p. 610.—Río Durango, Ecuador. Extreme southwestern Colombia and northwestern Ecuador. Deeper rufous than *unirufus*. Colour variation is apparently clinal along the Pacific coastal region and limits of the two subspecies are somewhat arbitrary.

Lipaugus lanioides (Lesson) 1844, *Echo du Monde Savant*, **11**(7), p. 156.—Rio de Janeiro, Brazil.

Lipaugus streptophorus (Salvin & Godman) 1884, *Ibis*, p. 448.—Roraima, British Guiana [= Venezuela].

Chirocylla uropygialis (Sclater & Salvin) 1876, *Proc. zool. Soc. Lond.*, p. 355.—Tilotilo, La Paz, Bolivia.

Conioptilon mcilhennyi Lowery & O'Neill 1966, *Auk* **83**, p. 3.—Balta, Río Curanja, Loreto, Peru.

Gymnoderus foetidus (Linnaeus) 1758, *Syst. Nat.*, ed. 10, **1**, p. 108.—Surinam.

Haematoderus militaris (Shaw) 1792, *Mus. Lever.*, **2**, p. 61.—Cayenne.

Querula purpurata (P. L. S. Müller) 1776, *Natursyst.*, suppl., p. 169.—Cayenne.

Pyroderus scutatus (Shaw) 1792, *Mus. Lever.*, **4**, p. 199.—Nova Friburgo, Rio de Janeiro, Brazil.

Subspecies:

P. s. scutatus. Southeastern part of the range of the species, in Brazil, Argentina and Paraguay. For the characters of the subspecies, see Table 8 (p. 145).
P. s. occidentalis Chapman 1914, *Bull. Am. Mus. nat. Hist.* **33**, p. 631.—San Antonio, Western Andes, Colombia. Western Andes of Colombia and western slopes of Central Andes, just extending into Ecuador.
P. s. granadensis (Lafresnaye) 1846, *Rev. Zool.* **9**, p. 277.—'Bogotá', Colombia. Remainder of the Colombian range of the species, and northern and western Venezuela.
P. s. orenocensis (Lafresnaye) 1846, *Rev. Zool.* **9**, p. 277.—Sierra de Imataca, Bolívar, Venezuela. Eastern Venezuela and northern Guyana.
P. s. masoni Ridgway 1886, *Auk* **3**, p. 333.—Pozuzo, Huánuco, Peru. Andes of northern and central Peru.

Cephalopterus glabricollis Gould 1851, *Proc. zool. Soc.*

Lond. **18**, p. 92.—Chiriquí, Panama.

Cephalopterus penduliger Sclater 1859, *Ibis*, p. 114.—Pallatanga, Chimborazo, Ecuador.

Cephalopterus ornatus G. Saint-Hilaire 1809, *Ann. Mus. Hist. nat. Paris* **13**, p. 238.—Barcelos, Rio Negro, Brazil.

Perissocephalus tricolor (P. L. S. Müller) 1776, *Natursyst.*, suppl., p. 85.—Cayenne.

Procnias tricarunculata (J. & E. Verreaux) 1853, *Rev. Mag. Zool.*, ser. 2, **5**, p. 193.—Bocas del Toro, Panama.

Procnias alba (Hermann) 1783, *Tab. Aff. Anim.*, p. 213.—Cayenne.

Procnias averano (Hermann) 1783, *Tab. Aff. Anim.*, p. 211.—Northeastern Brazil.

Subspecies:

P. a. averano. Northeastern Brazil.

P. a. carnobarba (Cuvier) 1817, *Règne Animal*, **4**, p. 172.—Trinidad. Northwestern part of the range of the species, in Venezuela, adjacent parts of Brazil and Guyana, and Trinidad. Differs from *averano* (in the adult male) in having pale grey (not white) body plumage.

Procnias nudicollis (Vieillot) 1817, *Nouv. Dict. Hist. nat.*, new ed., **8**, p. 164.—Nova Friburgo, Rio de Janeiro, Brazil.

Rupicola rupicola (Linnaeus) 1766, *Syst. Nat.*, ed. 12, **1**, p. 338.—Cayenne.

Rupicola peruviana (Latham) 1790, *Index Ornith.*, **2**, p. 555.—Chanchamayo, Junín, Peru.

Subspecies:

R. p. sanguinolenta Gould 1859, *Proc. zool. Soc. Lond.* **27**, p. 100.—Nanegal, Pichincha, Ecuador. Western Andes of Colombia and northwestern Ecuador. For characters of the subspecies, see p. 184.

R. p. aequatorialis Taczanowski 1889, *Warsz. Uniwers. Izv.*, no. 4, p. 19.—Machay and Mapoto, eastern Ecuador. Northern part of the range of the species east of *sanguinolenta*, south to Cajamarca, Amazonas and northern San Martín in Peru.

R. p. peruviana. Central Peru from southern San Martín to Junín.

R. p. saturata Cabanis & Heine 1859, *Mus. Heineanum*, **2**, p. 99.—Locotal, Bolivia. Southeastern Peru in Cuzco and Puno, and Bolivia.

Appendix 2
Scientific names of the cotingas and their derivations

Scientific names of birds, as of other animals, are conventional labels; their validity is governed by a set of internationally agreed conventions, and they need not be literally appropriate. Indeed some are positively misleading if taken literally, especially those based on the name of a place from which the bird was mistakenly thought to have originated. Nevertheless most scientific names are descriptive of the birds to which they are attached, some have interesting associations, and others are obscure and puzzling. The following list includes all currently valid names of cotingas (genera, species and subspecies) with notes on their origins and derivations.*

Names not capitalized are those of species and subspecies, and are followed by the name of the genus or species to which they belong in parentheses. Generic names are capitalized.

*L., Latin.   Gr., Greek.

aequatorialis (Rupicola peruviana) L. *aequatorialis*, equatorial. This subspecies was described from specimens collected on the eastern slopes of the Andes of Ecuador very near the Equator.

alba (Procnias) L. *albus*, fem. *alba*; white.

amabilis (Cotinga) L. *amabilis*; lovable, lovely.

Ampelioides Ampelion-like or Ampelio-like (Gr. suffix). This genus was considered by Verreaux, who erected it, to be intermediate between *Ampelion* (the name then applied to *Carpornis*) and *Heliochera* (the name then applied to *Ampelion*).

Ampelion Gr. ἀμπελίων, bird of the vine (ἀμπελίς), presumably a fruit-eater but identity obscure. (The forms *Ampelis* and *Ampelio* were also used by early authors, and were confusingly applied to several different cotinga genera.)

antioquiae (Ampelion rufaxilla) From Antioquia, the Department of Colombia where the type specimen was collected.

antoniae (Carpodectes) The species was discovered by José C. Zeledon, whose manuscript notes Ridgway used in describing it. Zeledon wrote: 'I have named this charming bird *Carpodectes antoniae*, after a dear sister whose death I mourn.'

arcuata (Pipreola) L. *arcuatus*; bent like a bow, curved; referring to the shape of the dark feather markings.

atra (Tijuca) L. *ater*, fem. *atra*; black.

atropurpurea (Xipholena) L. *ater*, *atro-*, black; *purpureus*, purple.

aureopectus (Pipreola) L. *aureus*, golden; *pectus*, breast.

averano (Procnias) A contraction of the Portuguese *ave de verano*, bird of summer. According to Buffon, who coined the name and gave this derivation in his *Histoire Naturelle des Oiseaux*, in Brazil the *averano*'s call is heard only during about 6 weeks of the summer, in December and January — a puzzling statement, as it seems much more appropriate for the Bare-throated Bellbird (*P. nudicollis*) of southeastern Brazil than for the Bearded Bellbird of the tropical northeast. But Buffon's description fits the Bearded Bellbird exactly; possibly, knowing neither of them at first hand, he simply attributed the local name to the wrong bird.

boliviana (Phibalura flavirostris) Refers to the country where the subspecies was discovered.

buckleyi (Laniisoma elegans) Named after Clarence Buckley, a nineteenth century collector who discovered many new birds in Bolivia and Ecuador.

cadwaladeri (Laniisoma elegans) Named after M. B. Cadwalader, Managing Director of the Academy of Natural Sciences of Philadelphia at the time when this subspecies was discovered.

Calyptura Gr. καλύπτω, to cover, conceal; οὐρά, a tail. Refers to the very short tail of this genus, which hardly projects beyong the tail-coverts.

carnifex (Phoenicircus) L. *carnifex*, executioner, torturer, hangman. Used fancifully by Linnaeus in reference to the blood-red of the male's plumage.

carnobarba (Procnias averano) L. *caro*, *carn-*, flesh; *barba*, beard. Refers to the fleshy wattles on the male's throat.

Carpodectes Gr. καρπός, a fruit; δέκτης, a receiver, one who takes.

Carpornis Gr. καρπός, a fruit; ὄρνις, bird.

castaneotinctus (Lipaugus unirufus) L. *castanea*, chestnut (the tree); *tinctus*, wetted, washed (as with a colour). Refers to the fact that this subspecies is more deeply rufous than other populations.

cayana (Cotinga) Of Cayenne (French Guiana), a country from which many early bird specimens reached Europe.

Cephalopterus Gr. κεφαλή, head; πτερόν, feather. A name coined by G. Saint-Hilaire, 'faisant allusion au grand nombre des pennes ou grandes plumes qui lui forment une huppe très-élevée sur la tête'.

chachapoyas (Pipreola riefferii) From Chachapoyas in Peru, type locality of this subspecies.

Chirocylla Gr. χείρ, hand; κυλλός, curved, crooked, esp.

of legs bent outwards by disease. Refers to the modified outer primaries, which are very short and outwardly curved.

chlorolepidota (Pipreola) Gr. χλωρός, green, greenish-yellow; λεπιδωτός, covered with scales, scaly. Refers to the scaly effect of the green feather-edges on the underparts of the female.

condita (Tijuca) L. *conditus*, stored away, hidden; referring to the fact that the type (and only known) specimen remained for 30 years in the Museum of Zoology at São Paulo before it was recognized as distinct from *Tijuca atra*.

confusa (Pipreola riefferii) L. *confusus*, mixed up, confused. Refers to the fact that this rather poorly marked subspecies is somewhat intermediate between *chachapoyas* and *riefferii*.

Conioptilon Gr. κονία, a fine powder; πτίλον, soft feathers or down under the true [i.e. contour] feathers. Refers to the powderdown feathers abundantly present over much of the body of this genus (note adapted from Lowery & O'Neill 1966).

Cotinga Brisson, who first used this name (1760, *Orn.* 2: 339,340), has a footnote: 'Cotinga, nom qu'on donne en Amérique à quelques especes de ce genre'. Presumably it was an Amerindian name; I have been unable to find out anything more about it.

cristata (Calyptura) L. *cristatus*, crested, from *crista*, a crest.

cryptolophus (Lipaugus) Gr. κρυπτός, hidden; λόφος, crest. Refers to the concealed, presumably erectile crown-patch.

cucullatus (Carpornis) Hooded, from L. *cucullus*, a cowl or hood.

decora (Pipreola aureopectus) L. *decorus*, becoming, proper; hence decorous, handsome.

Doliornis Apparently from Gr. δόλιος, deceitful, treacherous; ὄρνις, bird. Taczanowski, who coined the name, made no reference to its meaning.

elegans (Laniisoma) L. *elegans*, luxurious, fastidious; later, losing its bad meaning, fine or elegant.

festiva (Pipreola aureopectus) L. *festivus*, festive, gay; referring to the fact that the underparts of this subspecies are more extensively yellow than in neighbouring populations.

flavirostris (Phibalura) L. *flavus*, yellow; *rostrum*, beak.

foetidus (Gymnoderus) L. *foetidus*, evil-smelling. This feature of the species seems not to have been referred to by recent collectors.

formosa (Pipreola) L. *formosus*, beautiful.

frontalis (Pipreola) L. *frontalis*, adjectival form of *frons*, forehead; referring to the yellow patch above the bill, which distinguishes the female of this species from related species.

fusca (Iodopleura) L. *fuscus*, dark; referring to the generally dark black-brown plumage of this species.

fuscocinereus (Lipaugus) L. *fuscus*, dark; *cinereus*, ashy.

glabricollis (Cephalopterus) L. *glaber*, smooth, hairless; *collum*, neck (in scientific names of birds generally referring to throat).

granadensis (Pyroderus scutatus) From New Granada (Grenada), the old name for the country which is now Colombia.

Gymnoderus Gr. γυμνός, bare, naked; δέρος, a poetical form of δέρμα, skin.

Haematoderus Gr. αἷμα, blood; δέρος, a poetical form of δέρμα, skin (used here for the 'skin' in the ornithological sense of skin with feathers).

hopkei (Carpodectes) Named after Gustav Hopke, who discovered this species. Berlepsch, in naming it, expressed the hope that the honour thus done to Hopke would spur him on to further ornithological researches.

intermedia (Pipreola) L. *intermedius*, intermediate. Taczanowski, who named this species, considered it intermediate between *P. (riefferii) melanolaema* of Venezuela and *P. viridis* (now *P. intermedia signata*).

Iodopleura Iodo-, an adjectival form of Gr. ἴον, violet (the flower), and Gr. πλευρόν, side, flank.

isabellae (Iodopleura) This species was first collected by Eugène Thirion on the Rio Negro in southern Venezuela. Parzudaki, who described it, named it after the collector's wife, Isabelle.

jucunda (Pipreola) L. *jucundus*, pleasant.

kathleenae (Pipreola whitelyi) Named after Kathleen Phelps, wife of William H. Phelps, Jr, who accompanied the expedition to Ptari-tepui on which this subspecies was discovered.

lamellipennis (Xipholena) L. *lamella*, an unclassical diminutive form of *lamina*, a thin piece of wood, metal etc.; *penna*,. a feather. Refers to the flat, shiny feathers of the male plumage.

Laniisoma L. *lanius*, butcher, butcher-bird (shrike); Gr. σῶμα, body. Refers to the supposedly shrike-like form of this genus.

lanioides (Lipaugus) L. *lanius*, butcher, butcher-bird (shrike), with Gr. suffix: shrike-like.

leucopygia (Iodopleura pipra) Gr. λευκός, white; πυγή, rump. Refers to the fact that this form (originally described as a distinct species) is distinguished from *I. p. pipra* by its white rump bar.

Lipaugus Gr. λιπ- from λείπω, to leave, leave out, omit or (intrans.) to be wanting or lacking; αὐγή, light, brightness. Refers to the fact that this genus lacks bright or shining colours. In the original citation it was mis-spelt *Lipangus* and this spelling was followed in some early publications.

lubomirskii (Pipreola) Named after Prince Ladislas Lubomirski (1824–1882), a conchologist who organized the conchological collections of the Warsaw Museum and otherwise aided that institution.

maculata (Cotinga) L. *maculatus*, spotted. P. L. S. Müller, who described this species, wrote that it differs from *C. cotinga* by having five orange-coloured spots. Presumably he had before him a specimen in which the purple colour had in places been altered by heat (p. 22).

masoni (Pyroderus scutatus) Named after Professor O. T. Mason (1838–1908), Curator of the Department of Ethnology at the United States National Museum.

maynana (Cotinga) Linnaeus named this species, basing it on 'Le Cotinga des Maynas' of Brisson (1760, *Orn.* 2: 341). Brisson wrote: 'On le trouve dans le pays des Maynas', apparently referring to a tribe inhabiting a part of Amazonian Peru.

mcilhennyi (Conioptilon) Named after John S. McIlhenny of Baton Rouge, Louisiana, who sponsored the Louisiana State University 1964–65 Peruvian Expedition during which this species was discovered.

melanocephalus Gr. μέλας, black; κεφαλή, head.

melanolaema Gr. μέλας, black; λαιμός, throat.

militaris (Haematoderus) L. *militaris*, soldier-like, military. A name used for several bird species with red, or red and black, plumage.

mindoensis (Lipaugus cryptolophus) From Mindo in western Ecuador, where the type specimen was collected.

nattereri (Cotinga) Named after Dr Johann Natterer (1787–1843), who collected extensively in Brazil and discovered many new bird species.

nigricollis (Phoenicircus) L. *niger*, black; *collum*, neck, throat.

nitidus (Carpodectes) L. *nitidus*, shining, bright.

nudicollis (Procnias) L. *nudus*, bare; *collum*, neck, throat.

occidentalis (Pipreola riefferii, Pyroderus scutatus) L. *occidentalis*, western; in both cases referring to the Western Andes of Colombia, where these two subspecies occur.

orenocensis (Pyroderus scutatus) From the Orinoco (French, Orénoque), near the mouth of which this form was first collected.

ornatus (Cephalopterus) L. *ornatus*, adorned, ornate.

paraensis (Iodopleura isabellae) From Pará (Belém), the type locality of this subspecies.

pariae (Pipreola formosa) From the Paria peninsula of northern Venezuela, to which this subspecies is confined.

penduliger (Cephalopterus) L. *pendulum*, something that hangs; *gero*, wear, carry.

Perissocephalus Gr. περισσός, extraordinary, remarkable; κεφαλή, head.

peruviana (Rupicola) From Peru.

Phibalura This is a puzzling name. Without doubt it refers to the very long, forked tail (Gr. οὐρά, *-ura*), but there is no Greek word from which *Phibal-* can be derived. Vieillot, who coined the name, makes no reference to its derivation. Possibly the intended derivation was from L. *fibula*, a pin, splint (and other allied meanings), quite an appropriate word to describe the long, fine outer tail-feathers; but if so, the double mis-spelling is surprising.

pipra (Iodopleura) Lesson, who described this species, thought that it came from Ceylon and considered it to be intermediate between the pardalotes (Dicaeidae, a southeast Asian and Australasian family) and the manakins (Pipridae). He therefore named it *Pardalotus pipra*, to indicate its supposed affinities.

Pipreola Swainson, in defining this genus (in his treatment, a subgenus), distinguished it from 'the typical Piprae' [manakins] by the structure of the foot; it

seems that he coined a name that was simply a variation on *Pipra* in order to indicate affinity.

Porphyrolaema Gr. πορφύρεος, dark red, purple; λαιμός, throat.

Procnias Illiger, who originated the name, gave its derivation as '*a Procne in hirundinem mutata*' (from Procne, who was changed into a swallow), *-ias* being a familial or generic ending. Procne, a character from Greek mythology, was the daughter of Pandion and wife of Tereus.

pulchra (Pipreola) L. *pulcher*, fem. *pulchra*, beautiful.

punicea (Xipholena) L. *puniceus*, red or purple coloured.

purpurata (Querula) L. *purpuratus*, clad in purple.

Pyroderus Gr. πῦρ, fire; δέρος, a poetical form of δέρμα, skin. (cf. *Haematoderus*; the use of this word in *Pyroderus* is inappropriate, as only a small part of the 'skin' is red).

Querula L. *querulus*, full of complaints, querulous. Vieillot, who coined the name, evidently based it on Buffon's account. Buffon describes the bird, which he calls *Le Piauhau*, as moving about in bands, 'toujours en criant aigrement, *pihauhau*'.

ridgwayi (Cotinga) Named after Robert Ridgway, Curator of Birds at the Smithsonian Institution from 1880 to 1929. This is an unusual case of a bird named after the author who described it, the explanation being that Ridgway based his description partly on a MS by José Zeledon, the collector, who proposed the name for the new species.

riefferii (Pipreola) Named after a traveller, Herr Rieffer, who sent bird skins (Bogotá trade skins) back to Europe.

rubidior (Pipreola formosa) L. *rubidus*, red; comparative *rubidior*, redder. Refers to the fact that the male's throat is a more intense red than in the nominate race.

rubrocristatus (Ampelion) L. *ruber*, red; *crista*, crest.

rufaxilla (Ampelion) L. *rufus*, red; *axilla*, arm-pit. The name is not appropriate, as the upper and not the under-wing coverts are red-brown.

Rupicola L. *rupes*, rock; *colo*, to inhabit.

sanguinolenta (Rupicola) L. *sanguinolentus*, bloody, blood-red.

saturata (Rupicola peruviana) L. *saturatus*, filled, glutted; referring to the intense, saturated orange-red colour of this subspecies.

sclateri (Ampelion) Named after P. L. Sclater (1829–1913), for long a leading authority on South American birds.

scutatus (Pyroderus) L. *scutum*, shield; *scutatus*, armed with a shield. Refers to the shield-like red throat-patch.

signata (Pipreola intermedia) Past participle of L. *signo*, to mark, designate. Apparently intended to mean well-marked or distinct, as immediately after suggesting the name (a substitution for a former name, *viridis*, which was pre-occupied), Hellmayr refers to it as a well-marked form.

squamipectus (Pipreola frontalis) L. *squama*, a scale (of a fish); *pectus*, breast. Refers to the female plumage, in which the entire under-parts are yellow regularly barred with dark green.

streptophorus (Lipaugus) Gr. στρεπτοφόρος, wearing a collar.

stresemanni (Ampelion) Named after Erwin Stresemann (1889–1972).

subalaris (Lipaugus) L. *subalaris*, placed or carried under the arms (or in this case, wings); referring to the bright yellow under-wing feathers.

Tijuca Derivations of Indian names, as this is, are often uncertain. There are two possibilities: (1) *tî*=bill, *yúb*=yellow, a reasonable suggestion in that it fits the bird but etymologically doubtful; (2) *tijuca*= swamp, a word used in some Brazilian place names but not apt for a bird of montane forest. I am indebted to Dr Helmut Sick for this information.

tricarunculata (Procnias) L. *tres*, *tri-*, three; *caruncula*, a little piece of flesh, hence a wattle or caruncle.

tricolor (Perissocephalus) L. *tres*, *tri-*, three; *color*, colour. This is a puzzling name for a species which is rather uniform brown with black wings and tail, but in the Daubenton plate on which P. L. S. Müller based his description (*Planch. Enlum.*, pl. 521) the bird is shown as earth-brown above, and bright red-brown below, with black wings and tail, i.e. distinctly tri-coloured.

tschudii (Ampelioides) Named after J. J. von Tschudi (1818–1889), author of an important work on the birds of Peru. Tschudi had already described the species as *Ampelis cincta*, but the name *cincta*, being pre-occupied, had to be changed, and as often happens in such cases the new name proposed by G. R. Gray commemorated the original author.

unirufus (Lipaugus) L. *unus*, one; *rufus*, red, reddish – i.e. uniformly rufous.

uropygialis (Chirocylla) Adjectival form of L. *uropygium*, rump (from Gr. οὐρά, tail; πυγή, rump); referring to the conspicuous chestnut of the rump.

viridicauda (Pipreola arcuata) L. *viridis*, green; *cauda*, tail.

vociferans (Lipaugus) Present participle of L. *vociferor*, to cry out, cry aloud; referring to the very loud call of this species.

whitelyi (Pipreola) Named after Henry Whiteley, Jr (1844–1892), who discovered this species.

Xipholena Gr. ξίφος, sword; λαῖνα=χλαῖνα, upper garment, mantle. Refers to the modified sword-like feathers of the upper wing coverts.

Zaratornis Zarate, the locality in Peru where the bird was first discovered, and Gr. ὄρνις, bird.

Appendix 3

Notes on the distribution maps

The distribution maps are based almost entirely on specimens, supplemented in a few cases by reliable sight records. The following notes deal with points that are doubtful, obscure or of special interest.

Ampelioides tschudii (Map 13)

The unique Bolivian record is reported by Parker, Remsen & Heindel (1980).

Carpornis (Map 6)

The record of *C. cucullatus* from Rio Claro, Goias (Pinto 1944), is based on an old specimen in the British Museum (Natural History) collection and is probably unreliable; it is omitted. Two records of *C. cucullatus* from the extreme south of the range, in Rio Grande do Sul, are just off the map (west of San Lorenzo, about 31° 20'S, and Pelotas, 31° 45'S – the latter probably unreliable).

Cephalopterus (Map 26)

The record just south of the lower Orinoco is based on a specimen collected by E. André on the Caura River in November 1897, now in the American Museum of Natural History. This record has been consistently ignored in the literature; it was omitted, apparently inadvertently, by Berlepsch & Hartert in their report on André's collection (1902, *Novit. Zool.*).

Haematoderus (Map 28)

The westernmost locality (c. 70 km north of Manaus) is based on a sight record by T. E. Lovejoy and others (Lovejoy, pers. comm.).

Iodopleura (Map 4)

The most inland record of *I. pipra* (Lagoa Santa, Minas Gerais, 19° 38'S, 43° 53'W; Burmeister 1856) was doubted by Pinto (1944) but accepted by Camargo & Camargo (1964).

Laniisoma elegans (Map 2)

The single Colombian record (Fátima, Boyacá, Blake 1961) cannot be exactly located but is entered in the approximate area.

Lipaugus vociferans etc. (Map 20)

Lipaugus unirufus extends west in southern Mexico to just off the map (a little to the west of 95°W).

The single Peruvian locality for *L. fuscocinereus* is based on a recent specimen collected by T. A. Parker in the Department of Cajamarca, 5° 5'S, 79° 23'W (Specimen in LSUMZ).

Phoenicircus (Map 1)

The small scale of the map prevents a detailed indication of the distribution of the two species along the lower Rio Tapajós. *P. carnifex* has been recorded at seven localities on the right bank, and one (Villa Braga) on the left bank. *P. nigricollis* has been recorded at three localities on the right bank and two on the left bank. The occurrence of *P. nigricollis* at Marabá on the Rio Tocantins, mapped by Haffer (1970) on the basis of a specimen in the Museu Nacional, Rio de Janeiro, appears to be incorrect, as there is in fact no specimen in the Museu Nacional (H. Sick, *in litt.*).

Pipreola chloropelidota and *P. frontalis* (Map 12)

In addition to the localities mapped, both species have been recorded from Guilea, Santiago Zamora, Ecuador – a locality that cannot be traced.

Procnias (Map 29)

The only record of *P. averano* from Guyana based on a specimen (Adaroo River, specimen in Phelps Collection) is omitted, as the locality is untraceable. A sight record from Guyana (Kanuku Mountains, March 1970; pers. obs.) is also omitted. The northeastern Brazilian population formerly occurred in Pernambuco, where Marcgrave discovered the species, but the exact locality is unknown.

The two records of *P. alba* from the Rio Negro (Barcelos, and 20 miles up the Rio Negro from Manaus) almost certainly refer to stragglers. Occasional stragglers of *P. alba* (not shown) have also occurred in Trinidad (ffrench 1973). Wallace's sight record near Belém (Wallace 1853) is puzzling, since it is so far outside the normal range, and is omitted. For French Guiana there appear to be no more exact records than the general locality 'Cayenne', and a point is entered arbitrarily in the middle of the country.

The westernmost record of *P. nudicollis* in Brazil, and the only one from Mato Grosso (Faz. Taquari, R. Paraná; specimen in the Los Angeles County Museum) is not mapped, as the locality cannot be exactly traced.

Pyroderus (Map 25)

The Venezuelan record from Altagracia (specimen in Carnegie Museum) is from a place of this name between Upata and San Felix on the edge of the Sierra de Imataca, and not from the better known Altagracia on the Orinoco (K. C. Parkes, *in litt.*). Confusion between the two places has led to erroneous statements about the distribution of this species in Venezuela (e.g. Hellmayr 1929).

The single record from Ecuador (Guayupe, Imbabura, 1250 m; specimen in British Museum (Nat. Hist.) collected by L. Gomez) is shown in the approximate position; the locality is not exactly traceable.

Rupicola (Map 30)

The westernmost locality for *R. rupicola* (Araracuara, R. Caquetá) is based on a specimen in the Museo de Historia Naturale, Instituto de Ciencias Naturales (MHN (ICN)), Bogotá.

Xipholena (Map 17)

The northwesternmost locality shown for *X. punicea* (Hacienda Guadualito, Ribera R. Arauca, Arauca) is based on a specimen in the MHN (ICN) collection. Other far western and southwestern records are essentially as in Haffer (1970, fig. 7).

References

Allen, J. A. 1891. On a collection of birds from Chapada, Matto Grosso, Brazil, made by Mr Herbert H. Smith. *Bull. Am. Mus. nat. Hist.* **3**: 337–380.

Ames, P. L. 1971. Morphology of the syrinx in passerine birds. *Bull. Peabody Mus. nat. Hist.* **37**: 1–194.

Bangs, O. & Barbour, T. 1922. Birds from Darien. *Bull. Mus. comp. Zool. Harv.* **65**: 191–229.

Bates, H. W. 1863. *The naturalist on the River Amazons.* John Murray, London.

Beebe, M. B. & Beebe, C. W. 1910. *Our search for a wilderness.* Henry Holt & Co., New York.

Beebe, W. 1924. The rarest of nests in the tallest of grass stems. *Bull. N.Y. zool. Soc.* **27**: 114–117.

———— 1954. Discovered – the nest and egg of the Black-winged Bellbird. *Anim. Kingd.* **57**: 115–119.

Béraut, E. 1970. The nesting of *Gymnoderus foetidus. Ibis* **112**: 256.

Blake, E. R. 1961. Notes on a collection of birds from north-eastern Colombia. *Fieldiana Zool.* **44**: 25–44.

Bond, J. 1956. Additional notes on Peruvian birds II. *Proc. Acad. nat. Sci. Philad.* **108**: 227–247.

Brush, A. H. 1969. On the nature of "cotingin". *Condor* **71**: 431–433.

———— 1978. Avian pigmentation. Pp 141–164 in M. Florkin & B. T. Scheer (eds), *Chemical zoology*, vol. X. Aves. Academic Press, New York & London.

Buffetaut, E. & Taquet, P. 1979. An early Cretaceous terrestrial crocodilian and the opening of the South Atlantic. *Nature* **280**: 486–487.

Burmeister, H. 1856. Systematische Uebersicht der Thiere Brasiliens. Zweiter Theil. Vögel (Aves). G. Reimer, Berlin.

Burton, P. J. K. 1976. Structure and histology of the wattle in the White Bellbird (*Procnias alba*). *J. Zool., Lond.* **178**: 285–293.

Camargo, H. F. de A. & Camargo, E. A. de 1964. Ocorrência de *Iodopleura p. pipra* no Estado de São Paulo, Brasil, e algumas notas sôbre *Iodopleura isabellae. Papéis Dep. Zool. S. Paulo* **16**: 45–55.

Carriker, M. A. 1935. Descriptions of new birds from Bolivia, with notes on other little-known species. *Proc. Acad. nat. Sci. Philad.* **87**: 313–359.

Carvalho, J. C. M. & Kloss, G. R. 1950. Sôbre a distribuição do galo-da-serra "Rupicola rupicola" (Linnaeus, 1766), com observações de sua vida no habitat natural e em cativeiro. *Revta bras. Biol.* **10**: 65–72.

Chapman, F. M. 1926. *Phibalura flavirostris* Vieill. in Bolivia. *Auk* **43**: 99–100.

———— 1928. The nesting habits of Wagler's Oropendola (*Zarhynchus wagleri*) on Barro Colorado Island. *Bull. Am. Mus. nat. Hist.* **58**: 123–166.

———— 1929. *My tropical air castle.* Appleton, New York.

———— 1930. A new race of *Phibalura flavirostris* from Bolivia. *Auk* **47**: 87–88.

Chubb, C. 1921. *The birds of British Guiana*, vol. 2. B. Quaritch, London.

Cordier, C. 1943. The Umbrella Bird comes to the Zoo. *Anim. Kingd.* **45**: 3–10.

Cracraft, J. 1973. Continental drift, paleoclimatology, and the evolution and biogeography of birds. *J. Zool., Lond.* **169**: 455–545.

Crandall, L. S. 1945. The Umbrella Bird is not a dull fellow any more. *Anim. Kingd.* **48**: 109–112.

———— 1948. Notes on the display of the Three-wattled Bell-bird (*Procnias tricarunculata*). *Zoologica, N.Y.* **33**: 113–114.

Delacour, J. 1945. L'Oiseau-parasol (*Cephalopterus ornatus*). *Oiseau N.S.* **15**: 130–140.

Descourlitz, J. T. 1852. *Ornithologie brésilienne ou histoire des oiseaux du Brésil.* T. Reeves, Rio de Janeiro.

Ellis, H. R. 1952. Nesting behavior of a Purple-throated Fruit-crow. *Wilson Bull.* **64**: 98–100.

Everitt, C. 1963. Breeding the Black-throated Cotinga (*Pipreola riefferi*). *Avicult. Mag.* **69**: 141–144.

Eyton, T. C. 1861. Note on the anatomy of *Cephalopterus penduliger. Ibis* (1)**3**: 57–58.

ffrench, R. 1973. *A guide to the birds of Trinidad and Tobago.* Livingston Publ. Co., Wynnewood, Pa.

Fogden, M. P. L. 1972. The seasonality and population dynamics of equatorial forest birds in Sarawak. *Ibis* **114**: 307–343.

Fox, H. M. & Vevers, G. 1960. *The nature of animal colours.* Sidgwick & Jackson, London.

Friedmann, H. 1948. Birds collected by the National Geographic Society's expeditions to northern Brazil and southern Venezuela. *Proc. U.S. natn. Mus.* **97**: 373–570.

Garrod, A. H. 1876. On some anatomical characters which bear upon the major divisions of the passerine birds. Part I. *Proc. zool. Soc. Lond.* **1876**: 506–519.

Gilliard, E. T. 1938. The birds of Mt. Auyan-tepui, Venezuela. *Bull. Am. Mus. nat. Hist.* **77**: 439–508.

———— 1962. On the breeding behaviour of the cock-of-the-rock (Aves, *Rupicola rupicola*). *Bull. Am. Mus. nat. Hist.* **124**: 35–68.

Goeldi, E. A. 1894. On the nesting of *Phibalura flavirostris* and *Lochmias nematura. Ibis* (6)**6**: 485–494.

———— 1894–1900. *As aves do Brasil.* Alves & Co., Rio de Janeiro & S. Paulo.

Goodfellow, W. 1901. Results of an ornithological journey through Colombia and Ecuador. *Ibis* (8)**1**: 300–319, 458–480, 699–715.

Görnitz, K. & Rensch, B. 1924. Ueber die violette Färbung der Vogelfedern. *J. Orn.* **72**: 113–118.

Greenewalt, C. H. 1962. Dimensional relationships for flying animals. *Smithson. misc. Collns* **144**: 1–46.

Griscom, L. & Greenway, J. C. 1937. Birds of Lower Amazonia. *Bull. Mus. comp. zool. Harv.* **88**: 83–344.

Haffer, J. 1970. Art-Entstehung bei einigen Waldvögeln Amazoniens. *J. Orn.* **111**: 285–331.

———— 1974. Avian speciation in tropical South America. *Publ. Nuttall Orn. Club* No. 14.

Hagen, W. von 1938. On the capture of the Umbrella Bird (*Cephalopterus penduliger* Sclater). *Proc. zool. Soc. Lond.* **108**: 27–30.

Hagmann, G. 1907. Die Vogelwelt der Insel Mexiana, Amazonenstrom. *Zool. Jb. (Syst.)* **26**: 11–62.

Hamilton, J. F. 1871. Notes on birds from the Province of São Paulo, Brazil. *Ibis* (3)**1**: 301–309.

Haverschmidt, F. 1968. *Birds of Surinam.* Oliver & Boyd, Edinburgh & London.

———— 1977. The occurrence of the Crimson Fruit-crow *Haematoderus militaris* in Surinam. *Bull. Br. Orn. Club* **97**: 76.

Hellmayr, C. E. 1929. Catalogue of birds of the Americas. Part VI. *Field Mus. nat. Hist., zool. ser.* 13.

Hempel, A. 1949. Estudo da alimentação natural de aves silvestres de Brasil. *Archos Inst. Biol. S. Paulo* **19**: 237–268.

Holt, E. G. 1928. An ornithological survey of the Serra do Itatiaia, Brazil. *Bull. Am. Mus. nat. Hist.* **57**: 251–326.

Howe, H. F. 1977. Bird activity and seed dispersal of a tropical wet forest tree. *Ecology* **58**: 539–550.

———— 1980. Monkey dispersal and waste of a neotropical fruit. *Ecology* **61**: 944–959.

Howe, H. F. & De Steven, D. 1979. Fruit production, migrant bird visitation, and seed dispersal of *Guarea glabra* in Panama. *Oecologia* **39**: 185–196.

Ihering, H. von 1900. Catalogo critico-comparativo dos ninhos e ovos das aves do Brasil. *Rev. Mus. Paulista* **4**: 191–300.

———— 1914. Novas observações sobre ninhos e ovos de aves do Brasil. *Rev. Mus. Paulista* **9**: 420–448.

Kantak, G. E. 1979. Observations on some fruit-eating birds in Mexico. *Auk* **96**: 183–186.

Knox, A. G. 1980. Feather protein as a source of avian taxonomic information. *Comp. Biochem. Physiol.* **65B**: 45–54.

Koepcke, M. 1954. *Zaratornis stresemanni* nov. gen. nov. spec., un cotingido nuevo del Peru. *Publ. Mus. Hist. nat. Javier Prado Ser. A (Zoologia)*, no. **16**: 1–8.

———— 1958. Die Vögel des Waldes von Zarate. *Bonn. zool. Beitr.* **9**: 130–193.

Kopp, L. E. 1966. A taxonomic revision of the genus *Persea* in the Western Hemisphere (Persea–Lauraceae). *Mem. N.Y. bot. Gdn.* **14** (1).

Lack, D. 1968. *Ecological adaptations for breeding in birds.* Methuen, London.

Layard, E. L. 1873. Notes on birds observed at Para. *Ibis* (3)**3**: 374–396.

Lint, K. C. & Dolan, J. M. 1966. Successful breeding of the Orange-breasted Cotinga (*Pipreola jucunda*) in the San Diego Zoological Gardens. *Avicult. Mag.* **72**: 18–20.

Lloyd, C. A. 1895. Stray notes from Pirara. *Timehri* **9**: 220–232.

Lowery, G. H. & O'Neill, J. P. 1966. A new genus and species of cotinga from eastern Peru. *Auk* **83**: 1–9.

Luthi, H. 1970. Blick in die Natur: der geheimnisvolle Zaratornis. *Bol. Colonia Suiza en el Peru* **5**: 15–17.

Mayr, E. & Phelps, W. H. 1967. The origin of the bird fauna of the south Venezuelan highlands. *Bull. Am. Mus. nat. Hist.* **136**: 273–327.

Mayr, E. & Short, L. L. 1970. Species taxa of North American birds: a contribution to comparative systematics. *Publ. Nuttall Orn. Club* No. 9.

McKey, D. 1975. The evolution of coevolved seed dispersal systems. Pp. 159–191 in L. E. Gilbert & P. H. Raven (eds), *Coevolution of animals and plants.* Univ. Texas Press,

Lawrence & London.

Merizalde de Abuja, C. 1975. Reproducción en cinco especies de aves del Occidente del Ecuador. *Rev. Univ. Católica del Ecuador* **3**: 167–183.

Meyer de Schauensee, R. 1966. *The species of birds of South America.* Academy of Natural Sciences, Philadelphia, and Livingston Publ. Co., Narberth, Pennsylvania.

———— 1970. *A guide to the birds of South America.* Livingston Publ. Co., Wynnewood, Pennsylvania.

Miller, A. H. 1963. Seasonal activity and ecology of the avifauna of an American equatorial cloud forest. *Univ. Calif. Publs Zool.* **66**: 1–78.

Mitchell, M. H. 1957. *Observations on birds of southeastern Brazil.* Univ. Toronto Press, Toronto.

Morrison, A. 1948. Notes on the birds of the Pampas River valley, south Peru. *Ibis* **90**: 119–126.

Morton, E. S. 1973. On the evolutionary advantages and disadvantages of fruit eating in tropical birds. *Am. Nat.* **107**: 8–22.

Naumburg, E. M. 1930. The birds of Matto Grosso, Brazil. *Bull. Am. Mus. nat. Hist.* **60**: 1–432.

Niethammer, G. 1956. Zur Vogelwelt Boliviens. Teil III. Passeres. *Bonn. zool. Beitr.* **7**: 84–150.

Nicéforo, M. H. 1947. Notas sobre aves de Colombia II. *Caldasia* **4**: 317–377.

Novaes, F. C. 1978. Ornitologia do Território de Amapá, 11. *Publ. Avuls. Mus. Para. E. Goeldi* No. 29.

———— 1980. Observações sobre a avifauna do alto curso do Rio Paru de Leste, Estado do Pará. *Bolm Mus. Para. Emilio Goeldi, n. ser.,* **100**: 1–58.

Olalla, A. M. 1943. Algumas observações sôbre a biologia das aves e mamíferos sul-americanos. *Papeis Dep. Zool. S. Paulo* **3**: 229–236.

Olalla, A. M. & Magalhães, A. C. 1956. Pássaros. Fam. Rupicolidae, galos da serra, da rochas o do Pará. *Bibl. zool. S. Paulo* **2**: 26–40.

Olivares, O. M. 1958. Aves de la costa del Pacifico, Municipio de Guapi, Cauca, Colombia, III. *Caldasia* **8**: 217–251.

Olivares, A. & Hernandez, J. 1962. Aves de la Comisaría del Vaupés (Colombia). *Revta Biol. trop.* **10**: 61–90.

Olson, S. L. 1970. Specializations of some carotenoid-bearing feathers. *Condor* **72**: 424–430.

———— 1971. Taxonomic comments on the Eurylaimidae. *Ibis* **113**: 507–516.

O'Neill, J. P. & Parker, T. A. 1981. New subspecies of *Pipreola riefferii* and *Chlorospingus ophthalmicus* from Peru. *Bull. Br. Orn. Club* **101**: 294–299.

Parker, T. A. 1981. Distribution and biology of the White-cheeked Cotinga *Zaratornis stresemanni*, a high Andean frugivore. *Bull. Br. Orn. Club* **101**: 256–265.

Parker, T. A., Remsen, J. V. & Heindel, J. A. 1980. Seven bird species new to Bolivia. *Bull. Br. Orn. Club* **100**: 160–162.

Pelzeln, A. von 1868–70. *Zur Ornithologie Brasiliens.* A. Pichler's Witwe & Sohn, Vienna.

Penard, F. P. & Penard, A. P. 1910. *De vogels van Guyana (Suriname, Cayenne en Demerara)*, Pt. 2. F. P. Penard, Paramaribo.

Pereyra, J. A. 1951. Avifauna argentina. *Hornero* **9**: 291–347.

Peters, J. L. & Griswold, J. A. 1943. Birds of the Harvard Peruvian Expedition 1939. *Bull. Mus. comp. Zool. Harv.* **92**: 281–327.

Pinto, O. M. de O. 1944. Catalogo das aves do Brasil. Part 2. Dept. Zool., Secr. da Agricult., São Paulo.

———— 1953. Sobre a coleção Carlos Estevão de pelos, ninhos e ovos das aves de Belém (Pará). *Papéis Dep. Zool. S. Paulo* **11**: 111–222.

Quelch, J. J. 1896. Abstract of address on the birds of British Guiana. In *Papers presented to the World's Congress on Ornithology*. Charles H. Sergel Co., Chicago.

Reinhardt, J. 1870. Bidrag til kundskab om fuglefaunaen i Brasiliens campos. *Vidensk. Meddr dansk naturh. Foren.* 1–124: 315–454.

Richmond, C. W. 1893. Notes on a collection of birds from eastern Nicaragua and the Río Frio, Costa Rica, with a description of a supposed new trogon. *Proc. U.S. natn. Mus.* 16: 479–532.

Ridgway, R. 1905. A winter with the birds in Costa Rica. *Condor* 7: 151–160.

———1907. The birds of North and Middle America. Part IV. *Bull. U.S. natn. Mus.* No. 50.

——— 1912. *Color standards and nomenclature*. Washington, D.C., published by the author.

Russell, S. M. 1964. A distributional study of the birds of British Honduras. *Orn. Monogr. (A.O.U.)*, No. 1.

Salvin, O. & Godman, F. D. 1891. Biologia Centrali-Americana. Aves. Vol. 2. Taylor & Francis, London.

Schaefer, E. & Phelps, W. H. 1954. Aves de Rancho Grande. *Bol. Soc. venez. Cienc. nat.* 6: 3–167.

Schomburgk, R. 1848. *Reisen in Britisch-Guiana in dem Jahren 1840–1844*. Part 3. J. J. Weber, Leipzig.

Schönwetter, M. 1969. *Handbuch der Oologie*. Lieferung 16. Akademie Verlag, Berlin.

Schubart, O., Aguirre, A. C. & Sick, H. 1965. Contribuição para o conhecimento da alimentação das aves brasileiras. *Arqu. Zool.* 12: 95–249.

Schwartz, P. & Snow, D. W. 1979. Display and related behavior of the Wire-tailed Manakin. *Living Bird* 17: 51–78.

Sclater, P. L. & Salvin, O. 1875. On Venezuelan birds collected by Mr A. Goering. Part V. *Proc. zool. Soc. Lond.* 1875: 234–238.

——— & ——— 1876. On new species of Bolivian birds. *Proc. zool. Soc. Lond.* 1876: 352–358.

——— & ——— 1879. On the birds collected by the late Mr T. K. Salmon in the State of Antioquia, United States of Colombia. *Proc. zool. Soc. Lond.* 1879: 486–550.

——— & ——— 1880. On new birds collected by Mr C. Buckley in eastern Ecuador. *Proc. zool. Soc. Lond.* 1880: 155–161.

Sibley, C. G. 1970. A comparative study of the egg-white proteins of passerine birds. *Bull. Peabody Mus. nat. Hist.* 32: 1–131.

Sick, H. 1951. An egg of the Umbrella Bird. *Wilson Bull.* 63: 338–339.

——— 1954. Zur Biologie des amazonischen Schirmvogels, *Cephalopterus ornatus*. *J. Orn.* 95: 233–244.

———1955. O anambé prêto, *"Cephalopterus ornatus"* Geoffroy Saint-Hilaire (Cotingidas, Aves). *Revta bras. Biol.* 15: 361–376.

———1957. Rosshaarpilze als Nestbau-Material brasilianischer Vögel. *J. Orn.* 98: 421–431.

——— 1969. Aves brasileiras ameaçadas de extinção e noções gerais de conservação de aves no Brasil. *Anais Acad. bras. Cienc.* 41: 205–229.

——— 1970. Ueber Eier und Lebensweise der Weissflügel-Kotinga, *Xipholena atropurpurea*. *J. Orn.* 111: 107–108.

——— 1979. Zur Nistweise der Cotingiden *Iodopleura* and *Xipholena*. *J. Orn.* 120: 73–77.

Sick, H. & Teixeira, D. M. 1979. Notas sobre aves brasileiras raras ou ameaçadas de extinção. *Publções avuls. Mus. nac. Rio de J.*, no. 62.

Skutch, A. F. 1969. Life histories of Central American birds III. *Pacific Coast Avifauna*, No. 35. Cooper Orn. Soc. Berkeley, California.

——— 1970. The display of the Yellow-billed Cotinga *Carpodectes antoniae*. *Ibis* 112: 115–116.

——— 1976. *Parent birds and their young*. Univ. Texas Press, Austin and London.

Slud, P. 1960. The birds of Finca "La Selva", Costa Rica: a tropical wet forest locality. *Bull. Am. Mus. nat. Hist.* 121: 53–148.

———1964. The birds of Costa Rica. *Bull. Am. Mus. nat. Hist.* 128: 1–430.

Snethlage, E. 1908. Ornithologisches von Tapajoz und Tocantins. *J. Orn.* 56: 493–539.

Snow, B. K. 1961. Notes on the behavior of three Cotingidae. *Auk* 78: 150–161.

——— 1970. A field study of the Bearded Bellbird in Trinidad. *Ibis* 112: 299–329.

——— 1972. A field study of the Calfbird *Perissocephalus tricolor*. *Ibis* 114: 139–162.

——— 1973. Notes on the behavior of the White Bellbird. *Auk* 90: 743–751.

——— 1977. Territorial behavior and courtship of the male Three-wattled Bellbird. *Auk* 94: 623–645.

——— 1978. Calls and displays of the male Bare-throated Bellbird. *Avicult. Mag.* 84: 157–161.

Snow, B. K. & Snow, D. W. 1979. The Ochre-bellied Flycatcher and the evolution of lek behavior. *Condor* 81: 286–292.

Snow, D. W. 1962a. A field study of the Black and White Manakin, *Manacus manacus*, in Trinidad. *Zoologica (N.Y.)* 47: 65–104.

——— 1962b. A field study of the Golden-headed Manakin, *Pipra erythrocephala*, in Trinidad, W.I. *Zoologica (N.Y.)* 47: 183–198.

——— 1971a. Display of the Pompadour Cotinga *Xipholena punicea*. *Ibis* 113: 102–104.

——— 1971b. Notes on the biology of the Cock-of-the-rock (*Rupicola rupicola*). *J. Orn.* 112: 323–333.

——— 1971c. Observations on the Purple-throated Fruit-crow in Guyana. *Living Bird* 10: 5–17.

——— 1971d. Evolutionary aspects of fruit-eating by birds. *Ibis* 113: 194–202.

——— 1973a. Distribution, ecology and evolution of the bellbirds (*Procnias*, Cotingidae). *Bull. Br. Mus. nat. Hist. (Zool.)* 25: 369–391.

——— 1973b. The classification of the Cotingas. *Breviora*, no. 409.

——— 1975. *Laniisoma elegans* in Peru. *Auk* 92: 583–584.

———1976a. The relationship between climate and annual cycles in the Cotingidae. *Ibis* 118: 366–401.

——— 1976b. *The web of adaptation: bird studies in the American tropics*. Quadrangle, New York, and Collins, London.

——— 1977. Waltzing cotingas. *Anim. Kingd.* 80: 13–18.

——— 1980. A new species of cotinga from south-eastern Brazil. *Bull. Br. Orn. Club* 100: 213–215.

——— 1981. Coevolution of birds and plants. Pp. 169–178 in P. H. Greenwood (Gen. ed.), P. L. Forey (ed.) *Chance change & challenge. The evolving biosphere*. British Museum (Natural History) & Camb. Univ. Press, London & Cambridge.

Snow, D. W. & Goodwin, D. 1974. The Black-and-gold Cotinga. *Auk* 91: 360–369.

Snow, D. W. & Lill, A. 1974. Longevity records for some neotropical land birds. *Condor* 76: 262–267.

Strong, R. M. 1952. A peculiar pigmentation. *Auk* 69: 199–200.

Taczanowski, L. 1874. Description des oiseaux noveaux du

Pérou central. *Proc. zool. Soc. Lond.* **1874**: 129–140.

———— 1884. Ornithologie du Pérou. Vol. 2. Oberthur, Rennes.

Tashian, R. E. 1952. Some birds from the Palenque region of northeastern Chiapas. *Auk* **69**: 60–66.

Terborgh, J. W., Fitzpatrick, J. W. & Emmons, L. Bird and mammal species recorded at Cocha Cashu Biological Station and vicinity, Manu National Park, dept. Madre de Dios, Peru 1973 through 1979. *Publ. Mus. Hist. nat. Javier Prado.*

Thoresen, A. C. 1974. First Shrike-like Cotinga record for Peru. *Auk* **91**: 840.

Todd, F. S., Gale, N. B. & Van Oosten, J. R. 1972. El "Vaca del Monte". *Avicult. Mag.* **78**: 79–83.

Todd, W. E. C. 1950. Critical notes on the cotingas. *Proc. biol. Soc. Wash.* **63**: 5–7.

Völker, O. 1938. Porphyrin in Vogelfedern. *J. Orn.* **86**: 436–456.

———— 1952. Die Lipochrome in den Federn der Cotingiden. *J. Orn.* **93**: 122–129.

Vuilleumier, F. 1969. Field notes on some birds from the Bolivian Andes. *Ibis* **111**: 599–608.

Wallace, A. R. 1850. On the Umbrella Bird (*Cephalopterus ornatus*), "Ueramimbé", L.G. *Proc. zool. Soc. Lond.* **18**: 206–207.

———— 1853. *Travels on the Amazon and Rio Negro.* Ward, Lock & Co., London.

Warter, S. L. 1965. The cranial osteology of the New World Tyrannoidea and its taxonomic implications. Ph.D. thesis, Louisiana State University.

Wetmore, A. 1939. Observations on the birds of northern Venezuela. *Proc. U.S. natn. Mus.* **87**: 173–260.

———— 1972. The birds of the Republic of Panamá. Part 3. *Smithson. misc. Collns* **150**.

Wünschmann, A. 1966. Die Balz der Rotkropf-Kotinga *Pyroderus scutatus* (Shaw). *Gefied. Welt* **90**: 46–48.

Wyatt, C. W. 1871. Notes on some of the birds of the United States of Columbia. *Ibis* (3) **1**: 113–131.

Index

Page numbers in bold type refer to the main entries for the species